SUBSCRIPTIONS
International Review of Social History (ISSN 0020–8590) is published in three parts in April, August and December plus one special issue in December. Three parts plus one special issue form a volume. The subscription price (excluding VAT) of volume 58 (2013) which includes electronic access and delivery by air where appropriate is £176 net (US$301 in the USA, Canada and Mexico) for institutions; £48 net (US$78 in the USA, Canada and Mexico) for individuals ordering direct from the publisher and certifying that the journal is for their own personal use. Single parts and the special issue are £46 (US$79 in the USA, Canada and Mexico) plus postage. An electronic only price available to institutional subscribers is £146 (US$252 in USA, Canada and Mexico). EU subscribers (outside the UK) who are not registered for VAT should add VAT at their country's rate. VAT registered subscribers should provide their VAT registration number. Japanese prices for institutions are available from Kinokuniya Company Ltd, P.O. Box 55, Chitose, Tokyo 156, Japan.

Orders, which must be accompanied by payment, may be sent to a bookseller, subscription agent or direct to the publisher: Cambridge University Press, The Edinburgh Building, Shaftesbury Road, Cambridge CB2 8RU; or in the USA, Canada and Mexico: Cambridge University Press, Journals Fulfillment Department, 100 Brook Hill Drive, West Nyack, New York 10994–2133. Periodicals postage paid at New York, NY and at additional mailing offices. Postmaster: send address changes in USA, Canada and Mexico to International Review of Social History, Cambridge University Press, 100 Brook Hill Drive, West Nyack, New York 10994–2133.

Information on International Review of Social History and all other Cambridge journals can be accessed via journals.cambridge.org

Printed and bound by Bell & Bain Ltd, Glasgow, UK

international
review of
social history

Special Issue 21

Mutiny and Maritime Radicalism in the Age of Revolution: A Global Survey

Edited by Clare Anderson, Niklas Frykman, Lex Heerma van Voss, and Marcus Rediker

CAMBRIDGE
UNIVERSITY PRESS

University Printing House, Cambridge CB2 8BS, United Kingdom

Cambridge University Press is part of the University of Cambridge.

It furthers the University's mission by disseminating knowledge in the pursuit of education, learning and research at the highest international levels of excellence.

www.cambridge.org
Information on this title: www.cambridge.org/9781107689329

A catalogue record for this publication is available from the British Library

ISBN 978-1-107-68932-9 Paperback

Cambridge University Press has no responsibility for the persistence or accuracy of URLs for external or third-party internet websites referred to in this publication, and does not guarantee that any content on such websites is, or will remain, accurate or appropriate.

CONTENTS

Mutiny and Maritime Radicalism in the Age of Revolution:
A Global Survey

Edited by
Clare Anderson, Niklas Frykman, Lex Heerma van Voss,
and Marcus Rediker

IRSH 58 (2013), Special Issue, pp. 1–14 doi:10.1017/S0020859013000497
© 2013 Internationaal Instituut voor Sociale Geschiedenis

Mutiny and Maritime Radicalism in the Age of Revolution: An Introduction*

NIKLAS FRYKMAN

Department of History, Claremont McKenna College
850 Columbia Ave, Claremont, CA 91711, USA

E-mail: nfrykman@gmail.com

CLARE ANDERSON

School of Historical Studies, University of Leicester
3–5 Salisbury Road, Leicester LE1 7QR, UK

E-mail: ca26@leicester.ac.uk

LEX HEERMA VAN VOSS

Huygens Institute for the History of the Netherlands
Prins Willem-Alexanderhof 5, PO Box 90754, 2509 LT The Hague
The Netherlands

E-mail: Lex.HeermavanVoss@huygens.knaw.nl

MARCUS REDIKER

Department of History, University of Pittsburgh
3508 Posvar Hall, Pittsburgh, PA 15260, USA

E-mail: marcusrediker@yahoo.com

ABSTRACT: The essays collected in this volume demonstrate that during the age of revolution (1760s–1840s) most sectors of the maritime industries experienced higher levels of unrest than is usually recognized. Ranging across global contexts including the Atlantic, Indian, and Pacific Oceans as well as the Caribbean, Andaman, and South China Seas, and exploring the actions of sailors, laborers, convicts, and slaves, this collection offers a fresh, sea-centered way of seeing the

---

* The papers presented in this volume are the outcome of two conferences. The first was organized by the editors and Emma Christopher and held on 16–18 June 2011 at the International Institute of Social History in Amsterdam. The second was organized by the editors and held on 21–22 May 2012 at the Huygens Institute for the History of the Netherlands

confluence between space, agency, and political economy during this crucial period. In this introduction we contend that the radicalism of the age of revolution can best be viewed as a geographically connected process, and that the maritime world was central to its multiple eruptions and global character. Mutiny therefore can be seen as part of something bigger and broader: what we have chosen to call maritime radicalism, a term as well as a concept that has had virtually no presence in the literature on the revolutionary era until now.

The practice of mutiny is as old as warfare itself, but the concept and the word are of more recent provenance. Etymologically, mutiny derives from the Latin *motus* (motion or movement), which spawned the French word *émeute* (riot) and the German word *Meute* (mob), which in turn gave rise to *Meuterei*, the Dutch *muiterij*, the French *mutinerie*, and soon thereafter the English mutiny. The initial meaning of the word was diffuse, suggesting a general state of tumult, unruly discord, and social disturbance, but during the ferocious wars that tore apart the continent in the sixteenth and seventeenth centuries mutiny affixed itself more specifically to the collective rebellions that erupted with growing frequency inside Europe's hugely expanded armed forces. The Spanish army of Flanders, a massive force of 70,000 men, appears to have been especially afflicted, suffering no fewer than 37 major mutinies between 1589 and 1607, many of them lasting for multiple years and involving between 3,000 and 4,000 soldiers each time.[1]

Mutiny thus entered Europe's military vocabulary at a time when nascent nation-states began to transform their armies from chaotic collections of drifters, forced recruits, feudal retainers, and paid mercenaries into the standardized, tightly organized, and highly hierarchical war-making machines of the modern era. As part of this military revolution, war-workers were deskilled and turned into replaceable cogs through a program of extensive drilling based on the time and motion studies carried out by the Dutch military pioneers Maurice and William Louis of Nassau, subsequently refined and implemented with deadly success by the legendary Swedish warrior-king Gustavus Adolphus.[2]

---

in The Hague. The first conference was funded by the Royal Netherlands Academy of Arts and Sciences, the International Institute of Social History, the University of Pittsburgh, and Stichting Professor van Winterfonds. The second conference was funded by the University of Pittsburgh, the Huygens Institute for the History of the Netherlands, and Stichting Fonds voor de Geld- en Effectenhandel. We thank these institutions for their hospitality and generosity and the participants at both conferences for their comments on the papers.

1. Geoffrey Parker, "Mutiny and Discontent in the Spanish Army of Flanders 1572–1607", *Past & Present*, 58 (1973), p. 39.
2. Idem, *The Military Revolution: Military Innovation and the Rise of the West, 1500–1800*, 2nd edn (Cambridge, 1996), pp. 16–24.

At sea, the process of military standardization lagged behind by a few decades, but as European powers expanded their professional war-fleets in the second half of the seventeenth century they imposed naval articles of war to create the same strictly hierarchical form of organization that had already transformed their armies. All traces of collective decision-making, long a prominent element of North Atlantic maritime culture, were obliterated. The result was a micro-society that resembled tyranny in its purest form: "All that you are ordered to do is duty", an old salt advised the landsman Ned Ward at the turn of the eighteenth century. "All that you refuse to do", he continued, "is mutiny".[3]

The authoritarianism of the militarized work environment, which leaves no formal room for opposition short of all-out mutiny, explains in part why mutinous soldiers and sailors have repeatedly been in the most radically democratic, most militantly anti-imperialist vanguard of the great revolutionary movements that have thundered across the world in recent centuries: New Model Army mutineers at Putney in the mid-seventeenth century; sepoys at the start of the Indian Uprising in 1857; insurgent sailors at Kiel, which triggered the revolution that toppled the German Kaiser in 1918; seamen at Kronstadt who in 1921 challenged the increasingly authoritarian rule of the Bolsheviks; or, most recently, American GIs who, with their mass refusals, marches, protests, and anti-officer violence ("fragging"), undermined the war effort in Vietnam during the late 1960s and early 1970s.[4]

Until recently, the scarcity of reliable data has made it seem nearly impossible to estimate the actual incidence of mutiny during the age of sail. The events themselves are notoriously underreported, shrouded in "a double conspiracy of silence" since no one involved had an interest in their involvement becoming known – for officers it might result in a career-ending stigma, for the mutineers themselves in a life-ending sentence.[5] As a consequence we must assume that extant evidence represents only a small proportion of actual events. And yet, where quantifiable data has been uncovered and analyzed, the results have been perfectly astonishing. New work has revealed previously unknown

---

3. Quoted in Marcus Rediker, *Between the Devil and the Deep Blue Sea: Merchant Seamen, Pirates, and the Anglo-American Maritime World, 1700–1750* (Cambridge, 1987), p. 211.
4. James Holstun, *Ehud's Dagger: Class Struggle in the English Revolution* (London, 2000), pp. 192–256; C.A. Bayly, *Indian Society and the Making of the British Empire* (Cambridge, 1988), ch. 6; Michael Epkenhans, "'Red Sailors' and the Demise of the German Empire, 1918", in Christopher M. Bell and Bruce A. Elleman (eds), *Naval Mutinies of the Twentieth Century: An International Perspective* (London, 2003), pp. 80–105; Paul Avrich, *Kronstadt 1921* (Princeton, NJ, 1970); David Cortright, *Soldiers in Revolt: GI Resistance During the Vietnam War* (Chicago, IL, 1975).
5. James C. Scott, *Two Cheers for Anarchism: Six Easy Pieces on Autonomy, Dignity, and Meaningful Work and Play* (Princeton, NJ, 2012), pp. 8–9.

mutinies and other forms of resistance in the Indian Ocean convict trade.[6] Recent research in North Atlantic naval archives meanwhile suggests that at least one-third of European warships experienced some form of collective rebellion during the 1790s.[7] Perhaps even more impressively, the comprehensive Transatlantic Slave Trade Database demonstrates that approximately one in ten slave ships experienced a mutiny, some of them successful, most suppressed.[8]

The essays collected here build on such work, demonstrating unambiguously that during the age of revolution (1760s–1840s) most sectors of the maritime industries – not just warships, but convict vessels, slave ships, and merchantmen, sailing in the Atlantic, Indian, and Pacific Oceans as well as the Caribbean, Andaman, and South China Seas – all experienced far higher levels of unrest than is usually recognized. The authors range across global contexts: exploring the actions of sailors, laborers, convicts, and slaves, and offering a fresh, sea-centered way of seeing the confluence between space, agency, and political economy during this crucial period. They make clear that we must take seriously seaborne voyages as spaces for incubation and as vectors for diffusion of political radicalism.

In this respect, the volume uses evidence of shipboard mutiny to rethink the relationship between sea and land, as well as to foreground the era's multiple geographical centers and logics of resistance from below. We contend, in other words, that the radicalism of the age of revolution can best be viewed as a geographically connected process, and that the maritime world was central to its multiple eruptions and global character. And, in understanding the global and connected character of the age of revolution, as well as its maritime and subaltern dynamics, we seek to decenter Europe and North America in our analysis and also to rethink the era's temporality, which, these essays suggest, stretches at least into the 1850s.

MARITIME RADICALISM

Mutiny is part of something bigger and broader, what we have chosen to call maritime radicalism, a term as well as a concept that has had virtually no presence in the literature on the revolutionary era until now. But why

---

6. Clare Anderson, "'The Ferringees are Flying – The Ship is Ours!' The Convict Middle Passage in Colonial South and Southeast Asia, 1790–1860", *Indian Economic and Social History Review*, 41:3 (2005), pp. 143–186.

7. Niklas Frykman, "The Wooden World Turned Upside Down: Naval Mutinies in the Age of Atlantic Revolution" (Ph.D. thesis, University of Pittsburgh, 2010).

8. David Richardson, "Shipboard Revolts, African Authority, and the Atlantic Slave Trade", *William and Mary Quarterly*, 58 (2001), pp. 69–92. The Trans-Atlantic Slave Trade Database is available at www.slavevoyages.org, last accessed 14 June 2013.

is that so, given the near universal recognition of the ship as the most important tool of globalization before the emergence of air travel in the twentieth century? Why have events and processes that transpired onboard ship remained hidden for so long? And why has it been so hard to conceptualize maritime radicalism as a subject for historical study?

Part of the problem has been sources. Seafarers, like other poor people of the past, left relatively few records of their own: their speeches, songs, and yarns vanished on the wind, leaving few traces for historians to ponder. Because they traveled far and wide, whatever sources they may have left are often widely dispersed and not easy to locate; their "archive" is not conveniently national, and rarely if ever self-generated. Historians must therefore depend to a large extent on sources about dissident sailors and other workers generated by the authorities of the state, often as they sought to repress maritime radicalism of one kind or another. The difficulty of recovering the voices below deck through the writings of those who wielded power over their heads is greater still when insurgents and authorities spoke different languages, as was often the case with slaves, colonial subjects, labor migrants, and foreign-born sailors, such as lascars.[9]

There is also the problem of "terracentrism", the pervasive unconscious assumption or belief that history is made exclusively on land. Most scholars, like everyone else, see the oceans of the world as anti-spaces, as blanks that lie in between, and which are somehow unreal in comparison to the landed, national spaces that surround them. If maritime space is, to a considerable extent, "unthinkable", it therefore follows that radical action taken at sea would be rendered invisible.[10]

In *Between the Devil and the Deep Blue Sea* and *The Many-Headed-Hydra*, Peter Linebaugh and Marcus Rediker argued that within the Anglo-Afro-Hiberno Atlantic a coherent and effective maritime radicalism was embodied in a series of fugitive connections, over vast spaces and spans of time, based on the circulation of seafaring peoples and their experiences.[11] Its common characteristics included mobility and multi-ethnicity, both expressed in a potent phrase, the "motley crew". The guiding values and core practices of maritime radicalism were collectivism,

9. Transnationalism, the archive, and subaltern voice is explored in some detail in Clare Anderson, "Introduction to Marginal Centers: Writing Life Histories in the Indian Ocean World", *Journal of Social History*, 45 (2011), pp. 335–344.
10. Marcus Rediker, "Hydrarchy and Terracentrism", in Anna Colin and Mia Jankowicz (eds), *Hydrarchy* (Cairo, 2012), pp. 11–18; Marcus P.M. Vink, "Indian Ocean Studies and the 'New Thalassology'", *Journal of Global History*, 2 (2007), pp. 41–62.
11. Rediker, *Between the Devil and the Deep Blue Sea*; Peter Linebaugh and Marcus Rediker, *The Many-Headed Hydra: Sailors, Slaves, Commoners, and the Hidden History of the Revolutionary Atlantic* (Boston, MA, 2000).

anti-authoritarianism, and egalitarianism. Radical sailors routinely stood together ("one and all" was a favorite cry), elected their officers, and divided their resources equally. All of these values and practices were eloquently expressed through the "round robin", an instrument of protest used by sailors, who drew one circle within another, wrote their demands within the interior circle, and signed their names from the edge of the inner circle to the outer one, to disguise who had begun the petition, to take strength in numbers, and to limit the captain's violent power of retaliation.

As we shall see in the essays that follow, the elements of maritime radicalism were many, ranging from the individual and solitary to the collective and massive. Sailors ran away, alone and in groups – sometimes big groups. When they remained on their vessels they engaged in a variety of acts of resistance. They challenged their captains and other officers through what was called "sea-lawyering": they grumbled or "murmured", indicating displeasure in indirect ways. They devised and signed petitions such as the round robin. They disputed orders, maintaining that law or custom underwrote their refusal to do as commanded by their officers. Negotiations subtle or overt were commonplace at sea. More dramatic forms of maritime radicalism included machine-breaking (sabotage), work stoppage, strike, running amok, as well as mutiny.

Sailors also carried maritime radicalism ashore, where they engaged in a variety of actions ranging from sabotage to arson to strikes: the sailors of London organized a massive work stoppage in 1768, first damaging the rigging of their ships in acts of sabotage, then "striking" the sails, forcing commerce to a halt, and thus adding the word strike to the English language.[12] Seafaring people were also frequent and enthusiastic leaders and participants in port city mobs (against impressment, among other causes), igniting riots and larger insurrections. Seafarers, dockworkers, and maritime artisans played important roles in revolutions – in America, France, and Saint-Domingue. The first and third of these world-shaking events contained an anti-imperial dimension, demonstrating the part seamen and their many-sided radicalism might play in peoples' war.

In this volume maritime radicalism consists of the ensemble of actions that challenged prevailing relations of power, at sea and ashore, on three interrelated levels: first, the ship itself, which was its own social and political unit; second, the nation-state or empire that formulated and enforced the laws that governed the ship; third, the system of international capitalism within which nation-states, empires, and their ships operated.

---

12. Lex Heerma van Voss, "Introduction: Industrial Disputes, Strikes", in *idem* and Herman Diederiks (eds), *Industrial Conflict: Papers Presented to the Fourth British–Dutch Conference on Labour History, Newcastle upon Tyne* (Amsterdam, 1988), pp. 1–9.

The actors include naval and merchant seamen from around the Atlantic rim, Indian lascars, European and Asian convicts, and enslaved people from West Africa, the East Indies, and the Americas. The venues of maritime radicalism include vessels that ranged from the smallest canoe to the greatest three-masted ocean-going ship, as well as the docks, warehouses, waterfronts, and port cities beyond where these vessels congregated to embark and disembark people and commodities, sometimes people who were themselves considered commodities.

Events analyzed include maritime insurrections like those aboard the *Amistad* in 1839 and the *Creole* in 1841, as well as the maritime dimensions of larger upheavals, for example the American Revolution. Like mutineers, other agents of maritime radicalism could have three distinct though sometimes interrelated objectives. They could seek escape from, reform of, or revolution against ship, state, or capitalist economy. No single cultural tradition of maritime radicalism is posited; rather, we seek to understand how life and work at sea generated and transmitted radical action from below, and how seagoing passages served at times to preserve, revitalize, connect, and transform previous actions across time and vast spaces.

A GLOBALIZING WORLD

In the second half of the eighteenth and the first half of the nineteenth century, a number of colonial empires stretched out across the globe. European powers including Spain, Portugal, France, Britain, the Dutch Republic, Denmark, and Sweden traded in tobacco and sugar from the Caribbean, spices, cotton, and tea from south and east Asia, silver from Latin America, gold and slaves from Africa. To do so they conquered colonies large and small in all these areas, everywhere trying to force the local population or imported slaves and servants to produce the commodities in demand on the international markets. They built fortifications to protect their trading posts, ports, and shipping lanes, both from each other and from unconquered local forces.

Wars between European empires were frequently fought in the colonies, and their possession and the domination of the sea routes connecting them became an increasingly important reason to wage war in the first place. The War of Austrian Succession (1740–1748), the Seven Years' War (1756–1763), the American Revolutionary War (1775–1783), as well as the French Revolutionary Wars (1792–1802) and the Napoleonic Wars (1803–1815) were all fought on a world scale.

From the American Revolutionary War onward a strong ideological element was infused into these international conflicts, reaching an apogee in the French Revolutionary Wars, when the French often encountered ideologically inspired supporters in the countries in which they fought.

National and imperial boundary lines blurred. To give but one example from the essays that follow, after the Dutch Republic became the Batavian Republic in 1795 the French and their revolutionary Dutch Batavian allies went to war against the British and their own counter-revolutionary Dutch Orangist allies over the long-contested South African Cape Colony, pivotal gateway to the Indian Ocean, China, the Spice Islands, Australia, and the South Pacific beyond.

Colonial empires offered convenient places to stow away criminals and political opponents, and convicts were also used to expand imperial frontier zones. The Dutch East India Company locked up its political enemies far away from Indonesia on Robben Island, just off Cape Town.[13] The French deported to Guyana, its "dry guillotine", from 1795 onward.[14] The British sent convicts from Britain, Ireland, and the colonies to Australia, and from India to south-east Asia and the Andaman Islands.[15] As metropolitan labor markets strained under the weight of escalating demand for naval and merchant seamen, plantation workers, and infantrymen for the military defense of colonial outposts, imperial rulers used the law to generate a highly mobile, super-exploitable convict labor force to build and maintain the material infrastructure of expansion.[16]

Another solution was to impress, conscript, and crimp workers for military service, afloat and ashore.[17] A third was using a rising proportion of foreign-born workers both from around the Atlantic and beyond, as did the Dutch and British East India fleets.[18] A fourth was employing slaves as sailors and soldiers on board ships. The scramble for cheap labor in fact was so intense that even slaves on board slave ships were put to work, commonly performing household tasks such as preparing food, and at times sailing the ship or fighting off enemies.[19] After Britain

---

13. Kerry Ward, *Networks of Empire: Forced Migration in the Dutch East India Company* (Cambridge [etc.], 2009).

14. Miranda Spieler, *Empire and Underworld: Captivity in French Guiana* (Cambridge, MA, 2012).

15. Clare Anderson, *Subaltern Lives: Biographies of Colonialism in the Indian Ocean World, 1790–1920* (Cambridge [etc.], 2012); Ian Duffield and James Bradley (eds), *Representing Convicts: New Perspectives on Convict Forced Labour Migration* (Leicester, 1997).

16. Clare Anderson and Hamish Maxwell-Stewart, "Convict Labour and the Western Empires, 1415–1954", forthcoming in Robert Aldrich and Kirsten McKenzie (eds), *Routledge History of Western Empires* (London, 2013), pp. 211–242.

17. Ulbe Bosma, "European Colonial Soldiers in the Nineteenth Century: Their Role in White Global Migration and Patterns of Colonial Settlement", *Journal of Global History*, 4 (2009), pp. 317–336; Denver Brunsman, *The Evil Necessity: British Naval Impressment in the Eighteenth-Century Atlantic World* (Charlottesville, VA [etc.], 2013).

18. Jan Lucassen, "A Multinational and its Labor Force: The Dutch East India Company, 1595–1795", *International Labor and Working-Class History*, 66 (2004), pp. 12–39; Matthias van Rossum, "De intra-Aziatische vaart: schepen, 'de Aziatische zeeman' en ondergang van de VOC?", *Tijdschrift voor Sociale en Economische Geschiedenis*, 8:3 (2011), pp. 32–69.

19. Marcus Rediker, *The Slave Ship: A Human History* (London, 2008), pp. 268–270.

abolished the slave trade in 1807, it sometimes replaced "white" soldiers with liberated Africans from intercepted slave ships ("prize negroes"), whom naval authorities disembarked in colonies in the Caribbean or on Mauritius, where they were enlisted into the army or indentured for up to fourteen years.[20]

Sailing a large ship was expensive, and mercantile and naval authorities tried to economize on the number of hands and on the wages they paid them, as well as on the space, food, and drink available to both crew and human cargo. Discipline in turn was harsh, and the experience of the lash was broadly shared below deck. While on board, the material circumstances of slaves, convicts, and sailors often differed only by degree, and indeed mutinous convicts – though rarely slaves, as far as we know – sometimes received critical help from one or more crew members. Such shared experiences must at times have extended to soldiers in port and on shore, who also suffered from harsh discipline, low pay, and bad food, and, much like their comrades afloat, often had to resort to desertion or mutiny so as to escape military service.

Knowledge of the ocean-world's political geography – its shifting zones of slavery and freedom, imperial domination, and peripheral autonomy – was critical to mutineers, whether slaves, sailors, or convicts. Conquering the quarterdeck and becoming master of the ship was, after all, only the first step in a successful mutiny; after that, the ship had to be taken to a spot where the mutineers could sell it or at least get ashore safely. This meant that the mutineers either had to be able to navigate the ship themselves, or had to find someone from among the original crew willing and able to do so. During the late seventeenth and early eighteenth centuries, European mutineers had been able to continue sailing their ship as pirates, but by the mid-1720s, as the hold of the maritime empires over the seaways of the Atlantic tightened, this possibility disappeared from the northern hemisphere.[21] Elsewhere, of course, piracy was still an option, for instance in the South Pacific, which was only beginning to be integrated into Britain's carceral archipelago.

But in the late eighteenth-century Atlantic and Caribbean the option of fleeing towards autonomous zones was curtailed, and successful mutineers were forced instead to depend on a keen sense of where the authority or jurisdiction of one empire fizzled out and where that of a

20. Anita Rupprecht, "'When He Gets among His Countrymen, They Tell Him that He Is Free': Slave Trade Abolition, Indentured Africans and a Royal Commission", *Slavery and Abolition*, 33:3 (2012), pp. 1–21; Robert J. Steinfeld, *The Invention of Free Labor: The Employment Relation in English and American Law and Culture, 1350–1870* (Chapel Hill, NC, 1991).
21. Marcus Rediker, *Villains of All Nations: Atlantic Pirates in the Golden Age* (Boston, MA, 2005).

second one began, or, in the case of slave mutineers, where slavery still flourished and where it had been abolished already. All evidence suggests that such knowledge was available, for example, about abolitionist networks or the political and juridical circumstances which made it advisable to drop weapons and ships' papers overboard, and instead trust local authorities. We know little about the nature of the networks through which such information circulated, but it seems that they were kept up-to-date in rapid response to the constantly shifting political realities of a world consumed by war and revolution, in a world characterized by increased subaltern mobility and a rapidly expanding print culture.[22]

Both authorities and mutineers depended on news about political shifts to determine how forces had changed or which rules applied. As global contacts grew, so did faster communication, even before technical innovations added speed.[23] Official news, however, did not always spread with the same speed as proletarian communication networks. And this was not necessarily to the disadvantage of mutineers. For example, the sailors in the British squadron at the Cape knew about the Nore mutiny before their superiors did. These surreptitious lines of communication meant that revolutionary movements spread globally, even when authorities were at pains to prevent it: in the case of the Nore mutiny, from British home waters outward to the Mediterranean squadron, the Cape, the fleet in the Indian Ocean, and the *Hermione* frigate in the Caribbean.[24]

REVOLUTION AT SEA

Between the 1760s and late 1840s, revolutionary ferment broke out around the Atlantic world: erupting in multiple places, spreading inward and outward, and moving multi-directionally across Europe, the Americas, and the Caribbean. This resulted in a fundamental restructuring of states and empires. With American independence, Britain lost its North American colonies and turned subsequently to Asia. The French Revolution led to the abolition of the monarchy and the constitution of a new republic. And following the first and only successful revolution of enslaved peoples in world history came the birth of the independent nation of Haiti in 1804.

22. Julius S. Scott, "The Common Wind: Currents of Afro-American Communication in the Era of the Haitian Revolution" (Ph.D., Duke University, 1986).
23. Yrjö Kaukiainen, "Shrinking the World: Improvements in the Speed of Information Transmission, c. 1820–1870", *European Review of Economic History*, 5 (2001), pp. 1–28.
24. Niklas Frykman, "The Mutiny on the *Hermione*: Warfare, Revolution, and Treason in the Royal Navy", *Journal of Social History*, 44 (2010), pp. 159–187. See also Julius S. Scott, "Crisscrossing Empires: Ships, Sailors, and Resistance in the Lesser Antilles in the Eighteenth Century", in Robert L. Paquette and Stanley L. Engerman (eds), *The Lesser Antilles in the Age of European Expansion* (Gainesville, FL, 1996), pp. 128–143.

These profound political implications, and their relationship to the global economic restructurings of the Industrial Revolution in a range of national and imperial contexts, have led to this period being characterized as the age of revolution.[25] Since then, historians working from a range of perspectives have explored the intellectual history of the period; they have underscored the importance of proletarian radicalism in the production of these large-scale historical transformations; and they have unpicked some of their global relationships and connections, between and beyond the obvious sites of revolution in Europe, North America, and the Caribbean.[26] But few have taken pause to consider the human conduits of such connections, or the importance of oceans as both medium and site of revolution itself.

This volume seeks entry into these historiographical debates by doing just that, and by centering subaltern insurgency in an analysis that pays close attention to the mobility, circulation, and connection of radical ideas and action – often across vast distances. It aims to produce an analysis of the proletarian worlds of the seas and oceans which foregrounds their importance as cradles and conduits of radical thought and action, and their many connections to land-based radicalism and revolution.

The authors, in line with contemporary understandings, employ a broad definition of mutiny that includes all forms of collective resistance to the constituted authority aboard ship, from muttering and murmuring all the way to bloody massacre. In most cases, mutinies erupted as a result of conflicts over specific issues inherent in the experience of life and labor on board ship, in particular its disciplinary structure. In some cases, however, it grew as well from broader, transnational ideas concerning justice and rights that were central to the age of revolution. They included, as Christopher Magra shows in his essay on the mass resistance against British naval impressment in the years leading up to the American Revolution, the idea that humans are born free and have a right to remain so, that sovereignty resides in the people, and that violence in the defense of liberty against tyranny is entirely justified.

Such ideas were not new, of course; Magra traces their genesis back to the tumultuous democratic agitation of the English Revolution. The maritime radicalism of the American Revolution was in turn echoed by European naval mutineers a generation later. Niklas Frykman demonstrates that the lower-deck rebels of the 1790s found powerful inspiration in the most advanced democratic ideas of the revolutionary Atlantic, and

---

25. R.R. Palmer, *The Age of the Democratic Revolution: A Political History of Europe and America, 1760–1800*, 2 vols (Princeton, NJ, 1959, 1964); Eric Hobsbawm, *The Age of Revolution, 1789–1848* (London, 1975).
26. For a survey of recent work, see David Armitage and Sanjay Subrahmanyam (eds), *The Age of Revolutions in Global Context, c.1760–1840* (Basingstoke, 2009).

combined these with their own militant traditions to fuel a wholly unprecedented cycle of massive naval revolt.

Radical ideas and the autonomous political practices associated with them also flowed from beyond the European imperial orbit on to the lower deck. As Marcus Rediker forcefully argues, the Mende, Temne, and Kono mutineers on board the *Amistad* reconstituted a chapter of the West African Poro Society deep below deck in the hold of the slave ship, using its transplanted authority to forge iron bonds of solidarity and declare war on their captors. Similarly, Matthias van Rossum shows how, throughout the 1780s, Balinese slaves aboard Dutch East Indiamen brought with them a shared knowledge of amok, a furious, collective act of violent revolt which they deployed to devastating effect on board the *Mercuur* in 1782.

Shipboard unrest was not simply an extension or transfer of land-based struggles on to the sea, but rather the result of an amalgamation of geographically diffuse cultural traditions and political experiences in a highly concentrated, physically isolated, and immensely tension-filled environment, the like of which existed nowhere on land. In her essay on British convict transportation across the Indian Ocean, Bay of Bengal, and South China Sea, Clare Anderson illustrates the explosive and creative potential of a specifically maritime cosmopolitanism by showing how Indian peasant rebels, anti-imperial insurgents from across south Asia, and veteran Chinese pirates repeatedly pooled their martial knowledge to launch more than a dozen shipboard revolts in the declining years of the British East India Company's rule.

Cultural heterogeneity onboard ship could itself become a source of conflict, which in turn might precipitate mutiny, especially when class and ethnic or racial lines of division coincided, as they frequently did on slave ships, on European convict vessels sailing in Asian waters, or indeed the European owned and officered merchant ships crewed by Asian sailors that are at the center of Aaron Jaffer's fine-grained analysis of lascar resistance.

The extraordinarily large number of mutinies uncovered in these essays should not lead to the conclusion that overthrowing constituted authority on board ship was an easy thing to do, even in the age of revolution. Hamish Maxwell-Stewart demonstrates convincingly that convict vessels sailing from the British Isles to the Australian penal settlements were teeming with discontent, some of it of an explicitly radical political nature, and yet only 1 out of 830 voyages between 1787 and 1868 ended in a successful mutiny. But as Ian Duffield's essay suggests, would-be mutineers bided their time, waited patiently for their disembarkation in Australia, and then seized a convenient country vessel and put to sea as convict pirates in the South Pacific. The very ships designed to terrorize, remove, and reform European troublemakers inadvertently served to diffuse an insurrectionary spirit literally halfway around the world.

Nicole Ulrich shows that British warships did the same when they carried news of the 1797 fleet mutinies from home waters to southern Africa, where it promptly ignited a squadron-wide mutiny at the anchorage off Cape Town, which in turn sent a spark flying from ship to shore that connected naval mutineers to unruly KhoiSan laborers and slaves in the backcountry.

Authorities elsewhere took steps to guard against the danger of similar revolutionary contagion emanating from the open sea: the very same year that major naval mutinies raged in British home waters and off the Cape, Dutch authorities in cosmopolitan Curaçao built a new fort to protect the island's capital Willemstad, and carefully positioned its guns to threaten its own naval squadron in the bay below, which, as Karwan Fatah-Black recounts, had by now a well-earned reputation for troublemaking and political militancy.

On Curaçao, the revolutionary threat of maritime radicalism come ashore never fully materialized – divisions of race, class, nationality, and politics ran too deep – but a generation later it finally came into its own when mutineers on board the slave ship *Creole* sailed into Bermuda's Nassau harbour, where, as Anita Rupprecht movingly describes, they found a powerful, armed community of amphibious radicals, many of them former slaves themselves, who swarmed the ship and forced the colonial government to recognize the insurgents' freedom.

CONCLUSION

Maritime historians have long tended to naturalize early modern shipboard hierarchies, whether military or civilian – to see them as imposed by the physical environment of a large deep-sea-going sailing vessel itself, and as a consequence to treat mutinies as rare anomalies, unusual breakdowns, or failures of command that are blamed on the shortcomings of particular officers, the influence of individual troublemakers, or on the unusual hardships caused by shortages of provisions or space on a particular voyage. In a revealing contrast to the dominant analyses of the revolutions that brought down the ancien régime, explanations in fact have tended to focus on almost everything except the violent, tyrannical nature of shipboard society and the lower deck's well-founded, well-reasoned decision to countenance it no longer.

Taken together, the essays collected here offer a different narrative, one that demonstrates repeatedly and unambiguously the political maturity and radical autonomy of the lower deck, whether on board slave ships, convict ships, warships, or massive East Indiamen. In so doing they also suggest a new, sea-centered geography of the revolutionary era, a dense and expansive network, reaching across the globe, as well as forward and backward in time, a network of seafarers that brought together, amalgamated, and mutually stimulated struggles in vastly different and distant regions.

It is notable that this network almost perfectly coincides with the rapidly unfurling tentacles of European imperialism into the Indian Ocean region, to south-east Asia, and to Australia and the south Pacific in the late eighteenth and early nineteenth centuries. The adoption of a maritime perspective thus suggests strongly the insufficiency of conceiving of this period as simply one of Atlantic revolution. But how to conceptualize the era instead – how to make sense of its powerful dialectic of revolutionary overthrow and imperial expansion, how to delineate its full geographic reach, not just across oceans but deep into continental interiors as well, and how to map these connections in turn – goes well beyond the present volume to a new, even broader collective research agenda.

We opened this introductory essay with a brief genealogy of mutiny, for it is unrest at sea which constitutes the central theme of each essay in this volume. As the authors collectively make clear, the different levels of maritime radicalism were deeply connected, especially in the age of revolution – when a ship's captain, an imperial planner, and an international capitalist could all seem jointly tyrannical. Convict pirate, naval mutineer, and slave ship rebel, in turn, proposed dreams of freedom that were as expansive and widely open, as egalitarian and anti-national as the sea itself. During this age of revolution, in other words, the ship as both engine of capitalism and space of resistance was a mobile nodal point of great strategic importance, for both rulers *and* workers worldwide.

IRSH 58 (2013), Special Issue, pp. 15–34 doi:10.1017/S0020859013000242
© 2013 Internationaal Instituut voor Sociale Geschiedenis

The African Origins of the *Amistad* Rebellion, 1839

MARCUS REDIKER

Department of History, University of Pittsburgh
3508 Posvar Hall, Pittsburgh, PA 15260, USA

E-mail: red1@pitt.edu

ABSTRACT: This essay explores the *Amistad* rebellion of 1839, in which fifty-three Africans seized a slave schooner, sailed it to Long Island, New York, made an alliance with American abolitionists, and won their freedom in a protracted legal battle. Asking how and why the rebels succeeded, it emphasizes the African background and experience, as well as the "fictive kinship" that grew out of many incarcerations, as sources of solidarity that made the uprising possible. The essay concludes by discussing the process of mutiny, suggesting a six-phase model for understanding the dynamics of shipboard revolt, and showing how such events can have powerful historical consequences.

The *Amistad* rebellion is one of the most famous shipboard revolts in history. In 1839 fifty-three enslaved Africans rose up, killed two members of the Cuban slaver's crew, made prisoners their so-called "masters", José Ruiz and Pedro Montes, took control of the vessel, and sailed it to Long Island, New York. These self-emancipated rebels were then captured by the United States Navy, towed ashore, and incarcerated in New Haven, Connecticut, where their cause became a political controversy and a popular sensation, in the United States and around the Atlantic. In jail they built an alliance with American abolitionists and fought a long and ultimately successful legal battle to avert return to slavery in Cuba. Nineteen months after the revolt, they won their formal freedom before the United States Supreme Court and, eight months later, their repatriation to their native Sierra Leone. It was a major victory in the worldwide struggle against slavery.[1]

The *Amistad* rebellion was part of a massive Atlantic wave of resistance to slavery during the 1830s. David Walker's *Appeal [...] to the Coloured Citizens of the World* (1829) had emphasized the continuing relevance of Toussaint L'Ouverture and the Haitian Revolution to freedom struggles. Sailors, black and white, spread the revolutionary word by smuggling the pamphlet into

---

1. This essay draws on material presented in my book, *The Amistad Rebellion: An Atlantic Odyssey of Slavery and Freedom* (New York, 2012).

slave societies. Nat Turner led a bloody uprising in Southampton County, Virginia, in 1831, and Sam Sharpe followed with his "Baptist War" in Jamaica in 1831–1832. Enslaved Africans in southern Sierra Leone waged a prolonged revolt called the Zawo War against Spanish and African slave-traders. Other revolts, for example, in Brazil and Cuba, erupted against the backdrop of a growing abolitionist movement and indeed helped to make it possible. William Lloyd Garrison founded *The Liberator* in Boston in 1831 and Great Britain abolished slavery in its West Indian colonies in two stages, in 1834 and 1838. Shipboard revolts on the *Amistad* and the *Creole* in 1839 and 1841 were victorious exclamation points in this powerful cycle of rebellion.[2]

The *Amistad* rebellion also occupies a special place in the longer history of revolts aboard slave ships. Such risings were not uncommon, occurring on as many as one slaving voyage out of ten over the three and a half centuries of the gruesome trade in human bodies, even though slave ships were designed to make uprisings difficult, if not impossible, and slaving captains possessed a time-tested body of practical knowledge about how to prevent revolt, from the use of ethnic conflict to the application of torture and terror. *Successful* revolts, however, were extremely rare, which raises the question, how did the *Amistad* Africans do it? What follows is a narrative of the *Amistad* rebellion, beginning with a description of the schooner itself, followed by an account of what happened in the mutiny and an analysis of what made it successful. The essay suggests a model for understanding mutiny on slave ships and other kinds of vessels.[3]

THE REBELLION

The European deep-sea sailing ship, of which the slave ship was an important type, was the most important machine of what has been called

2. Henry Highland Garnet, *An Address to the Slaves of the United States of America* (Buffalo, NY, 1843); Peter Hinks, *To Awaken my Afflicted Brethren: David Walker and the Problem of Antebellum Slave Resistance* (University Park, PA, 1997); C.L.R. James, *The Black Jacobins: Toussaint L'Ouverture and the San Domingo Revolution* (New York, 1989; orig. publ. 1938); Kenneth S. Greenberg, *Nat Turner: A Slave Rebellion in History and Memory* (New York, 2003); Michael Craton, *Testing the Chains: Resistance to Slavery in the British West Indies* (Ithaca, NY, 1982); Adam Jones, *From Slaves to Palm Kernels: A History of the Galinhas Country (West Africa), 1730–1890* (Wiesbaden, 1983), pp. 89–94; João José Reis, *Slave Rebellion in Brazil: The Muslim Uprising of 1835 in Bahia* (Baltimore, MD, 1993); Robert L. Paquette, *Sugar is Made with Blood: The Conspiracy of La Escalera and the Conflict between Empires over Slavery in Cuba* (Middletown, CT, 1988); James Brewer Stewart, *Holy Warriors: The Abolitionists and American Slavery* (New York, 1996).
3. David Richardson, "Shipboard Revolts, African Authority, and the Atlantic Slave Trade", *William and Mary Quarterly*, 3rd series, 58 (2001), pp. 69–92, 73–74; David Eltis and David Richardson, *Atlas of the Transatlantic Slave Trade* (New Haven, CT, 2010), p. 189; Marcus Rediker, *The Slave Ship: A Human History* (New York, 2007), pp. 291–301. See also the Trans-Atlantic Slave Trade Database, available at http://www.slavevoyages.org/.

the age of sail, roughly 1450–1850. When mutineers seized such a machine, they took possession of a technology that combined unprecedented speed, mobility, and, because of their cannon, destructive power. Because such ships were highly variable in size and number of people aboard, the type of vessel and its various material characteristics shaped the way mutiny happened.[4]

The *Amistad* was a long, low schooner, a two-masted craft common around the Atlantic in the early nineteenth century. The vessel was small by the standards of the day, 64 feet long, 19 feet 9 inches wide. It was essentially a coastal trader, but it had made longer voyages from Cuba to Jamaica, and its coppered hull suggests the possibility of a transatlantic slaving voyage or two. Built for speed, with limited carrying capacity, the schooner could outrun most British ships policing the slave trade and hence became a preferred vessel after the commerce in bodies had been outlawed in 1807–1808 in Great Britain and the United States.[5]

Before departure from Havana on 28 June 1839, bound for Puerto Príncipe, Cuba, a region of burgeoning sugar plantations, Captain Ramón Ferrer filled the hold of roughly 6,600 cubic feet with a big, well-sorted cargo: the enslaved (49 men, 4 children) as well as manufactured goods for plantation use: cog wheels, iron castings, and mill rollers. The cargo also contained fabrics and clothes, items for everyday use (soap, iron pots, leather goods), and a huge amount of food: 600 pounds of rice, as well as bread, fruit, olives, sausages, and "fresh beef". There was much less on board to drink: only 6 casks of water. As it happened, in the days leading up to the voyage, ship captains in Havana were having "great difficulty of finding a sufficient quantity of water casks", as one of them put it. The shortage would have consequences.[6]

---

4. Rediker, *The Slave Ship*, ch. 2.

5. See Quentin Snediker's excellent article on the history of the vessel, "Searching for the Historic *Amistad*", *Log of Mystic Seaport*, 49:4 (1998), pp. 86–95, in which he cites Captain George Howland, "An Autobiography or Journal of his Life, Voyages, and Travels with an Appendix of his Ancestry", 1866, typescript 295, Rhode Island Historical Society, Providence, Rhode Island, and Temporary Registry #15, for the schooner *Ion*, ex-*Amistad*, New London Customs Records, RG36, National Archives at Boston, Frederick C. Murphy Records Center, Waltham, MA [hereafter NAB]. Howland bought the *Amistad* at auction on 15 October 1840.

6. For detailed accounts of the cargo, see *New London Gazette*, 28 August 1839; "Superior Court", *New York Morning Herald*, 24 October 1839; *The Intelligencer*, 27 October 1839; and the Libel of José Ruiz, 18 September 1839, US District Court for the District of Connecticut, NAB. On the scarcity of casks, see Captain J. Scholborg to R.R. Madden, Havana, 28 June 1839, West India Miscellaneous, 1839; vol.: Removal of the Liberated Africans from Cuba, Superintendent Dr Madden and Superintendent Mr Clarke, Foreign Office; Correspondence from Dr R.R. Madden, Mr D.R. Clarke, and the Foreign Office relating to the removal of the "Liberated Africans" from Cuba, 1839, Colonial Office (CO) 318/146, National Archives of the UK [hereafter NA]. The letter carried the same date as the *Amistad*'s loading and departure from port.

Unlike the large slave ships, the *Amistad* did not have a lower deck, where the enslaved would be jammed together overnight and in bad weather. It was a single-deck vessel with a hold, which measured 6 feet 6 inches from the top of the keel to the underside of the deck above, with headroom diminishing on both sides as the hull curved upward to meet the outer edges. The bulky cargo already stored in the hold left limited room for the human freight, which was jumbled in with, and on top of, the hogsheads, casks, and boxes. The enslaved, crammed below deck, had very little headroom. Indeed, the hold was so crowded that half of the captives would have to be quartered on the deck and forced to sleep in the open, overnight, in chains for the three-day voyage. The rest were fettered and kept below.

The deck of the *Amistad* was crowded, especially during the day, when 60 people (53 Africans, 5 crew members, and 2 passengers) inhabited its 1,200 square feet, much of which was devoted to the masts, the longboat, the hatchway, and other shipboard fixtures. The *Amistad* also lacked a barricado on the deck, a defensive bulwark behind which the crew could retreat in the event of an uprising and from which they could fire their muskets and pistols down on the insurgents. The *Amistad* did have a galley with a brick oven for the preparation of the captives' food – a telltale sign of its slave-trading purpose. It also had a large hatchway amidships for the easier movement of bodies above and below during the voyage. It had 10 sweeps (oars) for self-locomotion and easier maneuvering along the treacherous shoals and inlets of the north coast of Cuba.[7]

The voyage of about 300 miles began well, with a good wind. Yet Captain Ferrer, who had made the passage many times, knew that the winds could shift and that the usual three-day voyage could stretch to two weeks or longer. He immediately put the enslaved on short allowance, conserving food, and especially the understocked water, for the additional time they might be at sea. On the second day out, the small vessel ran in to a storm, no doubt terrifying all of the Africans on board, but probably not the experienced sailors, who would have known harder weather. Turbulence without was soon matched by turbulence within.

The first sign of trouble came early, when on the night immediately following departure "one of the sailors observed that the slaves were coming up from the hold of the forecastle, and that they made some noise, on which account the sailor reprimanded them and told them to be quiet and go down into the hold". This seemed innocent enough; "murmurings" and commotion were common on slave ships. Crowded conditions

---

7. Dwight P. Janes to Lewis Tappan, New London, 6 September 1839, Sierra Leone Papers, American Missionary Association, Amistad Research Center, New Orleans, Louisiana [hereafter ARC].

produced anger, frustration, and fights among the captives and with the crew. Currents of tension and violence coursed through all slaving vessels, including the *Amistad*.[8]

The hardware of bondage was part of the charge. Grabeau and Kimbo, both leaders in the resistance, remembered that "during the night they were kept in irons, placed about the hands, feet, and neck. They were treated during the day in a somewhat milder manner, though all the irons were never taken off at once". The captain and crew slapped manacles, shackles, and neck-rings on the captives, especially overnight because some of the prisoners slept near them, on the deck. Kinna remembered the neck-rings as a special humiliation: "Chain on neck – you know dey chain ox". Fetters turned human beings into property, but not without a struggle.[9]

Casual violence was commonplace on slaving vessels, and the *Amistad* was no exception. Captain and crew alike used whips, clubs, and fists to terrorize and control the captives. On the deck of any deep-sea sailing ship could be found many tools and other items that handily became instruments of violent discipline. Cinqué and Bau recalled, "The captain of the schooner was very cruel; he beat them on the head very hard with any thing he could catch." Cinqué remembered with fierce anger a time when the slave-sailor and ship's cook Celestino slapped him on the head with a plantain. The cook would pay dearly for his mistake.[10]

The *Amistad* Africans also complained that they were given too little to eat and drink on the voyage – "half eat half drink" was how Fuli described short allowance. In concrete terms this meant two potatoes and one plantain twice a day, in the morning and evening. The fare may have been enough for the children on board, but it was too little for the men. Kinna recalled that the captain "gives us but little eat". Cinqué and Bau added that they were kept "almost starved" – this on a vessel full of food.[11]

Water was an even greater source of strife. Grabeau and Kimbo recalled that "their allowance of food was very scant, and of water still more so. They were very hungry, and suffered much in the hot days and nights from thirst." The allotment of water was half a teacupful in the morning and half a teacupful in the evening. As the prisoners suffered, they watched the crew wash their clothes in fresh water. To make matters worse, Celestino taunted them by taking long drafts in front of them. Kinna recalled, "He drink plenty, long". On a craft sailing through the tropics in midsummer,

8. "The Amistad", *New London Gazette*, 16 October 1839.
9. "Narrative of the Africans", *New York Journal of Commerce*, 10 October 1839.
10. "Private Examination of Cinquez", *New York Commercial Advertiser*, 13 September 1839.
11. "Mendis Perform", *New York Morning Herald*, 13 May 1841. In collective memory the amount of food had shrunk by 1852 to half a plantain per meal; see Hannah Moore to William Harned, 12 October 1852, ARC, for a remarkable oral history of the event taken from survivors at the Mende Mission thirteen years after the event.

the Africans simply were not given enough water to support nature.[12] At least some of the captives seem to have been able to move around the vessel during the daytime, and they took matters into their own hands. They searched for water and they found it below decks. To satisfy their burning thirst, they tapped and drank it, without permission.

When they were caught, Captain Ferrer decided to teach everyone a lesson. At least five men – Fuli, Kimbo, Pie, Moru, and Foone – and perhaps as many as seven (Sessi, Burna) – were each, by turn, restrained and flogged.[13] "[F]or stealing water which had been refused him", Fuli "was held down by four sailors and beaten on the back many times by another sailor, with a whip having several lashes". He referred to the lacerating cat-o'-nine-tails, the primary instrument of power aboard a slave ship. The sailors then flogged the other four, then repeated the entire cycle of punishment four times on each person. In order to maximize the torture, the seamen, with Ruiz's permission, mixed together "salt, rum, and [gun] powder" and applied the burning compound to Fuli's wounds. Not surprisingly, for sailors used gunpowder in tattooing, the marks of the wounds on Fuli's back were still visible months later. Kinna pointed out another disagreeable use of the compound: "Rum, salt, powder – put togedder, make eat dis I tell you". Months later, one of the Africans was still "lame, so as hardly able to walk, as he declares from blows received on board the Amistad".

Tensions aboard the schooner escalated amid the hunger, thirst, violence, torture, and blood. As the Africans later announced, "They would not take it".[14] Shortly after the morning meal of Monday 1 July, Cinqué and Celestino squared off in a fateful encounter on the deck of the *Amistad*. Tension had been rising between the two. Celestino had cuffed Cinqué and had likely been greeted in return by fiery eyes of resistance. He expanded his campaign by taunting the proud prisoner, of whom it could have been said, "Dat man ha big heart too much".[15]

Because the two men shared no common language, Celestino communicated by signs and gestures – "talking with his fingers", as one African recalled – and the menacing cook's knife he held in his hand. In

12. "Mendis Perform".
13. Testimony of Cinqué, 8 January 1840, United States District Court, Connecticut, NAB; "Narrative," *New York Journal of Commerce*, 10 January 1840.
14. "Ruiz and Montez", *New York Commercial Advertiser*, 18 October 1839; "Mendis Perform", "Plans to Educate the Amistad Africans in English", *New York Journal of Commerce*, 9 October 1839; "To the Committee on Behalf of the African Prisoners", *New York Journal of Commerce*, 10 September 1839.
15. "Ruiz and Montez". The phrase in pidgin English used by liberated Africans in Freetown to describe a proud person such as Cinqué is recorded in Robert Clarke, *Sierra Leone: A Description of the Manners and Customs of the Liberated Africans; with Observations upon the Natural History of the Colony, and a Notice of the Native Tribes* (London, 1843), p. 11.

order to answer the questions that were on every captive's mind – where are we going and what will become of us at the end of the voyage? – Celestino drew his blade's edge across his throat: they were going to a place where they would all be killed. The cook then made a chopping motion with his knife to show that their bodies would then be hacked to bits by the white men. He took the imagined bits of flesh to his mouth: they would be eaten. He gestured to a cask of salt beef, implying that it was filled with the bodies of Africans from a previous voyage; he gestured again to an empty cask indicating that therein lay their fate. As Cinqué noted, "The cook told us they carry us to some place and kill and eat us". Kinna added that Celestino "with his knife, made signs of throat-cutting. &c., and pointed to the barrels of beef, and thus hinted to Cinquez, that himself and his companions were to be cut up and salted down for food like beef". He pointed to "an Island ahead where the fatal deed was to be perpetrated". His words had direct impact, although they did not ter-rorize and pacify, as he had hoped they would. Instead, they galvanized the Africans to action. Every account of the uprising told by any of the *Amistad* Africans emphasized the decisive importance of Celestino's threat as a catalyst of rebellion.[16]

That night, after the vexed encounter between Cinqué and Celestino, as the *Amistad* sailed past Bahia de Cadiz a little before midnight, a storm arose from the shore. Rain poured from a dark, cloudy, moonless sky. Ruiz remembered it as a "black night". High winds prompted Captain Ferrer to order all hands aloft to take in the topsails to reduce the power of the wind to buffet the vessel. In a couple of hours, the rain stopped and the storm abated. All of the crew and passengers, except the helmsman, retired and were soon "sunk in sleep".[17]

A bigger storm was brewing in the hold of the vessel. Celestino's murderous sign language had created a crisis among the captives. As Grabeau stated and Kimbo affirmed, his sinister threat of death and cannibalism "made their hearts burn". Kinna remembered, "We very unhappy all dat night – we fraid we be kill – we consider". Soon, "We break off our chains and consider what we should do". Crowded together in the hold of the ship, they debated what to do in the face of an unspeakably horrible mass death.[18] An "old man" named Lubos had earlier reminded everyone that "no one ever conquered our nation, & even now we are not taken by fair means". Someone, probably Cinqué, responded, "Who is for

16. *Farmer's Cabinet*, 19 November 1841; Joseph Sturge, *A Visit To The United States In 1841* (London, 1842), Appendix E, p. xliv; Moore to Harned, 12 October 1852; "African Testimony", *New York Journal of Commerce*, 10 January 1840.
17. "Mendis Perform"; "The Long, Low Black Schooner", *New York Sun*, 31 August 1839; "The Amistad".
18. "Narrative of the Africans"; "Mendis Perform"; *Youth's Cabinet*, 20 May 1841.

War?". Most were, but a small group of Bullom men held back, fearing to "make war on the owners of the vessel". Lubos asked whether they would rather be "slaughtered for Cannibals" or "die fighting for life". Only one of these choices was an honorable death.

Lubos carried the day and the decision for war was taken, but now the Africans faced a literally iron dilemma. How would they get out of the manacles, shackles, neck-rings, chains, and padlocks that rendered them unable to move about the ship? Cinqué later remarked that "the chain which connected the iron collars about their necks, was fastened at the end by a padlock, and that this was first broken and afterwards the other irons". Kinna also stated, "We break off our chains", but he later added a second, somewhat different description of what they did: Cinqué found a loose nail on deck and used it to pick the central padlock. Whether the locks were broken or picked, a substantial number of men were soon free of their chains and ready to fly into action, awaiting Cinqué's "signal for them to rise upon their vile masters and the crew".[19]

At 4 am the ship was in almost total darkness. Everyone was asleep except the sailor at the helm. Cinqué, Faquorna, Moru, and Kimbo climbed up from the hold through the hatchway and on to the deck. It is not clear whether they had to break open the grating or whether it had been left unlocked by mistake. They crept quietly toward Celestino – not Captain Ferrer – as the first and primary object of their wrath. He was sleeping in the ship's long-boat, which lay in the waist, on the larboard side, near the cabin. Along the way Cinqué picked up a belaying pin, or handspike, used to turn the ship's windlass, and his mates did likewise, quietly gathering weapons from the deck. They surrounded Celestino and clubbed him repeatedly with hard, crushing blows. Fuli later recalled, "The cook was killed first – was killed by Jingua [Cinqué] with a stick, while lying in the boat". Burna agreed: "He saw Cinguez strike the cook with a club, probably a handspike". During the beating, Celestino did not cry out or groan, did not make any sound at all, according to Antonio, the captain's Afro-Cuban cabin boy. The only sounds to be heard in the damp night air above the rolling of the sea and the creaking of the ship were the thuds of wood on flesh and bone.[20]

19. "Narrative of the Africans"; "Mendis Perform"; "Anniversaries – Amistad Freemen", *Youth's Cabinet*, 20 May 1841; John Warner Barber, *A History of the Amistad Captives, being a Circumstantial Account of the Capture of the Spanish Schooner Amistad, by the Africans on Board; their Voyage, and Capture near Long Island, New York; with Biographical Sketches of each of the Surviving Africans. Also, an Account of the Trials had on their Case, before the District and Circuit Courts of the United States, for the District of Connecticut. Complied from Authentic Sources, by John W. Barber, Mem. of the Connecticut Hist. Soc.* (New Haven, CT, 1840), p. 11; "The Amistad Negroes", *Farmer's Cabinet*, 19 November 1841; "The Amistad Captives", *Liberator*, 19 November 1841.
20. "African Testimony"; "The Case of the Africans Decided for the Present – Habeas Corpus not Sustained", *New York Morning Herald*, 25 September 1839.

Now began "the whooh", as Burna called the chaos of open rebellion that engulfed the small deck. The commotion woke up the captain, who was sleeping on a mattress not far away, as well as the rest of the crew, and Ruiz and Montes, who were in the cabin. Ferrer called out, "Attack them, for they have killed the cook". Amid the confusion and uproar, those under attack scrambled frantically in the dark for arms, grabbing whatever was close at hand; there was no time to load pistols or muskets. Captain Ferrer seized a dagger and a club and fought furiously to defend his vessel from capture. The two sailors, Manuel and Jacinto, who were supposed to be the armed guard to prevent what was now happening before their very eyes, threw themselves into the battle, one with a club, the other with no weapon at all. Montes armed himself with a knife and a pump handle, screaming all the while at the Africans to stop, to be still. The unarmed sailor yelled to Montes to get the dead cook's knife and give it to him. Ruiz grabbed an oar as he scrambled from his passenger's quarters, shouting "No! No!" as he came on deck. Ruiz then "stood before the caboose and halloed to the slaves to be quiet and to go down into the hold". They ignored the command of their former master; indeed, more Africans escaped their chains and joined the fray, now wielding fearsome machetes. Seeing that the situation was far beyond exhortation, Ruiz called to Montes to kill some of the rebels in order to frighten the rest and to restore order. He believed, wrongly, that the Africans were all "great cowards".[21]

At first the crew and passengers were able to drive the rebels from amidships beyond the foremast, and at this point Captain Ferrer, who desperately hoped that this was a rebellion of the belly, commanded Antonio to fetch some sea biscuit and throw it among the rebels in the hope of distracting them. He knew they were hungry – too little food had been a complaint since the voyage began. Antonio did as his master commanded, but the insurgents, he explained, "would not touch it". Antonio himself opted for neutrality: he climbed up the mainstays, where he would watch the struggle unfold, safely from above.[22]

As the battle raged, Captain Ferrer killed a man named Duevi and mortally wounded a second, unnamed rebel, which infuriated the other Africans and made them fight harder. He also wounded others, as Kale recalled: "Then captain kill one man with knife and cut Mendi

21. "The Long, Low Black Schooner"; "Case", *New York Morning Herald*, 22 September 1839; "The Amistad"; "The Case of the Captured Negroes", *New York Morning Herald*, 9 September 1839. On the little girls and their discovery of the cane knives see Madden to A. Blackwood, Esq., 3 October 1839, Correspondence from Dr R.R. Madden, Mr D.R. Clarke, and the Foreign Office relating to the removal of the liberated Africans from Cuba, 1839, Colonial Office (CO) 318/146, NA.
22. Interview of Antonio, "The Long, Low Black Schooner".

people plenty". Two of the rebels attacked Montes with an oar, which he grabbed and used to hold them off. Montes wrestled with the men until one of the sailors cried out that he should let it go or they would kill him. At this point, a blow to his arm caused Montes to drop his knife. He groped desperately around the deck in an effort to find it. Ruiz continued to scream at the rebels to stop fighting and go below, but they ignored him, soon disarming him of his own makeshift weapon.[23]

Suddenly the tide of battle turned – red. An insurgent wielding one of the machetes slashed one of the sailors, who cried out "Murder!" He and his crewmate saw not only defeat but certain death in the ever larger, machete-wielding mob, so they threw a canoe overboard. They would not have had time to lower the longboat, which was in any case heavy with the battered corpse of Celestino. They jumped into the water, leaving the remaining four to battle many times their number. Of one of the sailors, Kinna recalled: "He swim – swim long time – may be swim more – we not know". The two sailors, cut and bleeding, eventually crawled into the canoe and began paddling for land. They had about eighteen miles to cover and it was by no means certain they would make it.[24]

Someone now gave Montes "a powerful blow on the head with a cane knife, and he fell senseless on the deck". Stunned, with another deep wound on his arm and "faint from the loss of blood", he roused himself, staggered from the battle scene, and fell headlong down the hatchway. Once below, he remained conscious enough to crawl into a space between two barrels and hide beneath a canvas sail. It was a frail hope against death.[25]

On deck, Cinqué and the other leaders of the rebellion now surrounded Captain Ferrer in a fury of flashing blades. Faquorna apparently struck the first two blows, Cinqué the final, fatal one. Antonio testified, "Sinqua killed Capt with cane knife – see it with my eyes".[26] When the time for the death blow came, one of the brave combatants, Kimbo, proved to be squeamish: "When the Captain of the schooner was killed, he could not see it done, but looked another way". Slashed several times on his face and body, the captain collapsed on the deck, bloody, crumpled, and lifeless.

---

23. Kale to John Quincy Adams, 4 January 1841, John Quincy Adams Papers, Massachusetts Historical Society. Fuliwa stated, "Capt. Ferrer killed one of the Africans, Duevi by name, before the Africans killed him". See "African Testimony". Kinna later alleged that Captain Ferrer had killed two of the Africans. One of them, unnamed, seems to have died later of wounds inflicted by Captain Ferrer.
24. "Mendis Perform"; Ruiz: "The cabin boy said they had killed only the captain and cook. The other two he said had escaped in the canoe – a small boat". See "The Captured Slaves", *New York Morning Herald*, 2 September 1839.
25. "Mendis Perform".
26. Testimony of Antonio, 9 January 1840, United States District Court, NAB.

Figure 1. "Death of Capt. Ferrer, the Captain of the Amistad, July 1839". This most famous image of the *Amistad* rebellion was drawn by engraver John Warner Barber, who visited the Africans in New Haven Jail and depicted the rebels as identifiable individuals – Cinqué at the far left with the cane knife in hand, attacking Captain Ramon Ferrer, and the similarly armed Konoma at the far right, rushing into battle.
From A History of the Amistad Captives *(New Haven, CT, 1839). Courtesy of Marietta College Library. Used with permission.*

The rebels danced, yelled, and beheaded the captain in a carnivalesque moment of victory.[27]

They now went in search of Montes, whose ragged, heavy breathing gave away his hiding place below deck. An enraged Cinqué found him and swung at him twice with his cane knife, narrowly missing. Montes begged for his life, to no avail as Cinqué prepared to swing again, until Burna stayed his arm. Cinqué and Burna then carried Montes up to the deck, where he saw Ruiz, "seated upon the hen coop with both hands tied". He, too, was pleading for his life. The rebels laced the two Spaniards together, "making at the same time horrible gestures" and threatening to kill them. Someone dragged young Antonio down from the stays and tied him to the two other prisoners. After a little while, Ruiz recalled, the insurgents "made signs that they would not hurt me". The new masters of the vessel then locked their prisoners below as they went through the captain's cabin and also familiarized themselves with the cargo.[28]

With two dead, two overboard, and three disarmed, bound, and begging for their lives, an eerie silence came over the blood-stained deck. The rebellion was over. The social world of the *Amistad* had been turned upside down. The captain and cook had been killed, the sailors had been forced to

27. "The Long, Low Black Schooner"; "The Negroes of the Amistad", *New Hampshire Sentinel*, 2 October 1839. According to the oral history as relayed by Hannah Moore, "the ocean reverberated with the yells and frantic dances of a savage clan". See Moore to Harned, 12 October 1852.
28. "The Long, Low Black Schooner"; "Case".

jump overboard, and the slaveholders were now prisoners. Those who had once been slaves had won their freedom in a desperate armed gamble.

SOURCES OF SOLIDARITY

What made the *Amistad* rebellion possible, and what in the end made it successful? The answers to these questions lie in a set of common characteristics and experiences that served as bases for the rebels' collective action. Most of the commonalities were based in the West African cultures from which they came. Others had emerged during their various captivities, in Lomboko (the slave-trading factory where they had been taken for shipment), on the transatlantic Portuguese slave ship *Teçora*, in the Havana barracoons (where they stayed ten days), and on board the *Amistad*. Out of these experiences grew a solidarity manifested in the uprising.

Who were the rebels? They were a motley crew, consisting of at least ten different ethnicities or nationalities. Yet they shared an unusually large capacity for communication among themselves: almost two-thirds were Mende, several others could speak Mende, and almost all were multilingual, as was common in their region of origin. All came from societies in which they were accustomed to working together for the good of the whole. Almost all were commoners: several practiced communal rice farming; others were urban weavers.

Crucially, all came from communities governed by the Poro Society – the powerful all-male secret society that trained warriors, declared war, organized rites of passage, settled disputes, and maintained social discipline. When it was observed that Cinqué "had been accustomed to command", the meaning of the phrase was two-fold: he had military experience and discipline and he had wielded authority in the Poro Society, which was by far the most significant means of self-organization known by, and practiced among, the *Amistad* Africans, whether Mende, Temne, or Kono.[29]

The rebels also shared a set of profound experiences based on their common misfortune of enslavement. All had been expropriated from the land and enslaved, although by various means, whether judicial ruling, kidnapping, or military action. All had endured a long, debilitating march, by land and water, to the coast. All, except the four children, were young, strong, able-bodied men, who had been separated from the families and kinship systems that had previously governed their lives. The very characteristics that made them desirable as slaves, whose youthful labor power could be exploited, made them dangerous as potential rebels. All had been

29. Barber, *A History of the Amistad Captives*, pp. 8, 11, 13. For evidence of Cinqué's Poro marks, called "tattoos", see *Pennsylvania Freeman*, 26 September 1839.

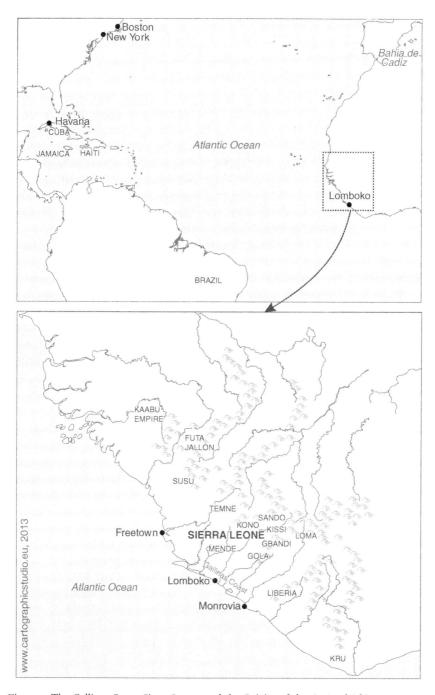

Figure 2. The Gallinas Coast, Sierra Leone, and the Origins of the *Amistad* Africans, c.1839.

imprisoned at Pedro Blanco's Fort Lomboko, on the Gallinas Coast. It was here that Cinqué and Grabeau met and began a conversation about freedom that would last several years. Grabeau testified that he "met the others for the first time" at Lomboko, where they began to take shape as a strange, new, accidental collective.[30]

All had experienced the slave ship and its Middle Passage, jammed together with 500–600 others in miserable circumstances for "two moons", many dying along the way, the survivors developing a "fictive kinship" that grew among the "brothers" and "sisters" of a common ordeal. Those bound for the *Amistad* wailed in anguish when they were separated from other shipmates on sale in Havana, and those who remained together repeatedly explained that "they were all brought from Africa in the same vessel", a powerful source of solidarity. Shared sufferings in the Havana barracoons and aboard the *Amistad* strengthened these ties.

The *Amistad* Africans, in sum, boasted commonalities of work, culture, government, enslavement, youth, geographic origins, sites of cooperation (factory, ship), and fictive kinship as "shipmates". In the broader context of the history of the slave trade, they exhibited unusually strong common experiences, social characteristics, and cultural connections, all of which combined to create a broad basis for collective rebellion, in a small place at a specific moment in time. They did not choose their way into the dilemma that confronted them aboard the *Amistad*, but they did choose their way out.

THE PROCESS OF SHIPBOARD REVOLT

Uprisings aboard slave ships (and, I would argue, on other types of ships) proceeded through six phases, some social, some technological. But they could – and did – break down, allowing the conspiracy to be discovered, and thereby to fail, at any point along the way. The phases were: forming an original core of rebels (what the Mende called *Ko-biye*, the attacking force, or vanguard, that would lead the rebellion); forming a collective that would carry it out; getting out of the irons (this phase would not apply to all mutinies); finding weapons; fighting the battle and seizing control of the ship; and eventually sailing the ship to freedom.

Cinqué and Grabeau, both Mende, constituted the original core of the rebels. The former was, in the idiom of the society from which he came, a "head war man", experienced and selected as such by his comrades in the hold of the *Amistad* in the run-up to the rebellion, which he subsequently led with bravery and success. The latter was apparently a high-ranking member of the Poro, evident from his extensive scarification and a fact offered later by someone who knew him in Mende country before his

30. "African Testimony".

enslavement: he was "connected with a high family, though poor himself". These two men thus represented a perfect combination of military, spiritual, and political authority as it existed on the Gallinas Coast and in its hinterlands – and, finally, in the displaced, mobile circumstances of the African diaspora aboard a slave ship in the northern Caribbean. Everyone on board would have recognized them immediately as leaders.[31]

Around these two leaders formed a secondary group: Burna, the third leading figure, and Moru – both Gbandi; Shule ("fourth in command, when on board the schooner") and Kimbo – both Mende; and Fa and Faquorna, nationality unknown. All had been warriors in their native societies. They now stepped forward because of their knowledge and experience of combat. They studied the ship and whispered their findings to each other in the hold. They wanted to know how the vessel worked, how many were the crew, what were their habits, what were their arms. (The crew was small; they kept no regular watch; they had muskets, pistols, and whips.) The warriors would have seen that the prospects for rebellion aboard the *Amistad* were much greater than they had been on the *Teçora*.[32]

The collective was formed (phase 2) through the organizing efforts of the *Ko-biye*, according to the principles of the Poro Society. Drawing on the host of experiences above, the collective came into purposeful existence during the meeting described by Kinna as the time when "we consider". During the "palaver" held in the hold, someone, probably Cinqué, asked, "Who is for War?". By the end of the meeting, the group had achieved unity, or, in Mende, *ngo yela*, which meant "one word" or unity. The oral history of the rebellion kept by the rebels themselves recalled their decision: all had "one word WAR!! and war immediately". They decided as a group to rise up, seize the ship, and sail home, or to die trying.

Even though a clear leadership had been established immediately before and during the uprising, the collective continued to meet and act together as the situation unfolded. As Ruiz noted, "a few days" after the rebellion the group met and officially chose Cinqué as their leader; he had earned the position through action, in the customary Mende way. They also allocated other positions among themselves: Sesse, who apparently had some seafaring knowledge (probably aboard the *Teçora*), would steer and "make sail". Foone would be the group's cook. Guided by Poro practice, the collective would be the sovereign decision-making power.[33]

These common experiences required a spark, a catalytic event, to bring them into full force. This lay in the confrontation between Cinqué and Celestino, which cannot be understood without a knowledge of Mende

31. *Vermont Chronicle*, 8 June 1842.
32. Barber, *History of the Amistad Captives*, p. 11.
33. *Ibid.*; Moore to Harned, 12 October 1852, ARC. On Grabeau's background, see *Vermont Chronicle*, 8 June 1842; Testimony of Antonio.

and neighboring cultures. Celestino's cannibalistic taunt resonated with a potent set of beliefs. In the interior of Sierra Leone, as elsewhere, it had been widely believed for decades that the strange white men who showed up on the coast in "floating houses" were cannibals. Enslaved Africans had on more than one occasion pointed to casks of beef as holding the flesh of previous captives and to puncheons of wine as holding their blood. West African slave-owners had long strengthened discipline in their own societies by threatening to sell slaves to the white men, who would, they explained, carry them across the "great waters" and eat them.

Since a large majority of the *Amistad* captives came from deep inland and had never seen white men, their ships, or even the sea, they took Celestino's threat of cannibalism seriously. Strengthening the grim prospect was another common belief, that cultural power could be wielded through the control and manipulation of body parts, which provided access to the world of malevolent spirits. Witches and sorcerers made special efforts to secure the body parts of famous warriors, whose hair, teeth, and bones might be used to create potent "medicine". Was Celestino a witch, a *honei*, who used his powers on behalf of the white men? Did Cinqué, as a warrior, feel especially threatened by the taunt? One of the main functions of the Poro Society was to punish, and at times to execute, witches and sorcerers who worked against the common good.[34]

Phase 3: how would the Africans get out of the irons – the manacles, shackles, neck-rings, chains, and padlocks – that rendered them immobile and unable to move about the ship? Whether the locks and chains were picked or broken, it was a matter of no small significance that two of the forty-nine enslaved men were blacksmiths, who knew the properties of iron intimately from their work. Sessi was described as "a blacksmith, having learnt that trade of his brother; he made axes, hoes, and knives from iron obtained in the Mendi country". When speed was crucial to avoiding detection, getting so many people out of irons was necessarily a communal undertaking.[35]

Phase 4 of the rebellion concerned the acquisition of weapons. At the beginning of the uprising the rebels used tools, handspikes, sticks (probably barrel staves), whatever they could find lying around on the deck. Then came a decisive discovery in the hold of the *Amistad*: a box of cane knives meant to be used by slaves in Puerto Príncipe, probably themselves. At the first trial of the *Amistad* Africans, for piracy and

34. W.T. Harris and Harry Sawyerr, *The Springs of Mende Belief and Conduct: A Discussion of the Influence of the Belief in the Supernatural among the Mende* (Freetown, 1968), p. 83; Jones, *From Slaves to Palm Kernels*, p. 185; Anthony J. Gittins, *Mende Religion: Aspects of Belief and Thought in Sierra Leone* (Nettetal, 1987), p. 122; Rediker, *The Slave Ship*, pp. 266–269.
35. *New York Journal of Commerce*, 10 October 1839; *New York Morning Herald*, 13 May 1841; *Youth's Cabinet*, 20 May 1841; Barber, *History of the Amistad Captives*, p. 11.

murder, a cane knife was presented as evidence to the grand jury and
described by a newspaper correspondent:

> [...] it is a most formidable weapon in the hands of a resolute man, [c]ould be
> wielded with deadly effect; it is about 3 feet long, 3 or 4 inches wide at the end,
> and narrowing until it enters the handle, where it is about one inch and half
> wide; the handle is of horn with a knob at the end.

The rebels transformed a tool of exploitation into its opposite – a tool of
emancipation.[36]

How the captives found their weapons of self-emancipation has long
been one of the mysteries of the *Amistad* rebellion. It so happens that
Havana-based British diplomat and Irish abolitionist, Richard Robert
Madden, knew how it happened and explained the process in a letter of
October 1839. Writing of the *Amistad*, he noted:

> There was much merchandize also on board, and amongst the rest a package of
> swords or machetes as they are called, which are used for cutting down canes.
> The female negroes of the party, true to their sex, indulged their curiosity in
> examining the contents of various packages around them whenever there was an
> opportunity, and faithful also to the communicative character of the fair part of
> humanity, they imparted the information they had acquired to their male
> friends, and the latter true to themselves, and faithful to one bold man among
> them who became their chief, they acted on it.

The "female negroes" were the three little girls – Margru, Kagne, and
Teme, each about nine years old. They were not, as Madden seems to
suggest, on a shopping expedition. They were, rather, trapped on a slave
ship, but they had freedom of movement that others did not have. They
used their intelligence, their ability to range freely, and their ability to
communicate to find the cane knives and inform their male shipmates of
the location, thereby making the successful rebellion possible.[37]

The battle for control of the ship, the fifth stage in the process of
mutiny, drew on two aspects of previous experience. First, warfare –
much of it connected to the slave trade – had been extensive in the
homelands of the *Amistad* Africans from the mid-1820s up to the moment
of their shipment out of Lomboko in April 1839. All of the men aboard
the *Amistad* would have been trained as warriors in defense of their villages and cities. Gnakwoi had been a "war boy" who fought with the
notorious mercenary warlord, Goterah. Cinqué and Bau explained that
"they had been in battles, in their own country, using muskets". They had
almost surely been soldiers in the army of King Amara Lalu, who fought

36. *New York Morning Herald*, 22 September 1839.
37. The *New Hampshire Sentinel* reported on 4 September 1839: "After killing the captain and
the mulatto, Joseph ransacked the cabin below, and having found a quantity of sugar knives,
armed the rest of the slaves."

the aggressive expansion of King Siaka, the paramount king allied with the
Spanish slave-traders. Grabeau had military experience of a distinctly
ironic, not to say contradictory, sort: he had, at one point in his life,
fought in a war against "insurgent slaves", not far from the American
colony of Liberia. He would now use his martial skills to fight as an
insurgent slave himself.[38]

The fundamental practices of Mende warfare were apparent in how the
uprising took place. The weapon of choice was a knife. Mende warriors
always preferred knives – the cutlass at home, the very similar cane knife
aboard the *Amistad*, the discovery of which must have seemed a gift of the
ancestral spirits. Moreover, they used typical Mende tactics: they used a
moonless night to launch a surprise guerilla attack (in Mende, *Kpindi-go*),
using war shouts and swinging their blades wildly in a successful effort to
make their opponents abandon position so that victory might be more
easily achieved. The goal of warfare was not slaughter but capture, of
people and place, both of which were quickly achieved on board the
vessel. They also performed a Mende war dance ritual, *kootoo*, as they
celebrated the killing of Captain Ferrer.[39]

The two sailors who jumped overboard during the mutiny and managed to get back to Havana pointed out another crucial experience: "the
Captain, owner of the schr., [Ferrer] was warned, previous to sailing, to
keep a look out for the negroes, as they had attempted to rise and take
the vessel in which they were brought from Africa". The subversive
experience of slave-ship revolt was thus already present aboard the
Amistad. Nothing more is known about that rebellion as it was not mentioned in any other documentation surrounding the *Amistad* case. Yet it is of
first significance that the veterans of a failed rebellion aboard the *Teçora*
would have another chance to get it right, and get it right they would.[40]

The sixth and final phase of the rebellion was perhaps the biggest
challenge of all. Could they sail the schooner to freedom? The decision
was taken to keep Montes alive because he knew how to navigate the
vessel. The original plan of revolt may not have included killing Captain
Ferrer, who might have been more useful in sailing the ship. As young
Kale explained to John Quincy Adams: "We never kill captain; he no kill
us". Even though Ruiz and Montes "made fools of us, and did not go to
Sierra Leone", as Cinqué explained, he and his comrades did learn to
handle the ship well enough to make it to a place that was not "slavery
country". They set sail, hauled anchor, used the boat, and managed to go
ashore at least thirty times during the voyage after the rebellion, all of

38. "Private Examination of Cinquez"; Barber, *History of the Amistad Captives*, pp. 8, 13;
Vermont Chronicle, 8 June 1842.
39. For the African background to the rebellion, see Rediker, *The Amistad Rebellion*, ch. 1.
40. Correspondence from Havana, *New York Journal of Commerce*, 25 July 1839.

which bespeaks no small amount of skill. Most of the places they anchored and went ashore remain unknown: did they go ashore in South Carolina or Virginia only to discover that these places *were* "slavery country"? Their ability to sail the ship may have owed something to the sickness of white crew members aboard the *Teçora*, a common problem on Atlantic slave ships, which was solved by bringing African men out of the lower deck and teaching them the rudiments of sailoring – how to hand, reef, and steer on a sailing ship.[41]

The successful rebellion aboard the slave schooner *Amistad* progressed through stages that would have characterized mutiny on other types of vessels: the formation of the core and the collective, the acquisition of weapons, the struggle for control of the vessel, and the effort to sail it to a free place. Only the enslaved and some indentured servants and convicts would have to free themselves of their fetters as a third stage. Naval and merchant sailors were not only unchained (unless in the bilboes as punishment), they were trained in the use of arms and frequently had pistols, muskets, and cannon at their disposal. They also had much higher levels of the necessary maritime skill to sail the vessel after capture. These were great advantages. Convicts, servants, and slaves, to have any hope of success, had to find weapons and comrades with some seafaring knowledge among them, and in many cases they did. A successful revolt on a slaver such as the *Amistad* would have been perhaps the most difficult of all mutinies to carry off.

CAUSES AND CONSEQUENCES

The planning and execution of the rebellion – and no less the long, dangerous, even tortuous voyage afterward – were great achievements. Acting on shared common experiences and West African precepts of self-organization, the *Amistad* Africans had done what few of the millions before them had done: waged a successful uprising aboard a slave ship, then sailed the vessel to a place where they might secure the freedom they had fought for and won. Their armed self-defense forced abolitionists, in America and around the world, to make revolutionary arguments in defense of their resistance and against the institution of slavery itself.

As Attorney Roger Baldwin explained to the justices of the Supreme Court, the *Amistad* "had been taken by force out of the hands of Spanish subjects, was not sailing under Spanish colors, had lost its national character, and was in the full possession of the Africans". John Quincy Adams made the same point before the same court: "The Africans were in possession, and had the presumptive right of ownership" of the *Amistad*; "they were on a voyage to their own native homes [...] the ship was

41. *New York Journal of Commerce*, 20 March 1841.

theirs". And of course the *Amistad* Africans themselves knew what they had achieved, even as posterity was beginning to paint them as hapless victims. Indeed, young Kale wrote to Adams, telling the great man exactly what he should say to the Supreme Court: "If court ask you who brought Mende people to America? We bring ourselves. Ceci hold rudder."[42]

The shock waves of the *Amistad* rebellion reverberated in many different directions – throughout the Caribbean and Brazil, where a successful revolt put the master class on the defensive; back to Europe, where monarchs, middle-class reformers, and workers took great interest in the case; to the Bahamas, where once-enslaved African Americans aboard the *Creole* would take their captured vessel to freedom in 1841; to Africa, where the *Amistad* rebels returned in January 1842, bringing missionary abolitionists and an international track of the Underground Railroad with them; and throughout America, where the movement against slavery took a radical turn, especially among African-American abolitionists, leading in a direct line to John Brown's raid on Harper's Ferry in 1859 and Civil War in 1861. The agency of fifty-three enslaved Africans on a small vessel in the northern Caribbean in 1839 rippled far and wide around the Atlantic.

42. *New York Journal of Commerce*, 23 February 1841 and 26 February 1841; Kale to John Quincy Adams, 20 March 1841. Note, however, that Kale wrote his letter on 4 January 1841, six months before Baldwin and Adams made their arguments in court.

IRSH 58 (2013), Special Issue, pp. 35–60 doi:10.1017/S0020859013000473
© 2013 Internationaal Instituut voor Sociale Geschiedenis

Orangism, Patriotism, and Slavery in Curaçao, 1795–1796*

K ARWAN F ATAH - B LACK

Institute for History, Leiden University
Doelensteeg 16, 2311 VL Leiden, The Netherlands

E-mail: karwan.fatah@gmail.com

ABSTRACT: The defeat of the Dutch armies by the French and the founding of the
Batavian Republic in 1795 created confusion in the colonies and on overseas naval
vessels about who was in power. The Stadtholder fled to England and ordered
troops and colonial governments to surrender to the British, while the Batavian
government demanded that they abjure the oath to the Stadtholder. The ensuing
confusion gave those on board Dutch naval vessels overseas, and in its colonies, an
opportunity to be actively involved in deciding which side they wished to be on.
This article adds the mutinies on board the *Ceres* and *Medea* to the interplay
between the Curaçao slave revolt of 1795 and the rise of the Curaçaoan Patriot
movement in 1796. The mariners independently partook in the battle for the
political direction of the island and debated which side they wished to be on in the
fight between the French Revolution and the British Empire.

INTRODUCTION

In 1795 the island of Curaçao was rocked by one of the larger slave revolts
of the age of revolution.[1] The revolt was closely connected with the
uprising in Saint-Domingue and the unstable political situation in the

---

* I am much indebted to the organizers of and participants in the seminar "Curaçao in the Age
of Revolutions", held at the Royal Netherlands Institute of Southeast Asian and Caribbean
Studies (KITLV) in the summer of 2010. That seminar and the edited volume subsequently
published lifted the case of Curaçao from that of a local and somewhat parochial history to one
with Caribbean and Atlantic relevance. My thanks go too to the organizers of and participants
in the two seminars on "Mutiny and Maritime Radicalism in the Age of Revolution" at the
International Institute of Social History (IISH) in Amsterdam and the Huygens Institute for the
History of the Netherlands (Huygens ING) for including the momentous events on the island
in the analysis.
1. David Geggus, "Slave Rebellion During the Age of Revolution", in Wim Klooster and Gert
Oostindie (eds), *Curaçao in the Age of Revolutions, 1795–1800* (Leiden, 2011), pp. 23–56,
40–49.

Netherlands, and both in their symbols and their songs the rebellious slaves referred favourably to the French and Haitian revolutions.[2] The uprising occurred during a tumultuous time, for August 1795 was not long after the Dutch Republic had been invaded by the French revolutionary army in January of the same year. During the invasion revolutionary associations had taken control of government in many Dutch towns and had formed the Batavian Republic, which existed from 1795–1806. Opposition to the revolutionary ferment crystallized around Stadtholder William V. The Stadtholder, the head of state of the Dutch Republic, was traditionally a member of the House of Orange. William V, with the help of a Prussian invasion led by his brother-in-law, had crushed an attempted revolution under the leadership of the Patriot movement in 1787. Now, in 1795, when the Patriot movement had regained momentum and Patriot exiles had returned to the Netherlands, the Orangists looked again to the Stadtholder to lead a counter-offensive. But the French invasion drove William V to Kew, London from whence he began working to undermine the newly founded Batavian Republic. He wrote letters to the governors of the Dutch colonies and overseas possessions asking them to surrender to British forces.

Given the context, in which the Patriot movement is associated with both the uprisings by enslaved and free non-Europeans in Curaçao, as well as with the violent overthrow of the Stadtholder in the Netherlands, we should expect (in line with the position taken by the "petit blancs" in Saint-Domingue during the French and Haitian revolutions) that the sailors and soldiers on board vessels of the Dutch navy in the port of Willemstad would stand firmly behind their Prince of Orange and favour continuation of the segregation of white and black. At first sight the soldiers and sailors would not stand to gain much if their patron – and with him the entire system of patronage within the military – were to be overthrown; and still less if non-white colonial subjects should gain a more equal position, for that would reduce the few privileges enjoyed by the military as a result of their European ancestry. And indeed, quite a few soldiers and sailors did rally behind the Prince and were easily mobilized against the slave revolt. However, their allegiance to the Orangists seems to have been neither wholehearted nor unanimous, with clear signs of divisions in individual ships and between the crews of different ships about whom to support in the conflict. Some were outspoken in support of the Patriots while others "voted with their feet" by joining forces with non-white Curaçaoans to plot desertion and ultimate escape from the colony.

---

2. Klooster and Oostindie, *Curaçao in the Age of Revolutions*, a collection of articles on Curaçao's turbulent history at the end of the eighteenth century, treats these issues in great detail.

What determined the loyalties of Dutchmen in those turbulent times? Were their choices politically motivated and, in keeping with this volume's main topic, was there a sort of maritime radicalism in the Dutch navy informing their limited support for the Prince of Orange and the "aristocracy of colour"? Our inability to hear the voices of the men involved effectively prevents any definitive answer to those questions, but it is still possible to reconstruct fragments of exchanges on board the naval vessels using a range of sources. Of primary importance to this article is the shipboard administration of the frigate *Ceres*. The lists of debts and accounts of the auctions of the belongings of men who had died or deserted tell us a lot about shipboard life. From the colonial archive much becomes clear about the context in which men chose to desert, to mutiny, or to accommodate the momentous political and social transformation taking place in their world. I will look at the economic position of sailors, their role in the slave revolt, and their acts of resistance throughout their stay in the port, and I shall devote special attention to their involvement in the political conflict between Orangists and Patriots within the island's government and military forces.

BALANCE OF POWER

As a trade-oriented nodal point with a secure natural harbour, Curaçao was strongly centred on Willemstad, the single urban core of the island and named after William II, Duke of Nassau and Prince of Orange, who had been Stadtholder when Curaçao was conquered and taken from the Spanish in 1634. A census of 1789 established that there were 12,864 slaves, 3,564 whites, and 3,714 free black and coloured Curaçaoans on the island and that most of them lived in and around the town: in fact 42 per cent of the slaves, 95 per cent of the whites, and nearly 90 per cent of the free non-whites lived in Willemstad. The whole urban population, including the free black, coloured, and enslaved Curaçaoans "worked in the commercial and maritime branches of the Curaçaoan economy".[3]

Fort Nassau (its building now a restaurant) overlooks the port of Willemstad, and any vessel sailing through the harbour mouth would have come within range of its cannons. The fort was built as Fort Republiek [Fort Republic] on a hill above the town covering its port. That it was completed in 1797 by a Patriot military committee which had assumed power through a coup d'état against the Orangists in December 1796 testifies to the dynamism of the Patriot government as well as to their will

3. Han Jordaan, "Free Blacks and Coloreds and the Administration of Justice in Eighteenth-Century Curaçao", *New West Indian Guide/Nieuwe West-Indische Gids*, 84:1–2 (2010), pp. 63–86, 79–80.

Figure 1. View on Willemstad around 1800, with Fort Republiek prominently on the hill in the background.
Library of Congress Geography and Map Division, Washington DC. Public Domain.

to organize the island's defences without relying on the Dutch navy.[4] The artillery placed in the fortress the same year was manned by coloured mariners recruited by the Curaçaoan Patriots of the Military Committee.[5] The transition from the pre-revolutionary Dutch-led defence of the island to their more locally organized National Guard highlights how rebellious actions by slaves, sailors, and citizens in the colony intersected and changed Curaçao profoundly in the context of an age of revolution. It is therefore very telling that in the nineteenth century the Dutch chose to change the name to Fort Nassau, as if to erase the memory of its anti-Orangist history.

In the late eighteenth century the dire state of the Dutch navy and the lack of colonial control over Curaçao's population, both free and enslaved, created a volatile situation on the island. The Patriot movement

4. J. Hartog, *Het fort op de berg. Gedenkboek bij het tweehonderdjarig bestaan van Fort Nassau op Curaçao* (Assen, 1996), pp. 3–13.
5. Han Jordaan, "Slavernij en Vrijheid op Curaçao. De dynamiek van een achttiende-eeuws Atlantisch handelsknooppunt" (Ph.D. dissertation, Leiden University, 2012), p. 219.

that took control of Curaçao in December 1796 was a complicated mixture of a Dutch movement for national centralization of the state, the revival of the glory of the Netherlands as a republic, and a local movement that wished to maintain the position of the island as a free port between the various Atlantic empires. In the context of the Haitian and French revolutions the various incarnations of the Patriot movement were also a vehicle for the emancipation of people who had until then been excluded from positions of power simply because they were not Europeans. By taking control, the islanders with more than just European ancestry became fully integrated in the island's defence organization, and the garrison and naval vessels became less vital to the port's defence.

The changed status of the naval vessels in the organization of the local defences signified a great change in the balance of power on the island. The navy had been the primary instrument of state power on the island, but was manned and directed primarily by people from the Dutch Republic rather than the Curaçao-based civilian militia. In the two years after the founding of the Batavian Republic the frigates *Ceres* and *Medea* moored in Willemstad became the focus of struggles over political direction as much as over the working conditions on board the ships themselves. Disagreement developed into running battles in the streets, desertions, disrupted public ceremonies, refusal of orders, and a mass discharge of the crew and garrison in July and August of 1796. While the slave revolt of 1795 has received a good deal of attention from historians, the 1796 Patriot coup d'état and the insubordination on board the *Ceres* and *Medea* are treated as afterthoughts (if they are mentioned at all). On close examination, however, the landside revolt by the enslaved Curaçaoans in 1795, the rise of the local variant of the Patriot movement, and the insubordination of soldiers and sailors in 1796 turn out to be closely linked.

Orangism in naval crews is usually used to explain why they were rowdy and insubordinate during the Patriot takeover of Curaçao.[6] The historiography has emphasized the support for the House of Orange found among common soldiers and sailors in Dutch service, but that support was by no means universal in the navy. Orangism, in fact, turns out to have been a phenomenon in the officer corps rather than among the lower ranks.[7] In the Dutch Republic, popular Orangism formed the template for opposition to civic regents who were abusing their economic and political power in the Dutch cities, while the dynamic of supporting a distant Prince of Orange against the brutish locals certainly did not create

6. T.H. Milo, "De Bataafsche Marine in Curaçao, 1795–1800", *Marineblad*, 51 (1936), pp. 326–345, 483–496.
7. Niklas Frykman, "The Wooden World Turned Upside Down: Naval Mutinies in the Age of Atlantic Revolution" (Ph.D. dissertation, University of Pittsburgh, 2010), pp. 168–169.

any deep-seated loyalty. During the series of revolts and wars grouped under the "age of revolution" the God-given right of royal families came into question, and in the Dutch Republic the mythical role of the princes of Orange-Nassau in delivering the provinces from unjust rulers came under serious challenge from the Patriots who, in opposition to the royal aspirations of Orange-Nassau, argued for a centralized republic.

Overseas, the split in Dutch politics and society took a different form. In Willemstad the faltering international power of the Dutch made the split between Orangism and Patriotism less about the question of centralized government and reduced it to the choice either for a British takeover of the island – favoured by the Orangists – or against it. Within the Patriot movement on Curaçao there was a division between those who wished to recreate the position of the port as a neutral and autonomously governed nodal point in the Caribbean, and those who hoped for radical social change which they thought would be helped by the arrival of the revolutionary French army.[8] In the context of a non-white population in the throes of emancipation, Patriotism denoted skin colour too,[9] making oppositional lower-deck Patriotism on board naval vessels all the more interesting as a phenomenon, breaching as it did both the dominance of Orangism and white racial solidarity as frames of reference for insubordinate sailors. Politically divided and unreliable, the naval crews were in the end distrusted by the local Patriots, who then chose to strengthen their defences independently of the navy.

CURAÇAO IN THE CARIBBEAN

Curaçao was not simply a little bit of Dutch society overseas; it was strongly influenced by the world at large through its connections within the Caribbean and the wider Atlantic. In the mid-1790s the political conflicts between the Orangists and both the pro-French and the more autonomy-oriented varieties of Patriot support intersected with the regional interests of the British, French, North American, and "perhaps a Haitian drive to export revolution", as well as "Venezuelan revolutionaries taking refuge in Curaçao". The interplay of a multitude of forces was the result of the island's "long-standing status as a free trade zone and the ties its inhabitants had developed around the region".[10]

In the seventeenth century Curaçao had been a hub for both legal and illegal slave trading to the Spanish colonies. The *asiento de negros* of the

---

8. Karwan Fatah-Black, "The Patriot Coup d'Etat in Curaçao, 1796", in Klooster and Oostindie, *Curaçao in the Age of Revolutions*, pp. 123–140, 127–130.
9. Jordaan, "Slavernij en vrijheid", pp. 229–235.
10. Gert Oostindie, "Slave Resistance, Colour Lines, and the Impact of the French and Haitian Revolutions in Curaçao", in Klooster and Oostindie, *Curaçao in the Age of Revolutions*, p. 11.

Spanish crown had been the formal agreement by which traders of the Dutch West India Company (WIC) could sell Africans to the Spanish mainland colonies. Before and after the formal *asiento* trade Curaçao functioned as an illegal slave market,[11] but with the rise of the commercial and military power of the English and French in the Atlantic, the WIC lost its *asiento* and, simultaneously, Curaçao's position as a hub in the Atlantic world declined. However, its natural harbour and proximity to Tierra Firme did ensure its position as an entrepôt where Caribbean goods could be collected before they were sent to Europe.[12]

The colony was closely connected to the wider Caribbean, and important trades in Curaçao were cacao from the Spanish colonies and indigo from the southern peninsula of French Saint-Domingue.[13] Southern Saint-Domingue saw successful indigo production by free coloureds, and the trading partners of the Curaçaoan merchants on Saint-Domingue were often former Curaçaoans.[14] Garrigus has detailed the career of Julien Raimond, including his contributions to racial reform during the 1780s and early 1790s and his commercial relations with Curaçao.[15] Such "contacts were strengthened through intermarriage between the well-to-do coloured families of both colonies". Preceding the slave revolt of 1795 there was a rumour that Rigaud, a mulatto general from southern Saint-Domingue, was on his way to lead a liberation struggle on Curaçao.[16] The actual general of Curaçao's rebellious slave army, Tula, was himself nicknamed Rigaud. Those who fled Saint-Domingue for Curaçao after the beginning of the 1791 slave revolt were cited by Curaçao's government as a troublesome element in the city.

Coloured Curaçaoans who maintained connections with their mother colony could be found in many different colonies dotted around the Caribbean.[17] Curaçaoan sailors and small traders or smugglers transmitted information within the wider Caribbean, and news of the revolt in Saint-Domingue or the French occupation of the Netherlands was more likely to be circulated to their families and friends by the seamen directly than by passengers on board foreign vessels. In the mid-1780s "sixty-eight

---

11. Johannes Postma, *The Dutch in the Atlantic Slave Trade, 1600–1815* (Cambridge, 1990), pp. 26–55.
12. Wim Klooster, *Illicit Riches: Dutch Trade in the Caribbean, 1648–1795* (Leiden, 1995).
13. Han Jordaan, "Patriots, Privateers and International Politics: The Myth of the Conspiracy of Jean Baptiste Tierce Cadet", in Klooster and Oostindie, *Curaçao in the Age of Revolutions*, pp. 141–169, 153.
14. Wim Klooster, "The Rising Expectations of Free and Enslaved Blacks in the Greater Caribbean", in Klooster and Oostindie, *Curaçao in the Age of Revolutions*, pp. 57–74, 67.
15. J.D. Garrigus, "Opportunist or Patriot? Julien Raimond (1744–1801) and the Haitian Revolution", *Slavery & Abolition*, 28 (2007), pp. 1–21.
16. A.F. Paula, *1795, De Slavenopstand op Curaçao: een bronnenuitgave van de originele overheidsdocumenten* (Curaçao, 1974).
17. Klooster, "Rising Expectations", p. 67.

vessels arrived annually in Willemstad from Saint Domingue", and the outbreak of the revolt in 1791 did not break the connection. Maritime labour was a central occupation for free non-whites, giving many families, neighbourhoods, and parishes access to news from around the Caribbean. The number of sailors was so large that when "a disappointing number of free coloureds reported for militia inspection on Curaçao on the first day of 1793, their captains explained the many absentees by reference to the trade with the French colonies, in which they were employed".[18] Because of the closeness of the shipping network it is no surprise that there was much revolutionary interaction between such places as Coro, Guadeloupe, southern Saint-Domingue, and Curaçao, nor that some leaders of the slave revolt in 1795 had spent time in Haiti.[19]

ENSLAVEMENT AND FREEDOM

Slaves were in a peculiar position on the island. The maritime orientation of the colony made slaves "a vital cog in the maritime commercial system", which simultaneously challenged their very enslavement by giving them "ample opportunities for escape into Caribbean and Atlantic maritime circuits". The seaborne nature of the colony's economy created a very particular relationship between the enslaved, the enslavers, and the sea. Slave owners "developed a temporary form of manumission" which was "pro forma, to go to sea"; it "freed enslaved sailors only when they were at sea, and was revoked when they returned to the port of Willemstad". Their "freedom" was a ploy to prevent their treatment as prize goods if a ship should happen to be taken by a privateer.[20]

Because of the many maritime connections, slave resistance on Curaçao mostly took the form of flight to Tierra Firme. The ties between Coro and Curaçao "dated from pre-Columbian times", and efforts to escape slavery between the two areas started immediately after the Dutch takeover of the island in 1634. The distance between Curaçao and present-day Venezuela can readily be covered in a canoe or the small sailing vessels commonly used along the Curaçaoan coast for fishing or transport between coastal plantations and Willemstad. From the register of escaped slaves kept by WIC officials it emerges that most were skilled and many – at least 85 of the 585 recorded – were "seafarers". After their flight they would stay in contact with those who remained on the island.[21]

Free non-white Curaçaoans had a reputation for rowdiness. Their food and housing were sometimes worse than those of the slaves and they

18. *Ibid.*, pp. 66–67.
19. Oostindie, "Slave Resistance", p. 16.
20. Jordaan, "Free Blacks and Coloreds", pp. 81–82.
21. *Ibid.*

were notorious for ganging together and clashing in town.[22] According to Jordaan,

> The lack of respect shown to Whites by non-Whites paired with uneasiness about the growing number of free Blacks and Coloreds and the numerical superiority of the black and colored population as a whole were translated into a series of rules and regulations designed to keep the entire non-white population under strict control, usually without distinction between slave and free.[23]

Non-whites were banned from gathering, playing music, carrying sticks, or going out after dark unless they carried a lantern. Impertinent behaviour by non-whites could be punished directly by dishing out a "single blow of a cane". Under the legal system introduced to the colony by the States General there was no official difference between free coloureds and free whites, although in practice free non-whites were treated similarly to slaves if they landed in court. One difference, which set Curaçao apart from its neighbouring colonies, was that there were relatively few restrictions on their economic activities.[24]

CONNECTIONS TO ATLANTIC REVOLUTIONS

Julius Scott specifically names the "black and brown Curaçaolians" causing trouble wherever their ships docked, resulting in legislation in Jamaica in the early 1780s forcing ships' captains "to take away such people as they bring into port".[25] Curaçaoans were furthermore "part of the floating population of a run-away logwood community in Santo Domingo in 1790". They were described as living "without God, law or King". The Pointe Coupée conspiracy of Louisiana "featured a Creole slave from Curaçao", who spread the rumour that the authorities were "awaiting at the Capital an Order of the King which declares all the slaves free", a common and effective rumour to fuel a revolt.[26] It is therefore no surprise that the slave revolt of August 1795 was led by slaves who used the imagery of both the Haitian and French revolutions and deployed arguments based on their intimate knowledge of political developments in the Dutch Republic.[27]

22. *Ibid.*
23. *Ibid.*
24. *Ibid.*
25. J.S. Scott, "Crisscrossing Empire: Ships, Sailors, and Resistance in the Lesser Antilles in the Eighteenth Century", in Stanley L. Engerman and Robert L. Paquette (eds), *The Lesser Antilles in the Age of European Expansion* (Gainesville, FL, 1996), pp. 128–143, 133–134.
26. Martín Lienhard, *Disidentes, rebeldes, insurgentes: Resistencia indígena y negra en América Latina. Ensayos de historia testimonial* (Frankfurt, 2008), pp. 97–98, cited in Klooster, "Rising Expectations", p. 67.
27. Oostindie, "Slave Resistance".

Because of the colony's close connections with regional ports belonging to other empires it was quite common for conflicts in the wider Atlantic world to be imported on to the island. When the American War of Independence (1775–1783) broke out, the Curaçaoan government had been obliged to take measures to prevent citizens of the warring nations from violently clashing with each other in the city, and enthusiasm for the ideology of the French Revolution was countered in a similar way in 1789.[28] News of the French invasion and founding of the revolutionary Batavian Republic in January 1795 arrived in Curaçao only after some delay, and by the time it did an ordinance had been issued forbidding the singing of French revolutionary songs and the wearing of decorations with French revolutionary slogans,[29] and in fact it was May before it was learned that there was peace, and an alliance with France.

Because of the peace between France and the Batavian Republic, Curaçao's local government was obliged to allow French privateers into its port, which made Curaçao a frequent stopover for the swarm of Guadeloupian privateers roaming the Caribbean. The French privateers had a significant impact on the local balance of forces in the colony. Guadeloupe was then under the leadership of Hugues, a specialist in privateering who increased his fleet from 21 to 121 vessels and attacked a stunning 1,800 ships between 1795 and 1798. But more important for Curaçao was that the crews of the privateers were black or coloured, "many of them ex-slaves", and many of their captains were free men "of African descent", which made these ships "a symbol as clear as the Republican tricolor".[30]

After the slave revolt of 1795 the fear of renewed unrest remained, especially in the town of Willemstad. The French privateers and their crews were always subject to blame, so that when a new revolt threatened to break out the "crews of the privateers were ordered not to have contact with the island's blacks". That was to no avail, however, and on the "day before Christmas, sailors of the French privateers provocatively paraded through the streets with banners and drawn sabres, and with hundreds of Curaçaoan blacks in their wake". The "French free negroes or *citoijens*" were also accused of holding gatherings and singing revolutionary songs, resulting in fights "between the French sailors and the

28. J.A. Schiltkamp and J.T. de Smidt, *West Indisch plakaatboek. Nederlandse Antillen, Benedenwinden: Publikaties en andere wetten alsmede de oudste resoluties betrekking hebbende op Curaçao, Aruba, Bonnaire. 1638–1782* (Amsterdam, 1978), p. 381.
29. Johannes Hartog, *Curaçao: Van kolonie tot autonomie* (Oranjestad, 1961), I, pp. 325–327, 322; Schiltkamp and de Smidt, *Plakaatboek*, p. 389.
30. Laurent Dubois, *A Colony of Citizens: Revolution & Slave Emancipation in the French Caribbean, 1787–1804* (Chapel Hill, NC [etc.], 2004), pp. 241–248.

garrison's Orangist soldiers".[31] A year after the revolt the commanders of one of the Dutch naval vessels complained about the "people of colour, both Negroes and mulattoes, who have been banned from carrying clubs, but are nevertheless carrying clubs. Yes, are so rude, that they do not step aside, and do not refrain from singing loudly those tunes and songs which are detrimental to the good peace and order."[32] The symbols of the French Revolution and the Patriots were intrinsically connected with the rising self-confidence of coloured and black Curaçaoans.

THE *CERES* AND THE *MEDEA*

Heavily armed sailing ships were still important instruments of war and state power in the late eighteenth century. The ability of the Dutch Republic's navy to project violence and fear across the globe had been unprecedented in the seventeenth century, but during the eighteenth century its effectiveness began to wane. The long period without any direct military conflict with its main maritime rival, Britain, had created a situation in which the size, importance, and technical superiority of the Dutch navy had declined in comparison with its direct competitors. The decline went untested for a long time until it received a devastating blow from the British during the Fourth Anglo-Dutch War (1780–1784). Despite some recovery in the late 1780s, the presence of the Dutch navy in the West Indies was rather limited, being composed mainly of convoying ships that would remain there on missions for some time before convoying back.[33]

In Willemstad there were two frigates, the *Ceres* – a frigate of 860 tons and 40 guns – and the command vessel *Medea* – a frigate of 800 tons and 36 guns – as well as a host of smaller vessels, such as sloops to keep watch and punts transformed into cannon platforms. F.J. Wierts was captain of the *Medea* and in command of the navy in the port. After the death of Captain A.T. Ditmers, Albert Kikkert was appointed captain of the *Ceres*. The crews of both ships were in poor condition, and for Captain Ditmers and many of the crew it was most probably their first time in the tropics. The men on the *Ceres* had served under Ditmers on the *Zeehond*, fitted out with 16 cannons. It is still unknown if those men had followed Ditmers from his previous appointment in command of the 20-gun *Bellona*, but his appointment to the *Ceres* was certainly a promotion, for

31. Nationaal Archief, The Hague, WIC, entry 2.01.28.01 inv. no. 139, Governor's journal, 4, 5, and 1–2 August 1795, 9 December 1795, 12 December 1795, 24 December 1795; cited in Jordaan, "Patriots, Privateers and International Politics", p. 155.
32. Nationaal Archief, The Hague, Departement van Marine, Journaal van den Burger A. Kikkert, Colonel & Capitein ter Zee commendeerende het Bataafsche Fregat Ceres, 18 Februari 1795–3 Juli 1799 [hereafter "Log of the Ceres"], entry 2.01.29.03 inv. no. 73, August 1796.
33. Jaap R. Bruijn, *The Dutch Navy of the Seventeenth and Eighteenth Centuries* (Columbia, SC, 2011).

it doubled the number of cannons at his disposal. After various cruises in the North Sea and through the English Channel, the *Ceres* crossed the Atlantic, arriving in Willemstad early in 1795.

European naval crews did not do well in the Caribbean, on occasion greatly reducing the effectiveness of European warships. During the crossing and once in Willemstad many on board the *Ceres* had died or were in hospital, with the rest hungry and in poor condition. Wierts had left the republic in July 1793 and during his stay in Willemstad the state of his vessel too deteriorated.[34] Commander Wierts asked Albert Kikkert on 18 February 1795 to take command of the *Ceres*. Kikkert had arrived in Curaçao for the first time in 1787 on the *Hector* and became part of the colony's ruling class of plantation owners after his marriage to Anna Maria van Uytrecht, one of the daughters of a wealthy family of planters.[35] Kikkert's plantation was exceptionally large for such a small island, which lacked the typical plantation production of tropical goods for the European markets such as could be found on the larger Antilles or in the Guyanas.

On the morning Kikkert took over his new command the vessel lay at anchor in the bay behind the city, and Kikkert found that his interim predecessor had engaged ten slaves and three coopers to work on board as replacements for the sick men. The *Ceres* had lost not only its captain and two of its next most senior officers, but some ninety-six other crewmen too, including some of its petty officers. The ship was relatively new, since it had entered service only in November 1793,[36] but when Kikkert came on board in February 1795 he noticed that it already smelled bad and the air between decks was stuffy at best. According to Kikkert's log the crew looked terrible – and he was referring to the ones not in hospital. They had sold all their clothes and the ship was "in the greatest disorder".[37] Forty men were laid up sick, nine had deserted. In fact, of the original ship's complement of 230, only 82 were still on board, "mostly boys and old sailors".

The lack of discipline on board was not the only problem Kikkert faced, for he also saw how poor the sailors were, and attributed their poverty to the detrimental role of the ship's *schrijver*. A *schrijver* was an accountant who could extend loans to captain and crew and was placed on board by the Admiralty to keep control of finances. Kikkert was shocked by the sums the crew had to pay the *schrijver* for their clothing.[38]

---

34. Milo, "De Bataafsche Marine", pp. 337–345.

35. Eric Penseel, "Gouverneur Albert Kikkert: 'Yiu di Krsou o Makamba?'" (M.A. thesis, Leiden University, 2011), p. 37.

36. "In dienst stellling van de Ceres", *Rotterdamse Courant*, 16 November 1793.

37. "[...] gantsch niet zindelijk en in de grootste disordre", "Log of the Ceres", 18 February 1795.

38. The price of clothing was so high "dat ik schrikte" [I was shocked]; *ibid.*

When he visited the hospital to see the *schrijver* of the *Ceres*, Kikkert was informed of the rules governing the extending of loans to sailors. On the ships of the Admiralty of de Maze, based in Rotterdam, it was customary for 40 per cent of each crew loan to be kept by the *schrijver*, so that when a sailor took out a loan of, say, 10 guilders he could spend only 6 of them. If the sailor wanted cash rather than clothes, the exchange rate for a *pathino*, or silver peso, was 88 *stuyvers*, an exchange rate highly unfavourable to the sailor. By comparison, for ships of the Amsterdam Admiralty the rate was said to have been set at 56 or 57 *stuyvers* per *pathino*.[39] The result therefore was that many Maze Admiralty crew members were heavily indebted while still too short of money to clothe themselves properly or supplement their meagre rations with local food and drink.

The crew of the *Ceres* were sinking ever further into debt as their time on board went on, and only the captain and his direct subordinates managed to stay out of even a small amount of debt. What had accumulated over the course of two and a half years affected practically all the common soldiers and sailors who had served on that particular ship until, by May 1794, the crew owed the *schrijver* a total of 1,157.90 guilders, while two years later, in July 1796, that figure had climbed steadily to 9,596.65 guilders. Of course not all the debtors were still on board, since many had died and others had simply deserted. When the possessions left behind by deceased or deserted crew members were auctioned off, they often fetched less than 10 guilders. The debt to the *schrijver* was universally loathed, making it the first matter that came up when Kikkert took command in 1795, and the clearest basic demand voiced by the crew during the tumultuous August days a year later.[40]

When Kikkert boarded the ship together with Commander Wierts, he tried to gain control of the crew by establishing discipline and organizing sanitation. The entire crew, including the skipper and the first mate, were required to do their share of watch-keeping, and he reorganized the *bak*s (division of the crew into mess tables) on board since there were no petty officers in any of the same *bak*s as the common sailors, which had given the sailors much room to create "many disorders". The crew had found ways to improve their poor economic situation somewhat, exploiting the inexperience of their officers and lack of oversight. When Kikkert came on board, Lieutenant Tichler informed him that the crew had managed secretly to break through the wall into the captain's private store. They had then opened the wine cases and no fewer than 3,000 bottles of wine

39. *Ibid.*, 9 August 1796.
40. Nationaal Archief, The Hague, Admiraliteits Colleges, Confereer-rolle van s'lands fregat van oorlog Ceres, onder commando van Cap. Anth Theod Detmers, entry 1.01.46 inv. no. 909–910; "Log of the Ceres", 9 August 1795.

had been stolen.[41] Given the sheer number of bottles, that amount of drink cannot have been consumed entirely by the crew but was most probably sold ashore in the city, or passed on to other ships for a profit.

Even though the *Ceres* was a new ship, much filth had been allowed to accumulate on board. Barrels standing below deck had begun rotting out at the bottom because of the dirt they were standing in.[42] The disease environment on the islands was far better than that of the plantation colonies, where malaria took a heavy toll on European crews and soldiers, but yellow fever was an ever-present threat in the Caribbean and was capable of crippling entire island societies very quickly. However, it is not clear what had struck the crew of the *Ceres*; the captain's log counts only the dead and the revenue from selling their belongings. Attempting to cleanse the air on board by running fresh water through the ship was one of the chief methods used by Kikkert to improve conditions below deck, but it is unclear if that helped. Perhaps the survivors among the crew recovered after simply proving better able to adjust to the tropical climate, but in any case they soon started coming back aboard from the city's hospital. Kikkert dismissed the slaves who had been hired and completely emptied the whole ship, and only after every item had been taken ashore and the ship thoroughly cleaned was everything put back. It might be that his actions had mostly symbolic value for Kikkert and were intended to emphasize his position as master of the ship, but over the course of the following weeks many crew members did go back on board. As soon as the ship and its crew were once again in good order the vessel was moved from inland water to the town, stationed opposite the command ship *Medea*.[43]

Not long after order had been restored on the *Ceres*, international military tensions required the crew to be battle ready and there seemed to be the possibility that they would have to sail out to take a group of merchantmen into convoy. When news arrived on the island that France had invaded the Dutch Republic and that the Batavian Republic had been founded, Commander Wierts ordered his ships to be alert to the possibility that British ships might attack the island. A new conflict would demand fresh troops, and Commander Wierts ordered Kikkert to hire as many crewmen as possible.[44] The next day, six new men came on board, all clearly local sailors.[45]

41. "Log of the Ceres", 7 March 1795 and 18 February 1795.
42. *Ibid.*, 19 February 1795.
43. *Ibid.*, 4 March 1795.
44. *Ibid.*, 26 May 1795.
45. On 27 May 1795 Kikkert hired Sebia Martin, Guan Bistie, Filip Daniel Verkade, Laxis Alercies, and Joseph Gregorie, and Guan Bologna came on board that day; Nationaal Archief, The Hague, Lijst van de voorgevallen veranderingen in de bemanning van de schepen, *Ceres*, entry 1.01.46 inv. no. 993.

Of the twenty-seven new men hired by Kikkert to replenish the ship's crew, ten were called Guan, three of them called some variation of Guan Francisco. These new sailors were local men, most likely of colour, and they were familiar with shipboard life on smaller inter-Caribbean vessels, and even more familiar with stories of revolts and uprisings, not just by slaves, but also by the freemen of Saint-Domingue. A month before the *Ceres* saw the new men board the ship, one such sailor, Simon Gomiz, by name, had been locked up by the governor, Johannes de Veer, because he refused to speak anything other than French, triumphantly announcing in that language of revolution that Saint Martin had fallen from Dutch power into French hands. The incident shows a glimpse of the defiant attitudes alive among Curaçao's sailors, transmitting news of the spreading French Revolution to their colleagues and other islanders.[46]

THE SLAVE REVOLT

From the standpoint of the slave revolt of 1795 Curaçao was wholly unsuitable for prolonged territorial conflict. Food, water, and fuel were limited. The slaves were unable to undermine the forces of the city and its navy, and so were forced to retreat to a barren part of the island. The revolt started as a strike of enslaved workers on the Knip plantation owned by C.L. van Uytrecht. As early as April 1795 Kikkert had, on one occasion, cause to order the *Ceres's* stern-mounted cannons loaded "against the murmuring by the negroes".[47] After the alliance with France, small privateer vessels began to appear in Willemstad almost daily.[48] Strike action by enslaved workers on the Knip plantation spread like wildfire to other plantations, resulting in a well-coordinated attack by a slave army quickly organized under the leadership of Tula.

The influence on the Curaçaoans of travellers' reports of rebellion and revolution is clear from interrogations carried out after the revolt, as well as from the report made by the Catholic priest, Jacobus Schinck.[49] Schinck told of the singing of French revolutionary songs, the same ones banned when free men from Willemstad were singing them, and prohibited to the privateer crews who had paraded with flags and weapons through the streets of the city. In one of the interrogations a slave named Claasje was accused of placing a Jacobin hat and a machete on the altar of a church on the island. The leaders of the rebellion assumed the names of

---

46. The incident took place in late April 1795; Jordaan, "Slavernij en vrijheid", p. 230.
47. "Zette twee stukken achter uit tegen het mompelen der negers", "Log of the Ceres", 23 April 1795.
48. *Ibid.*, 23–30 July 1795.
49. Nationaal Archief, The Hague, Oud Archief Curaçao, inv. no. 105, Minuut-notulen van de gewone en buitengewone vergaderingen van Directeur (Commissarissen) en Raden, 1791–1804, "Verslag van Pater Jacobus Schinck, 7 September 1795", no. 69, 10 September 1795.

Figure 2. Curaçao and the Caribbean in the late eighteenth century. The slave revolt of 1795 started at Plantation Knip and the main battle with the colonial troops from Willemstad took place near Porto Marie. In Willemstad the defences were greatly improved by the building of Fort Republiek on top of a hill overlooking the city.

generals in the Haitian uprising, with Tula most famously adopting the name of Rigaud, leader of the coloured rebellion in the south of Saint-Domingue, the area with which the free coloureds of Curaçao had intensive trade relations.

The Haitian experience had frightened the white elite on the island. Their fear was fuelled by stories told by the white refugees from Saint-Domingue who settled in Willemstad. The slaves were accused during the revolt of wanting to install "a government of negroes", suggesting that fear of a second Haiti haunted Curaçao, while the slaves themselves did their best to exploit the weakness of the white elite. They knew about the occupation of the Netherlands as well as the abolition of slavery in France, so that during the revolt in August 1795 the slave leader argued that the French occupation meant emancipation for Dutch slaves as well. As Tula, the general of the slave army, said: "We have been badly treated for too long, we do not want to do anybody harm, but we seek our freedom. The French blacks have been given their freedom, Holland has been taken over by the French, hence we too must be free."[50]

The Curaçao revolt was not exclusively a slave rebellion. Many free men and women participated in preparatory rituals, built barricades, ran

50. *Ibid.*

messages, and helped with the provisioning of the slave army. After the revolt began on Saint-Domingue, former Curaçaoans started to come back to their island, including some who had previously been banished from Curaçao. The rebels on Curaçao cemented their alliance by swearing an oath and drinking *awa hoeramentoe* [water of enchantment].[51] The ritual was led by two free men of colour who prepared the ritualistic drink by mixing rum with powdered animal horn. In the aftermath of the revolt there were many free black and coloured men among those arrested. Arrest by itself did not necessarily mean that an individual was actually involved in the rebellion, but among those who were caught the accusations ranged from theft to being present when the takeover of the island was plotted, cooking for the rebels, and hiding weapons in private houses. During the revolt of the slaves the mulatto and black divisions of the colonial armed forces largely refused to mobilize.[52]

The revolt quickly reached Kikkert's plantation, and indeed his stock of slaves would provide two of the four most important commanders of the slave army, namely Carpata and Wakkau. The other two were Louis Mercier from Saint-Domingue, sometimes called Toussaint, as the rearguard, and Tula, or Rigaud, who was in overall command. Kikkert on board the *Ceres* had sensed the impending slave rebellion, noting in his log in early August 1795 that "the negroes are being rowdy because of the many French Free Negroes or *Citoijenes*".[53] Just as in April, he ordered the cannons to be loaded with live ammunition and shrapnel, and road blocks were set up on the Altona hill and the Roodeweg as rumours of rebellions by natives on Aruba and slaves in Coro reached the island. The fighting that followed became a war of attrition, with the slaves' initial victories turning into a defensive retreat, leaving many of them dead. Throughout the second half of August and into September 1795 slaves were brought to town and put aboard the naval vessels to be imprisoned and, in the end, hanged. After a last stand on the Christoffelberg the slave army was routed. With gruesome symbolism the leader was executed with the other ringleaders in the most tortuous and elaborate manner.[54] After a month the core of the rebel army had been smashed, but it took many more months before most slaves had returned to the plantations.

51. J.H.J. Hamelberg, *De slavenopstand op Curaçao in 1795* (Willemstad, 1896), p. 123.

52. Westerholt reported "infamously bad behaviour among the Negro corps", cited in Paula, *1795*, p. 299. The army tried to mobilize fifty "free mulattoes" for the corps, but only twenty turned up; AZKGA, *Journalen van Curaçao*, February 1795–December 1797, no. 139, cited in Paula, *1795*, p. 34.

53. In his log he wrote "de negers thans door de menigvuldige Fransche Vrijnegers of Citoijenes hier ook wat baldadigheden doende", "Log of the Ceres", between 1 and 7 August 1795.

54. "Verslag van Pater Jacobus Schinck".

THE NAVY CRUSHES THE REVOLT

Militarily speaking, the slaves needed either to take the city or flee to
Coro if they were to be successful. Both options were barred by the
presence of the Dutch navy. Kikkert had reported that his ship was the
only holder of sufficient ammunition, so the *Ceres* provided the powder
for the armed forces marched against the slave army, while the garrison
and armed forces too were supplied by the ship. The trained crew of the
Ceres was mobilized to fight the slaves, while those who remained on the
ship worked long days preparing hundreds of cartridges to be sent over in
small boats to the troops, along with other supplies such as clothes to
replace garments that had been torn to pieces on the island's thorny
hedges.[55] The slave army was at a devastating disadvantage because it
lacked naval supply lines. On some days the crews on the *Ceres* made
more than 1,000 cartridges for the fighting troops on the island.

When the government heard of the strike on the Knip plantation the
initial plan was to drive the slaves back onto their plantation. However,
the next day news came that the rebels had taken possession of Kikkert's
plantation and that many slaves were joining the uprising. The rebels were
said to have caused major destruction and broken open storehouses. The
rebel army was reportedly 350-strong, although not well armed.[56] To
resupply the army a small boat was used called a *golette*,[57] which Kikkert
sent to his plantation, where he picked up no fewer than 80 of his own
slaves who had apparently not joined the uprising. Later the *golette* went
to pick up all that was left of the maize in the storehouse of Kikkert's
plantation to prevent it from falling into the hands of Tula's army.[58]

The leading troops, who had been sent to contain the strike around
Knip, were driven back by the rebels, so Captain Baron van Westerholt
tot de Leemcule of the army was sent with sixty-four men in a barque,
and Kikkert and Wierts sent sixty more men under arms with two officers
overland, to link up with Westerholt.[59] The second confrontation, later
known as the battle of Port Marie, ended in the imprisonment of twelve
rebels, who were sent to the city.[60] To protect the city, the colonial
administration had been forced to rely on the crews of merchant vessels.
The sailors from the frigates marched into battle with sixty mulattoes and
"free Negroes" to pull the ships' cannons up the roads and hillsides. Given
the seriousness of the slave revolt, Kikkert planned to take armed civilians

55. "Log of the Ceres", 23, 24, and 27 August 1795.
56. *Ibid.*, 18 August 1795.
57. *Ibid.*, 20 August 1795.
58. *Ibid.*, 25 August 1795.
59. *Ibid.*, 19 August 1795.
60. *Ibid.*, 20 August 1795.

to provide reinforcements for the officers inland, and to arm his new ad hoc troops he used arms from the arsenal, the ships, and privately owned weapons. There was no powder ashore, so the *Ceres* and *Medea* supplied the powder for the operation. In a way, Kikkert argued, the absence of powder on land was a good thing, since the slave army would not be able to acquire any.[61]

After the initial victories of the revolt, the rebels were beginning to suffer defeats at the hands of the ad hoc colonial forces. Scores of prisoners were being sent to the city, but it is uncertain, of course, whether the army simply arrested anyone they found wandering around the island or properly targeted enemy combatants. The large number of prisoners could not be kept in the town's fort, so the *Ceres* was used as a floating prison and prisoners were brought to Willemstad using the smaller vessels, in any case a safer way to transport the re-enslaved than marching columns of them across the island. The small vessels were used not only for transport; they played their part too in crushing the spirit of the rebels. The naval sloop sailed into port with prisoners on board and with a slave hanging from the bowsprit[62] – as it entered the port he was cut down. The *Ceres* held many people detained – at one time at least eighty suspected rebels – while they waited to be taken ashore to the fort by the public prosecutor P.T. van Teylingen, who tortured and questioned them.[63] When slaves were executed in the city an alarm was sounded and the ship's crew was sent ashore to provide cover for the execution.[64] A barque under the command of Lieutenant de Lange brought in more prisoners and reported that three of them had been hanged on board, and another man was hanged on a sloop before it returned to port.[65] The barque later came in with two of the leaders of the slave army, one of them Tula, and when the other two leaders were caught – both officially the property of Kikkert – the barque was again sent to pick them up.[66]

If they ever existed, detailed records of the violence on board the smaller vessels have been lost, but judging by the reports of the hangings on the small boats during voyages that took no more than a few hours the confined spaces on those small vessels must have been the scene of some truly horrific and vengeful violence. One can hardly imagine the impact of seeing the man hanging from the bowsprit of the sloop on those lining the

61. *Ibid.*, 21 August 1795.
62. *Ibid.*, 2 September 1795.
63. *Ibid.*, 1 September 1795; OAC 121, Resoluties van Directeur (Commissarissen) en Raden, 1790 – 1804, "Memorie van P.Th. van Teylingen", no. 65, 27 October 1795, in Paula, *1795*, p. 188.
64. "Log of the Ceres", 4 September 1795.
65. *Ibid.*, 19 September 1795.
66. *Ibid.*, 21 September 1795.

shore in the town. The last slave ship had arrived in Curaçao fully fifteen years before the revolt, but the tales of such ships must still have circulated among the enslaved, and the parallels with being kept on board the *Ceres* must have been obvious. The ordeal ended on 27 September 1795 with the elaborate torture and execution of the leaders of the revolt.

After the rebellion had been crushed and the initial celebrations were over, the problems on board ship resurfaced immediately. The slave revolt provided a distraction to the naval crews but it brought with it immediate experience of extreme violence on a scale that must have horrified the men. They were rewarded, and even received presents from citizens in Willemstad, 3 silver *pesos* and 6 *realen* each.[67] The bravest among them were rewarded with promotion, and *constaple* mate Frans Klaassen (still in irons for theft) was let off with no more than re-mustering with the rank of able seaman. Nevertheless, the on-board camaraderie and harmony proved to be short-lived.

From November 1795 the crew of the *Ceres* started to desert, and a number of incidents followed in quick succession until punishment turned harsher than it had been in the aftermath of the slave revolt. When a court martial was held to punish those who had been absent without leave, it resulted in the keelhauling of a boatswain and bottle master, who were put in irons until a chance came to banish them. Sailors started disappearing, as did soldiers; even a corporal chose to desert. Kikkert and his men were unable to retrieve the deserters, although they did discover that the sailors had paid money to be taken to Tierra Firme in a canoe. Since it is unlikely that anyone in town would have lent them the required sum, they might have used the money they received as reward for crushing the slave revolt as payment for their crossing to the Spanish Main.[68] In December a sailor tried to commit suicide because the captain had threatened to kick him to death – although that skipper was subsequently arrested and his discharge was requested by Kikkert for causing trouble among the petty officers. Both the captain concerned and the man who had attempted suicide were sent off the ship.[69] The *Ceres* was now missing 100 men from her full complement, and morale on board had fallen so far that civilians were brought on board to ensure that the crew would not surrender if the British attacked.[70]

Without the support of the navy's two frigates and their smaller vessels the course of the slave revolt would have been rather different, and indeed the navy's presence was an important reason for the failure of the slave revolt to conquer the island. By providing supplies for the armed forces,

67. *Ibid.*, 23 September 1795.
68. *Ibid.*, 2–16 November 1795.
69. *Ibid.*, 2–5 December 1795.
70. *Ibid.*, 13–15 February 1795.

prison space, and somewhere to store powder out of reach of the rebels, the navy effectively ensured that the slaves would be at a major disadvantage. The ships provided the infrastructure, firepower, and garrison troops, but, though their crews were thanked for their efforts, over the following months many of them chose to abandon ship.

POLITICAL INCLINATIONS

The colonial government of Curaçao had some experience with the spread of revolutionary feeling among the white, black, and coloured populations. By 1793 adherents of a revolutionary undercurrent on the island were organizing gatherings, with speeches for poor whites and free mulattoes, which on 21 May of that year prompted a ban on publicly speaking out against the House of Orange. It was forbidden even to listen to such speeches, and anyone who heard forbidden pronouncements and failed to inform the public prosecutor, Van Teylingen, were themselves liable to be punished. Clashes between soldiers and citizenry intensified after news arrived that the Dutch Republic had been invaded by the French. On 4 August 1795 an ordinance was issued forbidding freemen and "Negroes" from going about armed with sticks or clubs, and soldiers of non-commissioned rank were banned from bearing arms when not on duty. A curfew was imposed on the sailors, who were required to be out of the harbour no later than 9 o'clock in the evening, when public houses and dance halls had to close too,[71] although the harbour prohibition did not apply to crewmen of Dutch naval vessels.

Low morale was not limited to the *Ceres*, but for some reason the *Medea*'s crew seemed more prone to take collective action. The *Medea*'s crew clashed violently on the waterfront with men from a French privateer, frightening the privateer so much that it set sail and left the port.[72] To counter the "unruliness",[73] the crews of the *Ceres* and *Medea* were confined to their ships, and were further forbidden to associate with each other. The seaworthiness of both vessels deteriorated, and in March 1796 the *Medea* was deemed unfit to put to sea. The *Medea*'s crew became more and more Orange-leaning, until a yellow flag was raised over the *Medea* and some of them shouted "Hurrah". They looked into who among them was on the side of the Orangists or the Patriots. Kikkert heard from the captain of a freighter that the *Medea*'s crew considered themselves to be serving the Prince of Orange and that only a dozen of them thought otherwise.[74]

71. Hartog, *Curaçao: Van kolonie tot autonomie*, p. 324.
72. "Log of the Ceres", 13–24 January 1795.
73. *Ibid.*, "balstorigheid".
74. *Ibid.*

The geography of Willemstad is highly relevant to the episode that followed, in which the Orangists attacked the city's predominantly non-white neighbourhood. Willemstad lies at the mouth of the colony's natural harbour, which splits the town in two. In Punda, the old town, there is a fortress, Fort Amsterdam, which is still, in fact, the centre of the island's government today. It has historically always been a wealthier part of town, and it was where many of the warehouses stood. Geographically then, support for the French Revolution could be located on the other side of the city across the harbour, called the "Spanish side", also known as Otrabanda, which means "the other side" in Papiamentu. It was the less affluent part of the city, with many poor and coloured Curaçaoans, and with a synagogue which was seen as a hotbed of French-leaning revolutionaries.

Wierts, the Dutch naval commander and captain of the *Medea*, and one of his lieutenants, Robert Minors, were attacked in July 1796 by a violent mob wearing French cockades and most probably made up of crew members of French privateers, many of them non-white. Lieutenant Minors was killed and Wierts badly injured, and next day the incident sparked a response from the garrison in Fort Amsterdam. On their own initiative some soldiers left the fort and moved into Otrabanda. The officers were unable to control the soldiers, who organized incursions into Otrabanda in a spirit of revenge and again violently clashed with the crew of a French privateer. Patrols were sent after them to try to bring them back to the fortress, but to no avail. The soldiers were placed under curfew and banned from entering the city after 8 o'clock at night. However, the cannon shot meant to be fired from the fortress to indicate the start of the curfew was not sounded. In response the *Ceres* prepared for battle to prevent the plundering and burning of Otrabanda, and citizens approached the *Ceres* asking if they might spend the night there. The actions of the military speak of a very open anti-Patriot attitude, very possibly triggered by fear of the rise of the free coloured population, both in politics as well as in the defences, through their predominance in the crews of French privateers.

MUTINY

The transference of power from the Stadtholder to the Batavian Republic was a messy affair on the island, that resulted in a full-blown mutiny among the navy and garrison. On 7 August 1795 Wierts received the order from Admiral Braak in Suriname to change the oath under which the navy, garrison, and the government served. Wierts went aboard the *Medea* and read the *Articulbrief* (ordinance on military discipline), but when he asked if the crew were willing to swear the oath he was met with "a deep silence"[75]

---

75. "Een diep stilzwijgen", Nationale Vergadering van 16 December 1796, Rapport Wierts, cited in Milo, "De Bataafsche Marine", pp. 337–345.

from the officers, who bowed their heads to decline. In the end only the two openly Patriot officers were willing to swear the oath, along with the *schrijvers* and the surgeons, but the petty officers remained defiantly silent. The common sailors too declined, but at least they added an explanation: "we are released from one, then also from the other, we are free and therefore no longer in service".[76] Kikkert reported that "none of the crew wanted to take the new oath, but instead wanted to be released and to receive their due pay".[77] Wierts thought their response was led by the skipper. Kikkert, Wierts, and Heshusius, one of the loyal officers, pondered how to respond to the refusal, but finally decided to let the matter rest for a day.

Now it was time to go to the council and governor and get them to swear the new oath, but there too they met with an unpleasant surprise. The governor refused to take the new oath and so had to be replaced by a temporary governor, and when Wierts returned to the ship the next day he was presented with a letter from the entire crew telling him that they were released from the oath and were henceforth free. Now they wanted their pay, and they would decide for themselves if they wanted to return to service or not.[78] The mutineers also issued an ultimatum demanding satisfaction within twenty-four hours, "or else they would be forced to start in a different way".[79] At that moment the armed forces in the fortress again joined the "debate" by shouting rudely from behind their battery, so Wierts ordered one of the cannon to be loaded with shrapnel and shown to the soldiers, who responded by moving away only to return with field pieces. However, neither side opened fire, and it is unclear from the various reports who the loyalists were who loaded the *Medea*'s stern cannon. But whatever the truth, it was now clear to the commanders that the soldiers had no intention of taking the new oath. In fact, the garrison in the fort were the first to back their refusal with the threat of gunfire.

Despite the mutiny in the armed forces, Wierts called the governing council and the governor to meet in session and demanded they take the

---

76. "[…] zijn wij van het eene ontslaagen, dan van het andere ook, en dus vrij uit den dienst". *Ibid.*

77. Kikkert, who was there, wrote in the log "dog geene van de equipage wilde den nieuwen eed doen, maar zeiden van ontslagen te willen wezen met hunne afbetaling daarbij"; *Log of the Ceres*, 9 August 1796.

78. "[…] uit naam van de gantsche Equipage een zogenaamd Request gepresenteerd, en door de meest alle (eene weinige uitgezonderd) ondertekend, en beginnen eerstelijk met te zeggen: 'Wij moeten ons geld hebben, hetgeen wij verdiend hebben zo lang wij onder den voorgaande Eed gestaan hebben, nu zijn wij vrij van den Eed en wagten op onze betaling, en dan zullen wij zien wat ons te doen staat, of wij weder dienst zullen neemen, of niet'", in Milo, "De Bataafsche Marine", p. 340.

79. "[…] zeggende verder, resolutie op de zaak te willen hebben binnen 24 Uuren, of anders zouden genoodzaakt zijn, op eene andere manier te beginnen", in *ibid.*

oath of allegiance to the Batavian Republic. The governor, having served
the island since the 1750s, had already announced that he would use the
opportunity to retire, but two others resigned because they simply
refused to take the oath. A certain J.J. Beaujon was appointed temporary
governor in a letter from the National Assembly providing for a successor
in the event de Veer's position became vacant. The soldiers refused to
recognize the new governor and shouted "Hurrah for Orange" when
Beaujon was presented to them. The council quickly cancelled the
customary introduction of the new official to the city as the soldiers took
over Fort Amsterdam wearing orange ribbons. The soldiers and their
officers had been released from the old oath, although they did not
actually swear the new one. Now the *Ceres*, *Medea*, and the fortress were
all refusing to take orders from the military leadership, leaving the city
without regular defences.

The governor and his council had lost control over their armed forces
and the fort, as well as over the crew of the *Medea*, and because of the
Orangist occupation of the fortress the councillors dared not meet there.
As a counter-measure they sought to meet on board the *Ceres*; there the
crew said they would allow the meeting only if they were paid. The first
ship to be brought back under control was the *Ceres* on 12 August, when
a ship's council was held and it was agreed that the crew would be discharged and all immediately re-mustered. They would receive arrears of
pay within four days plus a golden Johannes – a Portuguese coin common
on the island and worth 22.50 guilders – as a gratuity if they rejoined
the service. Rations were to be increased and monthly pay raised by
8 *realen*.[80] In total, 80 men re-mustered to serve on the *Ceres*.

Meanwhile the soldiers were still openly resisting the new order, and
most of them were decked out in Orange colours. The *Medea*'s crew
refused point-blank to re-enter service because their ship was unsea-
worthy, and they feared that if they did remuster they would never return
to the Netherlands.[81] However, on 15 August the *Medea* abandoned its
mutiny and negotiated a mass discharge from Dutch naval service, since
none of the *Medea*'s crew wanted to return to service, and they came on
board the *Ceres* to request that they be allowed to depart on an American
brig. What amounted to a covert mass desertion by naval personnel was
effectively condoned, and the following week the thirty men of the
Ceres's crew who did not want to take the oath to the Batavian Republic
were likewise sent ashore. That week soldiers too began to submit to
discipline again and those who were still on board received their due pay.
The crews of the smaller vessels as well as the *Medea* were brought on

80. *Ibid.*, p. 342.
81. "Log of the Ceres", 9–16 August 1796; Milo, "De Bataafsche Marine", p. 343.

board the *Ceres*, the *Articulbrief* was read to them and they shouted "Vive la République" three times. They were then sent back to the *Medea*. When order had been restored, punishment for the Orangist ringleaders was mild.[82]

The unstable situation on the island continued after the mutiny in the armed forces had fizzled out, but the crisis moved to a conflict between the French-leaning and autonomy-oriented Patriots in the council. The civilian militia took an active role in trying to push the colony towards the French Revolution, or at least to purge Orangist influences from the local government. The civilian militia was re-formed into a National Guard by the Military Committee, something of great significance for it provided the colony with a locally based military force and mobilized the island on an unprecedented scale. The National Guard was expanded to about "1,100 officers and men, organized in six companies of infantry, three companies of cavalry, and four companies of artillery", on an island of 20,000 inhabitants.

The artillery was mainly made up of "free blacks and coloureds" recruited by Lauffer from the "seafaring population of the island". Maritime labour had made the sailors "familiar with the handling of the cannons aboard the ships". To encourage the experienced sailors "ship's captains, who were often light coloured '*mustees*', were given officer's ranks". That meant not only that non-whites were appointed to positions of command, but that they were dispersed over a number of divisions in an attempt to reduce "the power of the respective captains".[83] Lauffer, a keen strategist, cleverly used the available non-white sailors to supplement the armed forces loyal to the Patriots. He used them to outflank the Orangists, and allowed them aboard the naval vessels to ensure loyalty there. The most visible legacy of the Patriot government of Lauffer is Fort Republiek.[84]

CONCLUSION

The 1795 slave revolt was the largest single slave uprising in the Dutch Atlantic, but its repercussions among free and enslaved townspeople have only recently been documented. Research conducted by Han Jordaan on the position of the free people of colour within Willemstad has problematized the classical view of that group by revealing their high level of agency, their participation in a wide range of trading activities, and their assertive behaviour in local politics, society, and the law courts. But as a maritime nodal point, the permanent presence of ships of the Dutch

82. Sergeants Bulje and Bartels were sent off and it was left at that; "Log of the Ceres", n.d.
83. Nationaal Archief, The Hague, 2.01.28.01, West Indisch Comité, inv. no. 136, cited in Jordaan, "Patriots, Privateers and International Politics", p. 157.
84. Hartog, *Het fort op de berg*.

navy has never been considered part of the story. Even on this tiny island, with its highly mobile population, the worlds of land and water are often still regarded separately. Maritime lives and interconnections were constitutive to the slave revolt, providing those on the island with inspiring stories and examples that they used to press forward their agenda. It is strange that the crews of the Dutch naval vessels have remained invisible in this history because those same mariners independently took part in the following year's battle for the political direction of the island. The crews of the *Ceres*, *Medea*, and the garrison actively debated which side they wished to take in the fight between the French Revolution and the British Empire, and how they would ensure either an Orangist or a Patriot outcome on the island. That the crew of the *Ceres* did not default to the position of Orangism, and on the *Medea* too the Patriots had some following, brings into question the prevalent image that lower-deck mariners were Orangist by definition.

The ships under the command of the navy were crucial in staging the endgame of the attempted slave revolt. Maritime power provided the crucial advantage that the slave army could not match with perseverance and numbers alone. The ships supplied seasoned fighters and ammunition and made sure that the land forces were resupplied; the *Ceres* ensured that the rebellious actions by free blacks in the city were stopped. The ships later became the holding place of the rebels who were caught, as well as the stage for the dramatic hangings and scenes of terror.

While within the Dutch Republic and in its army and navy the terms "Patriot" and "Orangist" did not necessarily connote skin colour (and the Patriots had no colonial vision to speak of), in the colonial context of Curaçao those terms certainly did. Curaçao's connectedness to places such as southern Saint-Domingue and Guadeloupe, where the French Revolution was also contributing to the fall of the aristocracy of colour, profoundly changed what it meant to identify oneself as Orangist or Patriot. The founding of the Batavian Republic therefore had an unintended impact on the entitlement felt by non-whites in the colony, as well as the threat felt by some white people for whom Orangism became a flag to rally round. On the island the movement for autonomy was not especially explicit in its aims, but the reorganizing of the defences without that troublesome and volatile element of the Dutch naval ships and their crews speaks volumes.

IRSH 58 (2013), Special Issue, pp. 61–85 doi:10.1017/S0020859013000266

International Radicalism, Local Solidarities: The 1797 British Naval Mutinies in Southern African Waters

Nicole Ulrich

History Department, Rhodes University
Grahamstown 1640, South Africa

E-mail: n.ulrich@ru.ac.za

ABSTRACT: This article details the 1797 mutinies in the British Royal Navy in southern African waters at Simon's Bay and Table Bay at the Cape of Good Hope. Drawing attention to the intersections between international protest during the age of revolution and between local, African protest, it shows that the Cape mutinies were part of an empire-wide strike, and were rooted in the organizational traditions of naval sailors. Yet, these mutinies were also of local significance. They signalled the growing confidence, and radicalization, of the popular classes at the Cape, as sailors, KhoiSan labourers, and slaves all experimented with new strategies of rebellion. Realizing the fundamental class bias of custom and law during their struggles for improvements in wages and working conditions and for a more democratic workplace regime, naval sailors also contributed to a broader political dialogue at the Cape concerning the relationship between the imperial state, freedom, and rights.

INTRODUCTION

Towards the end of 1797, Thomas Kelly of the carpenters' crew on HMS *Jupiter* was ordered to appear before a court martial for mutinous behaviour. Kelly threatened that:

> [...] he was a Delegate and sent by [...] His Company and the Voice of the Ship's Company was not to be played with. He said that a man's life was not so easily taken away now as it was four months ago. The Prisoner desired me [Captain Losack] to recollect Simon's Bay and England, and that the Times were not now as the[y] had been.[1]

---

1. National Archives, Kew [hereafter NA], Admiralty Records [hereafter ADM], 1/5488, Minutes of Proceedings of a Court Martial Assembled and Held on Board His Majesty's Sloop *Rattlesnake* on Table Bay on Saturday the Ninth Day of December 1797, p. 288.

Kelly was referring to the 1797 mutinies by naval sailors at Spithead and Nore in Britain, and also to the mutinies that had taken place in southern African waters at the Cape of Good Hope. The Cape mutinies were not isolated protests, and this article examines both the local and international dimensions of the Simon's Bay mutiny (7–12 October 1797) and the Table Bay mutiny (7 November 1797).

The Cape mutinies were, at one level, inspired by, and in many ways resembled, the Spithead mutiny. As in the case of Spithead, sailors in Simon's Bay organized democratically across the squadron. Drawing on the rhetoric of "free-born Englishmen",[2] sailors attempted to hold their officers to account, and to force the Admiralty to implement significant improvements. However, the mutiny and subsequent court martial of one Captain Stephens, accused by sailors of oppression and neglect of duty,[3] radicalized sailors rather than reinforced their loyalty. The earlier notion that rights resided in English tradition and law no longer seemed appropriate, as sailors now questioned the legitimacy of naval custom and the courts, leading to the second mutiny in Table Bay. At another level, the mutinies at the Cape also signalled a further upsurge in local, popular resistance, and were followed by the Servants' Rebellion in 1799 and a revolt against slavery in 1808. All of these protests, which represent the Cape's age of revolution, posed a significant challenge to the existing order, as the popular classes experimented with new strategies and new ideas about the relationship between rights, freedom, and the imperial state.

THE CAPE COLONY

The Cape's popular classes consisted of slaves (either locally born, or imported from Asia, India, and other parts of Africa), indigenous KhoiSan labourers,[4] sailors, and soldiers mainly recruited from Europe. To understand how these labourers fitted together, it is necessary to briefly outline the Colony's history and political economy.

The Cape of Good Hope was colonized by the Dutch East India Company (the Verenigde Oost-Indische Compagnie, or VOC) in 1652, and moved into the British imperial orbit briefly from 1795–1803, and then decisively from 1806. The Colony, located at the southernmost tip of the African continent, straddled the Atlantic and Indian oceans and served as a junction between Africa, Europe, and Asia.

---

2. E.P. Thompson, *The Making of the English Working Class* (Harmondsworth, 1963), pp. 84–110.
3. NA, ADM, 1/5488, Letter of Charges Against George Hopewele Stephens of HMS *Tremendous*, 17 October 1797, p. 4.
4. I am using the term KhoiSan, as opposed to Khoisan, to emphasize that this term does not refer to a specific ethnic/racial group, and in order to give equal weight to the pastoralists (Khoi/Khoikoi) and hunter-gatherers (San people) included in the term.

The Cape's economy was divided into three sectors, each with a specific labour system. The Colony was established to function as a refreshment station for VOC fleets travelling between the Netherlands and Batavia (now Jakarta). Not surprisingly then, the urban economy was port-centred and dominated by the Company, the Colony's largest employer. There were about 3,000–4,000 Company servants stationed at the Cape.[5] The Company hired a small number of skilled workers and artisans, but the majority of these servants consisted of low-ranking sailors and soldiers who staffed the local garrison and fleet. They were bonded by 3–7-year contracts. Any attempt to break the contract, or to desert, was met with severe punishment and, in some cases, death. It is for this reason that these contracts can be characterized as a form of indenture, and the majority of the VOC's servants can be seen as unfree labour.

In addition to recruiting men from across Europe, especially Germany and Scandinavia, the VOC also increasingly relied on Asian sailors to crew homeward-bound ships. In 1792, out of the 1,417 sailors who sailed from Asia to Cape Town, 233 were Indians, 101 Javanese, and 504 Chinese.[6] Soldiers were equally diverse in terms of origin, and a separate KhoiSan regiment (the "Hottentot's Corps") augmented the local garrison, which included significant numbers of Germans and Scandinavians.[7] Added to this, the Company owned about 1,000 slaves, who served as domestic labourers or worked at the docks, on public works, and Company outposts. The rest of the urban population consisted of free burghers,[8] and small groupings of "free blacks"[9] involved in retail (running taverns, eating houses, and boarding houses), small manufacturing businesses, or fishing. They relied on the labour of privately owned slaves, or the "free" poor.

The second sector of the colonial economy comprised grape and grain farms, located in the fertile hinterland and worked by privately owned slaves, assisted by a small number of KhoiSan labourers. Compared to the plantations in the Americas, slave holdings at the Cape were relatively small. Few farmers owned more than 50 slaves at one time. Nevertheless, privately owned slaves still slightly outnumbered slaveholders. In 1773 the Cape Colony was home to approximately 8,902 private slaves (both urban and rural), compared with 8,465 free burghers.[10] By the beginning

5. N. Worden, E. van Heyningen, and V. Bickford-Smith, *Cape Town: The Making of a City* (Kenilworth, 2004), p. 49.

6. *Ibid.*, p. 51.

7. J. Parmentier and J. de Bock, "Sailors and Soldiers in the Cape: An Analysis of the Maritime and Military Population in the Cape Colony during the First Half of the Eighteenth Century", in N. Worden (ed.), *Contingent Lives: Social Identity and Material Culture in the VOC World* (Cape Town [etc.], 2007), pp. 549–558, 556.

8. Company servants released from their contracts to take up farming, and their descendants.

9. Freed slaves and convicts, and their descendants.

10. N. Worden, *Slavery in Dutch South Africa* (Cambridge [etc.], 1985), p. 11.

of the nineteenth century, about 40 per cent of slaves were locally born.[11] The remainder were imported. Slaves were initially sourced from parts of Indonesia and India, but towards the end of the eighteenth century the Company mainly sourced new slaves from East Africa, especially Mozambique. Successful wine and grain farmers became exceptionally wealthy. Together with licensed retailers and high-ranking VOC officials, they constituted the Colony's elite.

Finally, a stock-farming sector was located on the Colony's outskirts, and bled into an unsanctioned hunter-raider-trader economy on the colonial borderlands. This kind of farming required substantially less capital and labour than arable farming, but also yielded lower returns.[12] There was a grouping of wealthy stock farmers, but most were fairly modest, wandering pastoralists (*trekboers*). Although there were stock farmers who owned one or two slaves, they were dependent mostly on KhoiSan labour.[13] KhoiSan labourers preferred to accumulate resources over a relatively short period before returning to their pastoralist or hunter-gatherer communities, and they resisted entering into binding, long-term contracts. The bargaining power of KhoiSan was eroded by colonial dispossession, and violence, and they were increasingly forced into labour. In 1775 the first regulations *officially* indentured KhoiSan children.[14]

There is a tendency in the literature to treat the labourers associated with each particular sector as geographically and socially separate. Reflecting the persistent fixation on race in South African historiography even today, historians have also tended to treat different sections of the popular classes as distinct racial groups. However, there were always opportunities for labourers to move across sectors, or to other parts of the Colony, and, in so doing, to forge social connections that transcended race, nation, and ethnicity.

The most notable site of connection was the popular culture of leisure[15] that centred on the town's dockside taverns and eating houses. Including sailors, soldiers, and urban slaves, men and women from different races

11. R. Shell, *Children of Bondage: A Social History of the Slave Society at the Cape of Good Hope, 1652–1838* (Johannesburg, 2001), p. 47; J. Armstrong and N. Worden, "The Slaves, 1652–1834", in R. Elphick and H. Giliomee (eds), *The Shaping of South African Society, 1652–1840* (2nd edn, Cape Town, 1989), pp. 109–183, 132.

12. L. Guelke, "Freehold Farmers and Frontier Settlers, 1657–1780", in Elphick and Giliomee, *Shaping of South African Society*, pp. 66–108, 89, 92.

13. Including those who were partly descended from slaves, or Europeans, and acculturated KhoiSan known as *Oorlams*.

14. R. Elphick and V.C. Malherbe, "The Khoikhoi to 1828", in Elphick and Giliomee, *Shaping of South African Society*, pp. 3–65, 32.

15. For the early nineteenth century see A. Bank, *The Decline of Urban Slavery at the Cape, 1806–1843* (Cape Town, 1991). For the eighteenth century see N. Ulrich, "Counter Power and

and with different legal statuses were drawn together. It was also here that the local and the "foreign" drank, danced, gambled, and traded stories and stolen/smuggled goods.

Although rural labourers had fewer social opportunities, they were not totally secluded. Slaves and KhoiSan labourers, in both town and countryside, were hired out regularly. This allowed labourers from different workplaces and districts to mingle, and cross the urban–rural divide. As *pasgangers*,[16] sailors and soldiers stationed at the Cape worked on farms, and on occasion could also be found in the countryside. Finally, those living in more isolated parts of the Colony regularly met guides and wagon drivers, occupations dominated by KhoiSan, who must have played an integral role in disseminating local and international news and analysis.

Such opportunities for connection across the regionally based sections of the economy, together with a shared experience of exploitation under harsh labour regimes primarily predicated on the gallows, facilitated the emergence of a distinct popular culture from relatively early on in the Colony's history.[17] This culture was held together by social and familial bonds, and practices of mutual aid, creating the basis for a class-based identity, and broader political solidarity.

THE AGE OF REVOLUTION AT THE CAPE

Traditionally, scholars have treated the Cape as the harbinger of the later country of South Africa, into which it was incorporated in 1910, and the Cape has typically been studied in isolation from the wider world, with an emphasis on the exceptional nature of colonial society and the origins of apartheid in South Africa. More recently historians have started to criticize this treatment of the Cape as the first chapter in a nationally bounded past for obscuring its historical role as a node in imperial circuits of trade and labour.[18] This analysis can be extended – the Cape's unique location and its incorporation into the Dutch and British empires also ensured that the Colony was part of significant global developments. This study argues that the Cape was influenced and contributed to the age of revolution.

The age of revolution was a time of heightened political and social turmoil that unleashed far-reaching change. At the heart of this turmoil was an intense class conflict in which the popular classes played a leading

Colonial Rule in the Eighteenth-Century Cape of Good Hope: Belongings and Protest of the Labouring Poor" (Ph.D. dissertation, University of the Witwatersrand, 2011).
16. Low-ranking Company servants could pay the Company so that others could take on their duties while they earned money in other capacities.
17. Ulrich, "Counter Power and Colonial Rule", pp. 100–140.
18. The most notable study is K. Ward, *Networks of Empire: Forced Migration in the Dutch East India Company* (Cambridge, 2009). Also see the essays in Worden, *Contingent Lives*.

role in toppling *anciens régimes*, and in promoting radical political ideas.[19] The age of revolution was not confined to the North Atlantic.[20] Significant social conflict took place in parts of Asia and, as this article will show, in southern Africa. Due to the technologies of trade, transport, and communication of the time, the maritime world of ships and ports (such as the Cape of Good Hope) were absolutely central to the circulation of new, radical ideas, and dissemination of information amongst the popular classes about the toppling of imperial powers, monarchies, and the end of slavery.

At the Cape, the first manifestations of far-reaching political and social transformation can be seen in the late eighteenth century, with the decline of the VOC. An internal debt crisis, increasing competition from the British East India Company in the Indian Ocean, and losses sustained during the Fourth Anglo-Dutch War (1780–1784) all contributed. However, the Company's decline cannot be attributed only to external factors, and locally VOC rule was also undermined by fierce political contestation. Historians have noted the challenge spearheaded by the Cape Patriots, the gentry's rally for greater political representation, as well as that of the rebellious frontier free burghers, who dreamed of a republic.[21] Not previously acknowledged in the literature is that the popular classes at the Cape also mounted a series of profound challenges. This omission in the literature is curious, especially since these challenges proved much more destabilizing, and posed a serious threat to the existing order.

This omission in the literature arises from the insistence by many historians that the popular classes primarily resisted their conditions through "informal" and individualized forms of protest.[22] However, a broader conception of popular resistance – that includes an examination of individual *and* collective defiance – reveals that popular protest intensified from about the 1770s onwards.

Popular revolt was not necessarily land-bound. Mutinies on VOC ships that took place near the Cape were often tried locally. Those on land also believed that they could capture ships and sail to freedom. Ever since

19. This argument has already been made by: P.A. Kropotkin, *The Great French Revolution, 1789–1793* (London, 1909); C.L.R. James, *The Black Jacobins: Toussaint L'Ouverture and the San Domingo Revolution* (New York, 1938); P. Linebaugh and M. Rediker, *The Many-Headed Hydra: Sailors, Slaves, Commoners, and the Hidden History of the Revolutionary Atlantic* (Boston, MA, 2000).
20. C.A. Bayly, *The Birth of the Modern World, 1780–1914* (Malden, MA, 2004), pp. 89–91.
21. G. Schutte, "Company and Colonists at the Cape, 1652–1795", in Elphick and Giliomee, *Shaping of South African Society*, pp. 283–323. See also G. Schutte, *De Nederlandse Patriotten en de Koloniën: een Onderzoek naar hun Denkbeelden en Optreden, 1770–1800* (Groningen, 1974).
22. See R. Ross, *Cape of Torments: Slavery and Resistance in South Africa* (London, 1983); and N. Worden, "Revolt in Cape Colony Slave Society", in E. Alpers, G. Campbell, and M. Salman (eds), *Resisting Bondage in Indian Ocean Africa and Asia* (London [etc.], 2007), pp. 10–23.

soldiers from the local garrison, "a black convict", "two servants of freemen", and some slaves attempted to seize the *Erasmus* in 1659, protest in Cape waters mainly took the form of mass desertion by ship (or piratical seizure).[23]

By the 1780s, mutiny in Cape waters started to take on new dimensions, fuelling upper-class anxieties concerning the Asian crewmen upon which the Company was growing ever more reliant. In 1784 Chinese sailors on the *Java* mutinied, and a conspiracy was also uncovered amongst slaves on the *Slot ter Hoge* (travelling in the same fleet as the *Java*).[24] Officers on the *Slot ter Hoge* were particularly concerned that the conspiracy amongst slaves had spread to Asian sailors. This suggests that, as in the case of the North Atlantic, authorities felt threatened by alliances between slaves and sailors.

KhoiSan labourers also challenged their masters, and from the 1770s deserted in increasing numbers to join armed bands that raided frontier farms. By the 1780s some bands were several hundred strong, and in the 1790s there was a report of a band that had grown to almost 1,000.[25] Independent KhoiSan bands were often motley, including runaways from the Colony or neighbouring African communities, and were primarily motivated by a rejection of colonial rule and class exploitation. By the 1780s, anti-colonial action started to take on new forms when the prophet Jan Parel and 400 of his followers (mainly KhoiSan, but also a few slaves and free blacks in the Overberg region) combined millenarianism with a "revelation" of revolution.[26] Parel predicted that the world would end on 25 October 1788 (a year before the French Revolution), ushering in an era of utopian bliss, and the end of colonial rule.

Slaves also questioned their bondage. In the early 1790s, a number of cases were heard by the Council of Justice that showed that slaves no longer accepted the total authority of their masters, and they simply refused to conform to established practices of deference. One slave, Mentor van Mozambique, refused to greet any slave owner other than his own master and mistress,[27] thus rejecting the authority of the broader slave-owning community over individual slaves. Abraham van Macassar,

---

23. Johan Jacob Saar in R. Raven-Hart (ed.), *Cape Good Hope: 1652–1702: The First 50 Years of Dutch Colonisation as Seen by Callers* (Cape Town, 1971), pp. 58–67, 64–65.

24. K. van der Tempel, "'Wij, hebben amok in ons schip': Aziaten in opstand tijdens drie terugreizen op het einde van de achttiende eeuw", in J.R. Bruijn and E.S. van Eyck van Heslinga (eds), *Muiterij: Oproer en Berechting op Schepen van de VOC* (Haarlem, 1980), pp. 123–147.

25. S. Marks, "KhoiSan Resistance to the Dutch in the Seventeenth and Eighteenth Centuries", *Journal of African History*, 13 (1972), pp. 55–80, 74.

26. R. Viljoen, "'Revelation of a Revolution': The Prophecies of Jan Parel, *Alias Onse Liewe Heer*", *Kronos*, 21 (1994), pp. 3–15, 5.

27. Western Cape Provincial Archive [hereafter WCPA], 1/ STB/ 3/12, *Criminele Verklarringen*, 1786–1793, transl. in N. Worden and G. Groenewald, *Trials of Slavery: Selected*

even refused to greet his own masters, claiming that "if I do my work during the day and come home in the evening, that is enough".[28] Most astounding were the actions of Caesar from Madagascar, who demanded his *right* to speak when his owner objected to his insolence and ordered him to be quiet.[29] Convinced that even slaves had rights, Caesar exclaimed "I do not want to be silent, and I must retain my right to speak."[30]

Some sailors, soldiers, and slaves at the Cape could read and write, but they left little documentation of their movements, or ideas. There was also no press of any significance that reported on their actions. This means that we have to discern popular, political desires and conceptions of freedom from rebellious acts, or from government records, and the sporadic accounts of elites. Although our view of popular protest at the Cape is fragmented, it is clear that from the 1770s the popular classes rejected colonial rule and class exploitation, and sought to curb the authority of their masters.

ENTER THE BRITISH

The VOC was effectively closed in 1796. The Cape itself came under British occupation from 1795 to 1803 and again from 1806 to 1814, with an interim period of Batavian rule from 1803 to 1806. With British rule came political and economic change, including the introduction of a large number of new sailors and soldiers to the Cape.

Historians view the "transition period" (1795–1813) narrowly as a successive change in government, and stress institutional continuity in this period.[31] However, British rule represented a far greater change. The patrimonial system of the VOC was replaced by a new form of state-led imperialism, with a much more intrusive and centralized state under the direct control of the British War Office.

British authorities also championed the protection of private property and free trade, and a new class of British merchants soon arrived to exploit new trading opportunities. Through their linkages with London markets, these merchants played an important role in stimulating commerce and production, with access to credit and financial institutions.[32] Released from the monopoly of the VOC, local elites quickly pledged their allegiance

---

Documents Concerning Slaves from the Criminal Records of the Council of Justice at the Cape of Good Hope, 1705–1794 (Cape Town, 2005), p. 608.

28. WCPA, CJ 499, *Criminele Process Stukken*, 1792–1794, fos 419–421, transl. in Worden and Groenewald, *Trials of Slavery*, p. 618.

29. WCPA, CJ 796, *Sententiën*, 1790–1794, fos 279–284, transl. in Worden and Groenewald, *Trials of Slavery*, p. 614.

30. *Ibid.*

31. W. Freund, "The Cape under the Transitional Governments, 1795–1814", in Elphick and Giliomee, *Shaping of South African Society*, pp. 324–357.

32. T. Keegan, *Colonial South Africa and the Origins of the Racial Order* (Cape Town, 1996), p. 50.

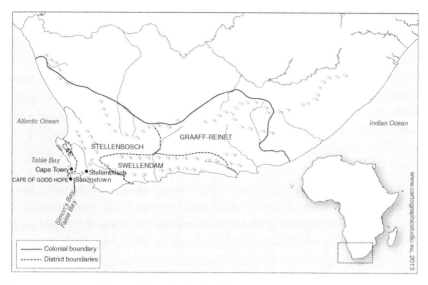

Figure 1. The Cape Colony during the first British occupation (1795–1803).
Based on a map in Elphick and Giliomee, Shaping of South African Society, *p. 326.*

to the British Empire and formed economic and even familial alliances with British merchants and high-ranking officials.

During the Napoleonic wars, the British did not view the Cape simply as a refreshment post, as the VOC had done, but also as a strategic military station. For instance, in 1797 the Earl of Macartney (Cape Governor from May 1797 to November 1798) wrote:

> Its chief importance to us arises from its geographical position, from its forming the master link of connection between the western and eastern world, from it being the great outwork of our Asiatic commerce and India Empire, and above all from the conviction, if in the hands of a powerful enemy, it might enable him to shake to the foundation, perhaps overturn and destroy the whole fabrick [sic] of our oriental opulence and dominion.[33]

In line with this military focus, local labourers were soon joined by thousands of additional sailors, and soldiers. It is estimated that the British garrison and navy consisted of roughly 5,000 and 3,000 men respectively.[34] Unfortunately there is no systematic study of these men at the Cape, but my preliminary examination of government records and

---

33. Letter from the Earl of Macartney to the Right Honourable Henry Dundas, Castle of Good Hope, 10 July 1797, in G.M. Theal (ed.), *Records of the Cape Colony, 1793–1811*, 7 vols (London, 1897–1905), Manuscript Documents in the Public Record Office, London, Printed for the Government of the Cape Colony) [hereafter RCC], II, p. 114.
34. Worden *et al.*, *Cape Town*, p. 93.

muster books indicates that "British" sailors and soldiers were a diverse lot and included Scots, Irishmen, northern Englishmen, Europeans (especially Dutch and Scandinavians), lascars from India, and a sprinkling of sailors recruited from the West Indies and the Americas.

Largely due to religious nonconformists, and to Enlightenment debates around equality, natural laws, and the inherent rights of man, increasing numbers of "respectable" men and women were convinced of the immorality of slavery.[35] One consequence at the Cape was the reform of the criminal justice system – one of the main instruments used to discipline labour at the Cape – and the repeal of legislation that permitted torture. For most elites, however, the aim was not to free labour but to regulate various forms of unfree labour more effectively. The trade in slavery flourished under British rule, and after the slave trade was abolished across the Empire a brisk trade in indentured servants shipped from Britain to the Cape emerged.[36] It is difficult to judge the exact numbers, but there are indications that at least some sailors in the Royal Navy stationed at the Cape were impressed.[37]

This continued reliance on unfree labour points to an important continuity – as under Dutch rule, most labourers at the Cape were unable to choose their employers or negotiate their wages. Although the most dreadful punishments and tortures had been abolished, the popular classes were still terrorized by harsh and violent measures of control and could still lose their lives if they resisted their masters.

BRITISH SAILORS

It would appear that naval sailors spent most their time on board, as their ships patrolled the seas. Since there are no studies of these men prior to this article, it is difficult to determine their relations with local labourers. However, we can most certainly identify two key sites of contact.

Much like low-ranking Company servants in the late eighteenth century, British sailors and soldiers became part of the dockside popular

---

35. M. Craton, J. Walvin, and D. Wright, *Slavery, Abolition and Emancipation* (London, 1976), pp. 195–199.
36. S. Newton-King, "The Labour Market of the Cape Colony, 1807–28", in S. Marks and A. Atmore (eds), *Economy and Society in Pre-industrial South Africa* (Hong Kong, 1980), pp. 171–207, 183.
37. In the court martial records, deserters continually avoided the harshest forms of punishment because they had not accepted the King's bounty, one indication that they had not joined the navy voluntarily. See, for instance, NA, ADM, 1/5487, Minutes of Proceedings of a Court Martial, 2 December 1796, pp. 19–29; or NA, ADM, 1/5487, Minutes of Proceedings of a Court Martial, 18 May 1797, pp. 237–242. There is also the pamphlet by the American Joshua Penny, who deserted at the Cape to escape impressments; J. Penny, *The Life and Adventures of Joshua Penny* (Cape Town, 1982), originally printed by the author in 1815.

culture of leisure. By the second British occupation (1806–1813), taverns and eating houses also became political spaces. It was, after all, in one of Cape Town's taverns that sailors and urban slaves planned the 1808 revolt against slavery, and recruited support from slaves working on farms.[38]

A second significant point of connection was desertion, which had always been, and continued to be, the most common form of popular resistance at the Cape. During both the first and second British occupations, the authorities issued proclamations offering pardons to deserted soldiers and sailors thought to be living in country districts.[39] Yet, such measures appeared to have little effect. Sailors and soldiers adopted a variety of strategies. Some were found work on frontier farms, and were absorbed into colonial society, while others roamed the Colony, relying on other slaves or labourers for support. There are also indications that some deserters joined the KhoiSan or fugitive bands on the colonial borderlands. For instance, Joshua Penny, an impressed sailor who deserted at the Cape, claimed to have lived with KhoiSan, as did the Irish sailor James Hooper, one of the sailors hanged for his participation in the 1808 revolt against slavery.[40] Travel writer Henry Lichtenstein, who travelled through the Cape during the Batavian period between 1803 and 1806, also confirms these strategies of desertion. He noted that when the Batavian governor, Jan Willem Janssens, toured the Cape he met a number of English deserters, "[s]ome concealed amongst the savages [KhoiSan], some among the colonists".[41]

The new wave of "British" deserters – and sailors and soldiers more generally – were increasingly associated with disorder. Governor Janssens shared these anxieties, and complained of the "extremely pernicious influence" of deserters on local inhabitants.[42] Even more alarming were the 1797 naval mutinies in Simon's Bay and Table Bay. There can be little doubt that it was these mutinies that initially, and unequivocally, allowed colonial authorities to link sailors and popular disorder.

THE SIMON'S BAY MUTINY

The Simon's Bay mutiny was inspired by the Spithead mutiny, which took place in April 1797 in English waters. The extent to which the democratic

38. N. Ulrich, "Abolition from Below: The 1808 Revolt in the Cape Colony", in M. van der Linden (ed.), *Humanitarian Intervention and Changing Labor Relations: The Long Term Consequences of the Abolition of the Slave Trade* (Leiden, 2011), pp. 193–222.
39. Proclamation by Francis Dundas, 26 February 1799, RCC, II, p. 375; and proclamations by Sir David Baird, 25 January 1806, RCC, V, p. 307; 16 May 1806, RCC, V, p. 421; and 15 August 1806, RCC, VI, pp. 25–26.
40. Penny, *Life and Adventures*, pp. 19–22.
41. H. Lichtenstein, *Travels in Southern Africa, in the Years 1803, 1804, 1805, and 1806*, 2 vols, transl. Anne Plumptre (Edinburgh, 1815), I, p. 391.
42. *Ibid.*

nature of sailors' organization and the crews' grievances in Simon's Bay resembled that of Spithead is truly remarkable, and suggests that sailors at the Cape drew on the well-established, egalitarian traditions of naval sailors that were further developed into forms of self-organization during the Spithead and Nore mutinies.[43] Although VOC crews had sometimes used their mutiny as a form of strike, this had not occurred in Cape waters. Thus, the Simon's Bay mutiny marked a distinct departure from previous modes of maritime protest in the region. Instead of killing their commanding officers and deserting, as had been done in the past, naval sailors forced their admiral to negotiate and implement reforms that improved their conditions.

The first signs of mutiny at the Cape started with "disturbances" on the *Vindictive* on 2 October 1797.[44] This was quickly quelled and the *Vindictive* separated from the rest of the squadron, which served only to enflame the sailors' desire for redress. Another warning of disquiet came on 5 October in the form of an unsigned letter dropped on the deck of the *Tremendous*. Addressed to Captain Stephens of the *Tremendous*, it stated that seamen on the *Rattlesnake* were being abused, and that to "keep disturbance from the fleet" this should be righted on every ship and that there must be no "Bad Usage" or mistreatment of the crew.[45] Stephens did not react, and on 7 October a jacket was attached on the jib-boom of each naval ship lying in Simon's Bay and, with the customary round of cheers, the *Tremendous, Trusty, Imperieuse, Braave, Rattlesnake, Chichester, Star,* and *Suffolk* rose in general mutiny.

This came in the wake of the Spithead mutiny in British waters, which was an astounding success.[46] There, a fleet-wide mutiny forced the Admiralty to negotiate, and sailors won numerous reforms, which were enacted by Parliament. Spithead delegates received a royal pardon and were officially honoured in the celebrations that followed.

---

43. For the egalitarian traditions of sailors see M. Rediker, *Between the Devil and the Deep Blue Sea: Merchant Seamen, Pirates and the Anglo-American Maritime World, 1700–1750* (Cambridge, 1987), and for self-organization at Spithead and Nore, see J.P. Moore, "'The Greatest Enormity That Prevails': Direct Democracy and Workers' Self-Management in the British Naval Mutinies of 1797", in C. Howell and R. Twomey (eds), *Jack Tar in History: Essays in the History of Maritime Life and Labour* (Fredericton, 1991), pp. 76–104.
44. Letter, *Rattlesnake* Company. It would appear to have been thrown on deck on 5 October 1797, RCC, II, pp. 162–163.
45. Letter, dropped on the quarterdeck of the *Tremendous*, 7 October 1797, RCC, II, pp. 161–162.
46. For the Spithead mutiny see D. Featherstone, "Counter-Insurgency, Subalternity, and Spatial Relations: Interrogating Court-Martial Narratives of the Nore Mutiny of 1797", *South African Historical Journal*, 61 (2009), pp. 766–787; C. Gill, *The Naval Mutinies of 1797* (Manchester, 1913); G.E. Manwaring and B. Dobrée, *The Floating Republic: An Account of the Mutinies at Spithead and the Nore in 1797* (London, 1935).

It is difficult to plot the "spatially stretched knowledge networks" of sailors that transmitted news of the Spithead mutineers' success to naval sailors at the Cape.[47] One source seems to have been the *Arniston*, which left Portsmouth in June and arrived at the Cape in August 1797.[48] (Interestingly, the *Arniston* was an English Indiaman, and not a naval ship, which indicates that merchant and naval sailors were somehow connected and that their networks overlapped.)

In the days preceding the Simon's Bay mutiny, the various ship's companies busied themselves passing letters between ships in the squadron and drawing up petitions, which mobilized the sailors around key demands. These letters give us some insight into the nature of the sailors' organization. At Spithead, each of the sixteen line-of-battle ships appointed two delegates to a central committee, and sailors took an oath to stay true to the cause.[49] Reflecting the egalitarian bonds and democratic practice that had developed amongst sailors across the Royal Navy, and which provided the basis for direct democratic practice and workers' control at Spithead,[50] the Simon's Bay mutineers also organized democratically. Like Spithead, they elected two delegates from each ship and were careful to build support across the squadron.

The company of the *Rattlesnake* initiated the correspondence between ships, but it was the close horizontal bonds developed between crewmen that laid the foundations for unity.[51] Sailors spent months, sometimes even years, together and regarded each other as brothers. In the *Rattlesnake*'s initial letter to the *Tremendous*, and in the subsequent letters passed between the various ships, sailors addressed each other as "brother".[52]

These sailors' impulse was democratic. The *Rattlesnake*'s company informed their brothers that they had canvassed grievances amongst each other, and that the majority on the ship were determined "to bring the Usurpers of our rights to a just account of their future Transactions, and make or Compel them to render us justice and better usage".[53] They called on the support of other companies, arguing that "having long laboured under their Yoke – we hope that on this determination of ours we will find you and our other friends agreeable to force those Usurpers into a more lenitive line".[54]

---

47. Featherstone, "Counter-Insurgency, Subalternity", pp. 766–787, 775.
48. Letter, Lady Anne Barnard, The Castle, Cape Town, 15 October 1797, in William Henry Wilkins (ed.), *South Africa a Century Ago: Letters Written from the Cape of Good Hope (1797–1801)* (London, 1910), p. 95.
49. Gill, *The Naval Mutinies of 1797*, p. 24.
50. Moore, "The Greatest Enormity That Prevails", pp. 84–85.
51. For more on these horizontal linkages see Rediker, *Between the Devil and the Deep Blue Sea*, and Linebaugh and Rediker, *The Many-Headed Hydra*.
52. Letter, *Rattlesnake* Company, RCC, II, p.162.
53. *Ibid.*
54. *Ibid.*

The *Rattlesnake* did receive support. Although those on the *Tremendous* had not experienced similar abuses, and even wrote that they "had no right to complain", they declared that "if you have bad usage we one and all will see you righted".⁵⁵ The company on the *Tremendous*, the flagship, did not only pledge solidarity but also coordinated the petitioning and mutiny.

The various companies' statements of complaint show sailors' views of what they regarded as acceptable terms of remuneration and discipline, and their understanding of justice. The grievances raised by the sailors of the Cape station were similar to those raised at Spithead, and centred on the quantity and quality of provisions, on working conditions, on punishment, and on the privileges of rank. Their demands dealt not only with issues related to the belly. Sailors in both English and Cape waters wanted to curb the power of their commanders, and they demanded a more democratic workplace in which sailors had a say in ship discipline.

In terms of rations, all the companies complained about the quality of bread and beef. Those on the *Imperieuse* indicated that they had received no butter or cheese since they arrived at the Cape, but only rice and sugar.⁵⁶ These were poor substitutes and were not given in adequate quantities. Similarly, the *Trusty's* company complained that there were no "greens or vegetables to be had and that the peas have been kept back".⁵⁷

Most companies believed that the weights and measures used to determine food allowance were fixed short. The seamen on the *Braave* insisted that the weights and measures had been short for eight to nine months and demanded that the purser "refund us the same".⁵⁸ The *Imperieuse* even declared the conduct of their purser, Mr Dennis, to be fraudulent, and that he "has much abused the confidence he had gained on his superiors to prejudice the navy".⁵⁹ Concerns were also raised that rations were being withheld without adequate restitution or payment. Of particular concern was that the liquor of all persons on the sick list – regardless of the nature of their disease – had been stopped. Although this liquor was supposed to be repaid in money within three months, some men had not been paid for up to a year.

The *Trusty* called for a stop to all "unnecessary work", such as "holy stoning and washing the decks in the middle of the day", while those on the *Braave* complained of "very irregular hours" of work, plus the late serving of food.⁶⁰ The *Rattlesnake* argued that two hours' personal washing a week was hopelessly inadequate, and demanded more recreation time.

55. *Ibid.*
56. *Imperieuse* Company's Grievances, RCC, II, pp. 171–172.
57. *Trusty* Company's Grievances, RCC, II, p. 170.
58. *Braave* Company's Grievances, RCC, II, pp. 172–173.
59. *Imperieuse* Company's Grievances.
60. *Trusty* Company's Grievances, and *Braave* Company's Grievances.

As at Spithead, sailors in Simon's Bay wanted the authority of their officers to be limited. While sailors were willing to put up with a certain amount of harsh language, they rejected rudeness and abusive language when undeserved. The *Rattlesnake*'s crew complained of being "oppressed by young and inexperienced officers, who learned command before they had learned obedience".[61] The crew drew attention to some of the tyrannical and unlawful punishments to which they had been subjected. For instance, a Mr Steward had commanded one man to "ride the spanker broom at sea, with a hand swab for a whip", and had another "lashed across their shoulders and their arms extended with a twelve pound shot hung at each end".[62] The company also chastised Mr Syms for his "arbitrary command and degrading speeches".[63] Sailors said that in the harbour Syms would command the hoisting of boats, lowered up to three or four times a night, only to please an "arbitrary ambition", which they believed to be "quite inconsistent with the laws of Britain".[64]

The *Rattlesnake*'s company made it clear: seamen would "allow laws to punish", but would not tolerate "tyrants to bear His Majesty's commission".[65] This company demanded that "captains or officers commanding or serving in any of His Majesty's ships shall not harass or oppress subjects of Great Britain in any scandalous or fraudulent manner, unbecoming the character of British officers".[66] They demanded that the punishment of all misdemeanours should be referred to a majority, with the captain as president, rather than being punished at will by officers.

Finally, sailors also questioned the privileges attached to rank. As the men on the *Rattlesnake* stated, "[w]e would wish as all defending one cause to have the same share that is allowed of provisions without any respect to be paid to any person, rank, or quality".[67] Expressed more plainly, those on the *Trusty* wanted some "redress respecting the different officers having the prime of the meat, and that they will have mutton only every third day the same as the ship's company".[68] The *Braave* expressed similar sentiments about the distribution of meat, complaining that "our officers have been found to take the advantage of us therein by choosing prime pieces".[69] Sailors clearly wanted to see a more equitable distribution of food on board.

61. *Rattlesnake* Company's Grievances, RCC, II, pp. 174–176, 174.
62. *Ibid.*
63. *Ibid.*
64. *Ibid.*, p. 175.
65. *Ibid.*
66. *Ibid.*
67. *Ibid.*
68. *Trusty* Company's Grievances.
69. *Braave* Company's Grievances.

The mutineers had the military advantage. The admiral was detained on the *Tremendous* and the troops that occupied the heights of Simon's Town were no match for the ships' formidable guns.[70] Pringle had little option but to deal with the sailors' grievances and negotiate a settlement. However, sailors' mistrust of authority ran deep. The sailors' delegates agreed to speak to the admiral, but insisted that "whatever you might have to say to us that you will send the same in writing and we will do the same in return".[71] A written record would serve as protection: it could be presented as evidence at court martial, and it prevented the admiral from playing the respective companies against their delegates, and from reneging on his promises.

At first Pringle conceded little. He explained that rations were scarce, that the serving of beef every day was "the custom that had always taken place at the Cape of Good Hope", and that the navy did not allow peas to be issued when beef was served every day.[72] The only concessions were that he would investigate the non-payment of the carpenters' crew, and that in future the ship's surgeon would decide when it was necessary to stop the liquor allowance of the sick.

The sailors stood firm. They asserted that "the people of this squadron has heard something of the conduct of His Majesty's Fleet in England, and the regulations that has taken place in consequence with regard to extra allowance of pay and provisions".[73] The companies wanted the same to be implemented in their squadron. They also appealed for a speedy remedy, and demanded that a general amnesty be extended to every individual in the squadron, including those on board the now absent *Vindictive*.

It should be noted that, much like the mutineers at Spithead, sailors in Simon's Bay were well disciplined and indicated that they would not permit "Pillaging, Pilfering or Riot, or bad Usage given by any of us to either party".[74] Probably being careful not to be labelled as treasonous – they had after all mutinied during a war – the sailors' letters declared their loyalty to the Crown and the British Empire, and indicated that they would return to duty in the case of enemy invasion.[75]

Pringle's explanations of scarcity aside, he was forced to make some changes. In his reply on 9 October, the admiral noted:

---

70. Letter, Lady Anne Barnard, p. 96.
71. Letter, Delegates [Enclosure R], RCC, II, p. 184.
72. Admiral's response to the *Tremendous* [Enclosure E], RCC, II, pp. 168–170, 169.
73. General Statement of the Grievances Complained of by the Different Ships' Crews of the Squadron, RCC, II, pp. 177–179, 178.
74. *Ibid.*
75. Second Letter, *Rattlesnake* Company, RCC, II, p. 163.

It is the pursers' duty to furnish perfectly good weights and measures, and it is that of the commanders to see that they do so, consequently when any deficiency is discovered and reported to the Captain, he must correct the same immediately, as the men are not to be defrauded.[76]

Pringle claimed that a survey of bread had already been ordered, and that he had given orders that the biscuit baked in future would be of the proper quality. Captain Stephens, he said, had already brought the poor quality of beef to his attention, leading to a public order in September that required the butcher and an officer from each ship to attend the killing of cattle. There was also a little rum left in the stores of the *Tremendous*, which could be served out if required, and should there be any complaints regarding wine and sprits a survey would be ordered and the bad liquor condemned. The tobacco at the Cape was too expensive, but the admiral indicated that should tobacco arrive that could be purchased at a reasonable price, it would be procured.

Even the question of class privilege was addressed to some extent. It had long been custom in the navy for officers to have choice cuts of meat, for which one pound in seven was charged. In line with the sailors' demands, the admiral ordered "that no such thing be permitted to take place in future".[77]

With respect to the fleet at home, Pringle confirmed that he had had no official communications regarding an increase of pay or provisions, but "wished to God" that the ships' companies had exercised patience and waited for such information from England, instead of turning their officers ashore and committing acts "highly repugnant to the laws of their country".[78] The admiral promised to implement official orders once received, and meanwhile appealed to the companies to recall their officers and return to duty. This would convince him of the propriety of the sailors' intentions and, he argued, smooth the way to a general amnesty.

Bargaining continued, but eventually the sailors were satisfied that the admiral would ensure that the quality of bread was improved, and that he would remedy other complaints. The main area of contention remained the fate of the obnoxious officers sent ashore at the start of the mutiny. The sailors believed that they had sufficient cause for complaint against these officers, and had resolved not to serve under them again "on any terms whatever".[79] However, the admiral was not prepared to undermine the authority of his officers. Mirroring the sailors' appeal to the law, he maintained that he did not have the authority to simply remove officers

---

76. Admiral's Response, [Enclosure N], *Tremendous* in Simon's Bay, 9 October 1797, RCC, II, pp. 179–181, 181.
77. *Ibid.*, pp. 179–181, 180.
78. *Ibid.*, pp. 179–181, 181.
79. Reply of the Delegates, [Enclosure O], RCC, II, p. 183.

without first legally investigating the complaints against them. Pringle appealed for the companies to recall their officers, and to bring forward complaints "in a manly and legal way".[80] Sailors at the Cape were distrustful of the courts, but eventually agreed to the courts martial of officers.

The sailors returned to duty on 12 October. The royal standard was hoisted on board the *Tremendous* "as a signal of good order and discipline being established in the fleet".[81] On the same day, the admiral issued a proclamation granting the pardon and general amnesty to all seamen and marines in the squadron "who so returned to the regular and ordinary discharges of their duty".[82]

CUSTOM AND RIGHTS

The court martial of the controversial Captain Stephens started a few weeks later, on 6 November, on board the *Sceptre* in Table Bay. This trial points to a notable shift in the sailors' understanding of rights. Their firm rejection of custom at Stephens's trial signalled a departure from the notion that their rights were rooted in British tradition.

Much like the sailors at Spithead, the sailors in Simon's Bay publically identified themselves as the "lawful and true born subjects of great Britain" and demanded that their "Primitive Rights" should be recovered.[83] In so doing, these sailors appear to evoke an earlier conception of rights that had previously been articulated by, for example, the Levellers during the English Revolution. According to E.P. Thompson, in the eighteenth century claims to be a "free-born Englishman" were cloaked in a rhetoric of liberty, were made by reference to past – and often local – laws and customs, and were made by radicals, patricians, and demagogues alike to justify a range of political agendas.[84] Such claims were not so much a demand for democracy as the affirmation of a distinct entitlement to the rule of law, and a shared rejection of absolute, arbitrary power by the state over the gentry and common people.[85] As noted by Thompson, this particular understanding of rights was fundamentally limited – it implied respect for the monarchy, the hereditary principle, and for the traditional property rights of landowners.[86]

When applied in the context of the Royal Navy, sailors questioned the arbitrary authority exercised by their officers, and called for the

80. Memorandum of the Admiral [Enclosure P], RCC, II, pp. 182–183, 182.
81. Letter from the Earl of Macartney to the Right Honourable Henry Dundas, Castle of Good Hope, 13 October 1797, RCC, II, pp. 86–187, 187.
82. Proclamation, by Admiral Pringle [Enclosure U], RCC, II, p. 186.
83. Letter, *Rattlesnake* Company.
84. Thompson, *The Making of the English Working Class*, p. 85.
85. *Ibid.*, pp. 87, 90.
86. *Ibid.*, p. 96.

implementation of the law. For instance, the sailors of the *Tremendous* objected to the list of articles read out on the quarterdeck, which appeared to be different from the Articles of War. The company stated that it did not have a problem with the "general tenor" of such articles that dealt with good order, discipline, and cleanliness.[87] However, the sailors were of the opinion that "no authority whatever has a right to pose new laws on them except that of the British legislature".[88]

Although sailors deployed this particular rhetoric of "free-born Englishmen", it appears that they also started to recognize the limits of a tradition-bound notion of rights when they specifically rejected the notion of naval custom during Stephens's trial. At the heart of this rejection was the belief that custom was a naked instrument of class oppression. For instance, in the charges brought against Stephens, the sailors noted:

> The Ships Company are aware that the Customs of the navy will be used in defence of this Charge and That the Ships Company does not appeal to Customs as it has been custom perhaps before the Existence of the British Navy for people in low situations to be opprest [*sic*] by those in power therefore the purpose of all laws has generally been to protect the weaker members of society.[89]

Correctly anticipated by the sailors, Stephens was a firm supporter of customs, and custom was integral to his legal defence. He argued that "most of the charges against me has been long sanctioned by custom and recommended as well as followed by officers the most distinguished in our service".[90] Stephens believed that rule through custom was unquestionable. He argued that, although sailors claimed to have long-standing grievances, they had never complained because they knew it was custom and "therefore to complain of them would appear frivolous and troublesome".[91] The captain believe that sailors respected custom above all else, and maintained that they had been misled by a few mischievous individuals "to delight in disorder and confusion" and so to follow the example of the fleet in England.[92]

However, even though the captain may have believed that the mutiny could be blamed on a few troublemakers, he admitted that relations between sailors and their officers were starting to change. He claimed that the 1797 mutinies had "removed the tie of Confidence between officers and men and instead there of have taken up distrust, and now nothing is heard of but grievance and complains formerly not known of".[93]

---

87. *Tremendous* Company's Grievances, RCC, II, pp. 164–168, 166.
88. *Ibid.*
89. NA, UK, ADM 1/5488, Charges to be Exhibited Against Captain George Hopewele Stephens Esq. Commander of His Majesty's Ship *Tremendous*, 28 October 1797, pp. 7–8.
90. NA, UK, ADM 1/5488, Captain Hopewele Stephens Defence, p. 76.
91. *Ibid.*
92. *Ibid.*
93. NA, UK, ADM, 1/5488, Minutes of Proceedings of a Court Martial, pp. 87–88.

Why had sailors at the Cape become so distrustful of naval custom? Common understandings of rights and obligations in the navy could – and in many instances probably did – serve as a basis for a moral economy shared by sailors and their officers, which sailors could deploy when conditions and rations deteriorated, or officers became too authoritarian. Joseph Price Moore argues that British naval sailors occupied and moved between two distinct worlds, namely a world of tradition, paternalism, and deference, which allowed for an economy shared by officers and crew, and the world of capitalist relations, which gave rise to new forms of action, such as the strike and a broader class identity.[94] However, in the case of the Cape, it seems that sailors were no longer able to reconcile these two worlds, and the harsh reality of capitalist relations, together with the need for a broader identity in line with sailors' unity, undermined any possibility of an economy shared by officers and crew, and eroded the legitimacy of British, or naval, custom as a basis for claiming rights.

First, officers continually evoked custom to deny sailors the most basic provisions on the one hand, and to justify their privileges on the other. Pringle complained that the Cape was in short supply of just about everything. In August 1797, just two months before the mutiny, he wrote about the "great distress of the squadron", and that he had never been able to procure bread sufficient for one month for the whole squadron.[95] Considering these shortages, it was probably just as well that the squadron was some 760 men short (excluding the 60 men in hospital whom he did not expect to recover and return to duty).[96] Added to this, the quality of slops, beds, and marine clothing was inadequate and Pringle complained that "the men are totally destitute".[97] However, the sailors did not appear to trust such claims of scarcity. They may have questioned the Navy's tardiness with regard to providing monetary compensation for short provisions, and there seemed to be enough food to supply East India Company ships on their way to St Helena. Indeed, the officers still seemed to enjoy reasonably good rations. Under these circumstances, custom became a justification for failing to meet the sailors' most basic needs, as opposed to a system of reciprocation and redress between officers and crew.

In the second instance, not everyone in the navy could claim to be British-born, nor free. As noted above, "British" sailors were a relatively motley lot. An identification as British subjects could accommodate the multi-racial and multi-national composition of sailors drawn from across

---

94. Moore, "The Greatest Enormity That Prevails", pp. 81–83.
95. Letter, Admiral Pringle to Evan Nepan Esq., *Tremendous* in Simon's Bay, Cape of Good Hope, 17 August 1797, RCC, II, pp. 152–155.
96. Letter, Pringle to Nepan, *Tremendous* in Simon's Bay, Cape of Good Hope, 25 August 1797, RCC, II, pp. 156–157.
97. *Ibid.*

the empire. Even so, this would require the replacement of the parochial rhetoric of "free-born Englishmen" with a more universal notion of rights. Customary "British" rights, in short, could not provide an adequate basis for unifying sailors – something more was required.

Finally, ideas of rights were in the process of being re-conceptualized in the writings of radicals such as Thomas Paine, as well as in the American Revolution (1776–1783) and the French Revolution (1789–1794). In this context, sailors questioned the limited notion that rights resided in British tradition and law, as they too were influenced by, and participated in, discussions regarding the more intrinsic origins of rights derived from Reason, God, or nature, rather than British history.

THE LIMITS OF REFORM

Like the Spithead mutiny, which was followed by the more radical mutiny at Nore, the Simon's Bay mutiny was followed by a second, more radical phase when naval sailors mutinied in Table Bay on 7 November 1797. It is more difficult to make sense of this mutiny, especially since the only petition drawn up was destroyed.[98] Nevertheless, the mutiny seems to represent sailors' growing suspicion, not only of class bias inherent in custom but also of the law in which they had placed so much hope just a few weeks previously.

Upper-class individuals such as Lady Barnard, wife of the Secretary of the Colony under the first British occupation, were sorry that a general amnesty had been granted to mutineers at the Cape. She claimed that "even the best-natured people wish the delegates to be made examples of to the Navy".[99] It soon became apparent that the court martial was not simply about restoring Captain Stephens's name; it was also a means of enabling officers and commanders to reassert their authority.

In spite of the sailors' insistence on the rule of law, they did not trust the courts. It is for this reason that they demanded some representation in cases dealing with sailors' discipline during the Simon's Bay mutiny – a demand the sailors failed to win. The limits of the courts as a basis for popular redress became apparent on 7 November, the second day of the trial, when the court held two sailors in contempt.[100] James Hay was apparently drunk, while James Willis – one the delegates from the *Tremendous* during the Simon's Bay mutiny – was accused of interrupting the court. Both were sentenced to one month's imprisonment.

The court's actions infuriated the sailors. Together with the *Jupiter* and the *Reasonable*, the *Sceptre* had just recently returned from St Helena.

98. NA, ADM, 1/5488, Minutes of Proceedings of a Court Martial, 30 November 1797, pp. 139, 147, 150–154.
99. Letter, Lady Anne Barnard, p. 98.
100. NA, ADM, 1/5488, Minutes of Proceedings of a Court Martial, pp. 33, 40.

Officers picked up a mood of rebelliousness amongst sailors on these ships.[101] The imprisonment of Willis provided the trigger for action and, with three cheers, sailors on the *Tremendous*, *Sceptre*, and *Rattlesnake*, now all in Table Bay, mutinied. They were joined by the *Crescent*, quarantined off Robben Island on account of a smallpox outbreak on board the Spanish slaver she had just taken as a prize.[102]

This time Admiral Pringle acted together with the Cape governor and the fiscal, the Cape's chief legal officer, to repress the mutiny. They had the military advantage, and aimed the guns of the Amsterdam Battery at the ships.[103] The mutineers were given an ultimatum: give up their leaders and return to order or they would be fired upon. Left with little option, the leaders were surrendered. After briefly being detained in the castle, they were tried by courts martial.[104] While the court found Captain Stephens to be innocent of the charges sailors had brought against him, four of the Table Bay mutineers were found guilty and sentenced to death.[105]

In spite of the success of the Spithead and Simon's Bay mutinies, much still had to change. Through unity and democratic organization, sailors were able to win real improvements in their basic conditions, but the power and privilege of the upper classes remained intact. Like those at the Nore, sailors at the Cape were quick to recognize the limits of such reforms and were radicalized. Like those at the Nore, mutineers at Table Bay were also punished harshly for daring to oppose their officers.

THE LOCAL CHALLENGE CONTINUES

The Cape's new rulers were able to win the allegiance of the elite, and used military force to crush rebel free burghers, but the popular classes would prove much more difficult to coopt, or even to defeat militarily. The 1797 mutinies signalled a further upturn in popular protest at the Cape, as well as the development of new popular political strategies. Like the mutineers, KhoiSan and slaves would also adopt new strategies that raised questions about the relationship between rights, the state, and freedom.

Unlike the Servants' Rebellion and the 1808 revolt against slavery, naval sailors did not demand their freedom or a change in government. Yet the Simon's Bay mutiny cannot easily be described as reformist, despite its seemingly more moderate demands. The sailors organized a mutiny across

---

101. NA, ADM, 1/5488, Minutes of Proceedings of a Court Martial, 9 December 1797, pp. 281–302.
102. Theal, "Digest of the Records", RCC, V, p. 39, and Letter, Pringle to Nepean, *Tremendous*, Table Bay, Cape of Good Hope, 27 November 1797, RCC,. II, pp. 206–208.
103. Letter from the Earl of Macartney to the Right Honourable Henry Dundas, 12 November 1797, RCC, II, pp. 202–203, 202.
104. Letter, Pringle to Nepean, *Tremendous*, 27 November 1797, RCC, II, pp. 206–208.
105. RCC, V, pp. 39–40.

the squadron during wartime – an act that could easily be interpreted as treasonous. In addition, some of their demands, especially those related to limiting officers' privileges and authority, and the creation of a more democratic and egalitarian workspace, were actually quite radical. Most significantly, the Simon's Bay and Table Bay munities were continuations of the remarkable experiment on the part of sailors with direct democracy and workers' control during the Spithead and Nore mutinies. Sailors had succeeded in using militant, democratic protest to engage the Admiralty and to force the state to make substantial changes.

Even though the Table Bay mutiny ended in the execution of radicals, mutinies continued to take place in Cape waters. These included a mutiny by soldiers on board the *Lady Shore* en route to Botany Bay; a mutiny by the crew of the *Princess Charlotte* belonging to the East India Company; and a mutiny on board HMS *Hope* in 1800, just off the coast of Madagascar.[106]

Just as significantly, the 1797 mutinies marked a growing confidence and radicalization of the popular classes at the Cape, which resulted in a further upturn in resistance and also the willingness to experiment with new strategies and ideas. From 1799 KhoiSan labourers deserted their masters on an unprecedented scale, only to raid outlying farms for arms, ammunition, and horses.[107] By the end of July 1799 KhoiSan bands were in control of the whole south-eastern part of the Graaff-Reinet district. They had succeeded not only in halting the latest colonial encroachments, but also in pushing the colonial border back. Unlike sailors, these rebels believed their freedom could be realized only by remaining independent. The British were seen neither as their rulers nor their allies, and rebels simply did not engage with the Cape's new imperial powers. They could not be enticed to return to the Colony by labour reform, nor could they be defeated militarily. It would not be until 1811–1812, when the British military established forts in the area, that the British were able to gain control over the eastern boundary of the Colony.

A third major protest took place in 1808, during the second British occupation.[108] The revolt included, besides slaves, a number of KhoiSan servants and two sailors, who, as noted above, played an integral part in

---

106. Letter, Macartney to Dundas, 7 July 1798, RCC, II, p. 274; Letter, War Office to the Earl of Macartney, Downing Street, 15 December 1798, RCC, II, p. 312; and Letter, Major General Dundas to Henry Dundas, Cape of Good Hope, 6 April 1799, RCC, II, p. 418; Letter, Vice Admiral Curtis to Evan Nepean, Esq., Lancaster, Table Bay, Cape of Good Hope, 6 January 1800, RCC, II, p. 18.

107. For a more detailed account see S. Newton-King and V.C. Malherbe, *The Khoikhoi Rebellion in the Eastern Cape (1799–1803)* (Cape Town, 1981).

108. For a more detailed account see Ulrich, "Abolition from Below", pp. 193–222, and N. Worden, "Armed with Swords and Ostrich Feathers: Militarism and Cultural Revolution in the Cape Slave Uprising of 1808", in Richard Bessel, Nicholas Guyatt, and Jane Rendall (eds), *War, Empire and Slavery, 1770–1830* (London, 2010), pp. 121–138.

organizing the revolt. It was not simply a slave revolt; it was a *revolt against slavery*, which drew in other sections of the popular classes. Rejecting gradual reform from above, or the amelioration of their condition, the 1808 rebels developed their own vision of immediate and complete emancipation from below. On 27 October, anti-slavery rebels invaded 34 farms in the wealthy grape- and grain-growing districts of the Zwartland, Koeberg, and Tygerberg.[109] With their tied-up masters in tow, more than 300 rebels marched to Cape Town to demand their freedom and, if necessary, topple the government.[110]

During the revolt, one of the rebel leaders, Abraham van de Kaap, declared "the insurgents the next day would hoist the bloody flag and fight themselves free".[111] The bloody flag, or red flag, has important maritime connotations and was traditionally hoisted by sailors in mutiny.[112] There is no conclusive evidence, but perhaps due to the connections between sailors, slaves, and KhoiSan, the 1808 rebels may have borrowed the symbol of the red flag from the 1797 Cape mutinies.

Through these three protests we see three very different conceptions of rights, freedom, and the state. Sailors in Simon's Bay pressed the Admiralty to implement reforms. However, sailors struggled to reconcile their officers' paternalism and the harshness of capitalist relations. Rejecting a narrow view of rights based on British custom and law, sailors mutinied a second time in Table Bay.

On the other hand, rebels in the Servants' Rebellion and the 1808 revolt did not believe that the imperial state could offer rights or freedom. KhoiSan rebels did not believe that the British government could meet their demands, and sought to realize their freedom by remaining independent and refusing to engage the state. Those who participated in the 1808 revolt also placed little faith in the colonial state. Like rebels in the American, French, and Haitian revolutions, they were determined to topple the government should their demand for freedom not be met.

CONCLUSION

The 1797 mutinies by British naval sailors were a major contribution to the age of revolution that altered the world forever. Naval sailors fused their established workplace traditions in the Royal Navy with their experiences at the Cape, and the Simon's Bay and Table Bay mutinies intensified class conflict and contributed to popular resistance at a global and local level. Perhaps the most notable development in these Cape

109. WCPA, CJ 802, p. 752.
110. WCPA, CJ 802, pp. 753–754.
111. WCPA, CJ 802, p. 759.
112. Manwaring and Dobrée, *Floating Republic*, p. 50.

mutinies is that they demonstrated that sailors were starting to develop new political understandings of their circumstances. Even though they were able to secure improvements, like their brothers at Spithead, these victories appeared to be hollow as long as class exploitation and oppression remained intact. It is within this context that we see sailors starting to break with the particular rhetoric of "free-born Englishmen", used during the Spithead and Simon's Bay mutinies, and question the notion that their rights and liberty resided in British tradition and the courts.

IRSH 58 (2013), Special Issue, pp. 87–107 doi:10.1017/S0020859013000230

Connections between Mutinies in European Navies

Niklas Frykman

Department of History, Claremont McKenna College
850 Columbia Ave, Claremont, CA 91711, USA

E-mail: niklas.frykman@cmc.edu

ABSTRACT: During the revolutionary 1790s, an unprecedented number of mutinies tore through the British, French, and Dutch navies. This simultaneous upsurge of lower-deck militancy in both allied and belligerent fleets was not coincidental, nor was it simply a violent expression of similar pressures making themselves felt on ships under different flags but all engaged in the same conflict. Instead, through manifold personal connections, men who circulated back and forth across the frontline, and through the gradual emergence of a common political ideology, mutinies across navies constituted a single radical movement, a genuine Atlantic revolution in this so-called age of Atlantic revolutions.

The revolutionary 1790s were the Atlantic's great age of mutiny. Shipboard riots, mass desertions, armed strikes, all-out insurrections, violence against officers, and even assassinations swept through Europe's wooden warships like a wildfire. In just over 10 turbulent years, the French, British, and Dutch navies alone experienced at least 150 single-ship mutinies, as well as half a dozen fleet mutinies that lasted from a few days to several months and involved between 3,000 and 30,000 men each time. The waves of mutiny that washed through the French, British, and Dutch navies in the 1790s were each exceptional, but the simultaneity with which they crashed into quarterdecks on both sides of the front was wholly unprecedented. At the end of the decade, between one-third and one-half of the 450 ships and 200,000 men deployed across the 3 fleets had experienced or participated in at least one mutiny, many of them in several, and some even on ships in different navies.[1] Put differently, by the

---

1. The numbers of men and ships are approximate, but based on figures in N.A.M. Rodger, *The Command of the Ocean: A Naval History of Britain, 1649–1815* (New York, 2004), pp. 608, 639. The number of mutinies is a conservative estimate. Many French and Dutch naval records have been lost. Additionally, mutinies were notoriously underreported to begin with, since neither officers nor crew in many cases had an interest in the navy administration getting wind of any irregularities on board their ships. Jonathan Neale suggests that the actual number of

late 1790s up to 100,000 experienced mutineers were spread across the lower decks of the French, British, and Dutch fleets, all of them men who had risked their lives to contest for power with one of the world's most entrenched autocracies, the European naval officer corps.

This was a major revolutionary movement, one perhaps, as the English commonist Thomas Spence demanded, that ought to be named in the same breath as the great convulsions of 1776 and 1789.[2] Despite its remarkable scale, however, the mutinous Atlantic has been nearly forgotten. The practice of writing north Atlantic histories primarily from national and imperial perspectives has led to the movement's segmentation and thus reduction, and ultimately has reinforced the assumption that events at sea were only of marginal importance even in this so-called age of Atlantic revolution. The present article will therefore attempt to once again join those national segments together, and shift the perspective from shore to sea, by first describing the similarities between mutinies in different navies; secondly, by recovering material connections between them; and finally, by tracing the outline of a common political ideology that emerged out of the mutinous Atlantic.

MUTINIES IN THE FRENCH, BRITISH, AND DUTCH NAVIES

For most of the eighteenth century, the French navy had enjoyed comparatively high levels of social peace on board its ships. Between 1706 and 1789, there were five times more mutinies on privateers than on warships, four and a half times more on merchantmen, and more than twice as many in the nation's fishing fleet. After 1789, the proportions changed completely: mutinies in the civilian and paramilitary maritime industries disappeared almost entirely, while in the navy they went, virtually overnight, from episodic to endemic.[3] These mutinies, however, did not correspond to the popular image, most famously epitomized by the 1789 mutiny on the *Bounty*, of a crew swiftly rising on the captain, permanently seizing power on board, and then disappearing with the ship over the horizon.[4] The decomposition of the French state apparatus, coupled with the

mutinies may have been as much as twenty times higher than those reported. See his "Forecastle and Quarterdeck: Protest, Discipline and Mutiny in the Royal Navy, 1793–1814" (Ph.D. thesis, University of Warwick, 1990), p. 25.

2. Thomas Spence, "The Restorer of Society to its Natural State", in H.T. Dickinson (ed.), *The Political Works of Thomas Spence* (Newcastle, 1983), pp. 69–92, 78.

3. Alain Cabantous, *La Vergue et les Fers: Mutins et Déserteurs dans la marine de l'ancienne France (XVIIe–XVIIIe s)* (Paris, 1984), pp. 13, 159–161.

4. The *Bounty* enjoys an extraordinarily rich literature. For a recent overview, see Donald Maxton, *The Mutiny on HMS Bounty: A Guide to Nonfiction, Fiction, Poetry, Films, Articles, and Music* (Jefferson, NC, 2008).

ideological redefinition of the nation, removed the necessity of running away and instead allowed discontented seamen to use mutiny as a way actively to participate in the republican reconstruction of the navy. They seized that opportunity with great enthusiasm and revolutionary élan.

Across the French Atlantic Empire – from Toulon to Saint-Domingue, from Martinique to Brest – tens of thousands on board the King's warships embraced popular sovereignty as the new principle of naval governance. Officers suddenly found their orders endlessly questioned, debated, and sometimes overruled by crews who self-confidently declared themselves to embody the national will and therefore to be answerable to no higher power, least of all one put in place by the old regime. Bourgeois port city radicals, themselves engaged in a struggle for municipal control with the old naval administrative corps, in most cases threw their support behind these claims, and thus was forged a powerful alliance that together spent four years tearing apart the once mighty Royale. Crews rioted through the streets of Toulon, Brest, and Le Cap; they ignored orders and refused to put to sea; they sabotaged their ships, threw admirals into prison, maimed and even murdered a number of officers. By 1793, the lower deck had become almost ungovernable. But then came the war. Under the pressure of Jacobin violence, blistering nationalistic propaganda, and top-down working-class friendly reforms, the back of French lower-deck insurrectionism broke. During the Thermidorian Reaction, and continuing into the Directory's reign, there was a sharp, destabilizing rise in the number of desertions instead.[5]

Like the pre-revolutionary French fleet, Britain's Royal Navy experienced relatively modest levels of collective unrest for most of the eighteenth century. But the 1790s were different (see Figure 1). Initially, the wartime rise in the number of mutinies was quantitatively no more dramatic than it had been during the mobilizations of the mid-1750s or late 1770s, but in the early 1790s the nature of mutiny itself was qualitatively different. In previous wars, mutinous seamen either came together in illegal shipboard assemblies or they simply rioted to give expression to their discontent. Experienced officers, in turn, usually took view that such mutinies, while most certainly disagreeable, in the end served a useful purpose in allowing for the periodic release of dangerous tensions that inevitably built up below deck. In response, they quietly addressed whatever triggered the mutiny, and noisily punished a few of the men so as to re-establish the appearance of proper subordination on board.[6]

5. The standard work on the navy during the French Revolution is William S. Cormack, *Revolution and Political Conflict in the French Navy, 1789–1794* (Cambridge, 1995).
6. N.A.M. Rodger, "Shipboard Life in the Old Navy: The Decline of the Old Order?", in Lewis R. Fischer *et al.* (eds), *The North Sea: Twelve Essays on Social History of Maritime Labour* (Stavanger, 1992), pp. 29–39, 32.

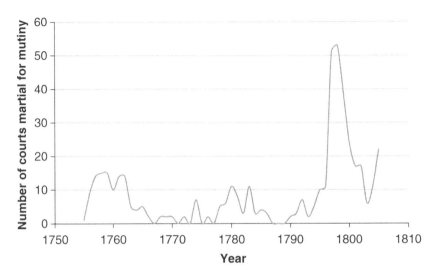

Figure 1. Courts martial for mutiny, British Royal Navy, 1755–1805
Digest and Analysis of Courts Martial, TNA: PRO (UK) ADM 12/24.

The mounting pressures of the international arms race combined with the first flames of revolution flickering around the Atlantic rim noticeably strained the navy's turbulent corporatism, and then led to its complete breakdown in the early 1790s. As soon as the fleet mobilized for war, the lower deck launched a series of rapidly radicalizing and increasingly militant strikes to demand seaworthy ships, the expulsion of cruel officers, better provisions, guaranteed shore leave, payment of outstanding wages, and other improvements to their working conditions. Unlike most previous eruptions, which had either been disorganized or relatively deferential, mutinies in the early 1790s tended to be both highly organized and extremely confrontational. The type of mutiny that first appeared on the *Winchelsea* in 1793 (and was subsequently perfected on the *Windsor Castle* and the *Culloden* in 1794, and on the *Terrible* in 1795) began with a moment of running amok, a brief period of furious but planned chaos below deck during which a hard core of mutineers quickly drove known loyalists up to the main deck, removed the ladders and secured the hatchways, and finally barricaded themselves in the stern of the ship by running in two of the great guns and pointing them aft, in the direction of the quarterdeck. Then they issued their demands.[7]

---

7. Court martial against men from the *Winchelsea*, The National Archives: Public Records Office (UK) [hereafter TNA: PRO (UK)], ADM 1/5330; court martial against men from the *Windsor Castle*, TNA: PRO (UK) ADM 1/5331; court martial against men from the *Culloden*, TNA: PRO (UK) ADM 1/5331; court martial against men from the *Terrible*, TNA: PRO (UK)

After a series of defeated single-ship mutinies, most of which ended with several men hanged, the lower deck's militant strike movement culminated in the famous fleet mutinies of 1797, when over 30,000 men on more than 100 ships immobilized the navy's home command for two whole months in the midst of the annual fighting season.[8] At the Nore anchorage, where the fleet mutinies peaked in late May, the mutineers developed a sophisticated committee system reminiscent of the revolutionary sections of Paris, elected a president, and proclaimed their ships a "floating republic".[9] It was the largest, best organized, and most sustained working-class offensive in eighteenth-century Britain. And it could not be contained to home waters. Revolts ripped through the Mediterranean squadron, then the Cape squadron, and finally reached even as far as the small Indian Ocean squadron stationed at Trincomalee six months after the original mutinies had been suppressed in England.

The crew of the *Suffolk*, at the time anchored in Colombo Roads, learnt about the fleet mutiny from an article in the 9 October 1797 issue of the *Bombay Courier*, and in response demanded the same concessions as those they imagined had been won at home, and then more (including jury trials to replace courts martial as well as the wholesale abolition of the current articles of war).[10] News of the fleet mutinies also spread to the Caribbean, where it fired the viciously violent mutiny on the *Hermione*, which in turn ushered in a new phase of lower-deck militancy.[11] Instead of the strike-like mutinies that had dominated the early years of the war, conspiracies and successful attempts to take over the ship, murder the officer corps, and then hand over the ship to the enemy now multiplied.[12]

In comparison with the French and British fleets, the Dutch navy appears to have experienced a higher level of unrest throughout the eighteenth century,

ADM 1/5331. For an analysis of the amok moment in its original context, see Matthias van Rossum's contribution to this volume.

8. For an overview of current scholarship on the fleet mutinies, see Ann Veronica Coats and Philip MacDougall (eds), *The Naval Mutinies of 1797: Unity and Perseverance* (Woodbridge, 2011).

9. Anon., *Memoirs of Richard Parker, the Mutineer; Together with an Account at large of His Trial by Court Martial, Defence, Sentence, and Execution and A Narrative of the Mutiny at the Nore and Sheerness, from its Commencement to its Final Termination* (London, 1797), p. 18.

10. Court martial against men from the *Kingfisher*, TNA: PRO (UK) ADM 1/5340; courts martial against men from the *St George*, TNA: PRO (UK) ADM 1/5340; court martial against men from the *Tremendous*, TNA: PRO (UK) ADM 1/5342; court martial against the men on the *Suffolk*, TNA: PRO (UK) ADM 1/5345. For mutinies at the Cape station, see also Nicole Ulrich's contribution to this volume.

11. Niklas Frykman, "The Mutiny on the *Hermione*: Warfare, Revolution, and Treason in the Royal Navy", *Journal of Social History*, 44 (2010), pp. 159–187.

12. Courts martial against men from the *Tremendous, Diana, Renomee, Caesar, Princess Royal, Haughty, Defiance, Glory, Ramillies, Queen Charlotte, Diomede,* and *Hope*, TNA: PRO (UK) ADM 1/5343, 1/5345, 1/5346, 1/5347, 1/5348, 1/5350, and 1/5351.

but even here the explosion of the 1790s was extraordinarily intense.[13] The combined French invasion and domestic revolution of 1794–1795 was greeted with mass desertions throughout the fleet. The following year, a squadron sent to secure the Cape of Good Hope colony surrendered to the British without firing a shot, in part because mutinies had broken out on several of the ships. Across the Atlantic, on the Suriname station, another squadron collapsed as low morale, miserable conditions, and high-handed, arrogant leadership triggered one mass escape after another, and also several murder plots. In the home command, things looked much the same. Approximately thirty crew members of the *Utrecht* were discovered in 1798 as they hatched a chilling plan to murder nearly every officer on board, fight their way past the shore batteries on Texel, and then sail for either Hamburg or England, depending on the winds. The following year, yet another fleet surrendered to the British amidst a violent, chaotic mass mutiny near the Texel anchorage. It marked the final, inglorious collapse of Batavian naval power.[14]

Though largely forgotten by later naval historians, the mutinies across the Dutch, French, and British fleets were not without consequence at the time. In the Batavian navy, where mutinies tended to be poorly organized and often lacked internal cohesion, the lower deck's chronic and violent disobedience nonetheless had the greatest impact. Not only was it a powerful check on the new regime's imperial ambitions and largely deprived its French ally of much-needed naval support against Britain, it also hastened the end of Dutch sea power in 1799, never again to be resurrected as anything other than a second- or even third-rate force. In France, by contrast, lower-deck insurgents rapidly moved beyond the exuberant chaos that accompanied the outbreak of revolution in 1789, proceeded systematically to clear nearly all remnants of the old regime from the fleet, and then pushed hard and successfully for a new, fundamentally

13. In contrast to the Dutch East India Company (VOC), there has been next to no research on mutinies and other forms of unrest in the pre-revolutionary eighteenth-century Dutch navy. The demographic and operational similarities between the two services in the later decades of the eighteenth century, however, suggest that the navy, like the VOC, probably experienced fairly high levels of social tensions aboard its ships. For mutinies on VOC ships, see Jaap R. Bruijn and E.S. van Eyck van Heslinga (eds), *Muiterij: Oproer en Berechting op Schepen van de VOC* (Haarlem, 1980).

14. Captain Donckum's report, Nationaal Archief, The Hague [hereafter NA (NL)], Inventaries van de Archieven van het Departement van Marine, 1795–1813, 2.01.29.01, inv. nr 451; Vice Admiral Engelbertus Lucas's dispatches, 20 August 1796, Captain Adjoint A.J. Knok's report, conclusions of the Council of War, 16 August 1796, NA (NL), Hoge Militaire Rechtspraak, 1795–1813 (1818), 2.01.11, inv. nr 221; Captain Lieutenant Ruijsch to Vice Admiral de Winter, 12 July 1797, NA (NL), Departement van Marine, 1795–1813, 2.01.29.01, inv. nr 236; courts martial against the men from the *Utrecht*, NA (NL), Hoge Militaire Rechtspraak, 1795–1813 (1818), 2.01.11, inv. nr 234; various interrogation minutes and reports, NA (NL), Hoge Militaire Rechtspraak, 1795–1813 (1818), 2.01.11, inv. nrs 236–242.

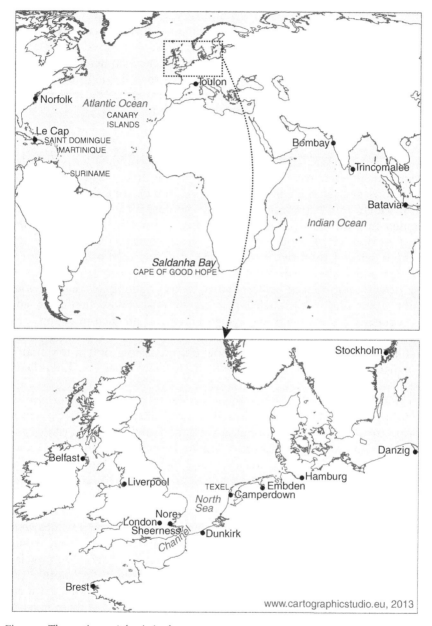

Figure 2. The mutinous Atlantic in the 1790s.

different regime of shipboard governance, a victory that, at least in the short term, probably made the French republican navy a stronger, more highly motivated fighting force than its royalist predecessor had been.

Only in Britain, finally, where mutineers struggled for years, where they developed highly militant and disciplined forms of mutiny, and in the end even mounted the single largest, most impressive insurrection of the whole period, had lower-deck insurgency comparatively little measurable impact on the war, other perhaps than driving up desertion levels, sharpening the manpower crisis, and scattering the runaways all over the Atlantic world, and sometimes beyond.

MOTLEY AND MOBILE MUTINEERS

Even though each navy's wave of unrest was first triggered by local conditions, and subsequently followed its own trajectory, the simultaneity with which this extraordinarily large number of mutinies suddenly erupted in both allied and belligerent fleets is notable. Yet despite the surge in disaffected, violent mutinies across navies, common crewmen on both sides of the front never stopped fighting each other with great courage and savage dedication. The British, in particular, excelled at the newly reintroduced close-combat melee fighting of the previous century, but now with much larger crews, vastly more firepower, and consequently a great many more men killed and maimed in action. The Battle of Camperdown, fought between the British and Dutch navies on 11 October 1797, marked a milestone: despite lasting only a few hours, proportionately it was the bloodiest engagement since the Four Days Battle of 1666.[15]

The British usually out-killed their enemies by a vast margin – from the Glorious First of June 1794 to the Battle of Trafalgar in 1805 by a proportion of about six to one – but against the Dutch at Camperdown the losses were more evenly balanced.[16] Unlike French and Spanish gun crews who were trained to aim for the masts and rigging, the Dutch adopted the British tactic of pounding the enemy's hull with broadsides until there were no longer enough men left standing to return fire. They battered each other for hours at very close range until finally the exhausted, slower-firing Dutch were forced to surrender. Most of their 16 ships were damaged beyond repair, some were on fire, and three of them would eventually sink. Of the 7,157 men who had sailed into battle, 620 now lay weltering in each other's gore across the blood-soaked decks; another 520 were already dead. The British, who had entered the fight with 8,221 men, overall suffered 228 men dead and 812 wounded, many of them invalids for life. On some of the ships the carnage was staggering. The *Ardent*,

---

15. Noel Mostert, *The Line Upon A Wind: The Great War at Sea, 1793–1815* (New York, 2007), p. 232.
16. Adam Nicolson, *Men of Honour: Trafalgar and the Making of the English Hero* (London, 2005), p. 20.

which had locked yardarms with the Dutch flagship *Vrijheid*, received 98 shots into her hull, lost 41 men dead and 108 wounded. The *Belliqueux* counted 25 dead and 88 wounded.[17]

Such slaughter does not call to mind the proletarian internationalism eighteenth-century deep-sea sailors are known for, nor does it suggest that the growing intensity and violence of their conflicts with the quarterdeck led naval seamen to reassess and readjust their national loyalties.[18] Looks, however, may well be deceiving. Before the battle there was in fact a fair amount of uncertainty among officers on both sides about whether their men could be relied upon to fight at all. As for the British, they were well aware that it had been only four months since the final collapse of the fleet mutinies in early June. Throughout the uprising, many of the mutineers had repeatedly sought to assure their officers that, as long as they were given "their Due", they once again would happily "go in search of the Rascals the Enemys of our Country".[19] But unfortunately, quite a few felt that they had not been given their due. Instead they had been made to suffer a veritable reign of terror once the officer class reconquered the quarterdeck. At least twenty-six men were executed, seventeen were sentenced to hard labor, five men were flogged through the fleet, and hundreds of others disappeared into various carceral institutions, including at least two men who were deported to the newly established penal settlements of New South Wales and Norfolk Island, both not far from where the crew of the *Bounty* had mutinied only a few years before.[20]

It was meant to be an awe-inspiring display of state terror, but did it work? Had the lower deck been cowed back into obedience? It was far from clear. In the four months between the final collapse of the fleet

17. William James, *The Naval History of Great Britain, from the Declaration of War by France, in February 1793; to the Accession of George IV, in January 1820*, 6 vols (London, 1837), II, pp. 75–89.

18. For lower-deck internationalism, see Peter Linebaugh and Marcus Rediker, *The Many-Headed Hydra: Sailors, Slaves, Commoners, and the Hidden History of the Revolutionary Atlantic* (Boston, MA, 2000), especially chs 5 and 7.

19. No. 29 (Note, Henry Long to the Lords Commissioners of the Board of the Admiralty, onboard the *Champion*, n.d.), papers found onboard of the *Repulse*, 12 June 1797, TNA: PRO (UK) ADM 1/727 C370.

20. Due to the incomplete and sometimes unclear documentation, historians disagree about the exact number of men punished, though all estimates are within a similar range. For a compilation of estimates, see James Dugan, *The Great Mutiny* (New York, 1965), pp. 389–390. My own figures are based on the partially incomplete "List of the Mutineers", TNA: PRO (UK) ADM 3/137. One of the two men sent to Australia was William Redfern, the *Standard*'s young surgeon's mate, who quickly earned a free pardon and went on to join the colonial ruling class as a major landowner, reformer, and medical pioneer. Redfern eventually had a neighborhood in Sydney named in his honor; "Convicts transported, 1787–1809", TNA: PRO (UK) HO 11/1; Bryan Gandevia, "Redfern, William (1774/5?–1833)", *Oxford Dictionary of National Biography*, at http://www.oxforddnb.com/index/52/101052448/, last accessed 6 August 2012.

mutiny at the Nore and the Battle of Camperdown, radical mutinies continued to erupt in both the home command and on stations abroad. Not even the men condemned to prison gave up. Several of them broke out of the dilapidated Marshalsea House of Correction and others joined members of the insurrectionary wing of the British democratic movement to launch a prisoner-rights campaign in Cold Bath Fields prison.[21]

If the British officer corps had some cause for concern when contemplating the loyalty of their men, their colleagues across the North Sea fared no better. In the months leading up to the battle, diffuse and violent unrest rippled through the fleet assembling at the Texel anchorage. In May, a British spy reported that the French "have so little confidence in the Dutch sailors and officers that they have shipped on board of every Dutch ship of the line such a number of French troops as they think sufficient to maintain discipline and enforce Patriotism".[22] But the cure, apparently, was worse than the disease for five months later, just before the battle, some of the French soldiers who were intended to enforce discipline on board instead conspired to assassinate the *Hector's* commander.[23] On the fleet's flagship, the *Vrijheid*, a sailor was executed two days later for murdering a soldier. He was sorry, he said before dying, for there were two more he would have liked to kill. On the *Wassenaar*, Gerrit Jan Nuvest, A. Franssen, and Jan Thyssen threatened to murder Lieutenant Preckels, who had sexually assaulted several men, including Nuvest, on whom he had tried to perform anal rape. On the *Kortenaar*, counter-revolutionary agitators were discovered with orange ribbons in their possessions, signifying loyalty to the deposed Stadtholder William of Orange, who from his exile in Kew had called upon Dutch troops to aid the British war effort against the revolutionary Batavian regime.[24]

If some of the Dutch sailors were thus eager to see the Royal Navy triumphant – or at least to see the Batavian fleet lose – one small group among them most likely was not: British ex-mutineers who had fled to the

---

21. Letter, William Cruchley to the Duke of Portland, 27 July 1797, TNA: PRO (UK) PC 1/44/156; Entry book for Admiralty prisoners, 1773–1799, TNA: PRO (UK) PRIS 11/15; List of pardoned mutineers sent to Coldbath Fields prison in preparation of their being sent to the hulks, TNA: PRO (UK) ADM 1/4173; "Statement of Thomas Aris", and "Second examination of Thomas Aris, 14 January 1799", Middlesex – Proceedings of the General Quarter Sessions in the Month of January 1799 respecting several Matters relating to the House of Correction for the said County and certain Prisoners confined in that Prison, London Metropolitan Archives [hereafter LMA (UK)] MA/G/GEN/450.
22. Letter, John Mitchell, Hamburg, 19 May 1797, TNA: PRO (UK) ADM 1/4172.
23. Letter, Vice Admiral Raders to the Committee for Naval Affairs, Texel, 9 October 1797, NA (NL) Departement van Marine, 1795–1813, 2.01.29.01, inv. nr 237.
24. Report, Vice Admiral de Winter, 4 October 1797, NA (NL), Departement van Marine, 1795–1813, 2.01.29.01, inv. nr 236; Jonathan I. Israel, *The Dutch Republic: Its Rise, Greatness, and Fall, 1477–1806* (Oxford, 1998), p. 1127.

continent following the collapse of the fleet mutiny at the Nore. During its final weeks, there was a lot of talk about taking the fleet to sea, but in the end only a small number of boats set off. One of these briefly dabbled in small-scale piracy in the Channel, but soon took a French privateering commission to go hunting for British merchantmen instead. Their ship, sailing out of Dunkirk, was called *Le Président-Parker* in honor of the executed former president of "the floating republic" at the Nore (Figure 3).[25] Much larger numbers of men simply trickled out of England alone or in small groups during the months that followed the collapse of the mutiny. Some went to America and caused trouble in the young US navy, others headed for the Low Countries.[26] In late July, one of the Admiralty's agents at Gravesend warned that a "practice has lately prevailed of many seamen embarking for Hambro' [Hamburg] or Embden [Emden], but in fact they go to Holland. [...]. I don't remember seeing such a number attempting to go out of the Kingdom as there has been for these three weeks or month past." He suspected that the ever-pragmatic Dutch had dispatched recruiting agents to make the rounds in London's sailor town, funneling men by way of northern German ports directly to Amsterdam.[27]

The Dutch, however, were not alone in taking the enemy's mutineers into battle, for at least one of the British ships at Camperdown was crewed in part by former Dutch mutineers. They had been part of a squadron that sailed from the Republic in February 1796 to reinforce the Cape Colony or, if it was already in British hands, to reconquer it instead. One of the ships had barely left the North Sea before the crew mutinied and surrendered to the British.[28] The rest of the squadron struggled on

25. Letter, Morard de Galles to the Minister of Marine, Brest, 11 Frimaire Year VI of the Republic, Service Historique de la Défense, Marine, Vincennes [hereafter SHM-V], BB/3/114, Service Général, Correspondance, Brest, 1797, f. 207.

26. Moreau de Jonnès, *Adventures in the Revolution and under the Consulate* (London, 1969), p. 157; "Captain Truxtun concerning mutinous assemblies on board US Frigate *Constellation*, 2 July 1798", in *Naval Documents Related to the Quasi-War between the United States and France*, 6 vols (Washington DC, 1935), I, p. 157.

27. "Extract from a letter from Gravesend, 26 July 1797, forwarded to Evan Nepean", TNA: PRO (UK) ADM 1/4173.

28. Captain Gerardus Donckum's second report, NA (NL), Inventaries van de Archieven van het Departement van Marine, 1795–1813, 2.01.29.01, inv. nr 451; "Relaas van de Ondergeteckende gecommandeert hebbende 't Bataafse Fregatt van Oorlog Jazon, wegens de overwelding en Aflopen daarvan door de Equipage op den 4e Junij 1796 geschied, omtrent op de Noordenbreidte van 53 Graden en 357 Graden 30 minuten Lengte, en vervolgens het Opbrengen van gen: Fregatt in een Vijandelijke haven aan de Westkust van Schotland gelegen", NA (NL), Inventaries van de Archieven van het Departement van Marine, 1795–1813, 2.01.29.01, inv. nr 451; court martial of Jacob Hillebrand, NA (NL), Hoge Militaire Rechtspraak, 1795–1813 (1818), 2.01.11, inv. nr 220; Transport Office, Letters to the Admiralty, 21 June 1796, and 2 February 1797, TNA: PRO (UK) ADM 98/107; Prisoners of War register, Edinburgh (and Greenock), 1796–1801, TNA: PRO (UK) ADM 103/111.

Figure 3. "Parker the Delegate, Sketch'd by a Naval Officer". Richard Parker (1767–1797), was executed for his role as President of the Delegates during the British fleet mutiny at the Nore. Some of his former comrades who managed to escape abroad during the chaotic collapse of the mutiny subsequently honored his memory by christening their French-licensed privateer *Le Prèsident-Parker*. *National Maritime Museum, Greenwich, UK. Used with permission.*

into the south Atlantic, continuously plagued by open disobedience, desertion, and even shipboard riots. Within days of dropping anchor in Saldanha Bay, approximately seventy miles north of the now British-occupied Cape, the Dutch ships were surrounded by a powerful Royal Navy squadron at sea and thousands of redcoats on land. Discipline completely disintegrated and chaotic mutinies erupted on several of the squadron's most powerful ships. Officers feared for their lives, many were ritually humiliated and several nearly murdered. When Vice Admiral Lucas called a council of war to determine whether to fight or surrender to the British, it was its unanimous conclusion that the crews were as likely "to shoot and kill their own officers as fire on the enemy".[29] It was the most shameful defeat in the history of the Dutch navy. Of the approximately 1,800 soldiers and sailors who had been part of the Dutch squadron, all but 300 joined the British. Some signed on with East India Company ships and others to work the docks at Cape Town. Quite a few went on board Royal Navy warships, and some of them ended up alongside British fleet mutineers on the ships that went out to meet the Dutch at Camperdown the following October.[30]

There was thus beneath the surface – or better, perhaps, below the main deck – an exchange of inter-naval mutinous experience taking place even during the most brutal battle of the whole period. The extent to which this occurred at Camperdown, as well as its neat symmetry, was perhaps unusual, but the circulation of insurrectionary experience back and forth across the frontline in itself was not. Deep-sea crews, whether employed in the civilian or military industries, were notoriously multinational, with average proportions of foreign-born men on board warships ranging from about 20 to 70 per cent, depending on the navy.[31] At any one time, in other words, there were tens of thousands who served under a flag that was not their own.

As the scale of warfare grew, and its full centrifugal force was brought to bear on the lower deck, these men began to circulate between different ships, different industries, and even different navies at ever-greater speeds. Sometimes they moved across the Atlantic commons by their own volition – perhaps by deserting from one ship and volunteering to serve

29. Vice Admiral Engelbertus Lucas's dispatches, NA (NL), Hoge Militaire Rechtspraak, 1795–1813 (1818), 2.01.11, inv. nr 221; the strength of the squadron at Gran Canaria, NA (NL), Hoge Militaire Rechtspraak, 1795–1813 (1818), 2.01.11, inv. nr 221.
30. Vice Admiral Engelbertus Lucas's dispatches, NA (NL), Hoge Militaire Rechtspraak, 1795–1813 (1818), 2.01.11, inv. nr 221; Letter, Capt. Lieut. Ruijsch to Vice Admiral de Winter, 12 July 1797, NA (NL), Departement van Marine, 1795–1813, 2.01.29.01, inv. nr 236; Letter, Admiral Elphinstone to the Admiralty, 1 November 1796, TNA: PRO (UK) ADM 1/55.
31. Niklas Frykman, "Seamen on Late Eighteenth-Century European Warships", *International Review of Social History*, 54 (2009), pp. 67–93, 71–73.

for higher wages on a second one – but, more frequently, they were tossed about by the vagaries of the international maritime labor market, with its multiple coercive recruitment systems, by the instability of life at sea, or simply by the miserable dislocations of wartime economic crisis. As a result, warships became like nodal points in a vast, ocean-spanning network of itinerant biographies, where men of many different backgrounds and with many different experiences temporarily came together, to work, live, and struggle side by side.

Few warships contained less than half a dozen nationalities, and many had double that or more. The mutinous crew of the Dutch *Utrecht* in 1798 included men from all over the Republic, as well as Belgians, Frenchmen, Spaniards, Italians, Austrians, Swiss, Germans, Danes, Swedes, Poles, Hungarians, Romanians, Ukrainians, Byelorussians, one Turk, one South African, one Bengali, and one Indonesian (from the island of Batavia, today's Jakarta).[32] And for some of them, this was not the first time, the first ship, nor even the first navy in which they stirred up trouble. Louwrens Perinay, a native Hungarian and one of the leading conspirators, promised that he would have no problem slitting the throats of lieutenants Block and van Solingen in cold blood: he claimed that while serving in the Russian Imperial Navy he had "participated in this sort of thing more than once before, during the war against the Turks".[33] Carl Ortmann, a native Pole from the great Baltic port of Danzig, was delighted to hear it; he pulled out a knife and promised the others: "Voila Guillotine – elle agira" [Here's the guillotine; it will do its work]. Before ending up in the Republic, where he came after being captured by the British off Norway, Ortmann had spent time working on a French cutter, where he presumably had learnt the language and picked up his bloodthirsty Jacobinism.[34]

State authorities were painfully aware of just how dangerous it could be to let experienced troublemakers circulate freely, especially after the suppression of the British fleet mutinies in the summer of 1797. In Britain, while the fleet mutinies were still raging on, concerns that its spirit might spread throughout the empire prompted an ad hoc executive committee of the imperial ruling class – including among its members the Prime Minister William Pitt, Hugh Inglis, Chairman of the East India Company, Thomas Raikes, Governor of the Bank of England, Richard Neaves, former Chairman of the Society of West Indian Merchants and the London Dock Company, and current director of the Hudson Bay Company, as well as

---

32. *Utrecht* muster book 1798, NA (NL), Departement van Marine: Monsterrollen, 1795–1810, 2.01.30, inv. nr 131.

33. Declaration of Fredrick Ballé, NA (NL), Hoge Militaire Rechtspraak, 1795–1813 (1818), 2.01.11, inv. nr 234.

34. Second interrogation of Carl Ortmann, NA (NL), Hoge Militaire Rechtspraak, 1795–1813 (1818), 2.01.11, inv. nr 234.

forty-six other men of similar caliber – publically to announce that any seaman unable to produce a certificate of good conduct from his former commander henceforth would be barred from working across all of Britain's maritime industries.[35] In Sweden, following a strike among the Stockholm iron-carrier corps, King Gustav IV Adolph henceforth forbade newspapers throughout the country from mentioning news of the events at Spithead and the Nore.[36] The next year, naval authorities in Brest expressed alarm at, and urgently sought to end, the daily interactions local fishermen had with British warships, as well as put a stop to the unsupervised circulation of foreigners in and out of the port.[37] Across the Atlantic, Captain Thomas Truxtun, rising star of the infant US Navy, linked the growing unrest among his own men in 1798 to the British mutinies the year before. "The Seamen of Great Britain", he fumed, "have sat such an Example of Infamy, that the Marine Laws of the United States, England, France, Spain, and Holland, as well as the Rest of the Maritime Powers of Europe, have been, and will still be made more severe in Consequence thereof." This was all for the good, he believed, for "it is in the Interest of all Parties at War, to pass Laws, and check such Proceedings, and it has been wise in them to do it".[38]

Truxtun's keen sense of quarterdeck solidarity, which extended effortlessly even across the frontline when it came to such matters as ensuring the smooth continuation of the war, was never quite matched by the motley mutineers below deck, despite their increasing mobility and heightened disaffection. Only in very rare circumstances did they refuse orders to fight each other, and there is only little evidence in either the French, British, or Dutch archives that they ever developed an explicit consciousness of being engaged in a common struggle that crossed the frontline. When they revolted, they did so over specific local grievances, or against specific officers. There is a fair amount of evidence, however, that in the course of these struggles they began to articulate a common political ideology – sometimes only in fragments, at other times in great detail – that appears to have been rooted, and to have grown out of, shared experience. That ideology we might call maritime or, better still, lower-deck republicanism.

35. "At a Numerous and Respectable Meeting of Merchants, Ship-Owners, and Insurers, and other Inhabitants of London, concerned in Commerce and Navigation, etc.", TNA: PRO (UK) ADM 3/137. I am grateful to Marcus Rediker for the wonderfully apt characterization of this group as an "executive committee of the ruling class".
36. Rolf Karlbom, *Hungerupplopp och Strejker 1793–1867: En Studie i den Svenska Arbetarörelsens Uppkomst* (Lund, 1967), pp. 41–42.
37. Letter, Brest, 21 Thermidor Year VI (8 August 1798), SHM-V, BB/3/133, Service Général, Correspondance, Brest, 1790, ff. 221–223.
38. "Captain Truxtun concerning mutinous assemblies on board US Frigate *Constellation*".

LOWER-DECK REPUBLICANISM

The mutineers' political ideas derived from several sources. Most important among these were the centuries-old traditions of maritime egalitarianism, forged at a time before the seventeenth-century emergence of specialized deep-sea battle fleets when shipping ventures, including marauding and war-making, were decentralized, cooperative undertakings with shared risks, relatively flat hierarchies, and forms of limited collective decision-making. These principles, which had assured common seamen a voice in the management of the ship, did not survive the professiona-lization of maritime warfare in the sixteenth and seventeenth centuries when coerced service and violently enforced hierarchies replaced the relative egalitarianism of the privateering fleets.[39] But the memory sur-vived, often deeply submerged, and occasionally it came gushing to the surface with torrential force. It is no coincidence, for instance, that naval mutineers during the 1790s repeatedly invoked piracy, that Patrick Tobin, after several times being denied his prize money, called "black colors as good as any", or that Colin Brown demanded "a roving commission", for among the pirate crews of the early eighteenth century they found within recent history a workable and successful model of equitable shipboard relations.[40] Many of the mutineers' central and recurring demands – for equal shares of prize money, for the election of officers and the limitation of their authority, for the company's right to determine or at least veto the ship's mission, for democratic jury trials, voluntarism, and contractual agreements – had all been realized among the pirates.[41]

The mutineers of the 1790s were also strongly influenced by the ideas of radical republicanism that swirled around the Atlantic in that decade. In fact, they used the language of the revolutionary era, as well as its forms of organization, with such frequency that the specifically maritime character of their struggles at times seems lost: they established "committees", selected "delegates", elected "presidents", addressed each other as "citizen", and spoke in terms of "natural rights", "consent", and "justice". To be sure, these were all political forms borrowed from the

39. Richard W. Unger, "Regulation and Organization of Seamen in the Netherlands and Germany before the Industrial Revolution", in Paul Adam (ed.), *Seamen in Society/Gens de mer en société*, 2 vols (Perthes, 1980), II, pp. 66–73; Peter Kemp (ed.), *The Oxford Companion to Ships and the Sea* (Oxford, 1976), s.v. "Oleron, The Laws of"; Travers Twiss (ed.), *Monumenta Juridica: The Black Book of the Admiralty*, 4 vols (London, 1871), I, pp. 89–133.
40. Trial of Patrick Tobin and Francis Matthew of the *Emerald*, 17 to 18 August 1797, TNA: PRO (UK) ADM 1/5341; Trial of Colin Brown, James Hayes, James O'Neale, Robert Gray, and Thomas Needs of the *Phoenix*, 3 to 7 July 1797, TNA: PRO (UK) ADM 1/5340.
41. Marcus Rediker, *Villains of All Nations: Atlantic Pirates in the Golden Age* (Boston, MA, 2004), pp. 60–82.

revolutionary movement on shore, explosive ideological contraband that had somehow found its way on to the lower deck.

Perhaps it was smuggled on board by the rising number of landsmen who were recruited in the late eighteenth century, men like Lawrence Cronin, a Belfast artisan whom the war had turned into a republican, and the tyranny on board the *Hermione* into a mutineer. Or perhaps someone like James Smart, who once had lectured at a meeting of the London Corresponding Society and was considered "a Scholar" by his shipmates.[42] Such men injected shipboard struggles with a broadly understood language in which to articulate political aspirations and grievances. The fiery enthusiasm with which that language was embraced below deck in turn suggests that its content corresponded closely to the egalitarian culture already there. Mutinous sailors thus had little difficulty integrating the ideas of radical republicanism with their own political traditions. A 1793 petition from the crew of the French frigate *Melpomene*, for instance, combined the traditional petition form of the round robin, in which the lower deck's egalitarian and collectivist ethos is expressed by signing names in a circle and thereby giving each equal prominence, with the language of radical republicanism: the petitioners referred to themselves as "the *sans culottes* composing the crew of the *Melpomene*", addressed themselves to "citizens, brothers & friends", and adorned the document with the slogans "Union and Fraternity" and "Liberty or Death".[43]

The repeated invocation of fraternity, or brotherhood, first in the address, then in the slogan, is important. Along with liberty and equality, it was one of the core universalist values of the revolutionary movement, one that expressed the ideal of solidarity with the entire human race. But it was also a value that resonated in particular with seamen who – torn from home, scattered across the world, and thrown together in close confinement with men from many nations – frequently emphasized their shared occupational identity by referring to each other as "brother tars". In contrast to the landed revolutionaries' principled but abstract embrace of fraternity, the "brotherhood of the sea" was a lived experience that on one level included the whole community of seafarers and thus enabled men to move between different ships and navies, and on a second level expressed itself on individual vessels in the creation of "fictive kinship" networks (or, in Marcus Rediker's words, "miniature mutual aid societies") that were especially strong if a crew had gone through

42. Frykman, "Mutiny on the *Hermione*", p. 172; court martial against men from the *Grampus*, TNA: PRO (UK) ADM 1/5340.
43. "Melpomene – Minerve, 1793 (An II)", Service Historique de la Défense, Marine, Toulon, Institutions de répression, Cour martial maritime, Procédures et interrogatoires, 1792–An XIV, 4 O 1.

combat together.[44] These bonds were invaluable before, during, and after a mutiny, when the strength of a crew's solidarity could mean the difference between life and death for everyone involved.

Radical republicanism held a further appeal for naval war workers. When revolutionaries spoke of tyranny, the horrors of slavery, and the blessings of liberty, naval war workers knew better than most what they were talking about. For them, "liberty" meant shore leave, a time when they escaped the coercion, the constant supervision, the twenty-four-hour work cycles, and the terroristic discipline of the lash, if only for a few hours. Commanders rarely entertained requests for leave, primarily to prevent desertion, and as a consequence hundreds of malnourished, overworked, and bored men remained cooped up in a tiny, wet space for months and years on end, which was one of the most important reasons why epidemic disease repeatedly tore through the lower deck and left thousands of victims in its wake. The slogan "Liberty or Death" was therefore not just a threat, not just a measure of the lower deck's determination, but also a simple statement of fact. The ever-present danger of death, moreover, as well as perhaps the likelihood of having to inflict it upon others, in turn contributed to the enthusiasm with which naval seamen embraced the ideas of consent and popular sovereignty. Seamen in the Batavian navy, perhaps because they were all volunteers and to a large extent foreign-born, were especially prone to justify mutiny by arguing that the post-revolutionary change of flags invalidated their prior agreement of service: they had not given their consent to serving the Batavian Republic.[45]

The issue of consent was also centrally involved when it came to the single-most important trigger of mutiny across all three navies: punishment. Again and again, sailors rose up and liberated a shipmate if they thought the punishment – by flogging, keel-hauling, running the gauntlet, or any other means – too severe or wholly unjustified. And significantly, mutinous crews during the 1797 fleet mutiny reeved yard ropes (used to hang men on board ship) in order to symbolize that they had reconstituted themselves according to the principles of the lower deck and from now on assumed the responsibility of maintaining good order themselves, an act mirroring the widespread erection of gallows in front of the houses of the French rural aristocracy in 1789.[46]

44. Marcus Rediker, *The Slave Ship: A Human History* (New York, 2007), pp. 230–231. The emergence of exceptionally strong group cohesion among warriors is a well-known phenomenon. For an analysis, see Richard Holmes, *Acts of War: The Behavior of Men in Battle* (New York, 1985), pp. 31–73.

45. "Relaas", NA (NL), Inventaries van de Archieven van het Departement van Marine, 1795–1813, 2.01.29.01, inv. nr. 451; Petition, 30 May 1797, NA (NL), West-Indisch Comité, 1795–1800, 2.01.28.01, inv. nr. 128.

46. John Markoff, *The Abolition of Feudalism: Peasants, Lords, and Legislators in the French Revolution* (University Park, PA, 1996), pp. 224–225.

This was more than just a confrontational gesture. Seamen were well aware that their collective security on board ship, especially when lying so close to shore as they did at the Nore, depended on strict discipline and careful attention to duty. The mutineers therefore took great care to maintain regular and good order among themselves, and they created democratically controlled courts to try men for a variety of offences, most commonly for drunkenness and neglect of duty.[47] In some cases, punishments were imposed "by the desire of the majority", in others following the verdict of a jury.[48] Often the mutinous crews went to great lengths to follow proper procedure when trying a man, formally swearing juries and witnesses to strict impartiality, and providing the accused with a competent councilor who pleaded on his behalf.[49] The courts were willing to recognize extenuating circumstances, even when they tried their former persecutors. The boatswain of the *Proserpine*, for example, argued that he had only followed orders when he had abused the crew, and this was enough to sway the court to commute his corporal punishment to ritual humiliation.[50] Others were not so lucky. Master's mate Edward Dawson of the *Monmouth*, along with the sergeant of marines and a midshipman, was found guilty of conspiring against the ship's company and therefore sentenced to three dozen lashes, which was exceedingly mild compared to the bloodthirsty punishments usually imposed by regular courts martial for the equivalent crime of mutiny.[51]

If the reeving of yard ropes symbolized the emergence of a new order in the fleet, the red flags that flew alongside of them were intended to show that it was here to stay, whatever it took. The red flag had several overlapping meanings in the late eighteenth century, but it usually indicated the intention to suspend temporarily peaceful means of conflict resolution in favor of brute force. Authorities on shore, for instance, sometimes used the red flag to announce martial law, and in the navy the "bloody colors" signified that a ship was prepared to give battle. The latter use of the flag had evolved from the medieval *baucans*, a thirty-yard-long solid red streamer that north European ships flew as they sailed into combat to indicate that no quarter would be given or

47. "No. 12", Papers found onboard of the *Repulse*, 12 June 1797, TNA: PRO (UK) ADM 1/727 C370.
48. Court martial of Dennis Sullivan et al., TNA: PRO (UK) ADM 1/5339.
49. "No. 9" and "No. 11", Papers found onboard of the *Repulse*, 12 June 1797, TNA: PRO (UK) ADM 1/727 C370.
50. Charles Cunningham, *A Narrative of Occurrences that took place during the Mutiny at the Nore, in the Months of May and June, 1797; with a few Observations upon the Impressment of Seamen, and the Advantages of those who are employed in His Majesty's Navy; also on the Necessity and Useful Operations of the Articles of War* (Chatham, 1829), pp. 13–14.
51. Court martial of Richard Brown et al., TNA: PRO (UK) ADM 1/5340.

taken, or, in other words, that it would be a fight to the death.[52] Pirates during the so-called Golden Age used the "bloody flag" to convey the same meaning, and they ran it up the mast if their prey refused to surrender at the sight of the black Jolly Roger.[53] During the great 1775 Liverpool sailors' revolt, lower-deck insurgents fought under the red flag as they bombarded the city's Mercantile Exchange.[54] It re-emerged at Spithead, where it occasionally flew from the masts of the mutinous fleet, but at the Nore "the bloody flag of defiance" was there from the beginning and it flew throughout. Sailors even brought it with them to shore and marched behind it during large demonstrations they organized at Sheerness.[55]

Unlike its earlier appearances during moments of emergency and struggle, there are signs the mutineers at the Nore embraced the red flag as a positive and permanent symbol of their ongoing fight for better conditions. One of their communiqués was signed with the slogan "Red For Ever" and an eyewitness reported that he had heard some mutineers shouting "Huzza for the red flag!".[56] This perhaps indicates that a substantial number of the mutineers no longer believed that they were engaged in a narrow corrective or restorative struggle for lost rights and paternalist class compromises but instead had begun to develop a consciousness of permanent opposition between themselves and their rulers, the have-nots and the haves, that pointed towards the vicious social conflicts of the industrializing nineteenth century. Many mutineers in addition wore red cockades fixed to their hats and caps, bringing together the red flag's combative maritime symbolism with the red of the French Revolution, which by the late 1790s had become an international symbol

52. W.G. Perrin, *British Flags: Their Early History, and Their Development at Sea; With an Account of the Origin of the Flag as a National Device* (Cambridge, 1922), pp. 160–161.

53. Rediker, *Villains of All Nations*, p. 83. Intriguingly, a red Jolly Roger has recently come to light which was first captured from North African pirates in 1780. See "Rare Crimson Jolly Roger Restored", BBC News Online, 20 June 2007, http://news.bbc.co.uk/2/hi/uk_news/england/hampshire/6222054.stm, last accessed 10 May 2010.

54. R.B. Rose, "A Liverpool Sailors' Strike in the Eighteenth Century", *Transactions of the Lancashire and Cheshire Antiquarian Society*, 68 (1958), pp. 85–92, 85; Rediker, *The Slave Ship*, p. 256.

55. Cunningham, *A Narrative of Occurrences*, p. 8; Anon., *The Whole Trial, and Defence of Richard Parker, President of the Delegates for Mutiny, &c. On board the Sandwich, and others of His Majesty's Ships, at the Nore, In May, 1797. Before a Court Martial, held on board the Neptune, of 98 Guns, Laying off Greenhithe, near Gravesend, on Thursday, 22d of June, 1797, and following Days* (London, 1797), pp. 4, 12, 34–35; court martial against the men from the fleet at the Nore, TNA: PRO (UK) ADM 1/5339.

56. "The Delegates of the Different Ships at the Nore Assembled in Council – to their fellow Subjects", Petitions 1793–1797, TNA: PRO (UK) ADM 1/5125; Anne Hawkins and Helen Watt, "'Now is Our Time, The Ship is our Own, Huzza for the Red Flag': Mutiny on the Inspector, 1797", *The Mariner's Mirror*, 93 (2007), pp. 156–179, 156.

of regicide, class warfare, and social renewal.[57] The mutineers were so successful in colonizing the meaning of the red flag that the navy dropped it entirely from its official *Signal-book for the Ships of War* in 1799, thus surrendering its powerful symbolism to the global labor movements of the nineteenth and twentieth centuries.[58]

CONCLUSION

The radical republican ideas of the mutinous Atlantic cropped up with increasing frequency throughout the 1790s. Perhaps in each case they were arrived at independently, but more likely they are evidence of cross-fertilization, of a homogenization of lower-deck culture and experience brought about by the circulation of thousands, perhaps tens of thousands, of men back and forth across the frontline. This never resulted in anything akin to the famous Christmas Truce of World War I, and in only one known instance was lower-deck action explicitly aimed at preventing a battle from taking place, and the reason was not the men's principled unwillingness to fight their brother tars.[59] Mutinies, with only a few exceptions, were not aimed at forcing the belligerents to sue for peace, but rather to demand drastic improvements in the conditions of war work.

And yet despite that, the history of naval mutiny in this period, its massive scale, its transcendence of national and imperial boundaries, its politically sophisticated radicalism, does not support the conventional view that links mass military service in the French Revolutionary and Napoleonic Wars with the transition of premodern patriotism into modern, belligerent nationalism. It would appear instead that the connections between mutinies in different European navies at the turn of the nineteenth century, as well as the mutineers' pioneering use of the red flag as a positive symbol, together raise the possibility that early working-class internationalism, with its dual strategy of pragmatic national claims-making and utopian cosmopolitan insurrectionism, may in part have had its origins in the revolutionary Atlantic, far out at sea, and deep below deck.

57. Court martial against the men from the fleet at the Nore, TNA: PRO (UK) ADM 1/5339; court martial against the men from the *Sandwich*, TNA: PRO (UK) ADM 1/5340.
58. Perrin, *British Flags*, p. 175.
59. Norman Hampson, "Une mutinerie anti-belliciste aux Indes en 1792", *Annales Historiques de la Révolution Française*, 22 (1950), pp. 156–159.

IRSH 58 (2013), Special Issue, pp. 109–130 doi:10.1017/S002085901300031X
© 2013 Internationaal Instituut voor Sociale Geschiedenis

"Amok!": Mutinies and Slaves on Dutch East Indiamen in the 1780s

MATTHIAS VAN ROSSUM

Faculty of Arts, VU University Amsterdam
De Boelelaan 1105, 1081 HV Amsterdam, the Netherlands

E-mail: m.van.rossum@vu.nl

ABSTRACT: In September 1782, a violent and partly successful mutiny of Balinese slaves shocked the Dutch East India Company (VOC). This article will reconstruct the history of the mutiny of the *Mercuur*, tracing its significance in the context of slavery, labour, war, and the series of "Asian mutinies" that occurred in the 1780s. The revolt of the Balinese sheds light on the development of amok as a tradition of resistance. The purpose of calling amok cannot only be explained as a direct, impulsive response to perceived injustice or violation of codes of honour. It functioned as a conscious call to arms, signalling the start of collective and organized resistance. The Balinese mutiny was both similar to and different from other European and Asian forms of revolt.

It must have been a spectacular and terrifying scene. On 11 September 1782 two groups of armed men faced each other across the deck of the ship *Mercuur*, sailing in the Sunda Strait between the islands of Java and Sumatra. A group of European and Javanese soldiers and sailors loyal to the Dutch East India Company (VOC) had taken up position on the poop deck, below them a gang of mutinous Balinese slaves stood their ground on the quarterdeck (Figure 1).[1] The mutineers were armed with cutlasses and muskets, while the company's men carried hand grenades as well as guns and cutlasses.

Jacob Wedelaar, the officer leading the armed forces summoned to suppress the Balinese mutineers, later stated that he had tried to convince them to surrender by offering them clemency. The captain of the Javanese soldiers had translated this by calling out the word "*ampong*". Perhaps some of the slaves were still in doubt. The German petty officer Hartwick

---

1. The translations of terms of specific locations on the ship are based on "Division of Space on a Mid 17th Century East Indiaman", available at: http://maritimeasia.ws/maritimelanka/topics/hullspace.html.

Figure 1. Javanese soldiers in Batavia. In the foreground, a Javanese general and his officers; in the background, Javanese soldiers practising drill.
Painted by Jan Brandes, 1779–1785. Rijksmuseum, Amsterdam. Public domain

Jurgen Walrade, one of the first to board the ship, recalled that three obviously uncertain mutineers were forced to remain in the ranks. Others were clearly ready to defend themselves. The Javanese Saptoe, facing the Balinese slaves, later testified that he was immediately attacked by one of the mutineers with "a drawn cutlass".[2] Walrade declared that the

2. All reports and records concerning the court case following the mutiny on the *Mercuur* can be found in the Court of Justice of Batavia section in the Dutch East India Company Archive, The Hague, Nationaal Archief [hereafter NA], Archief van de VOC, 1.04.02, no. 9515.

mutineers resisted "by throwing cannon balls"[3] that wounded the soldiers about the knees and legs. The offer of *"ampong"* had been declined very quickly by the mutineers on the lower deck, and their stance was reinforced by repeated and growing cries of "Amok!".[4]

Now facing the determination of the mutineers in person, Wedelaar ordered his men to open fire on the renegade slaves. The Europeans and the Javanese threw their grenades among the mutineers and attacked them with "small gun and cutlass".[5] According to Hartwick Jurgen Walrade, the attack went on for half an hour, coming to an end only after a fire started by the mutineers began to take hold of the ship. Both the forces trying to retake the ship and the mutineers were forced to leave the *Mercuur*, which was soon fully ablaze and promptly sank, so that the soldiers and sailors were forced to take to the boats. The slaves attempted to reach nearby shore. Only nine of them were picked up out of the water or from islands by the crew of the warship, and were sent for trial in Batavia.

The September 1782 mutiny on the *Mercuur* occurred during a pivotal period in history, at the height of the Fourth Anglo-Dutch War (1780–1784), which, for the Dutch, resulted in the loss of many of their Asian colonies and marked the rise of British maritime power. The mutiny was followed by revolts of Asian slaves and sailors on board the Dutch East Indiamen *Slot ter Hoge* (slaves, 1783), *Java* (Chinese sailors and possibly slaves, 1783), and *Haasje* (slaves, 1790). They are the only "Asian mutinies" on board VOC ships ever to have been described in the Dutch historiography.[6] The affair on the *Mercuur* was the largest of the series, and seems to have been the most serious threat to the authority of the Dutch East India Company.

It is remarkable that the mutiny on the *Mercuur* has received so little attention. Although songs were written about the German mutineers of the *Nijenborg* in 1763, for example,[7] and a poem was dedicated to the famous VOC official Daniel Radermacher, who was the victim of the revolt by the Chinese sailors on the *Java*,[8] news of the mutiny on the

---

All source quotations have been translated into English from the original Dutch text. The original will be provided in the footnote only where confusion might otherwise arise.

3. Original: "het werpen van kogels".

4. Officer Jacob Wedelaar referred to "het herhaald roepen van amok" [repeated cries of amok]. Petty officer Hartwick Jurgen Walrade referred to their refusal of the *"ampong"*, "door het herhaald roepen van amok aan teneemen" [by taking up the repeated cries of amok].

5. Original: "klein geweer en sabel".

6. K. van der Tempel, "'Wij hebben amok in ons schip': Aziaten in opstand tijdens drie terugreizen op het einde van de achttiende eeuw", in J.R. Bruijn and E.S. van Eyck van Heslinga (eds), *Muiterij. Oproer en berechting op schepen van de VOC* (Haarlem, 1980), pp. 123–147.

7. J.C. Mollema, *Een muiterij in de achttiende eeuw: Het afloopen van het Oost-Indische Compagnieschip Nijenborg in 1763* (Haarlem, 1933).

8. Van der Tempel, "Wij hebben amok".

Mercuur was mentioned only in the *Groninger Courant* of 1 July 1783. The report stated that a Danish ship had brought unconfirmed news that "a Dutch East India Company ship" lying before Batavia had been overrun by its slaves. The report in the paper did not mention the wrecking of the ship, but did say that only a few of the fugitive slaves had been recaptured.[9] It seems that, apart from that report, the Dutch East India Company successfully managed to keep the affair quiet. No eye-witness accounts were published, and in other newspapers the *Mercuur* was not mentioned by name.

Despite the contemporary and historical silence that has blanketed events on the *Mercuur*, the mutiny is both interesting and important. The uprising of seventy-nine Balinese slaves who were able both to fight and to operate a ship must have sent a terrifying message to the officials of the company, who immediately ordered an investigation into the treatment of Asians on board company ships throughout their settlements.[10] Furthermore, it ordered that slaves on warships be dispersed, and trained only as sailors, not soldiers, in order to "prevent accidents as on board the ship *Mercuur*".[11] That illustrates how the mutiny, interestingly enough, is pertinent not only to the tightening of VOC regulations on the slave trade and slave behaviour, but also to the VOC's increasing use of Asian labour at sea, which included both maritime and military manpower, and both free and unfree. The mutiny on the *Mercuur* therefore figures in the middle of what were then sometimes contradictory developments.

This article will reconstruct the history of the mutiny of the *Mercuur*, placing it in the context of slavery, war, and the series of mutinies that occurred in the 1780s, as well as the company's use of Asian military and maritime labour. At the same time, it will emphasize that such mutinies were not merely moments of blind aggression, nor were they the result of the abstract structural forces of sharpening class relations. Although both violence and structure are important, it is essential to note that mutinies are also moments of vigorous agency, moments of revolt by people who are normally dominated, ruled, or even abused. Mutiny might be a moment of ultimate and empowering refusal, the beginning of recognition that working and living circumstances do not have to be accepted passively but can be changed. The mutiny on the *Mercuur* brings to light precisely such a moment, when the Balinese slaves took their place on board ship – and for a short time had a role in history. This article, therefore, will try to listen closely to the voices of those otherwise silenced and forgotten Balinese slaves.

---

9. *Groninger Courant*, 1 July 1783, pp. 1–2.
10. Van der Tempel, "Wij hebben amok", p. 145.
11. J.A. van der Chijs, *Nederlandsch-Indisch plakaatboek 1602–1811*, X (Batavia, 1885–1900), p. 592.

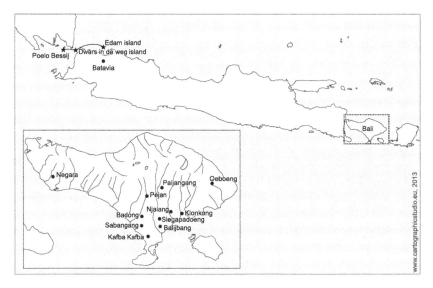

Figure 2. Java and Bali.

MARITIME LABOUR AND DIVERSITY

But first let us return to the mutiny. It all started early in the morning of 6 September when the *Mercuur* was lying off the island of Edam near Batavia. The crew of the *Mercuur* consisted of thirteen European and twenty-six Javanese sailors under the command of Captain Claas Roem, an experienced officer who had worked for the VOC since 1752.[12] In the summer of 1782, the crew was complemented by seventy-nine Balinese slaves all of whom – apart from a certain Likop, who belonged to the second equipage master, Willebrord Peusenswere – were the property of a private trading association called the "Societeit van de Cotter de Batavier". The slaves came from different regions seemingly from all over Bali rather than having one common area of origin,[13] although they appear to have been well aware of where each of them originated on the island. Such awareness perhaps indicates both extensive interaction within the group of slaves, which might naturally occur on board ship, as well as the importance of references to local origin in the process of identification (Figure 2).

Such a polyglot ship's company was not uncommon for the Dutch East India Company. The VOC acted as a truly multinational corporation,

12. "Generale Zeemonsterrol 1782", NA, VOC, no. 5230.
13. Several places were mentioned: Negara, Pejan, Balij Klonkong [Klungkung], Paijangang [Payangan or Pangyangan?], Oeboeng [Abang?], Balijbang [Beng?], Njalang [Nyalian?], Siegapadoeng [Singapadu?], Balij Kafba Kafba [Kaba-kaba?], Balij Badong [Badung?], and Sabangang [Tabanan?]. Present-day names of presumed places of origin are stated in brackets.

employing people from different continents and origins in the same functions and working environments. Besides the diverse north-west European workforce recruited by the VOC in the Dutch Republic, the VOC made extensive use of local Asian labour markets.[14] As a result, the personnel of the various VOC offices in Asia consisted of European and Asian employees. Asian or Eurasian workers might be employed as sailors, soldiers, writers, carpenters, smiths, or as simple unskilled workers. The VOC used both free and unfree labour, and a reconstruction by Jan Lucassen estimates employment of Asian labourers at 6,000 at the beginning of the seventeenth century rising to about 21,000 by the mid-eighteenth century.[15]

On board its ships the VOC employed European and Asian labour in mixed crews, leading to what must have been intimate contact between groups of different origin in closely confined working environments.[16] The employment of Asian maritime labour was on the rise especially in intra-Asiatic shipping. For the mid-seventeenth century there are numerous references to the employment of Chinese sailors, and from at least 1670 onwards there are references to the recruitment of Asian sailors in VOC reports,[17] and the continuous employment of Asian sailors can be traced in the annual reports of VOC personnel from 1691 onwards.[18]

14. J.R. Bruijn, "De personeelsbehoefte van de VOC overzee en aan boord, bezien in Aziatisch en Nederlands perspectief", *Bijdragen en mededelingen betreffende de geschiedenis der Nederlanden*, 91 (1976), pp. 218–248; I.G. Dillo, *De nadagen van de Verenigde Oostindische Compagnie 1783–1795: Schepen en zeevarenden* (Amsterdam, 1992); J. Lucassen, "A Multinational and its Labor Force: The Dutch East India Company, 1595–1795", *International Labor and Working-Class History*, 66:2 (2004), pp. 12–39; M. van Rossum et al., "National and International Labour Markets", in M. Fusaro and A. Polonia (eds), *Maritime History as Global History, Research in Maritime History*, XXXXIII (St John's, Newfoundland, 2010), pp. 47–72; M. van Rossum, "De intra-Aziatische vaart: Schepen, 'de Aziatische zeeman' en ondergang van de VOC?", *Tijdschrift voor Sociale en Economische Geschiedenis*, 8:3 (2011), pp. 32–69.
15. Lucassen, "A Multinational and its Labor Force", p. 15.
16. H. Ketting, *Leven, werk en rebellie aan boord van Oost-Indiëvaarders (1595–1650)* (Amsterdam, 2002). See also E. Goffman, *The Prison* (New York, 1961); P.E. Pérez-Mallaína, *Spain's Men of the Sea: Daily Life on the Indies Fleets in the Sixteenth Century* (Baltimore, MD, 1998); M. Rediker, *Between the Devil and the Deep Blue Sea: Merchant Seaman, Pirates, and the Anglo-American Maritime World, 1700–1750* (Cambridge, 1987).
17. Van Rossum, "De intra-Aziatische vaart", pp. 37–39, 48–52.
18. The *Generale Zeemonsterrollen* (maritime muster scrolls) are part of the *Generale Land- en Zeemonsterrollen*, an annual overview of personnel employed in Asia by the Dutch East India Company, both on land and at sea. During the seventeenth century several summaries had been produced based on estimates. In 1686 the VOC decided to construct an annual overview, the *Generale Land- en Zeemonsterrollen*. However, the first overview was not produced until 1691. The information in the *Generale Zeemonsterrollen* has been entered into a database containing a list of all VOC ships in Asia in June of every year in the period 1691–1791. No *Zeemonsterrollen* have survived for the years 1702, 1707, and 1792–1795. Although information varies in different periods, for most years the database provides information on the crew, their origin (European or Asian), location of recruitment, hierarchical structure, wages, and several other characteristics. For more information, see van Rossum, "De intra-Aziatische vaart", pp. 37–39.

In the period from 1670–1750 the Asian sailors employed on board ships active in intra-Asiatic trade were mainly of Indian origin recruited predominantly from Bengal. That did not necessarily mean that they all originally came from Bengal. Indian crews seem to have engaged in a wage labour relation which could last several years. In the second half of the eighteenth century the VOC increasingly recruited sailors of Chinese, Javanese, and Malayan origin, and the importance of Asian sailors to the intra-Asiatic shipping activities of the VOC increased continuously during the period, the proportion rising from just a few per cent in the second half of the seventeenth century to nearly 50 per cent in the second half of the eighteenth century.[19] It should be emphasized here that in general the VOC used more or less free wage labourers as sailors. The use of slaves as sailors by the VOC seems to have been marginal and resulted mainly from acute labour shortages caused by the Fourth Anglo-Dutch War.[20]

These are important findings for our assessment of Asian mutinies at the end of the eighteenth century. They show the importance of Asian labour to the Dutch East India Company and its shipping in Asia. The VOC had a long and involved experience with Asian sailors and with the employment of widely diverse crews on its ships. Furthermore, the company was experienced in employing slave labour in different environments, such as company workshops and households, but had much less experience with using slaves as crews for its ships. Of course, that does not mean that problems did not occur as a result of shipboard hierarchy, repression, or other factors. It does mean, however, that the trouble they had with Asian workers – free or unfree – cannot be explained simply by inexperience with Asian labour in general on the part of the VOC.

SLAVES AT SEA

Going back to the morning of 6 September 1782, we find some of the Javanese sailors, including Soeroe and Soelo, still at breakfast in the galley.[21] Another Javanese sailor was on watch for incoming vessels, and several other Balinese slaves testified to having been in the galley. Half of the group of slaves, however, were called on deck for exercises with Snaphaunce muskets under the command of the first mate, who was a European. Such intensive training involving slaves must have been a rather rare sight on company ships.

19. *Ibid.*
20. *Ibid.* Asian sailors seem even to have been employed on a relatively equal basis compared with European sailors. They were confined to more menial "common sailor" roles, but received more or less the same monthly wage: 7.5 guilders for an Asian sailor, and 9 guilders for an Asian sailor with military skills. European sailors were recruited in the Dutch Republic for wages varying from 5 to 11 guilders; soldiers were recruited for 9 to 10 guilders per month.
21. The Dutch original refers to the "bak".

Slaves were not absent from early modern shipboard life in Asia. Slavery and the slave trade were widely in existence throughout the Indian Ocean region.[22] On slave-trading routes therefore slaves might have been on board as human cargo, which in the case of the VOC company trade would have meant that slaves were on board in large numbers, as they were, for example, on the *Hogergeest* while it was attempting the direct voyage from the east coast of Africa to Batavia in 1684. The *Hogergeest* went off course and instead sailed along the coast of Malabar and on to Ceylon. During the voyage it was confronted with a conspiracy to revolt among the slaves, and was faced with the deaths from sickness of the captain, various other company employees, and 108 of the 274 slaves. That tragic voyage was reason enough to propose the abandonment of direct slaving voyages to Batavia and to set up the operation of a slave-trading route via the Cape of Good Hope.[23]

Besides slaves as company trading cargo, they were also often on board as the possessions of individual VOC employees. That is shown, for example, in the muster rolls that have been preserved for company ships sailing between Batavia and Deshima in the 1780s, on board 7 of which were registered 145 individually owned slaves. In 1781, the *Mars* had 103 sailors on board and 39 slaves who were individually owned, mainly by the higher-ranked company officers. Most of those slaves were owned by the Deshima director M.I. Titsingh, who owned fifteen of them, and the equipage master Dirk Jan Vinkemulder, who owned nine. But that other higher-ranked members of the crew also owned slaves is shown by the examples of the captain Hermanus Siedenburg with four slaves, officer Jochem Brandt who had two slaves, and the steward Federik Willem Recke with one.[24]

The private possession of slaves by VOC sailors and administrative personnel might have been motivated by status or convenience, but it was also a matter of money. Individually owned slaves could function as an important source of private trade for company servants. As with other types of private trade, the VOC tried to minimize and control what could be a profitable business. A regulation announced in 1776 for VOC captains stipulated that the maximum number of slaves that a captain was allowed to transport was eight, the maximum for the first mate being four.

---

22. M. Vink, "'The World's Oldest Trade': Dutch Slavery and Slave Trade in the Indian Ocean in the Seventeenth Century", *Journal of World History*, 14 (2003), pp. 131–177; R.B. Allen, "The Constant Demand of the French: The Mascarene Slave Trade and the Worlds of the Indian Ocean and Atlantic during the Eighteenth and Nineteenth Centuries", *Journal of African History*, 49 (2008), pp. 43–72.
23. W.P. Coolhaas (ed.), *Generale missiven van gouverneurs-generaal en raden aan Heren XVII der Verenigde Oostindische Compagnie*, IV (The Hague, 1960–1997), p. 744.
24. "Monsterrol van het schip Mars", NA, Archief van de Factorij Japan, 1.04.21, no. 1475.

The reason for the regulation was an excess of private slave trading, with one captain mentioned as having been found embarking as many as 131 privately owned slaves. In March 1778, the regulation concerning the private sale of slaves was sharpened to forbid the sale in Batavia of slaves over the age of 25 years. In December 1782, the regulation was tightened even further in order to reduce "the all too disadvantaging and too much flourishing private trade in slaves".[25]

As company trading goods, slaves on board VOC ships were sometimes put to work at sailors' tasks. In the 1680s the VOC stressed that during slave-trading voyages from the Cape to Batavia the slaves could "be trained for working on board the ship", as "these slaves would be very well suited to become good sailors".[26] Slaves with seafaring skills, whether acquired in company service or before their enslavement, seem to have had disadvantages as well as they were more prone to mutiny at sea. In 1686, seven illegally transported slaves rebelled during a voyage on the sloop *Steenbock* from Zolor to Coepang in the Indonesian archipelago. They murdered the assistant Hendrik Tiling and two sailors, forced the quartermaster and two other sailors off the ship, and sailed the vessel to Wolowea, taking the native wife of assistant Tiling and her female servant with them.[27]

FEAR AND CONTROL

The omnipresence of slaves, both at sea and on land, made their owners anxious. The VOC tried to control not only the trade in slaves, but also the possession and management of them, as well as the way slaves were expected to behave.

The regulation of March 1778 strove "to restrain the insolence and malevolence of slaves" such as would otherwise have led to rowdyism, robbery, and murderousness in and around Batavia. It was stressed that there should be severe punishment for any slave who offended or played his or her master false. It was announced that Christians were not permitted to have either their slaves or their children circumcised by "Mahometaanse Priesters" – Muslim "priests". Slaves were not allowed to ignite fireworks, and any slave who walked into Europeans or "people wearing hats" on purpose should be flogged – although with the exception of slaves walking in front of carriages with the task of warning or removing people in the street in order to prevent accidents. Slaves were not allowed to ride horses in the city,

25. Original: "overmatigen nadeligen en al te verre g'extendeerden particulieren handel in slaven". Regulations of 11 October 1776 and 17 December 1782; Van der Chijs, *Nederlandsch-Indisch plakaatboek*, pp. 49, 640.
26. Coolhaas, *Generale Missiven*, IV, p. 744. Original: "tot scheepsdiensten goeffent werden"; "daartoe die natie sigh zeer wel schicken wil en goede matrosen maackt."
27. *Ibid.*, V, p. 117.

even when they had the job of moving them from place to place, and they might not drink *arak* nor any other liquor in bars or pubs; nor were they allowed to enter Chinese gambling houses. Slaves were not allowed to sell any goods without permission, and extensive rules were formulated concerning slaves being on the street or out of their masters' houses in the evening, and with regard to the finding and return of runaway slaves.[28]

The fear of slaves was illustrated tragically by the events on the VOC ship *Slot ter Hoge*, sailing from Batavia to the Dutch Republic in the autumn of 1783, the year after the mutiny on the *Mercuur*. On the way to the Cape of Good Hope, Admiral Breton was warned by the slaves Floris and Wantrouw that there were rumours of a conspiracy among the slaves to run amok as they were being transported to the Cape as private trade goods.[29] After some inquiry, the information turned out to have come from the slave Fortuyn, and acting on his information the officers of the *Slot ter Hoge* imprisoned six slaves and began interrogating them – using torture – about the suspected plans for an uprising. Under pressure and begging to be pardoned, the slaves confessed and implicated others, which resulted in twenty slaves being accused of conspiracy. The officers decided in a ship's council to execute all of them directly by putting them overboard with their hands and feet tied.

It is clear that the ship's council sought support for their decision from the rest of the crew. The junior officers and the foremen of the different groups of European, Chinese, and Javanese sailors and Balinese slaves working as sailors were separately consulted and all agreed to the "sentence". However, subsequently, back in the Dutch Republic, the directors of the VOC did not approve the decision taken on the *Slot ter Hoge*, being displeased at the "informal" procedure followed and at the fact that the accusation of conspiracy had originated from only one of the slaves. The VOC directors apparently gained the impression that the whole event had been precipitated by collective fear rather than any real threat of mutiny.

Despite the directors' dislike of the course of events in 1783, the fear of slaves seemed not to have been an incidental phenomenon, but instead something structural. In June 1781, the same fear had been expressed in a proposal to provide for the company's urgent need of sailors. Their need for labour made it necessary not only to recruit more Asian sailors but also to try to employ slaves as sailors. The first experiment was intended to be done by employing "30 to 35 slaves from the craft quarters for every ship, in order to use them for work on homeward bound voyages after

28. "Plakaat ter beteugeling van de moetwil en insolentie der slaven", 31 March 1778, NA, VOC, no. 3504, fos 2042–2048.
29. The slave's name "Wantrouw" – meaning "Distrust" – is ironic in this case. It is important to note that (unless employed as sailors on board company ships) Asian subjects were not allowed to be taken to Europe without permission. Regulations on slaves were especially strict.

being trained in the profession of sailor".[30] The slaves would gain their freedom after completing two return voyages. However, it was stressed in the proposal that only the best and most able men should be chosen in order not to tempt the "murderous character of this nation", which could make the "slightest grievance" result in the most "horrible consequences" on board ship.[31]

SLAVES, SLAVING, SAILING

The Dutch had long experience both of slave trading and the employment of slave labour in the Americas and the East Indies alike.[32] The Dutch East India Company – and its personnel individually – participated in the slave trade from fairly early on. The Company, however, was one of many participants in a flourishing and complex trade. In the east Indian Ocean region slaves were exported from the east African coast to north-eastern Africa, Arabia, the Persian Gulf, and India. Sometimes African slaves would also be traded in the Indonesian archipelago and beyond. From the mid-eighteenth century slaves were increasingly traded to the Cape, Madagascar, Zanzibar, and other regions in Africa. Malagasy slaves were

30. Original: "30 a 35 uit het ambagtsquartier [...] voor ieder schip om, na alvoorens eenige tyd op de scheepen in het scheeps-werk onderweesen te zyn, vervolgens met dezelve naar Nederland te stevenen".
31. Original: "dat de keuse soude moeten geschieden uit de beste en bekwaamste, die veeltyds niet te missen zyn, als om dat de moordlust, zoo eygen aan die natie, over de minste ver-ongelyking akelige gevolgen op een schip zoude kunnen veroorzaaken". References from "Middelen ter voorziening in de behoefte aan matrozen voor Compagnie's retourschepen", 5 June 1781, Van der Chijs, *Nederlandsch-Indisch plakaatboek*, X, pp. 491–495.
32. On the slave trade and slavery in the Dutch East Indies see Vink, "World's Oldest Trade"; G.J. Knaap, "Slavery and the Dutch in Southeast Asia", in G. Oostindie (ed.), *Fifty Years Later: Antislavery, Capitalism and Modernity in the Dutch Orbit* (Leiden, 1995), pp. 193–206; R. Raben, "Cities and the Slave Trade in Early-Modern Southeast Asia", in P. Boomgaard, D. Kooiman, and H. Schulte Nordholt (eds), *Linking Destinies: Trade, Towns and Kin in Asian History* (Leiden, 2008), pp. 119–140; W.O. Dijk, "An End to the History of Silence? The Dutch Trade in Asian Slaves: Arakan and the Bay of Bengal, 1621–1665", *IIAS Newsletter*, 46 (2008), p. 16; Anthony Reid and J. Brewster (eds), *Slavery, Bondage and Dependency in Southeast Asia* (St Lucia, 1983); A. van der Kraan, "Bali: Slavery and Slave Trade", in Reid and Brewster, *Slavery*, pp. 315–340; B. Kanumoyoso, "Beyond the City Wall: Society and Economic Development in the Ommelanden of Batavia 1684–1740" (Ph.D., University of Leiden, 2011). Far more research has been conducted on the Dutch West Indies. See, for example, J. Postma, *The Dutch in the Atlantic Slave Trade, 1600–1815* (Cambridge, 1990); H. den Heijer, *Goud, ivoor en slaven. Scheepvaart en handel van de Tweede Westindische Compagnie op Afrika, 1674–1740* (Zutphen, 1997); P.C. Emmer, *De Nederlandse slavenhandel, 1500–1850* (Amsterdam, 2000); R. Paesie, *Lorrendrayen op Africa: De illegale goederen- en slavenhandel op West-Afrika tijdens het achttiende-eeuwse handelsmonopolie van de West-Indische Com-pagnie, 1700–1734* (Amsterdam, 2008); M. van Rossum and K. Fatah-Black, "Wat is winst? De economische impact van de Nederlandse trans-Atlantische slavenhandel", *Tijdschrift voor Sociale en Economische Geschiedenis*, 9 (2012), pp. 3–29.

shipped to Muslim markets, but also to the Cape, Batavia, and other European settlements.[33] Slaves from India were traded to the Indonesian archipelago as well as to the east of the Indian Ocean region. In the Indonesian archipelago multiple slave-trading routes existed, although slaves seem to have been "generally drawn from the eastern and northern part of the Archipelago, where Islam had not yet a firm foothold and weak polities were prone to internecine warfare and slave raiding".[34]

Destinations for the south-east Asian slave trade often included the major cities in the western part of the archipelago, with Batavia an important centre. The number of slaves imported to Batavia has been estimated at several thousand a year, and in the 1770s and 1780s, for example, contemporary estimates mention an annual import of some 4,000 slaves.[35] Most of those slaves were brought in by private European and Asian traders, by company personnel, or by illegal trade, so that the slave population of Batavia amounted to over 40,000 in 1779, out of a total population of 172,000. Slaves came from many different places, although most of them were from south Asia and the Indonesian archipelago, especially Bengal, Sulawesi, and Bali. The specific conditions and relations under which slaves lived varied significantly, and modes of unfree labour differed from slavery to debt bondage and from temporary to lifelong and hereditary "unfreedom".

No direct details are available of the specific type of slavery of the Balinese slaves involved in the mutiny on the *Mercuur*, although some information can be deduced from the context. Apart from the slave of the second equipage master, the Balinese slaves on the *Mercuur* consisted of a large group under the single general ownership of the Societeit van de Cotter de Batavier. Combined with their displacement from their direct social environment, that might indicate a more formal and definite type of slavery, and this seems to be confirmed by the decision the slaves took to rise up in order to flee. The north-easterly winds prevailing around Batavia in September might have influenced the westward course taken by the ship after the mutiny, although that naturally took the slaves further away from Bali. Apparently they were willing to take their chances elsewhere.

Definite forms of slavery were not exceptional for Bali, where slavery was also widespread in the indigenous society. In Bali, many slaves were owned by the rulers and the aristocracy and worked as servants or on the land.[36] It is unclear how far the Balinese slaves on the *Mercuur* were

---

33. G. Campbell, "Slavery and the Trans-Indian Ocean World Slave Trade: A Historical Outline", in H. Prabha Ray and E.A. Alpers (eds), *Cross Currents and Community Networks: The History of the Indian Ocean World* (Oxford, 2006), pp. 286–305.
34. Raben, "Cities and the Slave Trade ", p. 132.
35. *Ibid.*, p. 131.
36. Van der Kraan, "Bali: Slavery"; Knaap, "Slavery", p. 195.

already accustomed to their position as slaves, and that might well have been an important factor in the mutiny since recently enslaved men can be expected to be more prone to revolt than those who have become more accustomed to being slaves. Furthermore, it should be noted that the Balinese origin of the *Mercuur* slaves might not have been entirely random. As Bali was a Hindu society and most of the free company personnel were either Christian or Muslim, employing slaves specifically from that island might have been important to the company policy of "divide and rule".

The outbreak of the Fourth Anglo-Dutch War at the end of 1780 had rendered VOC navigation between the Dutch Republic and the East Indies difficult. As a consequence, the VOC faced shortages of European labour in Asia and the proposal of June 1781 to employ slave sailors on homeward-bound ships was one of the solutions. It is uncertain if the experiment had been put into effect, but only six months later the company decided to adopt more drastic measures. In January 1782 it was proposed by the Governor General "to experiment with" buying Balinese slaves in order to explore whether it "would be possible to educate them in sailing".[37] It was decided to buy around 100 *kloeke*: (strong) Balinese aged fifteen to twenty-five years old, and to turn them into sailors.[38]

Only a few months later the Balinese slaves were placed on board the *Mercuur*. They were to be trained in the work to be done on board ship, "as well as to handle cannons and Snaphaunce muskets",[39] and for this training the slaves appear to have been divided into different groups.

A CALL FOR AMOK

So there they were, early in the morning of 6 September 1782, exercising with the Snaphaunce muskets. The slaves had been divided into well-trained and less well-trained groups, and the better trained slaves were made to exercise first as an example to the others. After that it was time for the less well-trained slaves to exercise, but as they began their drills one of them, Njoman of Njalang, apparently failed to hold his head in the right way. The first mate, training the slaves, corrected Njoman roughly with "a blow to the head" and "by turning his head", which infuriated Njoman. He grasped the barrel of his Snaphaunce musket by the muzzle end and took a swing at the head of the mate, crying "Amok!" as he did so.

From then on the situation developed quickly. The call for amok was taken up by the Balinese slaves, who were "calling amok as with

---

37. Original: "een preuve te neemen"; "of het mogelyk zy die landaard aan den zeedienst te gewenne".
38. "Plaatsing Balinese slaven als matrozen op Comp: oorlogschepen", 18 January 1782, Van der Chijs, *Nederlandsch-Indisch plakaatboek*, X, p. 592.
39. Original: "zo wel met het canon als de snaphaan te leeren manouvreeren".

one voice".[40] Djoedoe from Balijbang declared that the call for amok was repeated by "a crowd".[41] Likop from Balij Paijangang declared that "amok has been called for by everyone present on deck and having exercised".[42] Several of the slaves joined in beating the first mate with their Snaphaunce muskets,[43] while the mate, surprised and wounded, staggered to the captain's cabin. The Balinese slaves followed him into the cabin with "Snaphaunce muskets and cutlasses in their hands" and beat him to a pulp.[44] In his statement before the Court of Justice, the slave Likop stated that he had afterwards found the first mate on the floor, lying dead with his "head crushed and a large wound in the throat".[45]

In the meantime, the slaves spread all over the ship, storming the powder magazine and cutting the anchor rope. The European and Javanese sailors did not put up a fight but fled the ship almost immediately. The Javanese sailors Kappar, Soeroe, and Soelo declared that they either jumped or fell from the ship, that they took hold of a plank and swam to the island of Edam, or they were picked up by the crews of smaller boats which happened to be passing.[46] The Europeans took flight in a small boat and were pelted with *koogels* (which can mean either bullets or cannon balls), bottles, and other items. The ship was soon completely in the hands of the mutinous slaves.

The mutiny was marked by a clear division of tasks. Weapons were handed out and mutineers were assigned to their roles. Likop was assigned to the kitchen, Djoedoe and Galantrik seem to have been in charge of the cannons – and of firing on the warship *'s Compagnies Welvaren* that was soon in pursuit of the *Mercuur*. Sisoepa and Interan were in charge of the wheel, Tedoen and Loewas of the remaining small boat. Leadership seems to have been divided by Njoman from Njalang and Doekoetoet from Balij Klonkong. It is not quite clear who had the upper hand. Djoedoe claims that Doekoetoet had made himself leader of the mutinous slaves and that Njoman had "also commanded".[47]

---

40. Original: "als uijt eenen mond amok is geroepen".
41. Original: "een menigte".
42. Original: "door alle geagter op geweest zijnde en geexerceert hebbende balijsche slaven als uijt eenen mond amok is geroepen".
43. Later, in his testimony before the Court of Justice, Djoedoe from Balijbang confessed to having called for amok and to having beaten the first mate. Likop stated that it had been Passak from Pejan, Tjimoen from Sabangang, Ketoet from Bebong, and Sittend and Djoedoe from Balijbang.
44. Original: "snaphaanen en houwers in de hand".
45. Original: "het hoofd verbrijsseld en een groote wond in de keel".
46. The Javanese sailors Soeroe and Soelo stated they were in the galley ("bak" or "galjoen") of the ship at the time of the mutiny – the same place as the slave Tedoen claims to have been (and from where, according to Djoedoe's statement, he took a "rijst stamper", a rice masher, as a weapon).
47. Original: "mede gecomandeert".

Mewa from Balij Negara claimed that Doekoetoet was alone in his leadership – and mentioned that he walked around the ship with a "parasol".[48] Tedoen and Likop mention only the leading role of Njoman.

Likop described an atmosphere of intimidation. He claimed the leadership of Njoman in the mutiny was based largely on fear, stating that he was first forced to help with the attack on the fleeing Europeans, and after that he was forced to work in the kitchen preparing food for the others. Furthermore, Likop stated that slaves attempting to flee were threatened and that Passeer from Balij Kafba Kafba was killed trying to escape. The emphasis on the intimidating leadership of Njoman might have served to downplay Likop's own role in the mutiny, for, after all, he was suspected of attacking company employees at both the beginning and end of the mutiny. We should bear in mind too that Likop was the slave of the second equipage master and seems to have been the only slave who was not part of the group owned by the Societeit van de Cotter de Batavier. At the same time, however, it is not unlikely that coercion might very well have been an integral part of enforcing and sustaining cohesion and loyalty during the mutiny.

Two interesting things about the beginning of the mutiny remain to be noted. The slaves seem to have been in possession of "cutlasses"[49] almost immediately when the fight broke out between the exercising slaves and the first mate. Likop declared that the cutlasses were brought on deck by "one of the youngest slaves",[50] while Djoedoe mentions that the cutlasses came from a "case" on deck,[51] that had been opened by "a young Balinese slave". The speed with which the cutlasses appeared in the drama raises questions. Was it an indication of prior preparations for the mutiny? Or was it quick thinking and alert assistance by the boy who was used to a servile role in an adult environment?

The VOC officials at least found the scenario of a prepared revolt not unlikely. In the trial of the nine mutineers brought to the Court of Justice significant attention was paid to the start of the mutiny and the origin of the weapons used. The fear of a "conspiracy" to run amok was also crucial to the events on the *Slot ter Hoge*. The confessions to conspiracy made by the slaves should be addressed with caution as they were obtained by torture. Nevertheless, the possibility that amok was premeditatedly organized by sailors or slaves was identified not only by the authorities but by the slaves and sailors themselves. The question figures prominently in the statements of Javanese sailors about a mutiny on board a Macao

48. Original: "sombreel".
49. Original: "houwers".
50. Original: "door een der jongste balijsche slaaven die den stuurman had opgepast een menigte op het dek zijn gebragt en door de overige opgenomen".
51. Original: "geweerkist die op het dek stond".

ship in 1783 near Pisang, south of Malacca. Interrogated before the Court
of Justice of Batavia, three Javanese mutineers declared that, after a dispute over payment of wages and threats by the captain that he would
impress them as soldiers on Macao, "Sie Dolla, one of them, had advised
them, quietly, to make *amok*". The next evening, "at eight o'clock", two
of the Javanese had "called *amok*".[52] The eleven mutineers killed several
Europeans and Chinese – the Macao sailors on board fled.

The same strategy could very well have been employed by the Balinese
slaves on board the *Mercuur*. The assistance of the young slave and the
joint call for amok would fit perfectly in that scenario. The mishandling of
the musket by Njoman could have served as a method of provoking
maltreatment by the first mate. The furious reaction of Njoman, the strike
at the first mate and the call for amok therefore served to signal the start
of the mutiny. The ready availability of weapons and the reasonably high
level of organization that characterized further developments during the
mutiny might also point to the scenario of a planned uprising.

The navigational skill of the Balinese slaves is another intriguing aspect.
The slaves managed to set sail almost immediately after the mutiny.
They overran the ship near the island of Edam in the roads of Batavia,
where the first attempt to retake the vessel was made by the warship *'s
Compagnies Welvaren*. The slaves then set sail westwards in the direction
of the Sunda Strait – in the opposite direction to their home island of
Bali. Near the island "Dwars in de Weg" a second attempt was made
to recapture the ship but, successful in resisting the second assault, the
mutineers sailed or perhaps drifted even further west.[53] They were at
the latitude of the island "Poelo Bessij, lying just under the highlands
of Lampong" (south Sumatra) when the third and final attack took
place.[54]

It is unclear whether the two sails of the *Mercuur* had already been set
before the mutiny, or if it had been done by the slaves themselves directly
after the mutiny. Likop claimed that the slaves sailed with "the two sails
that had already been set". Djoedoe, however, claimed that the two sails
"were set on the order of Njoman and Doekoetoet". Mewa at first
claimed that he was below deck, but later stated that he and others had
helped with handling "the sails and the cannon". Tedoen stated the two
sails were already set when he came on deck and that later he helped

---

52. Original statement by the Javanese sailors Salieden, Kadol, and Boejang: "Dat op die
drijgementen, een van hun met naame Sie Dolla, hun in stilte had aangeraeden om amok te
maken. Dat vervolgens 's avonds de klokke agt uuren door voorm. Saleedien en Sie Dolla Amok
was geroepen geworden"; NA, VOC, 1.04.02, 9515.
53. It seems that during the second attack the top of the mast of the *Mercuur* was blown off.
54. "Poelo Bessij" refers to the present-day island of Pulau Sebesi, near Lampung (South
Sumatra).

"in taking care of the sails".[55] Whether or not the sails had already been set before the mutiny, the slaves' ability to resist their attackers for five days and to navigate from Edam to Poelo Bessij seems to indicate a rather high level of organization and seamanship.

The mutiny on the *Mercuur* seems to have been a revolt against more than just shipboard hierarchy and violence. In the mutiny the Balinese freed themselves from the status of slave. They established a new social order that was in many ways an inversion of the normal situation. The slaves used their newly gained freedom to eat more diverse food (ships' biscuit, fish, and meat), but also to open the sailors' chests to look for liquor and European clothes. Ashore, slaves were not allowed in bars and taverns but after the mutiny they gained access to beer, wine, and distilled "white liquor".[56] The "European" clothes[57] found on board led to a carnivalesque sort of costume play. Doekoetoet was described as using a *sombreel* – a parasol or sun-hat – as a sign of his leadership and Djoedoe admitted that he had donned a white "shirt" or *baaijtje* (Figure 3).[58] Intarang, Loewas, and Mewa were said to have worn white trousers. The imprisoned slaves disagreed about Likop's clothes: Djoedoe declared Likop wore a white shirt, Tedoen states he had white trousers, while Mewa declared he had a red *baaijtje* and black trousers.

This defiance of social and ethnic categorizations did not last. After five days, early in the morning of 11 September 1782, the mutiny was broken. After two failed attempts to repossess the ship the European and Javanese soldiers managed to climb up the rear of the vessel and take the poop deck, from where they launched their attack on the mutineers. The ruthless reckoning of Jacob Wedelaar with the mutinous Balinese slaves seems completely in line with VOC regulations stating that renegade slaves who refused to surrender "should be killed in the best way possible".[59] Both the soldiers and the Balinese slaves were forced to leave the ship as fire engulfed it. Only nine slaves were picked up from the sea and nearby islands. A few other mutineers were mentioned as having died during the mutiny and subsequent fighting. Perhaps some slaves drowned trying to reach shore, but it is likely that a large number of the seventy-nine slaves did manage to escape. If so, the mutiny was, at least in part, successful.

55. Original: "mede op de zeilen te hebben gepast". Tedoen furthermore claimed to have done nothing else than attend the sails and keep an eye on the warship. He stated that he stopped doing so when Njoman ceased giving orders.
56. Original: "witte soopjes".
57. Original: "Europeesche kleederen linnen en ander goed".
58. Original: "hembt of baaijtje" (a *badjoe*: jacket or shirt).
59. Original: "neer te maken en van kant te brengen", "op de best mogelykste wyze", "Plakaat ter beteugeling van de moetwil en insolentie der slaven", 31 March 1778, NA, VOC, no. 3504, fos 2042–2048.

Figure 3. A young slave with a parasol.
Painted by Jan Brandes, 1779–1785. Rijksmuseum, Amsterdam. Public domain.

The events might have sent an important message to slaves and other workers concerning the possibilities of revolt.

The nine mutineers who were finally brought to trial in Batavia showed little solidarity. Likop was one of the first to make a statement. As early as 12 October, a few days before the interrogation of the European and Javanese crew members, he seems to have confessed to the events of the mutiny more or less voluntarily. He gave court officials detailed information with which they could interrogate the other mutineers. Djoedoe, Mewa, and Tedoen were interrogated as a group. It seems there might have been a short-lived attempt to "hold the line" under questioning, with the three stating that they were not certain of the course of events and that they were unaware of the role of their fellow mutineers. Soon, however, Mewa confessed that Djoedoe had indeed been one of the slaves who joined the assault on the first mate. After that, solidarity broke down and the men confessed to the mutiny pretty freely.

BLOODY ENDINGS

The mutiny on the *Mercuur* in 1782 was the first of a small series of mutinies by slaves and Asian sailors on homeward bound VOC ships and must have been an impressive event. The Balinese slaves murdered a first mate and took possession of a company ship. They held out for a number of days and made their way to South Sumatra chased by a warship. The *Mercuur* was eventually set on fire and sank and the VOC tried to hush up the events. The only news report, in the *Groninger Courant*, did not name the ship and was based on information from a Danish vessel. Despite that, the affair must have had a significant impact. It is most likely that some at least of the Balinese mutineers did manage to escape. Accounts of the mutiny and its repression might have been given by the runaway slaves, but also by the Europeans and Javanese who returned to Batavia. The mutiny of the *Mercuur* might have been an inspiration for the mutinies and conspiracies on the *Slot ter Hoge* (1783), the *Java* (1783), and the *Haasje* (1790).

It is uncertain, however, if all this should lead us to speak of an "age of mutinies", although a few other references to mutinies are indeed known for the period. The mutinies of Europeans, however, were mostly en route from Europe to Asia, as in the case of the mutiny on the *Gerechtigheid* (1782), the *Venus* (1782), and the *Barbestein* (1786). Mutinies by Asians occurred while ships were lying off Batavia (*Mercuur*), or en route from Asia to the Cape (*Slot ter Hoge, Java, Haasje*). Other mutinies by Asians occurred outside the service of the VOC as well, for example on a Macao ship in 1783 near Pisang, south of Malacca – where eleven Javanese sailors, one Malayan, and a Moor rebelled against the Europeans and Chinese on board,[60] or the mutiny by Asian passengers on the *Vrouwe Agatha*, a ship hired by the VOC and sailing from Batavia to the Cape in 1792.[61] These mutinies seem to have been related to wartime pressure on

60. NA, VOC, 1.04.02, 9515.
61. Cape Town Archives Repository, South Africa, Resolutions of the Council of Policy of Cape of Good Hope, C. 204, pp. 6–57.

labour markets and working conditions. Perhaps tales of mutiny inspired others. It is impossible, however, to trace direct links between the different mutinies.

Mutinies by both Asians and Europeans seem to have occurred regularly throughout the history of the VOC, those in the 1780s conceivably being part of a series of revolts during the Fourth Anglo-Dutch War and later. There seem to have been earlier concentrations of mutinies and revolts too. The 1680s, for example, saw a noticeable series of mutinies when slaves rebelled on the VOC ship *Hogergeest* in 1684, the Dutch private sloop *Steenbock* in 1686, and another privately owned Dutch vessel, also in 1686. Furthermore, Christian Asian sailors mutinied on a VOC *pantjalang* in 1688 and Chinese and Javanese sailors rebelled on a private vessel belonging to Dutchman Jacob Janssen de Roy in 1691. However, it is uncertain if and how these different mutinies were related. A thorough reconstruction of mutinies in Asian and other seas would be an interesting way forward as such research could reveal peaks in mutinies over time and place, and might reveal patterns.

Returning to the late eighteenth-century Asian mutinies, there seem to have been some important differences between the mutiny on the *Mercuur* and the role of slaves in later incidents. First, the position of the slaves was completely different. The Balinese slaves on the *Mercuur* were enslaved labourers trained for military and maritime tasks. The slaves conspiring or revolting on the *Slot ter Hoge*, *Java*, and *Haasje* were the property of highly ranked individual crew members, presumably functioning as servants or as "cargo" for private trade. A group of slave sailors were also on board the *Slot ter Hoge*, but they apparently agreed to the death sentence of the slaves suspected of conspiracy. Second, the mutinies on the *Java* and the *Haasje* resulted in a careful and secretly planned killing of European officers at some moment when they would be most vulnerable – after nightfall, during dinner, or in their sleeping quarters. On the *Mercuur*, the mutiny ignited on deck and in broad daylight. In both cases cruel treatment does seem to have been an important factor in the mutinous behaviour.

Once freed from their normal hierarchy by a violent moment of revolt, the mutiny on the *Mercuur* developed in a controlled manner. The homogenous background of the slaves, all of whom were Balinese, and their status as slave sailor-soldiers might have been an important factor in shaping the course of events. The slaves seem to have had a rather high level of organization and of maritime and military skill. According to the statements given, the mutineers accepted a form of personal leadership (Njoman, Doekoetoet) and division of tasks. Discipline on board was enforced by coercion and the threat of killing, and at least one slave was indeed killed for trying to leave the ship. The immediate availability of weapons and the collective response of the slaves to the call for amok might be indications of preparations made for the mutiny. Meanwhile, the aim of the mutiny seems not to have been to return to Bali but to gain freedom by taking over command of the ship. The mutineers set sail for south Sumatra, presumably using the north-eastern winds prevailing in September. In the meantime, the slaves celebrated their temporarily gained freedom on board ship with a somewhat carnivalesque inversion of the social order.

The open and shared outcry for amok in the case of the *Mercuur* is striking and brings into play an interesting issue. From the nineteenth century onwards, amok has been generally defined as an irrational – and often individual – act of violence performed by "native" men. The *Encyclopædia Britannica* in 1911 portrayed it as "homicidal mania".[62] The nineteenth-century Dutch linguist P.J. Veth used a very similar definition that tended to explain the phenomenon in a psychological way, describing it as an instance of "rage", leading native men to kill everyone standing in their way. According to Veth amok would be closely related to *mata glap* – a situation in which someone would be blinded by fury. He referred to the "calling of amok" as a phenomenon that emerged from such a desperate and misguided state of mind.[63] Others have framed "running amok" as not completely irrational, but nevertheless an individual act – as "a culture-specific syndrome wherein an individual unpredictably and without warning manifests mass, indiscriminate, homicidal behavior that is authored with suicidal intent".[64]

The process of pushing the phenomenon into a narrow psychological framework continued throughout the twentieth century. Researchers went in "search of the true amok" in Malay culture, and found that "both the subjects and the Malay culture view amok as psychopathology".[65] In a 1999 article, a distinction was made between two types of amok related to different psychological disorders. Studying the present-day occurrences of amok, Manuel L. Saint Martin stated that "beramok is plausibly linked to a depressive or mood disorder, while amok appears to be related to psychosis, personality disorders, or a delusional disorder".[66]

In contrast then to received wisdom from the nineteenth to the twenty-first century, the events presented in this article show that there is evidence to rethink the psychological definition of amok as individual and irrational rage. On board the *Slot ter Hoge* amok appears to have been a conscious act of revolt, which according to the reports took the form of a "conspiracy" to run amok among the slaves. The Dutch officers referred

62. "Amuck, Running", *Encyclopædia Britannica* (11th edn, 1911).
63. P.J. Veth, *Uit Oost en West. Verklaring van eenige uitheemsche woorden* (Arnhem, 1889).
64. J.C. Spores, *Running Amok: An Historical Inquiry* (Athens, OH, 1988), p. 7.
65. J.E. Carr and E. Kong Tan, "In Search of the True Amok: Amok as Viewed Within the Malay Culture", *The American Journal of Psychiatry*, 133 (1976), pp. 1295–1299.
66. M.L. Saint Martin, "Running Amok: A Modern Perspective on a Culture-Bound Syndrome", *Primary Care Companion to The Journal of Clinical Psychiatry*, 1:3 (1999), pp. 66–70.

to "murder or massacre under the name of amok".[67] The mutiny on the Macao ship in 1783 seems to have been planned the day before the "calling of amok" occurred. On the *Mercuur* as well, amok took the form of a full-blown mutiny. These mutinies and conspiracies show amok as a collective and rational act. The amok played out by the Balinese slaves is revealed as a conscious and rational act of defiance, and so we can see some light thrown on a tradition of resistance that was rather different from the "traditional" late-colonial perception of amok.

The Asian mutinies on board Dutch East Indiamen at the end of the eighteenth century establish amok as an indigenous claim to resistance. The moment of amok might be linked to notions of honour, as noted by Nigel Worden.[68] At the same time, however, the purpose of calling amok clearly goes beyond readiness to defend honour or reclaim self-worth. At the start of the mutiny, the direct individual response to perceived injustice or violation of codes of honour (a blow to the head) is taken over by peers in the group. At the end of the mutiny, facing armed troops, the mutineers again collectively cried out for amok. The "call" for amok was not then an act of an enraged lone killer, but played a key role in the mobilization of the group of mutineers. It functioned as a conscious call to arms, as a battle cry as well as a call for solidarity. Collectively rising against authority, the Balinese slaves seem to have employed the call for amok both as a defence of basic morals against maltreatment and as a way of gaining their freedom.

In its manifestation, the uprising shows similarities with other forms of conscious revolt, especially European maritime mutinies. The capture of the ship, the decision to set sail with the aim of gaining freedom, and the temporary inversion of social order are characteristics found in other mutinies. The level of organization and possible preparation are striking and interesting aspects. On the other hand, the Balinese mutiny on the *Mercuur* seems to have had a much more violent beginning than many other mutinies. Amok might well have been a pluriform but distinct tradition of resistance, with similarities to European-style mutinies. This seems to open up a promising area for fruitful future research, which could shed light on the development of amok as a tradition of resistance with distinctive cultural patterns, but we should keep in mind links and comparisons to other European and Asian forms of revolt. Such research will also enable us to understand better the historical interplay between local and global influences on traditions of revolt, as well as the transformation of fluid indigenous traditions into static "colonial" and "psychologized" categories.

67. Van der Tempel, "Wij hebben amok", p. 130.
68. N. Worden, "Public Brawling, Masculinity and Honour", in *idem* (ed.), *Cape Town: Between East and West. Social Identities in a Dutch Colonial Town* (Hilversum, 2012), pp. 194–211.

IRSH 58 (2013), Special Issue, pp. 131–151 doi:10.1017/S0020859013000291
© 2013 Internationaal Instituut voor Sociale Geschiedenis

Anti-Impressment Riots and the Origins of the Age of Revolution*

CHRISTOPHER P. MAGRA

Department of History, University of Tennessee
915 Volunteer Blvd, Knoxville, TN 37996-4065, USA

E-mail: cmagra@utk.edu

ABSTRACT: This essay details the relationship between anti-impressment collective actions, the American Revolution, and the age of revolution. Naval impressment represented the forcible coercion of laborers into extended periods of military service. Workers in North American coastal communities militantly, even violently, resisted British naval impressment. A combination of Leveller-inspired ideals and practical experience encouraged this resistance. In turn, resistance from below inspired colonial elites to resist British authority by contributing to the elaboration of a political discourse on legitimate authority, liberty, and freedom. Maritime laborers stood on the front lines in the struggle for freedom, and their radical collective actions helped give meaning to wider struggles around the Atlantic world.

Seafarers William Conner, Michael Corbet, Pierce Fenning, and John Ryan were Irish Americans living and working in Marblehead, Massachusetts, the foremost fishing port in British North America. On 22 April 1769, they were homeward bound from Cadiz, Spain on board the *Pitt Packet*, a brig that belonged to Robert "King" Hooper, a wealthy fish merchant in Marblehead, with a load of salt to be used in the colonial fisheries. Benjamin Caldwell, captain of HMS *Rose*, was stationed outside Marblehead's harbor. Caldwell ordered the *Pitt Packet* to strike sail and await inspection. He then sent Lieutenant Henry Gibson Panton with several armed seamen to board the *Pitt Packet* to force men into naval service, a practice known as impressment. The Irish-American workers locked themselves in the brig's hold. Panton ordered the door to the hold

* The author would like to thank all of the participants at the 2011 Maritime Radicalism conference and the members of the 2012 Maritime Radicalism workshop for their constructive feedback on early drafts of this essay. Funding from the Department of History, University of Tennessee, and the International Institute of Social History in Amsterdam, the Netherlands, made travel to these meetings possible.

to be broken down, and the press gang rushed in. Conner, Corbet, Fenning, and Ryan stood amidst piles of salt armed with fishing implements, ready to defend themselves. A tense standoff ensued. Corbet grabbed a harpoon and a handful of salt. He threw a line of salt before the press gang and swore that any man that crossed it would die. Panton stepped over the line. Corbet launched his harpoon at the Lieutenant, hit him in the neck, and severed his jugular. While some of the press gang attacked the Marblehead mariners, others carried Panton up to the main deck, where he bled to death. After a short fight, the gang overwhelmed and arrested the Irish Americans, who were arrested and tried for murder in a specially convened Vice Admiralty court in Boston, Massachusetts.[1]

On the other side of the Atlantic, impressed sailors were organizing a mutiny on their way to the Nore in March 1771. The Royal Navy was mobilizing for what was presumed to be another war with France. A press gang at Newcastle had captured 160 maritime laborers. These pressed men were being transported by sea to HMS *Conquestador* at the Nore. John Falkingham, captain of the *Conquestador*, reported that he only "received 85 men". The remaining 75 pressed men, along with 2 volunteers, had "risen against the crew" of the transport vessel, "the *Active* tender", en route to the Nore. The savvy mutineers "destroyed the lists which were sent by Captain Bover [the regulating captain in charge of the Newcastle press gang]". These lists recorded names and places of residence. After seizing control of the vessel, the mutineers "obliged the [*Active*'s] pilot to carry her into the Port of Whitby; by which means, seventy seven Impressed men and Volunteers made their Escape".[2] Separated by an ocean, workers whose lives revolved around the sea resisted the Royal Navy and thereby helped to usher in the age of revolution.

Historians have now studied the radical dimensions of the age of revolution for over fifty years, but the maritime nature of radical ideas and actions has for the most part been neglected.[3] When anti-impressment

1. L. Kinvin Wroth and Hiller B. Zobel (eds), *Legal Papers of John Adams*, 3 vols (Cambridge, MA, 1965), II, pp. 275–335. For coverage in the *Boston Evening Post*, the *New York Journal*, and the *Pennsylvania Chronicle*, see Oliver Morton Dickerson (comp.), *Boston Under Military Rule, 1768–1769, As Revealed In A Journal of the Times* (Westport, CT, 1971), pp. 94–95, 104–105.
2. The National Archives, Kew, UK (TNA), Records of the Navy Board and the Board of Admiralty (ADM), 106/1197/239.
3. Recent work on the radicalism of the age of revolutions includes Alfred F. Young, Gary B. Nash, and Ray Raphael (eds), *Revolutionary Founders: Rebels, Radicals, and Reformers in the Making of the Nation* (New York, 2011); David Andress, *The French Revolution and the People* (London, 2006); Gary B. Nash, *The Unknown American Revolution: The Unruly Birth of Democracy and the Struggle to Create America* (New York, 2005); and Sibylle Fischer, *Modernity Disavowed: Haiti and the Cultures of Slavery in the Age of Revolution* (Durham, NC, 2004). An exception to the neglect of maritime radicalism is Peter Linebaugh and Marcus

collective actions are discussed in relation to the American Revolution that opened the age of revolution, they are commonly portrayed as apolitical affairs in which angry workers on the margins of mainstream society simply wanted to avoid unwholesome military service and familial separation.[4] Only a few historians have maintained that maritime laborers had a political consciousness and acted on it. This consciousness has been described as "liberal", in the modern sense of the term, as workers were willing to wait for change to occur.[5] Peter Linebaugh and Marcus Rediker stand apart in their insistence that the workers engaged in eighteenth-century anti-impressment riots were motivated by radical ideas.

Their work highlights the ways in which ideas about egalitarianism and freedom circulated around the Atlantic world during the long and uneven transition to capitalism. Such ideas, combined with a shared experience with capitalist expropriation and exploitation, linked merchant mariners, pirates, slaves, and even those involved in anti-impressment collective actions into one transatlantic, many-headed proletariat that resisted Herculean efforts on the part of a ruling class to keep workers in check.[6]

This essay presents a sea-centered portrait of the radical ideology and behavior associated with anti-impressment collective actions in colonial America on the eve of the American Revolution. These actions were public, and therefore relatively well-recorded, illuminating the ways in which maritime radicalism (radical ideas and behavior directly related to life at sea) influenced the revolutionary movement that brought about an independent United States of America and ushered in the age of revolution.[7] Life and work at sea was central to radical actions and beliefs

Rediker, *The Many-Headed Hydra: Sailors, Slaves, Commoners, and the Hidden History of the Revolutionary Atlantic* (Boston, MA, 2000).

4. See, for example, Denver Brunsman, "Subjects vs Citizens: Impressment and Identity in the Anglo-American Atlantic", *Journal of the Early Republic*, 30 (2010), pp. 557–586; Keith Mercer, "Northern Exposure: Resistance to Naval Impressment in British North America, 1775–1815", *Canadian Historical Review*, 91 (2010), pp. 199–232; Nicholas Rogers, *The Press Gang: Naval Impressment and its Opponents in Georgian Britain* (London [etc.], 2007); Paul A. Gilje, *Liberty on the Waterfront: American Maritime Culture in the Age of Revolution* (Philadelphia, PA, 2004); N.A.M. Rodger, *The Wooden World: An Anatomy of the Georgian Navy* (London, 1986); and Pauline Maier, *From Resistance to Revolution: Colonial Radicals and the Development of American Opposition to Britain, 1765–1776* (New York, 1972).

5. Jesse Lemisch maintains that colonial maritime laborers who resisted impressment were "liberal" not "radical". Workers wanted change. They demanded that the very old use of state power to appropriate labor come to an end. The crucial point for Lemisch, however, is that the colonial maritime laborers that rioted against British naval impressment were "patient" and they were "not willing to destroy the present system to achieve a better one". See Jesse Lemisch, *Jack Tar vs John Bull: The Role of New York's Seamen in Precipitating the Revolution* (New York, 1997), p. xix.

6. Linebaugh and Rediker, *The Many-Headed Hydra*.

7. The term "radical" in this essay refers to actions that contemporaries perceived as being subversive, or potentially subversive, to the existing order of things. Christopher Hill, an expert

from below that helped push colonial elites, the so-called Founding Fathers, into armed rebellion against the British Empire. Maritime laborers' radicalism inspired both fear and conviction in elites that the world might be turned upside down.

Sea power provided the means for the expansion of the British Empire across the Atlantic world. In waters teeming with pirates, privateers, and enemy warships, a strong navy made it possible for commerce, communication, and conquest to extend out from Albion's island shores over the course of the 1600s and 1700s. In the words of John Evelyn, an English writer and a commissioner in charge of tending to wounded seamen during the Second Anglo-Dutch War,

> To pretend to Universal Monarchy without Fleets was long since looked upon as a politic[al] chimera [...] whoever commands the ocean, commands the trade of the world, and whoever commands the trade of the world, commands the riches of the world, and whoever is master of that, commands the world itself.[8]

British naval expansion could not have occurred without the coercion of maritime labor. There has long been a consensus among historians of the early modern British navy that impressment was integral to manning efforts.[9] Nicholas Rogers has made the most concerted effort to quantify impressment. He concludes that of the 450,000 men who served in the British navy between 1740 and 1815, 40 per cent were pressed.[10] In other words, nearly half of Britain's combat strength was coerced into military service over this 75-year period.

Eighteenth-century eyewitnesses also saw impressment as vital to manning the British fleet. John Nicol, a common Scottish tar who served

---

on early modern radicalism, wrote that radical ideas such as Gerard Winstanley's mid-seventeenth-century call to put the poor first, represented a "subversion of the existing social order". See Christopher Hill, *The World Turned Upside Down: Radical Ideas during the English Revolution*, (4th edn, New York, 1991), p. 38. By collective resistance, I refer to group behavior based on mutual understanding and assent, as opposed to individual action predicated solely upon self-interested motives not shared by others.

8. John Evelyn, *Navigation and Commerce, Their Origin and Progress* (London, 1674), pp. 15–17, 32–33.

9. Denver Brunsman, "Men of War: British Sailors and the Impressment Paradox", *Journal of Early Modern History*, 14 (2010), pp. 9–44; Mercer, "Northern Exposure"; Rogers, *Press Gang*; Stephen F. Gradish, *The Manning of the British Navy During The Seven Years' War* (London, 1980); Daniel A. Baugh, *British Naval Administration in the Age of Walpole* (Trenton, NJ, 1965); Neil R. Stout, "Manning the Royal Navy in North America, 1763–1775", *American Neptune*, 23 (1963), pp. 174–185; Richard Pares, "The Manning of the Navy in the West Indies, 1702–63", *Transactions of the Royal Historical Society*, 20 (1937), pp. 31–60; and John Robert Hutchinson, *The Press-Gang Afloat and Ashore* (London, 1913). N.A.M. Rodger stands apart from this consensus. In an investigation of the muster books of five random warships from the Seven Years' War, he concludes that only 15 per cent of the men had been pressed; Rodger, *The Wooden World*, app. III.

10. Rogers, *Press Gang*, pp. 5, 40.

in the Royal Navy in 1776, observed "I was surprised to see so few who, like myself, had chosen [naval service] for the love of that line of life. Some had been forced into it by their own irregular conduct but *the greater number were impressed men*".[11] In 1775, at the start of the American Revolution, Vice Admiral Samuel Graves, commander of the British North American squadron stationed off Massachusetts, reported in a letter to Philip Stephens, Secretary of the Admiralty Board, that "Necessity obliges me, contrary to my inclination, to use this method to man the King's Ships".[12] Judge Serjeant Foster adjudicated a very important legal case in 1743 in which a mariner killed a naval officer while resisting impressment. Foster famously ruled against the mariner and defended the institution of impressment. In his ruling, Foster stated:

> This Question touching the Legality of Pressing Mariners for the Public Service is a Point of very great and National Importance [...]. As to the Point of Public Safety, it would be time very ill spent for me to go about to prove that this Nation can Never be Long in a State of Safety, Our Coast defended and our Trade protected, without a Naval Force Equal to All the Emergencies that may happen. And how can We be Secure of such a Force? [...] I do not know that the Wisdom of the Nation has hitherto found out any Method of Manning our Navy, less inconvenient than Pressing; And at the same time Equally sure and Effectual.[13]

The British navy could not have safeguarded shipping lanes and maintained key Atlantic stations over the course of the eighteenth century without impressment. Without the ability to regularly patrol key strategic points in the Atlantic world, transatlantic shipping would have been put at greater risk. Increased risk meant higher maritime insurance rates for shippers, and it meant a reduction in the degree of predictability that was a key component of the free flow of goods. In short, without a sufficiently manned navy, Britain's maritime empire would have been vulnerable.

Like mutiny, resisting impressment was highly subversive in the context of the eighteenth-century British Atlantic world. A 1759 Act of Parliament erased any distinction between evading impressment and desertion.[14] The same act stipulated financial punishments, incarceration, transportation, and forced military service for those found to be aiding and abetting this "desertion".[15]

---

11. Tim Flannery (ed.), *The Life and Adventures of John Nicol, Mariner* (New York, 1997), p. 26. Emphasis is my own.
12. "Vice Admiral Samuel Graves to Philip Stephens, Secretary of the British Admiralty", *Preston*, Boston, 20 February 1775, in William Bell Clark *et al.* (eds), *Naval Documents of the American Revolution*, 11 vols to date (Washington DC, 1964), I, p. 98.
13. "Mr. Serjeant Foster's Argument concerning Pressing of Seamen, 1743", The National Maritime Museum, Caird Library, Greenwich, UK [hereafter NMM], Hartwell papers (HAR)/5.
14. NMM, Personal Papers of Sir Gilbert Elliot, Treasurer of the Navy, 1722–1777, ELL/9.
15. *Ibid.*

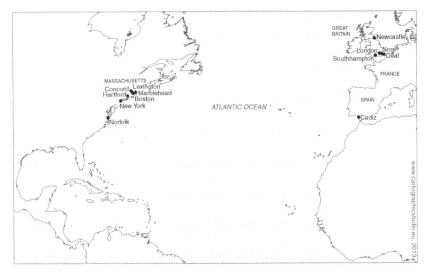

Figure 1. Atlantic coastal communities, c.1775.

For those who actually "deserted", the removal of the distinction between impressment and desertion meant death. George II's 1757 royal proclamation made desertion a capital crime.[16] Why, then, were maritime laborers willing to use violence to resist British naval impressment? Why would British subjects even consider murdering a British naval officer? Answers to these questions made for a revolutionary era.

In North American coastal communities, workers were engaged in a variety of radical actions during the 1760s and 1770s that helped bring about the American Revolution. Maritime laborers joined Sons of Liberty organizations; they threatened Stamp Tax collectors and customs agents with physical violence, and they destroyed private property.[17] Tar, a nautical weatherproofing agent, became a subversive weapon in the hands of maritime mobs that tarred and feathered British officials.[18] Maritime laborers in colonial ports converted ship masts into liberty poles to celebrate the repeal of offensive British legislation. The same workers then rioted whenever British soldiers stationed in North American cities tore down these liberty poles. In what has come to be known as the Battle of Golden Hill, thousands of mariners in New York City engaged in armed combat with British soldiers on 19 January 1770 following the removal of

16. NMM, "By the King, A Proclamation, For giving Encouragement to Seamen [...]", ELL/9.
17. See Benjamin L. Carp, *Defiance of the Patriots: The Boston Tea Party and the Making of America* (New Haven, CT, 2010); and Maier, *From Resistance to Revolution*.
18. Benjamin H. Irvin, "Tar, Feathers, and the Enemies of American Liberties, 1768–1776", *The New England Quarterly*, 76 (2003), pp. 197–238.

the local liberty pole.[19] And, to be sure, there was resistance to naval impressment such as the *Pitt Packet* affair. Collectively, workers' resistance in the streets generated a public discussion about the nature of British imperial authority. This resistance and discussion made policies such as the Stamp Act unworkable, and ultimately caused the British imperial machine to grind to a halt.

Certain preconditions made anti-impressment collective actions more likely to occur, the first of which was increased impressment itself. The British navy was most likely to press maritime laborers into military service during wartime.[20] According to Rogers, impressment was statistically most likely to occur over the course of the first year of a war, when demand for labor was exceptionally high, naval wages were notoriously low, and volunteerism was pitifully insufficient.[21] At the start of the Seven Years' War, for example, the number of men mustered into the British navy jumped more than threefold, from 9,797 in 1754 to 29,268 in 1755.[22] Military mobilization increased press-gang activities and generated unusually high levels of resistance.

The state of the economy in and around a port also bore on the frequency with which workers resisted impressment. The fact that wages in the private sector increased during periods of conflict made maritime laborers especially motivated to resist being forced into military service at this time. Left to their own devices, maritime laborers could have secured unusually high wages. As a London newspaper writer explained in 1775 "The cruelty of issuing press warrants has been long and justly complained of. The English tars, brave as they are, have no objection to be paid."[23] Impressment effectively cut workers' wages at a time when labor was scarce and pay high. During the eighteenth century, the primary focus of this essay, wartime wages on merchant vessels typically stood at on average 50–60 shillings per man, per month. At the same time, an able-bodied naval seaman earned 24 shillings per month.[24] Workers still resisted impressment when wages were low and jobs were scarce in the private sector. During peacetime in 1770 outside London, for example, it was reported that a mariner shot a naval officer "dead on the Spot" after the officer and a press gang came after

19. Richard Ketchum, *Divided Loyalties: How the American Revolution Came to New York* (New York, 2002), pp. 224–236.

20. Historians of the Royal Navy agree on this point: N.A.M. Rodger, *The Command of the Ocean: A Naval History of Britain, 1649–1815* (London, 2006), esp. pp. 395–396; Baugh, *British Naval Administration in the Age of Walpole*, esp. pp. 147–240; and Gradish, *The Manning of the British Navy During the Seven Years' War*, esp. pp. 54–86.

21. Rogers, *Press Gang*, p. 42.

22. Rodger, *The Command of the Ocean*, app. VI, p. 638.

23. "News from London", dated 21 July 1775, *Virginia Gazette*, 5 October 1775.

24. Baugh, *British Naval Administration in the Age of Walpole*, p. 229.

the sailor.[25] Men never wanted to be coerced into naval service, in peacetime or wartime. Yet losing the ability to earn higher than normal wages in the private sector during wartime gave workers extra incentive to resist impressment.

The nature of a ship captain's authority, on a merchant vessel and on a warship, also impacted the likelihood that anti-impressment actions would occur. The captain of a merchant vessel may have abused his crew, making them unruly, and even openly hostile. The abusive captain could then offer up such mariners to nearby naval officers, who would press the men. In 1775, at the start of the Revolutionary War, British General Thomas Gage wrote to Vice Admiral Samuel Graves to ask the naval commander to ban the impressment of seamen off the army's transport ships, which were hired merchant vessels bound for New York to get supplies for the army. The vice admiral denied this request. Graves explained that "We never impress the Transports people but in Cases of very bad behavior and at the Master's Request".[26] In 1740, "sturdy Fellows belonging to a [merchant] Ship near Southampton [England], having refused to go the Voyage without a Rise of Wages, left their Vessel. Upon which, the Master thereof gave Scent of them to a Press Gang, who, with the Assistance of some Constables, in short, seized them".[27]

A vindictive naval commander could also abuse his authority and press men out of spite or personal animosity. After the Committee of Safety in Marblehead, Massachusetts, confiscated some of Graves's personal effects that had been imported into the coastal community in violation of the Continental Congress's non-importation agreement, the British vice admiral stationed a warship outside Marblehead's harbor, "pressed several Men", and, according to a naval officer at the scene, Graves wanted "to burn their Town".[28] In either civilian or military cases, the nature of the captain's authority and the ways in which he wielded power could increase the activity of the press gang, which would provide additional opportunity and incentive for resistance.

In addition to these preconditions, a combination of deep-seated beliefs and practical experiences prompted maritime laborers to resist British naval impressment around the Atlantic world. They drew on the ideals of

---

25. *New York Gazette*, 26 November 1770; *Pennsylvania Gazette*, 29 November 1770; *Essex Gazette*, 11–18 December 1770; *Boston Post Boy*, 17 December 1770; *Connecticut Gazette*, 21 December 1770.
26. "Vice Admiral Graves to General Thomas Gage", Boston, 11 June 1775, in Clark *et al.*, *Naval Documents of the American Revolution*, I, p. 656.
27. *Boston Evening Post*, 14 April 1740.
28. "Diary of Lieutenant John Barker", entry dated Boston, 8 February 1775, in Clark *et al.*, *Naval Documents of the American Revolution*, II, pp. 81–82.

the Levellers, a radical political group of the mid-seventeenth-century English Revolution that originally protested enclosure and the expropriation of labor. The expansion of the Royal Navy began under Charles I, and the use of impressment to man the burgeoning fleet drew the Levellers' ire and contributed to the outbreak of civil war. Eventually, the Levellers promoted radical ideas such as popular sovereignty, the freedom of conscience, individual liberty, religious toleration, and equality before the law.[29] The demand for individual liberty was especially subversive in a deferential, hierarchical, corporatist society such as seventeenth-century England. Individual rights threatened to subvert the top-down structure of society.

Throughout the 1640s, the Levellers defended individual freedoms in their opposition to the government's use of impressment. This was a collective defense of individual rights. "The matter of impressing and constraining any of us to serve in the wars, is against our freedom", they wrote. There was "nothing more opposite to freedom", or no greater form of slavery, Levellers believed, than naval impressment. For this coercion violated "every man's Conscience", and it brought "hazards [to] his life" on a daily basis.[30] Following a string of anti-impressment collective actions, the "Seamen belonging to the Ships of the Commonwealth of England" were made to explain the motives behind their riotous behavior to Oliver Cromwell in 1654. The seamen, like their Leveller contemporaries, stated that they viewed the naval impressment that had continued under Cromwell's rule as a form of "thralldom and bondage". The maritime laborers did not believe they owed deference to state institutions, including the government and the military. Rather, they viewed themselves as "freemen of England", and they understood impressment as violating "the Principles of Freedom and Liberty" which were their natural rights. For such men, the state's abuse of these rights prompted their collective resistance.[31] As a group, they were willing to defend individual rights against thralldom.

Levellers such as Thomas Rainborough were outspoken in their denunciation of various forms of slavery. During the Putney Debates, Rainborough decried the impressment of soldiers and sailors as nothing less than a form of bondage. He equated the forcible appropriation and distribution of poorer English laborers to overseas colonies with African slavery. And he called for

29. For more on the Levellers, see Michael Mendle (ed.), *The Putney Debates of 1647: The Army, the Levellers, and the English State* (London, 2001); and Hill, *The World Turned Upside Down*.

30. Don M. Wolfe (ed.), *Leveller Manifestoes of the Puritan Revolution* (New York, 1944), pp. 80, 95, 227, 287, 347, 405.

31. *To his Highness the Lord Protector: the humble petition of the sea-men, belonging to the ships of the Commonwealth of England* (London, 1654).

the end of the enslavement of Africans.[32] These arguments generated a language of freedom and helped build anti-slavery sentiment in England that reinforced and justified militant resistance to press gangs.

Although elites forcibly suppressed Rainborough and other Levellers, maritime conduits helped to spread Leveller logic beyond Albion's shores to the wider Atlantic world. Sailors on merchant vessels, privateers, and warships routinely carried news and information across the ocean and effectively established a systematic English Atlantic communication network.[33] Colonists living around the Atlantic world were made aware of Leveller activities and the events of the Civil War.[34] Captured Levellers were also transported to work and die on overseas plantations.[35] The ideas that they shared were passed down from generation to generation.

Radical Leveller language was expressed in colonial American resistance to naval impressment as demonstrated in 1769 by the *Pitt Packet* affair. The court proceedings and the newspaper coverage that this sensational event generated offer an uncommon window into the radical motivations behind workers' resistance to impressment in colonial America just prior to the Revolution.[36]

Like the Levellers, Corbet and his mates collectively believed impressment into British naval service was a form of state-sponsored slavery, and that they were fighting for nothing less than their liberty from oppressive authority. James McGlocklin, a cook who worked with the Irish-American mariners, testified that Corbet and his mates responded to the press gang's command to come up on deck by stating "they were Freemen born free, and would not go aboard a Man of War".[37] James Siley, a British marine, and a member of the press gang, and John Roney, the master mariner on the *Pitt Packet*, both testified they heard Corbet and his mates "say they wanted nothing but their Liberty".[38] Peter Bowen and William Peacock, midshipmen on the British warship, testified

---

32. Linebaugh and Rediker, *The Many-Headed Hydra*, ch. 4, esp. pp. 109–111.

33. Ian K. Steele, *The English Atlantic, 1675–1740: An Exploration of Communication and Community* (London, 1986). For more on the particular role sailors played in this communication network, see Julius S. Scott, "Afro-American Sailors and the International Communication Network: The Case of Newport Bowers", in Colin Howell and Richard Twomey (eds), *Jack Tar in History: Essays in the History of Maritime Life and Labour* (Fredericton, NB, 1991), pp. 37–52.

34. See Carla Gardina Pestana, *The English Atlantic in an Age of Revolution, 1640–1661* (Cambridge, MA, 2007).

35. Linebaugh and Rediker, *The Many-Headed Hydra*, ch. 4.

36. For the proceedings of the Vice Admiralty court that tried the Marblehead mariners, see Wroth and Zobel, *Legal Papers of John Adams*, II, pp. 275–335. For newspaper coverage of this event, see Dickerson, *Boston Under Military Rule*, pp. 94–95, 104–105.

37. Wroth and Zobel, *Legal Papers of John Adams*, II, p. 320.

38. *Ibid.*, pp. 309, 319.

Corbet and his mates "said they were resolved to die, sooner than be pressed on Board a Man of War".[39] It was reported in a New York newspaper that:

> This Outrage of the Press Gang, so far from intimidating, increased the Reso-
> lution of the Men to die, rather than surrender themselves to such a lawless
> Banditti; and indeed their whole Conduct seemed to manifest an Abhorrence of
> being forced on board a Man of War, and that they preferred death to such a Life
> as they deemed Slavery.[40]

Patrick Henry was not the only colonist to maintain a liberty-or-death ethos. Thomas Hutchinson, Royal Governor of Massachusetts, wrote that "The seamen had shut themselves up in the fore peak, and had furnished themselves with harpoons, and other weapons [...] and swore they would die before they would be taken, and that they preferred death to slavery."[41]

Freedom and liberty were deeply ingrained in eighteenth-century American seafarers' lexicon, no less than in Levellers' hearts. A Massachusetts newspaper reported that at the start of 1769 mariners in Boston referred to British warships as "wooden prisons".[42] Christopher Prince, a Massachusetts mariner pressed into the British navy at the start of the Revolutionary War similarly referred to life "on board of a British [naval] vessel and under the command of British subjects" as "thralldom".[43] For maritime laborers, resisting impressment was a public, radical commentary on the legitimacy of British authority that was deeply rooted in seventeenth-century English political ideas.[44] Militant anti-impressment collective action was not simply a localized effort to fend off a press gang. Just as the Levellers viewed impressment as an infringement of natural rights and an indication of the abuse of state power during the English Revolution, colonial American maritime laborers equated impressment with state-sponsored slavery prior to the American Revolution.[45]

39. *Ibid.*, pp. 294, 300.

40. *New York Journal*, 22 June 1769.

41. Thomas Hutchinson, *The History of the Province of Massachusetts Bay, From 1749 To 1774, Comprising A Detailed Narrative of the Origin and Early Stages of the American Revolution* (London, 1828), p. 231.

42. *Essex Gazette*, 7 March 1769.

43. Michael J. Crawford (ed.), *The Autobiography of A Yankee Mariner: Christopher Prince and the American Revolution* (Washington DC, 2002), p. 59.

44. According to Paul Gilje, it was only *after* the American Revolution that many sailors internalized political ideology and became politically conscious. *Prior* to the Revolution, sailors lived for the moment and their notions of liberty reflected very practical daily concerns associated with shore leave. See Paul A. Gilje, *Liberty on the Waterfront: American Maritime Culture in the Age of Revolution* (Philadelphia, PA, 2004).

45. For more on the ways in which radical ideas connected seventeenth-century English dissenters and eighteenth-century American revolutionaries, see Margaret C. Jacob and James R. Jacob (eds), *The Origins of Anglo-American Radicalism* (Boston, MA, 1984); and Staughton Lynd, *Intellectual Origins of American Radicalism* (New York, 1968).

Popular perceptions of press gangs were directly related to the ways in which workers conceived of the nature of government authority. Benjamin Franklin, a prolific writer, one of the most democratic Founding Fathers, and a man who lived in port cities most of his life, amplified the voices of maritime laborers on this score. Echoing the Levellers, Franklin wrote that impressment took away people's natural freedom. He emphasized that impressment was especially exploitative, as it occasioned "the Loss of Liberty and Hazard of Life". By using force against its own people, the British government had become corrupt and tyrannical. It was turning free wage laborers into slaves. In no uncertain terms, Franklin linked British naval impressment and the legitimacy of the British state: "If impressing Seamen is of Right by Common Law, in Britain, Slavery is then of Right by Common Law". Giving voice to the concerns of many, Franklin hammered home the old Leveller saw that there was "no Slavery worse than that Sailors are subjected to", because of the constant dangers of death. For Franklin, and for the thousands of maritime laborers whose shoulders he stood on to shout, any government that defended and utilized impressment "doth not secure Liberty but destroys it".[46] Repeated attempts to press colonial maritime laborers helped to convince colonists in and out of doors that their government had lost its legitimacy.

Impressment also raised workers' political consciousness beyond the shores of North America, helping maritime laborers associate British authority with tyranny. In England, John Stradley was pressed into naval service near London at the end of the American Revolution. Of this impressment, Stradley wrote, "I was stolen away [...] and locked down in the hold with a sentinel over me with a drawn sword as if I had been a thief or a Murderer". Upon finishing his naval service, Stradley wrote, "I got Clear of that miserable situation of a seafaring life [...]. I again rejoiced in my liberty and thought it a great happiness to be free from [...] the Constraint of Tyrannical Officers".[47] John Nicol, who was pressed into the British navy during the French Revolutionary Wars, referred to impressment as "a bondage that had been imposed upon me against my will".[48] On both sides of the Atlantic, workers were concerned

---

46. Franklin's Remarks on Judge Foster's Argument in Favor of the Right of Impressing Seamen, 1781, in *The Papers of Benjamin Franklin*, at http://www.franklinpapers.org/franklin/framedVolumes.jsp, last accessed 23 April 2013. For more on Franklin's democratic politics, see Gary B. Nash, "Philadelphia's Radical Caucus that Propelled Pennsylvania to Independence and Democracy", in Alfred F. Young, Gary B. Nash, and Ray Raphael (eds), *Revolutionary Founders: Rebels, Radicals, and Reformers in the Making of the Nation* (New York, 2011), pp. 67–86.
47. NMM, Copies of Volumes and Documents – Transcripts (TRN)/38.
48. Flannery, *The Life and Adventures of John Nicol*, pp. 162–163.

about liberty, and these concerns had a direct bearing on popular political perceptions of British authority and resistance to impressment.

Practical experience at sea informed collective resistance as well as deep-seated popular beliefs about natural rights and good government. Naval service was a life-or-death proposition that brought abstract political concepts home to poorer, uneducated laborers. Rigid forms of discipline, low pay, work-related hazards, and lengthy periods away from home all made warships into schools of hard knocks in which workers became politicized. In 1654, maritime laborers explained to Cromwell that their anti-impressment riots had been partially caused by the "great hardship" associated with naval service. This included death, wounds, and sickness: "Sea-men having sacrificed themselves [i.e. died in the line of duty]; and some of our limbs are mangled, and blood spilt [...] besides great diseases and distempers, sometimes occasioned through bad Victual".[49] These rioters were men with prior naval experience who resisted in order not to be forced back into naval service.

Feeding naval seamen proper provisions remained habitually problematic for the British navy throughout the early modern era.[50] Bad food continuously generated bad blood between naval seamen and the navy. The navy also gained a widespread reputation for brutal forms of discipline. Physical forms of abuse that included floggings were not uncommon. There was also psychological abuse associated with confinement.[51] Maritime laborers around the Atlantic world were also well aware that the British navy did not pay well. Massachusetts royal governor William Shirley explained this fact to Commodore Augustus Keppel in 1755. Shirley informed Keppel that it would be very difficult to man the fleet in Boston "for the King's usual Pay".[52] That same year, Captain Housman Broadly informed Vice Admiral Edward Boscawen "there will be no getting Seamen at New York or Boston to come up early in the Spring upon the Wages allowed in the Navy".[53]

---

49. *To his Highness the Lord Protector.*

50. One of many examples that could be provided on this score comes from TNA ADM 51/71/2, Captain's Logs for the *Assistance*, Captain Richard Edwards, between 22 May 1753 and 29 March 1754. Captain Edwards recorded in his logbook: 29 July the food was surveyed and "Condemned as not fit for men to Eat, nor to be Kept on board, being a nuisance to the Ship's Company". The rotten food was "thrown overboard into the Sea". For an overview of the British navy's logistical challenges, see David Syrett, *Shipping and Military Power in the Seven Years War: The Sails of Victory* (Exeter, 2008).

51. John Nicol noted various forms of harsh discipline during his eighteenth-century service in the Royal Navy; Flannery, *The Life and Adventures of John Nicol.*

52. TNA ADM 1/480, Letters from Admirals on the North America station from 1745–1777, Letter from Governor William Shirley to Commodore Augustus Keppel, Boston, 20 May 1755.

53. TNA ADM 1/480, Letters from Admirals on the North America station from 1745–1777: Letter from Captain Housman Broadly to Edward Boscawen, Vice Admiral of the *Blue*, Oswego, 15 February 1755. According to Daniel A. Baugh, an authority on British naval administration, the navy did not increase wages for seamen at all between 1686 and the start of the American Revolutionary War. These meager earnings appeared worse during wartime, when

This reputation preceded press gangs into ports, and it contributed to workers' willingness to resist impressment. Maritime laborers' resentment toward impressment thus represented the confluence of radical ideas and lived experiences. This resentment contributed to militant collective resistance to naval impressment.

There were, of course, peaceful, law-abiding ways of protesting naval impressment that did not pose a threat to the status quo in eighteenth-century colonial America. Even in the midst of a 1768 anti-impressment riot in Boston, local elites calmly held a town meeting and pursued formal avenues of protest. Town Selectmen, elected local officials, resolved to send a deferential letter to Massachusetts' Royal Governor, Francis Bernard, requesting that the governor use his authority to have the naval officer in charge of the recent impressment removed from the area. Naval impressment had been illegal in North America since a 1708 parliamentary ban on the practice. The town leaders then published Bernard's negative response in the local newspaper.[54] Elites held another town meeting and further resolved to send "instructions" to their representatives in the Massachusetts legislature.[55] The Selectmen even resolved to forward their protests to their lobbyist in Parliament, only to wait patiently for a response.[56] The goal of all these protests was not to upset the balance of the standing social or political order, but simply to convey dissatisfaction to the proper authorities through formal channels in the hope that superiors would be the ones to effect change.

There were also widespread, conservative sorts of crowd actions that American colonists could have employed in reaction to impressment. Humiliation by charivaris and rough music, for example, were common eighteenth-century communal methods of defending moral economies.[57] Theoretically, colonial American communities could have publicly shamed naval officers into submission. These traditional shaming rituals seem to have worked best, however, when they targeted community members, which excluded British naval officers in colonial America. By and large, colonial American maritime laborers did not adopt elite or popular conservative means of protesting naval impressment on the eve of

merchants and privateers doubled or tripled standard pay rates to attract workers. See Baugh, *British Naval Administration in the Age of Walpole*, p. 229.
54. "News from Boston dated June 20, 1768", *Virginia Gazette*, 14 July 1768.
55. *Ibid.*
56. *Ibid.*
57. Peter Burke, *Popular Culture in Early Modern Europe* (New York, 1978); Natalie Zemon Davis, *Society and Culture in Early Modern France* (Palo Alto, CA, 1975); Dirk Hoerder, *Crowd Action in Revolutionary Massachusetts, 1765–1780* (New York, 1977); George Rudé, *The Crowd in History: A Study of Popular Disturbances in France and England, 1730–1848* (New York, 1964); and E.P. Thompson, *Customs in Common: Studies in Traditional Popular Culture* (New York, 1991).

the American Revolution. They engaged in direct action to effect change themselves. They did not petition politely for contemplative consideration of a list of grievances, and they did not wait patiently for a response from superiors. They angrily demanded immediate change, and they were willing to use violence to bring it about.

Collective anti-impressment actions had common phases, just like shipboard rebellions. First, a core of a few individuals agreed to fight against a press gang that was known to be operating in a port. We know this because of the bounties placed on ringleaders, and the financial rewards that were offered for information leading to their arrest or capture. In the aftermath of the Knowles anti-impressment riot in Boston in 1747, William Shirley, the Massachusetts Royal Governor, wrote to the Admiralty to inform them that he had proposed "the immediate issuing of a Proclamation for dispersing the Mob, and Discovering and Apprehending the Ringleaders and others concerned in it". Shirley's proclamation included a "Reward to be given" for information leading to the ringleaders' arrest.[58] Following an anti-impressment riot in Deal, England in 1755, the Admiralty publicly offered "a Reward of Two Hundred Pounds for the discovering, apprehending, and prosecuting of all, or any three or more of the Persons who were *principally* guilty of the several Offenses aforesaid".[59]

The principals then formed a collective, which could range in size from a small group to several hundred maritime laborers. In June 1765 a New York City mob burned the tender of HMS *Maidstone* on the city commons after press gangs had swept through the colonial port.[60] It was reported that:

> Tuesday Evening last, about Nine o'Clock, his Majesty's Ship the *Maidstone*'s Boat was taken from one of the Wharves, by a Mob consisting chiefly of Sailors, Boys and Negroes, to the Number of above Five Hundred, haul'd up through Queen-Street to the Common, at the upper End of the Town, where they burnt her, in the Circle of the exasperated Tumult, which I believe every sensible Man in Town much regrets, and am persuaded was out of the Power of the Authority to prevent her Fate, as it was but a few Minutes from the Time of their taking her to her being in Flames.[61]

By comparison, there were only four mariners involved in the *Pitt Packet* resistance, in which Corbet was clearly the ringleader.[62] All such maritime collectives prepared for self-defense.

---

58. TNA ADM 1/3818/289.
59. "Letter from the Admiralty Office, dated March 24, 1755", *London Gazette*, 25 March 1755 (emphasis my own).
60. A "tender" was a small vessel attached to a large warship, used in impressment raids.
61. *Newport Mercury*, 10 June 1765.
62. As a member of the Marine Committee, John Adams recommended Michael Corbet for a captain's commission in the continental navy because of the leading role the mariner played in

Militant maritime laborers were willing to use violence to protect their freedom. They often destroyed the navy's property. Commodore Charles Knowles authorized press gangs to operate in Boston in 1747. Forty men were taken off the streets by force and chained below decks in tenders that made their way to warships as the well-documented Knowles Riot broke out in Boston. In this collective action, maritime laborers rioted for three days. A mob captured British naval officers, held them hostage, and generally seized control of the colonial port city. Colonial mariners even took and set fire to one of the tenders that belonged to the navy.[63] Similarly, Lieutenant Thomas Laugharne of the sloop *Chaleur* pressed five men from various vessels outside New York City in 1764. New Yorkers formed a mob and burned the *Chaleur*'s tender in front of the port's meeting hall.[64] One year later, a New York City mob burned the tender belonging to HMS *Maidstone* on the commons after press gangs had swept through the port.[65]

Then, in the summer of 1768, American colonists in Boston, Massachusetts, rioted following three consecutive instances of impressment. Repeated impressment had "raised the resentment of the populace", and united colonists in opposition to British imperial authority. The "people in town" were "in great agitation". Notices were "posted up in diverse parts of the town requesting the Sons of Liberty to meet at Liberty Hall". Sons of Liberty flags "were flying on [the] Liberty Tree" in Boston.[66] A mob of some 2,000 angry people, many of them sailors, dragged one of the navy's tenders from the waterfront to Boston's liberty tree. The mob conducted a mock Vice Admiralty Court and condemned the navy's property, then carried the boat to the commons and set it ablaze.[67] In each case, colonists collectively confiscated and destroyed British naval property – the hated tender. These vessels, like Charon's boat that crossed the river Styx in Greek mythology, were symbols of the separation of life and death. Burning these symbols, especially in front of a liberty tree, represented a powerful plebian celebration of life and freedom. Setting fire to a tender was akin to burning a larger naval warship in effigy, on a miniature scale.

the *Pitt Packet* affair; Phillip Chadwick Foster Smith (ed.), *The Journals of Ashley Bowen (1728–1813) of Marblehead*, 2 vols (Portland, ME, 1973), I, pp. 208–209, fn 4.

63. Letter from Governor Shirley to the Admiralty, Boston, 1 December 1747, ADM 1/3818/285. For more on the riot, see Denver A. Brunsman, "The Knowles Atlantic Impressment Riots of the 1740s", *Early American Studies*, 5 (2007), pp. 324–366; William Pencak and John Lax, "The Knowles Riot and the Crisis of the 1740s in Massachusetts", *Perspectives in American History*, 10 (1976), pp. 163–214.

64. Lemisch, *Jack Tar vs John Bull*, p. 27.

65. *Ibid.*

66. "News from Boston", dated 16 June 1768, *Virginia Gazette*, 14 July 1768; *Boston Post Boy*, 20 June 1768; *New York Gazette*, 27 June 1768; *Pennsylvania Gazette*, 30 June 1768.

67. "News from Boston", dated 23 June 1768, *Virginia Gazette*, 21 July 1768. For more on this event, see Hoerder, *Crowd Action in Revolutionary Massachusetts*, pp. 164–184.

Such militant behavior set these collective actions apart from more polite, refined forms of political protest that involved town meetings, resolutions, memorials listing grievances, formal avenues of power, and waiting. Moreover, crimes against property were especially prosecuted in Anglo-American parts of the world. As Peter Linebaugh has demonstrated, the Crown and Parliament became increasingly active in inventing capital crimes and prosecuting offenders to preserve property rights over the course of the early modern era.[68] Riot acts were also established to preserve domestic tranquility and protect property from destruction. Burning naval property violated this sense of propriety and these laws, and it did so in a very public and overtly political manner. Destroying the navy's property on the commons, or before government-owned town halls, was highly subversive in a deferential hierarchical imperial world.

Maritime collectives also arrested press gangs. A mob of maritime laborers in Norfolk, Virginia, forcibly resisted being compelled to serve in the British navy in 1767. The armed sloop *Hornet* sailed into Norfolk on 5 September, and Captain Jeremiah Morgan landed with a press gang of around thirty men. Morgan had received press warrants authorized by King George III legitimizing naval impressment. After imbibing "a little Dutch courage" at a local tavern, Captain Morgan and his armed press gang "proceeded to that part of the town resorted to by seamen". The press gang attempted to strong-arm American colonists into joining the navy. The gang had captured several men when the local watch raised an alarm, and a mob of around 100 port denizens turned out and forcefully fought off Morgan and his crew. The press gang retreated to the *Hornet* in the face of this resistance, but not before colonists seized 30 of the naval seamen and placed them under arrest in the port's jail for the weekend.[69] It is likely that the maritime laborers involved in this affair were members of the Norfolk Sons of Liberty.

American maritime laborers were also willing to use intimidation to defy what was popularly perceived as a corrupt British government. On 2 February 1775, HMS *Lively* sat at the harbor mouth outside Marblehead, Massachusetts. Vice Admiral Samuel Graves, commander of the British fleet on the North American station, had ordered "the *Lively* at Marblehead, to raise men for the Squadron", and Graves "directed Captain [Thomas] Bishop of the *Lively* to press thirty Seamen". The Vice Admiral acknowledged in an official communication that Marblehead was "a place extremely violent in supporting and carrying into execution the Resolutions and Directions of the Continental Congress respecting

---

68. Peter Linebaugh, *The London Hanged: Crime and Civil Society in the Eighteenth Century* (London, 2003).
69. "News from Norfolk", dated 5 September 1767, *Virginia Gazette*, 1 October 1767.

the Non-importation Agreement".[70] By this, Graves meant that Marbleheaders had gone so far as to impound some of his personal effects that had been imported into the coastal community. Captain Bishop then stopped privately owned commercial vessels entering Marblehead's harbor, and he ordered his Lieutenant, William Lechmere, and several of the *Lively*'s crew to press maritime laborers into naval service.

Lechmere faced stiff resistance. According to HMS *Lively*'s logbook, which Captain Bishop maintained, "At 2 a.m. manned & armed the Pinnace and Cutter sent to Marblehead to Impress men at 9 ye Boats retd with 10 Men".[71] Ashley Bowen, a Marblehead resident who had worked in the cod fisheries and on locally owned merchant vessels before becoming a sailmaker, recorded in his diary that on 2 February 1775 the British man of war *Lively* "pressed ten men out of the vessels in our harbor". But, Bowen quickly noted, "Our people got 6 of them back again".[72] The "people" who attempted to rescue the pressed mariners were most likely maritime laborers who worked in the port's commercial fishing industry. An observer described the activity involved in the return of one of these six detainees:

> The Admiral issued press-warrants at Marblehead [...]. At first the people of Marblehead had determined on rescuing any pressed men; accordingly, after Mr. Lechmere, Lieut. of the *Lively*, had pressed two hands from on board a vessel coming in, on his return he was surrounded by eight or ten whale boats manned and armed; he called to them at their peril to keep off, which they did at a distance of two boats' lengths; they asked him if he had pressed any men out of the vessel he had boarded, which he answered in the affirmative; they bid him deliver them up without making any resistance; on his refusal, they pointed their pieces [i.e. weapons, most likely fowling pieces] into his boat, and Mr. L[echmere] ordered his men to do the same; one of the impressed men took this opportunity and leaped overboard; Mr. Lechmere snapped his piece at the man, which miss fired, and he was taken up by the whale boats; the other man was immediately secured, and without further opposition carried on board the *Lively*.[73]

The other five Marblehead mariners were probably rescued through similar acts of intimidation.

---

70. "Vice Admiral Samuel Graves to Philip Stephens, Secretary of the British Admiralty", HMS *Preston*, Boston, Massachusetts, 20 February 1775, in Clark *et al.*, *Naval Documents of the American Revolution*, I, p. 98. For more on the 1774 Continental Association that the Continental Congress established and that local committees of safety and inspection enforced, see T.H. Breen, *American Insurgents, American Patriots: The Revolution of the People* (New York, 2010), especially ch. 6.

71. Smith, *The Journals of Ashley Bowen*, II, p. 427.

72. *Ibid.* For more on Bowen, see Ashley Bowen, *The Autobiography of Ashley Bowen (1728–1813)*, Daniel Vickers (ed.) (New York, 2006).

73. "A Private Letter from a Gentleman at Boston, Dated Feb. 19, 1775", *Morning Chronicle and London Advertiser*, 8 April 1775, in Clark *et al.*, *Naval Documents of the American Revolution*, I, pp. 93–94.

The resistance of the Marblehead mariners made regional headlines. Newspapers in Boston, Massachusetts, and Hartford, Connecticut, reported that Graves had "arbitrarily treated" colonists in a port "mostly dependent on trade and navigation". Two months before more famous events at Lexington and Concord, the newspapers maintained that this affair "must convince the American colonies, that had they not nobly resolved to maintain and defend their rights and liberties, the most insignificant officers of the crown would have been authorized and encouraged to insult them". The Marblehead mariners were held up to the public as ideal patriots "determined to defend themselves against these unjustifiable proceedings".[74]

Colonial American maritime laborers were even willing to kill to defend their individual freedoms. The crew of the American privateer *Sampson* fired a "volley of musketry" against a press gang from HMS *Winchester* in August 1760 near New York City, killing four British seamen.[75] In the case of the 1769 *Pitt Packet* affair discussed above, the four Irish-American maritime laborers banded together and fought against the press gang until Corbet grabbed a harpoon, launched the weapon, and killed Panton, the naval officer. John Adams defended the mariners and got them acquitted on the basis of justifiable homicide in self-defense. Adams believed that British naval impressment raids were more powerful in raising Americans' political consciousness regarding the tyranny of their government than the Boston Massacre, in which he defended the British soldiers. In Adams's words, "Panton and Corbet ought not to have been forgotten". The Founding Father added, "Preston and his soldiers ought to have been forgotten sooner".[76]

Impressment also contributed to various mid-to-late eighteenth-century mutinies. Indeed, resistance to impressment might be considered pre-emptive mutiny. Coerced military service enraged maritime laborers to the point that they were willing to violently overthrow the command of naval vessels at sea. In addition to the mutiny that took place near the Nore mentioned above, there were four separate occasions in which maritime laborers who had been captured by the British navy off the coast of Great Britain and confined below deck on tenders during transport to waiting warships rose up and violently seized control of the naval transport vessels.[77] On two other occasions, crews of privateers near

---

74. *Massachusetts Spy*, 16 February 1775; *Connecticut Courant*, 20 February 1775.
75. Lemisch, *Jack Tar vs John Bull*, pp. 13–14.
76. Charles Francis Adams, *The Works of John Adams, Second President of the United States*, X, (Boston, MA, 1856), p. 210. Captain Thomas Preston was in charge of the British soldiers who fired upon the mob in the Boston Massacre.
77. "Extract of a Letter from Portsmouth [England]", dated 26 May 1755, *Virginia Gazette*, 5 September 1755; TNA ADM 1/924, E. Boscawen, 21 February 1757; TNA ADM 1/920, enclosed letter to E. Hawke, 3 June 1755; and (1771) TNA ADM 106/1197/239.

London mutinied upon learning that their captains were going to allow press gangs to board their vessels.[78]

Such militant behavior struck terror into the hearts of elites, who feared a world turned upside down. William Douglass, a Boston physician, witnessed the Knowles anti-impressment riot and expressed his concern to the public that "this Tumult might have increased to a general Insurrection". He warned his readers that allowing the masses to overturn the social order, if only for a few days, posed the serious risk of mob rule or anarchy.[79] In New York City, a local elite writing under the pseudonym "Anti-Licentiousness" responded to the anti-impressment activities of the Sons of Liberty in that port city in 1775 by warning the public,

> [...] let us not establish the sway of a mob [...]. Many fellow-citizens have been deluded by the cry of liberty, which has been held up to them as the reason for these violences [...] so daring a violation of the good order and police of the City, so flagitious an insult on Magistracy, and contempt of the laws, ought not to be passed over with impunity; for let us remember, that the restraints of the law are the security of liberty.[80]

The fear sailors prompted in elites makes clear the subversive nature of their actions. Just as ship captains feared mutiny and the loss of their vessels, those with social standing feared insurrections that threatened their place in the standing order of things.

Maritime radicalism also inspired revolution. In 1776, Thomas Jefferson listed naval impressment as one of the foremost grievances Americans had with the British government in the Declaration of Independence. The Founding Father wrote that the British government "has constrained our fellow Citizens". These citizens had been "taken Captive on the high Seas". Like the mariners at Marblehead, Massachusetts, they were forced to serve in the British navy at the start of the Revolutionary War in 1775, and they were made "to bear Arms against their Country, to become the executioners of their friends and Brethren, or to fall themselves by their Hands".[81] Impressment had become a *casus belli*. Thomas Paine, the famous revolutionary firebrand, wrote in his widely read *Common Sense* that "the present mode of impressing men" represented a powerful, intuitive justification for revolution.[82]

In sum, maritime laborers were militantly willing to defend freedom against tyranny, the central struggle of what would become the age of

78. TNA, Records created and inherited by the Treasury Board, 1/392/1.

79. "News from Boston", dated 17 November 1747, *New York Gazette*, 11 January 1748.

80. "Letter to Mr. Rivington", dated New York, 19 April 1775, in Peter Force (ed.), *American Archives*, Series 4, 6 vols (Washington DC, 1837–1853), II, p. 349.

81. "The Declaration of Independence", at http://www.loc.gov/rr/program/bib/ourdocs/DeclarInd.html, last accessed 5 May 2012.

82. Thomas Paine, *The Complete Writings of Thomas Paine*, Philip S. Foner (ed.), 2 vols (New York, 1945), I, p. 11.

revolution. The motivations behind this militancy involved radical ideas and practical experience directly related to life at sea. Workers were willing to kill, mutiny, intimidate, and destroy property to achieve their goals. Many of the struggles against impressment were victories. Sailors liberated their "Brother Tars"; they repelled and in some cases jailed press gangs, demonstrating for all to see that freedom could, and should, be won and defended. By this process anti-impressment collective actions had a disproportionate influence on the larger movement toward revolution in the American colonies and beyond. Workers' militancy gave rise to the Declaration of Independence, not vice versa. Mariners thus helped to bring about the American Revolution and to inaugurate the world-shaking revolutionary era.

IRSH 58 (2013), Special Issue, pp. 153–175 doi:10.1017/S002085901300028X
© 2013 Internationaal Instituut voor Sociale Geschiedenis

"Lord of the Forecastle": *Serangs*, *Tindals*, and Lascar Mutiny, c.1780–1860*

AARON JAFFER

*Department of History, University of Warwick
Coventry, CV4 7AL, UK*

E-mail: A.Jaffer@oxon.org

ABSTRACT: This article focuses on the diverse body of seafarers from the Indian Ocean region known as "lascars". Very little is known about mutiny amongst those employed aboard European merchantmen during the age of sail. Private voyage journals and other sources offer scattered glimpses of demonstrations, strikes, and assaults on officers. Lascars used such tactics to air grievances, resist unpopular orders, and extract concessions from their superiors. They also took part in more serious forms of mutiny, in which they murdered captains, commandeered ships, and expropriated cargoes. The depositions taken in connection with such incidents provide an unparalleled window on to their working lives. Labour intermediaries known as *serangs* and *tindals* feature prominently in these various disturbances. The unique position they occupied enabled them to undermine European officers and even depose captains. Their involvement in shipboard uprisings serves as a reminder of the ways in which mutiny could be staged, manipulated, and controlled.

INTRODUCTION

There is now an extensive literature devoted to "lascars", a fluid term used to describe sailors from the Indian Ocean region employed on European vessels. Although sometimes used only to denote south Asian seafarers, it might also include those of south-east Asian, Arab, or African origin.[1]

* Research for this article was supported by generous grants from the Arts and Humanities Research Council, the William Edwards Educational Charity, and the Economic History Society. I would like to thank those who commented on my paper at the "Mutiny and Maritime Radicalism in the Age of Revolution" conference in June 2011 and subsequent workshops. I am also grateful to David Arnold, Margaret Makepeace, Michael H. Fisher, Gopalan Balachandran, and others who kindly read drafts.
1. For a discussion of the various terms used to describe different non-European seafarers, see David A. Chappell, "Ahab's Boat: Non-European Seamen in Western Ships of Exploration and Commerce", in Bernhard Klein and Gesa Mackenthun (eds), *Sea Changes: Historicizing the Ocean* (London, 2004), pp. 75–89.

Lascars who visited or settled in Britain have been studied in great detail.[2] Lascar employment after the advent of steam shipping has also received much attention.[3] Historians have examined various forms of protest and disorder carried out by lascars in a range of contexts, including ship-burning in Indian ports, rioting in London, disputes with the East India Company, resistance to missionary activity, attempts to combat discrimination, and discontent aboard steamships.[4] The existing scholarship includes some discussion of mutiny, although this has mostly been confined to incidents that took place during the twentieth century. These include protests by non-European crews during World War II and the Royal Indian Navy mutiny of 1946.[5] Much less is known, by contrast, about shipboard unrest amongst lascars during the age of sail.[6]

This article focuses on episodes of lascar mutiny which occurred on sailing ships from the late eighteenth to the mid-nineteenth century. During this period lascars were to be found on a range of different vessels, including slavers, whalers, convict transports, and warships. The most widespread use of lascar crews, however, was on British merchantmen trading to Indian Ocean ports. East India Company ships, which made the long voyage between Britain and India, were forced to hire lascars in order to replace the huge numbers of European sailors lost to disease,

2. Conrad Dixon, "Lascars: The Forgotten Seamen", in Rosemary Ommer and Gerald Panting (eds), *Working Men Who Got Wet: Proceedings of the Fourth Conference on the Atlantic Canada Shipping Project, July 24–July 26, 1980* (St John's, NF, 1980), pp. 265–281; Rozina Visram, *Ayahs, Lascars and Princes: Indians in Britain 1700–1947* (London, 1986); Michael H. Fisher, *Counterflows to Colonialism: Indian Travellers and Settlers in Britain 1600–1857* (Delhi, 2004).

3. Ravi Ahuja, "Networks of Subordination – Networks of the Subordinated: The Ordered Spaces of South Asian Maritime Labour in an Age of Imperialism (c. 1890–1947)", in Ashwini Tambe and Harald Fischer-Tiné (eds), *The Limits of British Colonial Control in South Asia: Spaces of Disorder in the Indian Ocean Region* (Abingdon, 2009), pp. 13–48; Gopalan Balachandran, *Globalizing Labour?: Indian Seafarers and World Shipping, c.1870–1945* (Delhi, 2012).

4. Michael H. Fisher, "Finding Lascar 'Wilful Incendiarism': British Ship–Burning Panic and Indian Maritime Labour in the Indian Ocean", *South Asia*, 35 (2012), pp. 596–623; Shompa Lahiri, "Contested Relations: The East India Company and Lascars in London", in H.V. Bowen, Margarette Lincoln, and Nigel Rigby (eds), *The Worlds of the East India Company* (Woodbridge, 2002), pp. 169–181; Shompa Lahiri, "Patterns of Resistance: Indian Seamen in Imperial Britain", in Anne J. Kershen (ed.), *Language, Labour and Migration* (Aldershot, 2000), pp. 155–178; M. Sherwood, "Lascar Struggles Against Discrimination in Britain 1923–45: The Work of N.J. Upadhyaya and Surat Alley", *Mariner's Mirror*, 90 (2004), pp. 438–455; Balachandran, *Globalizing Labour?*, ch. 6.

5. Tony Lane, *The Merchant Seamen's War* (Manchester, 1990), ch. 7; Dipak Kumar Das, *Revisiting Talwar: A Study in the Royal Indian Navy Uprising of February 1946* (Delhi, 1993).

6. For a description of unrest aboard the *Lady Campbell*, see Amitav Ghosh, "Of Fanás and Forecastles: The Indian Ocean and Some Lost Languages of the Age of Sail", *Economic and Political Weekly*, 43 (2008), pp. 56–62, 60–62.

impressment, and desertion.[7] Country ships or privately owned vessels which traded between Asian ports also relied heavily on lascars, typically employing a small number of European officers to manage a predominantly lascar crew.[8] The lascars who worked aboard these vessels are often over-looked in the existing literature because many never left the Indian Ocean region. It is impossible to determine exactly how many lascars were employed aboard British ships at any one time. A conservative estimate put this figure at between 10,000 and 12,000 in 1855.[9]

Lascars served under their own petty officers. The most important of these was the *serang*, whose duties corresponded to those of a boatswain. He was usually assisted by one or more *tindals*, who acted as boatswain's mates and were headed by a *burra-tindal*. These intermediary figures have been the subject of much discussion amongst historians of maritime labour. Gopalan Balachandran and Ravi Ahuja have provided particularly wide-ranging studies of their activities as recruiters, disciplinarians, creditors, and trade unionists during the era of steam shipping. This has shed light on the problems they caused their employers, the ways in which they were portrayed by contemporaries, and the limits of their power.[10]

The role that *serangs* and *tindals* played in unrest on board sailing vessels remains unexplored. After discussing the position such figures occupied on board ship, this article examines their involvement in various types of mutiny. These included commonplace confrontations with officers, as well as more serious forms of shipboard uprising.

SERANGS AND *TINDALS* ABOARD SAILING VESSELS

Serangs and *tindals* enjoyed various privileges aboard merchantmen. Above all, they were given much higher wages than their subordinates. Lascars shipping out of Bombay, for example, received Rs 7 per month at the end of the eighteenth century, whereas *tindals* were paid Rs. 10–12 and *serangs* Rs 20.[11] Some travellers claimed that *serangs* also wore visible

---

7. Michael H. Fisher, "Working across the Seas: Indian Maritime Labourers in India, Britain, and in Between, 1600–1857", *International Review of Social History*, 51 (2006), Supplement, pp. 21–45, 26.

8. Anne Bulley, *The Bombay Country Ships, 1790–1833* (Richmond, 2000), ch. 13.

9. Visram, *Ayahs, Lascars and Princes*, pp. 52–53.

10. Gopalan Balachandran, "Searching for the *Sardar*: The State, Pre-Capitalist Institutions, and Human Agency in the Maritime Labour Market, Calcutta, 1880–1935", in Burton Stein and Sanjay Subrahmanyam (eds), *Institutions and Economic Change in South Asia* (Delhi, 1996), pp. 206–236; Ravi Ahuja, "Mobility and Containment: The Voyages of South Asian Seamen, c. 1900–1960", *International Review of Social History*, 51 (2006), Supplement, pp. 111–141, 132–137.

11. Bulley, *Bombay Country Ships*, p. 234.

symbols of their rank.[12] Herman Melville described a flamboyantly dressed *serang* aboard a fictional country ship in *Redburn*, who "was arrayed in a red army-coat, brilliant with gold lace, a cocked hat, and drawn sword".[13] Regrettably, few visual representations of lascars have survived from the age of sail. One rare exception, a set of watercolours produced by Robert Temple in the early nineteenth century, depicts a well-robed *serang* (Figure 1) and a more modestly clad, barefoot lascar (Figure 2).[14] The allocation of space may have been another marker of status amongst lascar crews. George Earl, an experienced seafarer, wrote of lascars who "always sleep on deck, as the small forecastle appropriated to their use will scarcely contain their boxes, and if any space should be left, it is monopolized by the serang".[15]

Language barriers between officers and lascars rendered the use of intermediaries particularly important. Some Europeans managed to become proficient in the languages of their crews. Seasoned captains, such as John Adolphus Pope, became adept linguists who were able to issue complex orders to their lascars.[16] Using Roebuck's fascinating dictionary and phrase-book, Amitav Ghosh has explored the unique lexicon that emerged during such encounters.[17] Despite cases of adaptation, however, complaints about the difficulties of communicating with lascars were very common. When James Innes was travelling as a supercargo along the coast of China in 1836 he became irate at the situation aboard the *Fairy*. He complained that "we have six Manila men who cannot speak one word of anything except bastard Span[ish], we have eight Lascars who know nothing of anything except Bengalee, our mates and app[rentice]s speak solely English".[18] *Serangs* and *tindals* were employed to bridge these linguistic divides. On board some vessels they would have been the only lascars able to communicate with the captain.[19]

12. James Wathen, *Journal of a Voyage, in 1811 and 1812, to Madras and China; Returning by the Cape of Good and St. Helena in the H.C.S. the Hope, Capt. James Pendergrass* (London, 1814), p. 10.

13. Herman Melville, *Redburn: His First Voyage*, 2 vols (London, 1849), II, p. 22.

14. Robert Temple, "Serang, or Cockswain of a Bombay Pilot Boat", "A Klassee, Sailor" (1810–1811), watercolours, WD315, British Library, London [hereafter BL].

15. George Windsor Earl, *The Eastern Seas, or Voyages and Adventures in the Indian Archipelago, in 1832-33-34, Comprising a Tour of the Island of Java – visits to Borneo, the Malay Peninsula, Siam, &c.; also an Account of the present State of Singapore, with Observations on the Commercial Resources of the Archipelago* (London, 1837), p. 82.

16. Anne Bulley, *Free Mariner: John Adolphus Pope in the East Indies, 1786–1821* (London, 1992), p. 58.

17. Ghosh, "Of Fanás and Forecastles", pp. 58–60; Thomas Roebuck, *An English and Hindoostanee Naval Dictionary of Technical Terms and Sea Phrases, As Also The Various Words of Command Given In Working a Ship, &c. With Many Sentences Of Great Use At Sea; To Which Is Prefixed A Short Grammar Of The Hindoostanee Language* (Calcutta, 1811).

18. James Innes, "Diary of James Innes" (1833–1834), 19 December 1833, MS JM/A7/231, Cambridge University Library [hereafter CUL].

19. Balachandran, "Searching for the *Sardar*", p. 210.

Figure 1. *Serang,* or cockswain of a Bombay pilot boat.
The British Library Board, D40013-59 WD 315 no.59. Used with permission.

The position occupied by *serangs* and *tindals* could vary considerably from ship to ship. The area of discipline is particularly representative of this. Lascar petty officers were entrusted with the task of punishing their sub-ordinates, preventing them from deserting, and containing unrest.[20] The customary response to any disturbance amongst lascars would have been to call one of these figures on deck. Those who remained loyal to their employers featured prominently in the suppression of mutiny. When two Malay lascars belonging to the *Sagor* began stabbing their shipmates in 1826, the ship's *serang* was summoned immediately. He failed to stop the muti-neers throwing the captain overboard but was the only member of the ship's company to offer them any resistance.[21]

For every captain who allowed his *serang* to be "lord of the forecastle", however, there were others who chose to interfere.[22] Friction between Europeans and lascar petty officers could result from differing approaches to punishment. Captain George Bayly, for example, described the steps he took when he found one of his *tindals* beating some new recruits: "I called the Tindal and told him I had not been accustomed to see the rope's end at work on board of my Ship and gave orders that the scene of the evening should never be repeated."[23]

The use of violence by *serangs* and *tindals* undoubtedly provoked resistance amongst their subordinates, although this rarely appears in the archives. As Ahuja states, "there were probably numerous instances when lascars clashed with serangs [...]. Such conflicts usually remained unrecorded as most of them were resolved or suppressed informally on board ship."[24] A diary kept aboard the *Lady Campbell*, an East Indiaman travelling to Calcutta in 1825, provides a rare example of such con-frontations. Robert Ramsay, the author, described how:

> [...] the Serang [...] having ordered one of his men to work, on the man's refusing, struck him, the man resented it, and a contest ensued; the 1st Mate gave the Serang a rope's end and desired him to beat the man, which was done, the Serang treating him over the head & face; the man caught the Serang by the hair, which was coiled up on his head, and pulled him by it.[25]

---

20. Ahuja, "Mobility and Containment", pp. 135–136.

21. Evidence of Marco Muntro, 14 September 1826, Proceedings of a Court Martial on two Malays reputed to have murdered Mr Langley, owner of the *Sagor*, and a lascar, Home Miscellaneous [hereafter HM], H/669, p. 603, India Office Records [hereafter IOR], BL.

22. *Colburn's United Service Magazine and Naval and Military Journal*, 3 vols (London, 1847), II, p. 115.

23. Quoted in Pamela Statham and Rica Erickson (eds), *A Life on the Ocean Wave: The Journals of Captain George Bayly, 1824–1844* (Carlton South, VIC, 1998), p. 246.

24. Ahuja, "Mobility and Containment", p. 135.

25. Robert Ramsay, "Journal of a Voyage from Gravesend to Calcutta by a Cadet in 1825", 3 January 1825, JOD/5, National Maritime Museum, London [hereafter NMM].

The *tindal* made no attempt to assist his superior during this scuffle, as was his duty, causing the mate to reprimand him for his conduct. His retort hints at another threat to the authority of serangs. According to Ramsay, "the Tindal replied it was not his business, that the Serang was in the wrong; and that he was not a countryman of the Serang's".[26] *Serangs* often had problems managing the diverse crews under their supervision and could easily fall victim to groups of lascars who shared a common background.[27]

The financial control that the *serang* sometimes exercised over his lascars has been discussed in great detail. As has been shown, it was customary for him to take charge of a crew's wages and pay them after making his own deductions, a practice which gave him considerable opportunity to swindle his subordinates. Many *serangs* also maintained complex ties of debt with their lascars.[28] Only occasionally are we given an insight into the ways in which these relationships affected the maintenance of order on board sailing vessels. A commander named Andrew Cheyne, for example, implied that the *serang*'s position as creditor could be used as a lever to undermine the authority of the captain. During a trading voyage in 1843 he accused one of his lascars of theft, claiming that the man had "at the Serang's suggestion broken open my desk, and abstracted 20 dollars to pay the Serang some gambling debt".[29] The corrupt practices of *serangs* were sometimes cited as a motive for violence against them. When a group of lascars belonging to the *Newport* killed their *serang* during a voyage from Madras to Penang in 1797, newspapers claimed that they had been defrauded by him shortly after joining the ship.[30]

Both the captain and the *serang* could play a part in the religious life of a crew. As was the case in other trades, the captain's spiritual outlook could have a significant impact on the tenor of a voyage. He could grant religious holidays, dictate what form of public worship took place, and forbid behaviour that he deemed to be immoral.[31] Captains of an evangelical bent may have used their position to preach to Muslim and Hindu lascars. A passenger travelling from Batavia to Dover aboard the *Bengal Merchant* in 1815 described the master's habit of making the crew attend divine service. In one diary entry he complained "that ridiculous thing of reading the Prayers of the Church of England to the Lascars, Chinamen, Malays

26. *Ibid.*
27. See, for example, *Calcutta Gazette*, 15 February 1798, p. 1; Evidence of Shaik Hussain, 6 September 1826, Proceedings of a Court Martial on two Malays reputed to have murdered Mr Langley, owner of the *Sagor*, and a lascar, HM, H/669, p. 604.
28. Ahuja, "Networks of Subordination", pp. 28–29.
29. Quoted in Dorothy Shineberg (ed.), *The Trading Voyages of Andrew Cheyne, 1841–1844* (Canberra, 1971), p. 293.
30. *Calcutta Gazette*, 15 February 1798, p. 1.
31. Margaret S. Creighton, *Rites and Passages: The Experience of American Whaling, 1830–1870* (Cambridge, 1995), pp. 102–104.

Figure 2. *Klassee*, i.e. sailor.
The British Library Board, D40013-50 WD 315 no. 50. Used with permission.

(unacquainted with the Language) again took place, and which in my humble opinion must tend to bring the Protestant religion into contempt".[32]

Religious concerns associated with food were often cited as a potential cause of conflict between lascars and their European officers. When Charles Nordhoff, the American journalist and writer, recalled his time on a country ship, he claimed that "so slight a misdemeanour on the part of any of the Europeans as handling any of their cooking utensils, or drinking from their water cask, would produce an instantaneous remonstrance".[33] Officers undoubtedly became frustrated with attempts to maintain ritual cleanliness. Storing food separately, keeping eating spaces apart, and allowing lascars to butcher their own animals would have presented many difficulties aboard a cramped sailing vessel.[34] Europeans also implied that religious strictures against certain foodstuffs had no place at sea. Captain Crawford of the *Investigator* expressed surprise at the refusal of Muslim sailors to eat turtle "even when in a dying state from the Scurvy and suffering under the greatest privations on board ship".[35] Other commanders are reported to have complained about the practice of fasting during Ramadan on the grounds that it hampered a crew's ability to work.[36]

Captains permitted their lascars to hold various religious festivals at sea. These involved feasting, music, and processions.[37] Anthony Mactier described one which took place during the voyage of the *Surat Castle* to India in 1797. The ceremony, which may have been associated with Muharram, featured lascars who "intoxicated themselves with Opium and wounded their breasts and other parts of the body with Swords [,] dancing all the while to the Sound of the Tom Tom".[38] The licensed disorder

32. [Anon], "Journal of a Voyage in the *Bengal Merchant*, from Batavia to Dover via the Cape and St Helena" (1815), 2 July 1815, RUSI/NM/162, NMM.

33. Charles Nordhoff, *Nine Years a Sailor: Being Sketches of Personal Experience in the United States Naval Service, the American and British Merchant Marine, and the Whaling Service* (Cincinnati, OH, 1866), pp. 228–229.

34. For a discussion of similar issues in relation to an earlier period, see A. Jan Qaisar, "From Port To Port: Life on Indian Ships in the Sixteenth and Seventeenth Centuries", in Ashin Das Gupta and M.N. Pearson (eds), *India and the Indian Ocean, 1500–1800* (Calcutta, 1987), pp. 331–349, 336–340.

35. John Crawford, "A Diary kept on board the Honourable Company's Surveying Ship INVESTIGATOR by J. Crawford, her Commander" (1818–1819), 9 December 1818, MS 353, National Library of Australia, Canberra.

36. Edward Thomson, *Our Oriental Missions*, 2 vols (Cincinnati, OH, 1870–1871), II, p. 38.

37. Alexander Gardyne, "Journal of the ship RELIANCE from Deal to Calcutta, 1827–28, kept by Alexander Gardyne, passenger", 16 April 1828, IGR/27, NMM; Edward James, *Brief Memoirs of the late Right Reverend John Thomas James, D.D., Lord Bishop of Calcutta; particularly during his Residence in India; gathered from his Letters and Papers* (London, 1830), pp. 1–2.

38. Anthony Mactier, "Journal of a Voyage to India" (1797–1798), 20 December 1797, RCMS 63/9, CUL. For a discussion of similar rituals performed by lascars in London see Fisher, *Counterflows to Colonialism*, pp. 161–162.

associated with such occasions may have provided lascars with a means of releasing tension. Whether they ever turned sour or got dangerously out of hand is unknown. As Margaret S. Creighton has shown, this was always a risk when allowing "Crossing the Line" festivities to take place.[39]

Serangs appear to have taken centre stage during many of these events. Certain ceremonies involved the *serang* leading his men aft to pay their respects to the captain.[40] "On the first evening the new moon makes its appearance", wrote George Bayly whilst in command of the *Hooghly*; "all hands dress themselves in their best garments and headed by the Serang come aft on the quarter deck, make their salaam to the Captain and Officers and return forward on the opposite side of the deck".[41] Regrettably, observers seldom described the manner in which these gestures were delivered or whether the occasion was ever used to surreptitiously insult the captain.[42] A passenger travelling to India aboard the *Reliance* in 1828 drew attention to the garb worn by *serangs* and *tindals* during a similar ceremony. Alexander Gardyne declared that the petty officers on board his ship "were positively irresistible, the Grand Turk himself could not have made a greater dash than did Serang Ally & his Vizier Abraham".[43] Although many of these customs reaffirmed the authority of the captain, they could also highlight his distance from the crew whilst cementing the *serang*'s position at its head.

LASCAR PROTEST AT SEA

Balachandran has argued that lascar crews aboard steamships rarely adopted violent or demonstrative means of improving their conditions. "Mutinies", he writes, "may have worked in certain circumstances on eighteenth century sailing vessels. But they had become unsustainable in the more regulated late-nineteenth century steam environment."[44] Ascertaining whether mutiny, or indeed any form of protest, was "sustainable" aboard sailing vessels is very difficult. Roebuck considered it necessary to include two vernacular terms for mutiny – *dunga* and *fusad* – in his dictionary, both of which were probably translated as "riot" or "disturbance".[45] To what extent they were used by lascars and how they were understood remains unclear.

39. Creighton, *Rites and Passages*, pp. 121–123.
40. E.g. [Anon], "Journal of a Voyage from Port Glasgow to Bombay and the Persian Gulf" (1828), MS 9594, p. 12, National Library of Scotland, Edinburgh.
41. Quoted in Statham and Erickson, *Life on the Ocean Wave*, p. 247.
42. Cf. David Arnold, "Salutation and Subversion: Gestural Politics in Nineteenth-Century India", in Michael J. Braddick (ed.), *The Politics of Gesture: Historical Perspectives* (Oxford, 2009), pp. 192–211, 206.
43. Gardyne, "Journal of the ship RELIANCE", 17 April 1828.
44. Balachandran, *Globalizing Labour?*, p. 266.
45. Roebuck, *An English and Hindoostanee Naval Dictionary*, p. 74.

Reconstructing the events to which these words were applied is hindered by a lack of available source material.

Acts of shipboard protest seldom appear in official documents. The logs of East Indiamen contain scraps of information relating to collective demands for better food, assaults on officers, and other disorderly incidents. Such entries rarely provide detailed information on these occurrences, whilst inconsistent log-keeping practices preclude any attempt to estimate their frequency.[46] Lascar unrest was sometimes mentioned in newspapers and official correspondence if it resulted in court action or was linked to a more serious disturbance. Collective refusals to work by the crews of the *Governor Raffles* in 1813 and the *Wilhelmina* in 1819, for example, were recorded only because they were the prelude to murderous attacks against captains.[47]

Private sea journals contain a wealth of information on lascars.[48] They often provide the best insight into everyday protest, since diarists wrote about mundane conflicts between officers and crew that would otherwise have passed unrecorded. Helenus Scott kept a detailed diary of the time he spent on the *Natalia*, a large Danish ship travelling from Bengal to Suez in 1779. The retired East India Company surgeon made numerous references to the vessel's lascar crew. He described the meagre rations on which they subsisted and accused the captain of being "a selfish ill bred fellow who thought of nothing but himself, his own ease, convenience and gluttony". He also noted the man's unsympathetic reaction when one of the lascars fell overboard.[49] Of particular interest is his account of a protest which took place towards the end of the voyage. Having been employed all day in the ship's boat, "the lascars [...] took sulk, threw down their oars, and refused to work nor would either threats, promises, or offers of money prevail on them to take them up again".[50]

As Scott's account suggests, lascars employed aboard sailing ships used the collective withdrawal of labour to express discontent and bargain with their officers. Singing may have played a part in this process. Lascars and other maritime workers across the Indian Ocean used rhythmic chants whilst rowing, loading cargo, and performing other strenuous tasks. As in other contexts, they were probably used to coordinate slowdowns.[51]

---

46. See, for example, the *Cuvera*, 24 March 1799, L/MAR/B/369A; *Arran*, 27 July 1800, L/MAR/B/520A; *Buckinghamshire*, 3 March 1817, L/MAR/B/18A, Ships' Journals, IOR.
47. *Calcutta Gazette*, 3 March 1814, p. 1; Statement of James Nicholls or Nicholas, 2 August 1819, Board's Collections [hereafter BC] 17222, p. 82, F/4/635, IOR.
48. Ghosh, "Of Fanás and Forecastles", p. 60.
49. Helenus Scott, "Journal of a Journey by the Red Sea and Egypt from Bombay to England, 1799", 10 May 1799, Scott Family Papers, VII, A2266, Mitchell Library, State Library of New South Wales, Sydney.
50. *Ibid.*, 23 May 1799.
51. Creighton, *Rites and Passages*, p. 131.

The inability of officers to understand these songs would have made them a powerful means of disrupting work.[52] Comments made by travellers also suggest that they may have contained obscenities or were even intended to annoy Europeans.[53]

Serangs and *tindals* were well placed to organize strikes.[54] They occupied an important position within the highly integrated system of sailing-ship labour and could obstruct the efficient running of a vessel by mistranslating instructions, refusing to relay orders to their subordinates, or simply commanding their men to stop working. This is illustrated by a work stoppage orchestrated by a *tindal* belonging to the *Centaur*. The incident was described by Jane Penelope Herring, the captain's wife, who made the following diary entry for 21 June 1850:

> Had a regular mutiny on board this morning [...] the man that was the first cause of it was told to do something on which he was incompetent & when apprehended he took out his knife [...] Mr. Blunt [the first mate] ordered him in irons when the [...] Tindal called all his men [...] & forbid them to work till he should be released, & as Mr. Blunt did not wish the work to stop, especially as Tony [the captain] was not on board he made him free at which they all went to their duty again.[55]

The *tindal's* victory was short-lived. When the captain returned to the vessel, the man was punished. In response to this, one of the other *tindals* armed a portion of the crew with bamboo sticks and led a brief assault on the officers.[56] This demonstrates the ease with which minor protests by lascars could descend into violence.

Serangs and *tindals* could play a key role in the process of negotiation between captain and crew. Such figures, as scholars have shown, acted as spokesmen for their subordinates.[57] Disputes over pay, welfare, safety, and other issues could easily become confrontational. When the *Bombay Merchant* arrived at Al-Mukalla on the Arabian coast in 1821, an argument broke out between Captain Hyland and his *serang*. They had reportedly been quarrelling for a number of weeks. According to newspapers:

> On their arrival at Maculla, the Serang went into the Captain's cabin, and asked for leave to go on shore with the rest of the crew. This was refused, the Captain

52. Ramsay, "Journal of a Voyage from Gravesend to Calcutta", 7 April 1825 (second entry, p. 85); Bulley, *Bombay Country Ships*, p. 228.
53. R.C. Oakley, "Journal of a Voyage from England to Bombay by way of Cape of Good Hope and back by Way of Egypt" (1828–1829), 19 October 1828, D/PLR/F52, Dorset History Centre, Dorchester.
54. Balachandran, "Searching for the *Sardar*", p. 210.
55. Jane Penelope Herring, "Private Journal of JANE PENELOPE HERRING. Being the Personal Log of a Voyage in the 'CENTAUR'" (1849–1850), 21 June 1850, Mss Eur C 925, India Office Private Papers, BL.
56. *Ibid.*
57. Ahuja, "Mobility and Containment", p. 133.

saying, that only one at a time could be allowed to leave the vessel. An altercation ensued, and several of the crew were seen assembled aft on the vessel's deck.[58]

The crew ignored the captain's commands, and what had begun as a request for shore leave quickly turned violent:

> [...] the Serang ordered the boat to be hauled up alongside, on which the Captain threatened to fire into her, if any one got into her and put off. The Serang and some of the crew laid hands on the Captain, who extricated himself with some difficulty from them. [The captain] then ordered the Sookhannee [helmsman] to bring up the irons to confine the Serang; the Sookhannee refused, and the Serang said they would put the Captain in irons. The Chief Officer then brought up the irons, which the Serang carried off, and going forward, armed himself with a broken oar, threw down some bamboos for the crew, and made use of strong language. The crew went on shore in the boat, leaving the Captain, the Chief Officer, and two others in the ship.[59]

Faced with such a complete breakdown of order and unable to secure aid from the local ruler, the captain decided to abandon the vessel and return to India with another ship. The *serang* took charge in his absence, sailed back to Bombay, and disposed of the cargo to the satisfaction of its owners, adding insult to injury by arriving before his former commander. Hyland labelled the incident as "insurrection and piracy", but British officials refused to treat it as such.[60]

Although it did not always have such dramatic consequences, the ability of *serangs* and *tindals* to incite violence could clearly pose a serious threat to the captain's authority. Troublesome petty officers could be replaced mid-voyage, although this depended on the availability of suitable replacements from amongst the crew.[61] Punishing such figures could also prove difficult. Gardyne described a mutiny that erupted aboard the *Reliance* when lascars showed solidarity with two of their *serangs*:

> After Tea this evening we were considerably alarmed by the whole body of our Lascars rushing forward & threatening violence. It appears that orders had repeatedly been given that they should have no lights after 6 O'Clock, this order they had, it seems, determined to violate this evening; the consequence was the 2 Serangs, or chiefs, were taken & put in Irons upon the Poop where they called up their men to a rescue who all instantly obeyed the summons, & a scuffle ensued.[62]

58. *The Asiatic Journal and Monthly Register*, XIV (London, 1822), p. 98.
59. *Ibid.*
60. The Memorial of Henry William Hyland, late master of the Grab Ship Bombay Merchant, 26 September 1821, Bombay Public Proceedings [hereafter BPP], 3 October 1821, P/345/65, p. 1887, IOR.
61. See for example Shineberg, *The Trading Voyages of Andrew Cheyne*, p. 293.
62. Gardyne, "Journal of the ship RELIANCE", 17 November 1827.

The captain decided to make an example of the head *serang*, who was flogged in the presence of the entire ship's company. All other lascars charged with mutiny were acquitted, apparently in belief that "the punishment about to be inflicted upon their Leader would produce the desired effect".[63] Whether this was a common response to unrest is unclear, although it is far from unlikely, given prevalent ideas about the status of *serangs* amongst their crews.[64] Although no attempt was made to disrupt the flogging, Gardyne implied that something of a tense atmosphere prevailed aboard the vessel for a few days afterwards. Awoken by loud noises in the middle of the night, he described his reaction as follows: "I was immediately on my legs with my hands upon my [...] Gun, supposing, (as I heard no wind nor other indications of a storm,) that our black friends in the forecastle had arisen to avenge the affront offered them on the person of Serang Ally."[65]

Serangs could exercise considerable control over what was communicated to the captain, hindering the ability of lascars to make personal appeals. This predicament was well expressed by a man called to give evidence at London's Old Bailey in 1857. The first mate of the *Dominion* stood accused of abusing lascars during a voyage from India. The captain sought to refute these charges and at one point implied that appeals could be made directly to him, alleging that "when the men had anything wrong, they complained to me". These words were contradicted by a lascar named Moyadeen. When questioned by the court about the process of airing grievances, he replied "the *serang* and the Burrah Tindal were over me; how could I go to the captain – it was the *serang* I should make the complaint to".[66]

Mutiny could provide lascars with a means of circumventing their petty officers. Successful acts of collective protest would have been dangerous without the collusion of a *serang* or *tindal*, but not impossible. When the *serang* of the *Charlotte Jane* ignored complaints made by his subordinates, they took matters into their own hands. The ensuing mutiny was recorded by Julius Berncastle, a passenger travelling aboard the 750-ton country ship from Bombay to China in 1849. Having worked all night in the rain, the lascars became angry when the mate ordered them to a new task instead of allowing them to eat breakfast: "one and all of them refused to go on with the work, and came aft in an insolent manner, to complain to the Captain, as it appears they had done to the Serang, without his giving a due

63. *Ibid.*, 19 November 1827.
64. Balachandran, "Searching for the *Sardar*", p. 210.
65. Gardyne, "Journal of the ship RELIANCE", 23 November 1827.
66. Evidence of William John Green, evidence of Moyadeen, Trial of John Greer, 26 October 1857, t18571026-1004, Old Bailey Proceedings Online [hereafter OBPO], available at http://www.oldbaileyonline.org

consideration to their reasonable demand".[67] This attempt by the lascars to express their complaint quickly turned violent. According to Berncastle, this was the result of a misunderstanding between officers and crew: "The mate, being the only one who understood their language, without going into the case, reported it as an act of open mutiny, pushed them forwards hastily, and several blows were exchanged. Their numbers being overpowering, the cutlasses were called for, not knowing how it would end."[68]

The mutiny was eventually suppressed by force. The captain's desire to punish those involved was probably tempered by fear of provoking another revolt. In a classic show of punishment, one of the mutineers was tied up in preparation for a flogging before being given a last-minute reprieve. The captain then addressed the crew's original complaint, promising that their meals would not be interrupted again. The *serang*, meanwhile, was summoned to the quarterdeck and reprimanded for ignoring the concerns of his lascars.[69] Faced with conflicting demands from their subordinates and superiors, *serangs* and *tindals* could thus find themselves in difficulty. As Samita Sen has remarked in reference to factory labour of a later period, the intermediary's peculiar position was "derived from the tightrope he walked between the employers and the workers – at moments of crisis he could be caught in the crossfire".[70]

SEIZING THE SHIP

Lascars were also involved in more serious forms of mutiny, in which they murdered captains, commandeered ships, and expropriated cargoes (Figure 3). These premeditated attempts to take control of vessels mostly conform to Cornelis J. Lammers's description of "seizure of power" movements.[71] References to such incidents appear as far back as the early eighteenth century, official records noting uprisings aboard the *Mary Galley* in 1713, the *Recovery* in 1755, and the *Tryal* in 1767.[72] Country ships appear to have been particularly vulnerable, since their commanders had few defences against

67. Julius Berncastle, *A Voyage to China: Including a Visit to the Bombay Presidency; the Mahratta Country; the Cave Temples of Western India, Singapore, the Straits of Malacca and Sunda, and the Cape of Good Hope*, 2 vols (London, 1850), I, p. 270.

68. *Ibid.*, pp. 270–271.

69. *Ibid.*, pp. 271–272.

70. Samita Sen, *Women and Labour in Late Colonial India: The Bengal Jute Industry* (Cambridge, 1999), p. 127.

71. Cornelis J. Lammers, "Strikes and Mutinies: A Comparative Study of Organizational Conflicts between Rulers and Ruled", *Administrative Science Quarterly*, 14 (1969), pp. 558–572, 563.

72. York Fort to Court of Directors, 10 September 1713, Sumatra Factory Records, VIII, G/35/8, fos 233v–234r; Fort William to Court of Directors, 8 December 1755, para. 145, Letters Received from Bengal [hereafter LRB], E/4/23; Fort William to Court of Directors, 31 December 1767, para. 11, LRB, E/4/28, IOR.

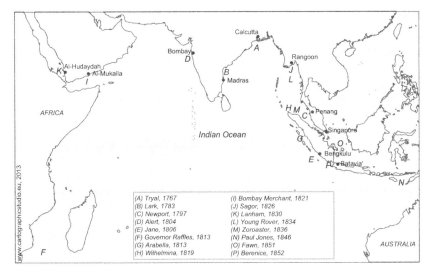

Figure 3. Selected ships with mutinous lascar crews.

sudden attack. Nordhoff claimed to have seen a structure resembling the *barricado* of a slave ship aboard one vessel – "stretching across from the mainmast to each rail, ten feet high, which was put up every evening at sunset, and abaft of which no Lascar was allowed to come at night" – but there is no evidence to suggest that this was a widespread practice.[73] Beyond their ability to take ships, the Indian Ocean region offered lascars a vast constellation of ports, islands, and kingdoms in which to shelter. Fugitive mutineers can be traced to areas of Hadramaut, India, Burma, Sumatra, and Java.

White sailors tended to side with their captains during these uprisings. They served in small numbers aboard country ships, and evidence suggests that many were treated leniently.[74] Nonetheless, collaboration between Europeans and mutinous lascars was not unknown. When several lascars were put on trial for attempting to seize the *Queen of the Teign* in 1853, attention was drawn to an English sailor named David Fairfold, who had failed to assist his officers in supressing the mutiny. It transpired that he had promised to help the mutineers sail to California once they were in control. Evidence given by the captain hints at how the man had come to be on familiar terms with his south-east Asian shipmates: "I had occasion to disrate Fairfold during the voyage [...] I sent him forward with the Lascars – he slept in the same part of the ship with the Lascars by way

73. Nordhoff, *Nine Years a Sailor*, p. 228.
74. Robin Craig, Ann Nix, and Michael Nix (eds), *Chronometer Jack: The Autobiography of the Shipmaster, John Miller of Edinburgh (1802–1883)* (Dunbeath, 2008), p. 28.

of punishment".[75] Accounts of lascars sharing plunder with Europeans can also be found amongst the records.[76]

From the 1780s onwards the East India Company began to keep increasingly detailed files on mutiny. Although these reports are often fragmentary, they provide an unparalleled window onto the working lives of lascars. Investigations involved taking lengthy depositions from captains, mates, servants, slaves, and suspected mutineers. Lascars touched on a wide range of subjects when interrogated, including their previous voyages, their wives ashore, their relations with sailors from other regions, and their dealings with Indian Ocean rulers. They sometimes used the opportunity to denounce their former commanders, complaining that they had been "unable to bear the beating and maltreatment of the Captain and mate", "irregularly paid, badly fed and often punished", or subject to commanders who "beat every Person in the Ship's Company for every trifling occasion".[77] Other lascars admitted that the lure of valuable cargoes of gold, silver, or opium had induced them to mutiny.[78]

Mutiny narratives are always difficult documents to interpret. As in other contexts, such testimony was heavily shaped by the judicial process.[79] Lascars concocted elaborate stories to explain their actions, made attempts to distance themselves from their former shipmates, and subtly altered the accounts they gave to downplay their own involvement.[80] The leadership of *serangs* and *tindals* was undoubtedly subject to exaggeration by their shipmates. Prosecutors, meanwhile, were under great pressure to convict those who were caught. Apprehending mutineers could be a difficult, lengthy, and expensive undertaking. British agents were often forced to use bribery and intimidation to recover fugitives.[81]

75. Evidence of William Tapling Stooke, Trial of Alie and Ahalt, 24 October 1853, t18531024-1116, OBPO.

76. The Declaration of Franciso DeCosta, 22 July 1783, Madras Public Proceedings [hereafter MPP], 21 August 1783, P/240/57, IOR.

77. Further Examination of John Henrick, 22 October 1834, BC 64350, p. 72, F/4/1581; Statement made by Pedro de Vas, 22 September 1836, BC 69433, p. 664, F/4/1724; The Declaration of Millapillee Niersemloo, 22 July 1783, MPP, 21 August 1783, P/240/57, IOR.

78. See, for example, Prisoner's Defence, 14 September 1826, Proceedings of a Court Martial on two Malays reputed to have murdered Mr. Langley, owner of the *Sagor*, and a lascar, HM, H/669, p. 604.

79. Kim A. Wagner, *Thuggee: Banditry and the British in Early Nineteenth-Century India* (Basingstoke, 2007), ch. 1.

80. See, for example, Prisoner Draman's Statement, 19 May 1819, BC 17222, pp. 13–23, F/4/635; information taken before Thomas Dunman, Justice of the Peace for Singapore, 27 December 1844, Bengal Judicial Proceedings [hereafter BJP], 5 March 1845, no. 164, P/142/29, IOR.

81. See, for example, Forbes & Co. to James A. Grant, Secretary to Government, 2 March 1805, BC 3486, pp. 34–36, F/4/182; Translation of a letter from Mr Pringle to the Governor of Suhar, 16 December 1804, BPP, 21 June 1805, P/343/24, pp. 3612–3613, IOR.

Officials bemoaned the costs of sending suspects to courts endowed with the necessary Admiralty jurisdiction to try them.[82] Faced with these obstacles, it would have been convenient to cast lascar petty officers as ringleaders. Only the better documented cases of mutiny allow a detailed examination of the ways in which they were able to use their position to depose captains.

Claims that *serangs* and *tindals* were able to bring about uprisings are difficult to dismiss. Evidence suggests that such figures could employ various means to incite their men to seize ships. When the *Jane* was captured by French privateers off Bengkulu in 1806, Captain Jansen relied upon his *serang*, named Ismail, and two *tindals* to retake the vessel. The lascars under their command appear to have been motivated less by a sense of loyalty to the British than by the *serang*'s promise to share out the ship's cargo.[83] After overpowering the French, Ismail and the *tindals* took possession of some gold dust that was on board and gave portions of it to the crew. A small quantity was even presented to the French sailors, apparently to placate them. Jansen tried to stop this redistribution, but was powerless to do so.[84] The incident provides a rare example of how lascars responded to conflict between European powers in the Indian Ocean, in this case by exploiting it to their advantage. More research is needed into this area, particularly in order to address claims that lascars were invariably "useless in action".[85]

Mutiny revealed the dangers of delegating the use of violence to intermediaries at sea. If a captain allowed one of his subordinates to become the most feared man aboard ship, he placed himself in an extremely dangerous position. Few cases illustrate this better than that of the *Lark*, a snow-brig seized during its voyage along the Coromandel Coast to Madras in 1783. Captain Dean's crew appear to have been in an unsettled state for at least a week prior to his murder at the hands of the *serang*. One sailor later made the particularly revealing claim that, during this period, another member of the crew had tried in vain to incite a mutiny. He deposed that "the Captain found fault with the Cussab [deck steward] for serving out more water than the fixed Allowance and struck him a blow on the Face [...] the Cussab thereupon called to the Ship's Company to assist him in his Defence but none came".[86]

82. For example, T. Parr, Resident at Fort Marlborough, to George Udny, President of the Board of Trade, 1 February 1806, BJP, 10 July 1806, no. 15, P/129/25, IOR.
83. *Calcutta Gazette*, 18 June 1807, p. 4.
84. Deposition of Monsieur Bernelot and Monsieur des Places, examination of Ismail Serang, examination of the Second Tindal, examination of the First Tindal, Monsieur Jenistreé's deposition, Monsieur Latoore's deposition, 5 January 1807, BJP, 19 June 1807, no. 51, P/129/36, IOR.
85. C. Northcote Parkinson, *War in the Eastern Seas, 1793–1815* (London, 1954), p. 343.
86. The Declaration of Franciso DeCosta, 22 July 1783, MPP, 21 August 1783, P/240/57, IOR.

The night that Dean was killed witnessed a similar confrontation. Shortly before it took place, the *serang* tried to embolden the crew by giving them alcohol. This was obtained from the cargo and served out in an almost ceremonial manner:

> [...] the Syrang [...] procured a Gimlet from Jack a Slave Boy belonging to the Captain and gave it to a Sea Cunny called Francisca [*sic*] DeCosta who went down into the hold and drew a small Tissal or pot of Arrack which he brought up to the Forecastle where the such part of the Ship's Company who were off duty drank of it & the Syrang sent the Cussab to call the others to come down and drink likewise.[87]

The *serang* then went on deck, apparently with the intention of provoking the captain. A boy employed as cook described what took place when Dean enquired about the time:

> The Captain [...] came upon the Poop and asked the Syrang how many Glasses it was? who said it was three Glasses but the Captain said it was only two and struck the Syrang a blow on the Face from whence he bled [,] the Captain and Syrang afterwards came struggling together from the Poop on the Deck where they both fell down and the Syrang called to the Ship's Company to assist him and the Tindal in the meantime flogged the Hands with a Rope commanding them to go and they accordingly went [and] seized the Captain by the Hair of his head [,] his legs and Arms and threw him overboard.[88]

Animosity between lascar petty officers and their superiors could play an important role in mutiny. Evidence suggests that *serangs* and *tindals* who had been humiliated by Europeans were sometimes able to foment uprisings as a form of retaliation. A mutiny which took place on board the *Fawn* near Singapore in 1851 was attributed to personal conflicts of this nature. Witnesses drew attention to a beating the *burra-tindal* had received at the hands of the mate shortly before the mutiny. The *burra-tindal*, who appears to have led the attack against the ship's officers, was reported to have pushed other members of the ship's company aside in his determination to find the mate.[89] As in the case of the *Lark*, accusations were made that threats had been used to persuade other lascars to participate. One account claimed that "the tindal went round to each man asking what side he was going to be on, threatening that if he was on the Captain's side, the tindal and his people would kill him".[90]

---

87. The Declaration of Millapillee Niersemloo, 22 July 1783, MPP, 21 August 1783, *ibid.*
88. The Declaration of Vaspillee Chimboodie, 22 July 1783, MPP, 21 August 1783, *ibid.*
89. *The Singapore Free Press and Mercantile Advertiser*, 12 December 1851, p. 3; *The Straits Times*, 16 December 1851, p. 3.
90. *The Singapore Free Press and Mercantile Advertiser*, 17 October 1851, p. 2.

Once in control of a vessel, lascars began overturning many aspects of established shipboard order.[91] Mutineers are reported to have destroyed logbooks, slept in the cabins of captains, and divided cargo amongst themselves.[92] Lascars usually executed their European officers, sometimes boasting to their shipmates about these acts of revenge. Crew members from the *Arabella* claimed that the lascar who murdered their captain in 1813 proclaimed "your Captain has plenty of fat, which I have let out".[93] Those who were spared were put to work about the ship. An English sailor from the *Paul Jones* complained that, after seizing the ship in 1846, mutinous lascars had ordered him to "wash down the Decks, and then to cook breakfast for them".[94] Rape may also have been used to settle scores during mutiny, as implied by restrained courtroom reports of lascars "lying on the Captain's lady".[95] The bodies of dead Europeans were thrown unceremoniously into the sea. What mutineers did with those of lascars killed during fighting is unclear, although a deposition from one case suggests that they were treated with more respect. A lascar from the *Zoroaster* claimed during interrogation in 1836 that "the Corpse of [the tindal] was removed into the Cuddy, placed on the Table, and covered with a sheet".[96]

It was not uncommon for *serangs* to take control of commandeered vessels, indeed some mutinies merely brought about a change at the highest levels of a ship's hierarchy. When lascars seized the *Alert* during a voyage from Calcutta to Bombay in 1804, one of their *serangs* appears to have adopted the role of captain. Having sailed the vessel to Al-Mukalla, he told the local authorities that all the Europeans had died at sea. An informant soon provided the British with an alternative version of events, claiming that "on the Passage this Sultaun Syrang with some of his Gang had rushed into the Cabin when the Captain and Officers were at Table after dinner and murdered them every one and assumed the Command of the Vessel and directed & disposed of every thing as he pleased".[97]

---

91. Cf. Clare Anderson, "'The Ferringees are Flying – The Ship is Ours!': The Convict Middle Passage in Colonial South and Southeast Asia, 1790–1860", *Indian Economic and Social History Review*, 42 (2005), pp. 143–186, 170–171.

92. The Declaration of Vaspillee Chimboodie, 22 July 1783, MPP, 21 August 1783, P/240/57; The Voluntary Deposition of John Parr Seaman respecting the murder on board the "Paul Jones", 25 November 1846, BC 120312, pp. 13–14, F/4/2319, IOR.

93. Examination of Muhummed Serrif, 6 November 1813, BJP, 19 July 1814, no. 6, P/131/42, IOR.

94. The Voluntary Deposition of Henry Gray Seaman respecting the murder on board the "Paul Jones", 25 November 1846, BC 120312, p. 18, F/4/2319, IOR.

95. *The Straits Times*, 16 December 1851, p. 3.

96. Statement made by Pedro de Vas, 22 September 1836, BC 69433, p. 665, F/4/1724, IOR.

97. Robert Henshaw, Customs Master, to James A. Grant, Secretary to Government, 20 December 1804, BC 3486, p. 3, F/4/182, IOR.

The ability of *serangs* and *tindals* to supplant captains was strengthened by the considerable sailing experience and "local knowledge" which they possessed.[98] Navigational skill could play a major role in mutiny.[99] Lascars were sometimes forced to divert commandeered vessels hundreds of miles in order to find refuge from British retribution. Those who seized a ship without being able to navigate soon encountered problems. Officials claimed that the mutinous crew of the *Tryal* had "continued a long while at Sea without knowing where they were", until they drifted towards Balasore and were caught in 1767.[100] Mutineers from the *Young Rover* were forced to go to their captain, whom they had imprisoned in the hold, to ask for advice on how to get to Rangoon in 1834.[101] The most daring mutineers made attempts to sell their plundered cargoes. When the *Lanham* was seized in 1830, her crew called at Al-Hudaydah to dispose of textiles and other goods. Suspicion was soon aroused by "the manner in which the Syrang [...] who now Commands her lavished money".[102]

Serangs and other leading mutineers may have mimicked the appearance of their former captains. As Clare Anderson has demonstrated, this highly symbolic act was a recurring feature of mutiny aboard convict vessels.[103] The case of the *Berenice*, a British barque commandeered en route to Sydney in 1852, provides a striking example of such behaviour. Having killed their captain, the crew sailed to Java but were soon caught by the Dutch. A detailed report was sent to the British, claiming that the "situation held by Ali, who was *Serang* [...] together with his influence over the conspirators, placed him, both during, and after the commission of the crime, at the head of the plot". Whether this was an exaggeration on the part of Batavian officials is impossible to determine, particularly without access to the original court transcripts. The report also charged him with dividing plunder, commanding others to wash blood from the decks, and ordering the destruction of the vessel. In a particularly damning passage, he was accused of aping the dead captain. "Chests were forced open, and the contents taken out and laid before Ali, who had dressed himself in the Captain's clothes and seated in his chair, telescope in hand, enacted the part of the Commander of the Vessel."[104]

98. Fisher, "Working across the Seas", p. 24.

99. Marcus Rediker, *Between the Devil and the Deep Blue Sea: Merchant Seamen, Pirates, and the Anglo-American Maritime World, 1700–1750* (Cambridge, 1987), p. 229.

100. Fort William to Court of Directors, 31 December 1767, para. 11, LRB, E/4/28, IOR.

101. Examination of Justo, 21 October 1834, BC 64350, p. 78, F/4/1581, IOR.

102. J.C. Hawkins, Commander of HCSW *Clive*, to J. Pepper, Commander of HCSW *Coote*, 1 February 1830, BPP, 17 August 1830, no. 4, P/12/53, IOR.

103. Anderson, "'The Ferringees are Flying – The Ship is Ours!'", p. 171.

104. Translation of a letter from the Governor General of Netherlands India to the Governor of Prince of Wales Island, Singapore and Malacca, 24 October 1854, BC 189636, pp. 3–9, F/4/2692, IOR.

Lascar crews were able to commandeer European ships throughout the last eight decades of East India Company rule, yet the scope for doing so diminished dramatically as the nineteenth century progressed. Sailing vessels could easily be worked and navigated by lascars, whereas the engineering skills required to operate steamships were closely guarded by Europeans.[105] In addition, safe havens for mutineers in the Indian Ocean gradually disappeared with the extension of imperial control over the region's ports, coastal territory, and shipping. The associated expansion of road, rail, and telegraph networks would have further hindered the ability of fugitive lascars to evade capture.[106]

CONCLUSION

Studying lascars as migrants can have the effect of obscuring the time they spent afloat and risks placing too much emphasis on the experiences of those who journeyed to Britain. Reconstructing mutiny and other events that took place at sea presents many difficulties due to the fragmentary nature of the available source material. Such occurrences were recorded sporadically in private diaries, ships' logs, official correspondence, and newspapers. These documents provide little more than scattered glimpses of shipboard life and its day-to-day conflicts. The most prevalent forms of mutiny were probably demonstrations, strikes, and scuffles with officers. It is clear that lascar crews used these tactics to air grievances, resist unpopular orders, and extract concessions from their superiors. Evidence suggests that such action was a familiar feature of labour relations on sailing vessels. Disputes arose from issues common to all seafarers, such as discipline and welfare, as well as from those which were culturally specific to lascars, such as ritual cleanliness.

Serangs and *tindals* could play a pivotal role in everyday protest. As was the case aboard steamships, their spheres of responsibility often overlapped with those of the captain. Their seafaring ability, linguistic skills, use of physical punishment, financial control over their subordinates, and their place in the religious life of a crew made them alternative centres of authority. This position could enable them seriously to undermine their European officers. Heading deputations, interfering with work routines, and inciting violence were some of the means by which they could disrupt shipboard order.

Serangs employed aboard sailing vessels were arguably amongst the most powerful of all labour intermediaries. Under certain circumstances, they were able to depose captains and assume command of ships. They were,

105. Kenneth McPherson, *The Indian Ocean: A History of People and the Sea* (Delhi, 1993), pp. 236–237.
106. Michael Pearson, *The Indian Ocean* (London, 2003), ch. 7.

of course, irrelevant to some mutinies and killed during others. Their leadership was also exaggerated by prosecutors and their former shipmates. Nonetheless, allegations that they could engineer crises, exploit disaffection to further their own ends, or use coercion to incite uprisings were not without foundation. Their involvement in shipboard uprisings serves as a reminder of the ways in which mutiny could be staged, manipulated, and controlled.

IRSH 58 (2013), Special Issue, pp. 177–196 doi:10.1017/S0020859013000308
© 2013 Internationaal Instituut voor Sociale Geschiedenis

"Those Lads Contrived a Plan": Attempts at Mutiny on Australia-Bound Convict Vessels

H A M I S H   M A X W E L L - S T E W A R T

Faculty of Arts, University of Tasmania
Sandy Bay, Hobart, Tasmania 7001, Australia

E-mail: hmaxwell@utas.edu.au

ABSTRACT: Between 1787 and 1868 a total of 830 convict vessels left the British Isles bound for the Australian penal colonies. While only one of these was seized by mutineers, many convicts were punished for plotting to take the ship that carried them to the Antipodes. This article will explore the circumstances that shaped those mutiny attempts and the impact that they had on convict management strategies.

Now confined in a dismal hole those lads contrived a plan
To take possession of that brig or else die every man
The plan it being approved upon we all retired to rest
And early next morning boys we put them to the test [...].[1]

It took four months for a convict ship to beat a passage from the British Isles to Australia. The fastest route hugged the coast of Africa until the Cape Verde Islands were reached and then swung out towards Brazil. After passing Rio de Janeiro, transport vessels altered course, swinging south-east out into the Atlantic to pick up the roaring forties – winds that would propel the ship and its convict cargo past the tip of Africa and across the Southern Ocean to Australia. While this route was faster than the alternatives, it had the disadvantage of placing the transport vessel within easy reach of South America – a continent where a man or woman might reinvent themselves. It was while off that coast that the ship was at its greatest risk of mutiny.

Yet the obstacles that would-be mutineers had to overcome were considerable. Every male convict vessel carried a detachment of at least thirty British regulars. A surgeon superintendent was also placed on board charged with maintaining hygiene and discipline. The ship itself was adapted for the voyage. A prison was formed below where the

---

1. Fourth stanza of the *Cyprus Brig*, a ballad celebrating the seizure of the *Cyprus* brig in 1829 while en route from Hobart Town, Van Diemen's Land, to the Macquarie Harbour Penal Station.

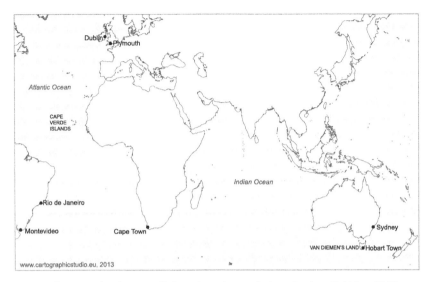

Figure 1. The route taken by Australia-bound convict vessels departing from British and Irish ports.

convicts could be secured in divisions, and hatches and other access routes were patrolled. An extension of landside power, convict transports formed a crucial link between metropolitan and colonial institutions. On board, conspiracies tested that link. While the voyage provided an opportunity to socialize convicts into their new role as penal labourers, those who plotted mutiny contested this process. Confrontations at sea thus had consequences on land, shaping both labour extraction and resistance patterns in convict Australia.

To seize a vessel was one thing, but to sail it was another. George Scantlebury and William Philip, convicts on board the transport *Argyle*, were accused of plotting to take the vessel when they were found to have an "epitome" in their possession. They admitted that they had used this small notebook to mark the ship's way – it was a habit that they had formed long ago, both men being accustomed to the sea.[2] Their fate was sealed when other convicts came forward to substantiate the charge. They were soon joined in irons by ten of their comrades all accused of conspiring to take the *Argyle* by force and sail her to South America.

Before being convicted and sentenced to life for maliciously setting fire to his own vessel, Philip had been employed in the coasting and foreign trade for twenty-five years.[3] According to a testimonial written by a former employer, during that time he had "carried away no mast, lost no

2. Tasmanian Archive and Heritage Office [hereafter TAHO], CSO1/539/11703.
3. TAHO, Con 18/3, p. 63, and Con 31/35, p. 64.

cable nor anchor". As a Mr Osborne wrote from Philip's hometown of Padstow, Cornwall: "He is a good sailor[,] an able mariner and a person I verily believe is deserving of encouragement".[4] Encouragement, however, was something that the colonial government was little inclined to extend to those accused of mutiny. Indeed, the recommendations that the Governor of Van Diemen's Land received on behalf of Philip and his fellow mutineers only served to confirm that they did indeed possess the necessary means to carry away a transport vessel to some destination beyond the pale of the empire.[5]

In desperation the twelve men turned to the *Argyle*'s surgeon in the hope that the man who had treated their ailments during the voyage might intercede on their behalf. Yet they were mistaken in thinking that the attention that Henry Brock had expended exploring their skin and gums for blotches and other scorbutic signs meant that he could be persuaded to extend his duty of care to non-medical matters. Now the vessel was in port, Brock informed the Colonial Secretary that the conduct of the petitioners had been so bad that he could only recommend their cases on account of the length of time they had remained closely confined in irons. He suggested that their punishment "should be as lenient as is consistent with the ends of justice".[6]

Indeed, if the truth be known, Brock had been alert to the possibility of a plot before the *Argyle* had even departed from Plymouth. He had received a confidential communication from the Naval Board "respecting a plan on the part of some of the convicts […] to Seize and take possession of the ship on the voyage out". The ringleader of the supposed plot had been prevented from sailing, but five of his fellow conspirators had been embarked from the *Captivity* hulk. Brock was instructed to maintain "an unremitting and vigilant watch", to make sure that the five were distributed amongst different messes, and to ensure that they were not exercised on deck at the same time. The news that it had been the "evil intension" of the conspirators to obtain laudanum from the hospital with which to lace the food or grog of the guard meant that the medical stores had to be particularly well guarded.

In the event, a similar communication had been sent by Horse Guards to Lieutenant Gillam, the officer in charge of the forty-strong military detachment. Both men were instructed to ensure that the "best understanding" was "cultivated" amongst all officers on board. As it was put to Brock: while "harmony of conduct and feeling is at all times due to the King's Service on the part of the officers serving in different departments,

4. TAHO, CSO1/539/11703.
5. TAHO, Con 18/3, p. 34, and the National Archive, UK [hereafter NA], ADM 101/04/05.
6. TAHO, CSO1/539/11703.

it is so in a more special degree under the circumstances in which you are placed".

Although it was Gillam's job to secure the vessel, it was Brock who was in charge of discipline. As well as attending to the health of those on board, he had to ensure that the ship was kept clean and orderly. The surgeon superintendent was thus ably equipped to play the role of government spy. He did more than just scrutinize the bodies of his convict charges searching for signs of infectious disease, lice, and deficiency disorders. He searched their belongings too on the specific instructions of the Naval Board, looking for files and knives, although he appears not to have appreciated the dangerous use to which Philip's epitome could be put. When on deck he watched the prisoners at work, secreting himself in the Steward's pantry, a place that afforded a secluded view of the quarterdeck.[7] He had also been instructed by the Admiralty to collect information "respecting the persons in this country who have been chiefly instrumental in the destruction of property by fire etc." – a reference to the Swing Riots which had recently rocked the southern counties of England.[8]

It may seem somewhat strange that Brock should be asked to lend his support to the task of "unmasking Swing", to borrow a phrase from Edward Gibbon Wakefield's pamphlet on the causes of the regional uprising.[9] While more than 480 followers of the mythical "Captain Swing" were transported to Australia, none were shipped aboard the *Argyle*.[10] As Rudé and Hobsbawm point out, however, there was a tendency in the aftermath of the disturbances for public opinion to draw a distinction between "Swing" the machine-breaker and "Swing" the incendiary. The former was generally seen as a disaffected rural labourer, the latter as an altogether more sinister figure. Arsonists generally struck by night. Their activities were not infrequently condemned by those who engaged in daylight collective protest who had something of an interest in disassociating themselves from nocturnal "outrages". This helped to reinforce the distinction in the public imagination between the misguided, disillusioned "peasant" – an object of some sympathy – and the itinerant criminal who by clandestine means sought to stoke the fires of rural discontent.[11] It was evidence of the latter that Brock was ordered by the

7. *Colonial Times*, 7 September 1831.

8. TAHO, CSO1/539/11703.

9. E.G. Wakefield, *Swing Unmasked, or, the Causes of Rural Incendiarism* (London, 1831).

10. George Rudé, *Protest and Punishment: The Story of the Social and Political Protesters Transported to Australia, 1788–1868* (Melbourne, 1978), pp. 114–115, and D. Kent and N. Townsend, *The Convicts of the Eleanor: Protest in Rural England, New Lives in Australia* (London, 2002).

11. E.J. Hobsbawm and G. Rudé, *Captain Swing* (Harmondsworth, 1985), pp. 201–202.

Naval Board to look for amongst the sweepings of the supposedly idle (and predominantly urban) poor shipped to Australia on the *Argyle*.[12] Any "authenticated intelligence" he gained through probing with words, rather than scalpel, he was requested to communicate in person on his return to England.[13]

Were the perpetrators of rural terrorism indeed strangers to the countryside? Was it "well-dressed men in a green gig" – or itinerant Irish vendors of leather straps – who sought to spread fear via the tinderbox before disappearing into the metropolis to boast of their deeds to less peripatetic criminal acquaintances?[14] If Brock ever found evidence to support the rumours circulating in England, then he appears, despite his instructions, not to have communicated this. After his convict informants had been disembarked in Hobart Town, Brock's card table and sofa bed were loaded onto a lighter. He had no immediate plans to return to Britain and, like many surgeon superintendents, sought to use his appointment to assist his own migration to the colonies.[15]

Brock's political masters are hardly likely to have been disconcerted by this failure to follow his instructions to the letter. After the *Argyle* departed the government received confidential reports from other quarters confirming that "the stories about strangers in gigs" were just that. The rumours were dispelled by the results of on-the-ground investigations, rather than those conducted clandestinely in the prisons and sickbays of transport vessels. As the report to the County Fire Office in London concluded: "in almost every instance, wherein conviction has taken place", the arsonist "has been a servant of the sufferer or person living near to him, acting under some motive of revenge".[16]

It used to be commonplace to argue that transported convicts were largely apolitical. As McQueen memorably put it: "it is misleading to clothe the convicts in the aura of class struggle since for its first fifty years Australia did not have a class structure, but only a deformed stratification which had itself been vomited up by the maelstrom which was delineating class in Britain".[17] They shared, as Robert Hughes emphatically put it, "other traits with *lumpen* workers, chiefly a loathing of authority". This, however, marked the limits of their political aspirations. As he elaborated:

> They played no role whatsoever in the radical disturbances of the day. Tribal loyalties could be fanatically strong among them, and they stuck together

12. See, for example, E.G. Wakefield, *Facts Relating to the Punishment of Death in the Metropolis* (London, 1831).
13. TAHO, CSO1/539/11703.
14. Hobsbawm and Rudé, *Captain Swing*, pp. 201–202.
15. TAHO, CSO1/539/11703.
16. Hobsbawm and Rudé, *Captain Swing*, p. 202.
17. H. McQueen, "Convicts and Rebels", *Labour History*, 15 (1968), pp. 3–30, 24–25.

against the peeler, the beak and the pink chaplain in his "cackle tub", as the prison pulpit was known. "The more you value your number one, the more careful you must be of mine [...] regard for number one holds us altogether, and must do so, unless we should all go to pieces in company." Fagin's words sum up the ethos of loyalty among thieves.[18]

Dickens's fable of life amongst an imagined criminal underworld is one of a number of tropes that have been employed to package the transported.

Some of the most powerful chains used to restrain and control those lagged to Australia were words. These include the term "convict", used to identify the unfree while simultaneously underscoring the extent to which their personal failings were responsible for their diminished civil status. Like plantation racism, "convictism" thus served to identify the transported as subjects fit for exploitation. It also helped to distinguish them from those who had arrived in the colonies as free men – effectively making prisoners less fully human.[19] Any attempt by the transported to challenge their condition merely confirmed them as at best ungrateful and at worst wicked and depraved. No wonder that they fiercely resisted the term "convict", preferring to be referred to as servants, bondsmen, prisoners, and even slaves.[20]

Convictism has cast long shadows. There has been a tendency in the literature to see the acts for which convicts were prosecuted while under sentence as indicators of their recidivist propensities,[21] despite the fact that overwhelmingly the charges laid against prisoners were what is technically called "status offences" – that is offences that could only be committed by those under sentence. Absconding is a good example. Those who were free could not be prosecuted under the same legislation. Even after the passage of the draconian Masters and Servants Act of 1837, they could not be flogged, ironed, and incarcerated in penal stations and female factories for movement offences.[22] This is critical since systems of exploitation are underpinned by sanctions aimed at limiting freedom of movement. Without the ability to move, the bargaining rights of workers are crucially undermined.[23]

18. R. Hughes, *The Fatal Shore* (London, 1988), p. 174.
19. For a description of how racism played a similar role in the plantation world, see G.M. Fredrickson, *Racism: A Short History* (Melbourne, 2002), p. 73.
20. H. Maxwell-Stewart, "'Like Poor Galley Slaves [...]': Slavery and Convict Transportation", in M.S. Fernandes-Dias (ed.), *Legacies of Slavery: Comparative Perspectives* (Newcastle, 2007), pp. 48–61, 56–57.
21. See, for example, J. Hirst, *Freedom on the Fatal Shore: Australia's First Colony* (Sydney, 2008), p. 64.
22. M. Quinlan, "Australia, 1788–1902: A Workingman's Paradise?", in D. Hay and P. Craven (eds), *Masters, Servants, and Magistrates in Britain and the Empire, 1562–1955* (Chapel Hill, NC, 2004), pp. 219–250.
23. See, for example, C. Crais, *The Making of the Colonial Order: White Supremacy and Black Resistance in the Eastern Cape, 1770–1865* (Johannesburg, 1992), pp. 125–146.

It has been necessary first to liberate convicts from the ideological shackles that have been used to set them apart from other categories of labour, before it has been possible to reconstruct the extent to which their actions provided an effective challenge to the state. The post-1988 reappraisal of convicts as transported workers has played a crucial role in this process.[24] As long as convicts were seen as members of a "deformed stratification" who led lives that were distinctively different from those of the working class proper, it remained difficult to see their brushes with the colonial state as anything other than actions that merely confirmed their criminality. Thus, Hirst sought to use the colonial careers of the transported Swing Rioters as a means of demonstrating the manner in which a convict's "disposition" was important in determining their fate. In his view the Swing Rioters were victims of circumstance accustomed to work "in the fields or village workshops". As such he thought that it was revealing that they had a remarkably "good" record of colonial behaviour. This contrasted favourably with the number of charges racked up by their more criminal counterparts. This, he concluded, provided stark testimony of both the fairness of the system of transportation and the recidivist tendencies of the majority of its charges.[25] The alternative explanation is that, as the Swing Rioters were disproportionately composed of agricultural labourers – men whose labour was in demand in the colonial labour market – they were better treated than some of their fellow convicts who possessed less readily utilized skills.[26]

Since Atkinson's pioneering work in the late 1970s, it has become commonplace to argue that convicts shaped their circumstances through their day-to-day negotiations with their masters and the state.[27] Yet, in contrast to the reassessments of convict interactions with their penal managers on land, the voyage to the Antipodes remains a largely unexplored space.

Attempts at mutiny on convict transports are said to be rare. It is the case that out of over 830 convict voyages from Britain and Ireland to the Australian penal colonies only one, the *Lady Shore*, was ever successfully seized. While threats and rumours of mutiny are said to have been commonplace, these have been attributed to a "combination of overreaction by the crew, boasting by convicts, and the intelligence – accurate or exaggerated – offered by informants".[28] While the notices placed in colonial newspapers have ensured a high degree of visibility for convict

---

24. See, in particular, S. Nicholas and P.R. Shergold, "Convicts as Workers", in S. Nicholas (ed.), *Convict Workers: Reinterpreting Australia's Past* (Cambridge, 1988), pp. 62–84.
25. Hirst, *Freedom on the Fatal Shore*, p. 63.
26. H. Maxwell-Stewart, *Closing Hell's Gates: The Death of a Convict Station* (Sydney, 2008), pp. 155–158.
27. A. Atkinson, "Four Patterns of Convict Protest", *Labour History*, 37 (1979), pp. 28–51.
28. A. Brooke and David Brandon, *Bound for Botany Bay: British Convict Voyages to Australia* (Kew, 2005), p. 142.

absconders on land, their would-be maritime counterparts accused of plotting to seize transport vessels have remained more difficult to identify.

The majority of those accused of conspiring to mutiny on the passage to Australia were sent to penal stations on arrival. Those considered less culpable were merely detailed to chain gangs. While inquiries were sometimes held in Hobart or Sydney, trials were rare. One reason for this was that there was considerable doubt about the authority of colonial courts to try convicts for an offence committed on the high seas.[29]

While the journals kept by the surgeon superintendents on the voyage to Australia can be revealing, they are often restricted to medical matters. It was, after all, in a surgeon's interest to downplay any disciplinary issues that might have occurred during the voyage since it was possible that these would reflect badly on the organization of the vessel and jeopardize the £50 bonus he was due for supervising an orderly passage.[30] While it has been argued that the threat of mutiny was inflated by the manner in which some convicts sought to lay false charges in the hope of receiving rewards that would ameliorate their own conditions, the evidence suggests that surgeons were wary about putting vessels into lockdown on the basis of unsubstantiated hearsay.

In line with the bulk of medical opinion then current, most surgeon superintendents believed in miasma theory – in short that disease was spread by the smell of corrupt or fetid matter. They thus placed great weight on the degree to which fresh air should be circulated through the prison. Regular airing kept smells down and helped to ensure that confined spaces did not become damp. It was for this reason that the decks were often dry scrubbed – water being thought of as an agent that promoted atmospheric deterioration. Surgeon superintendents also placed much store in exercise. This they thought was crucial to the maintenance of their convict charges. Security threats inevitably compromised carefully orchestrated hygiene regimes and were therefore unwelcome. Rather than taking convict informers at face value, many surgeons were sceptical about tales of plots. Joseph Steret on board the *Bardaster* went as far as to dish out forty-eight lashes to one of his convict charges "for stating that there was a Mutiny on board", when the surgeon's own investigations failed to find supporting evidence of such a conspiracy.[31]

Colonial officials themselves often found it difficult to get to the bottom of what had occurred at sea. On the *Eleanor*, a vessel that conveyed many of the 1830 Swing rioters to Sydney, the guard reacted to a sudden rush towards the prison door by firing and killing two convicts

---

29. *Cornwall Chronicle*, 10 September 1842.
30. C. Bateson, *The Convict Ships, 1787–1868* (Glasgow, 1959), p. 21.
31. TAHO, Con 31/2, p. 24.

and wounding two more. At the subsequent inquest considerable doubt arose as to whether there had been an attempt to seize the vessel. Some thought that the prisoners had surged forwards to acquire biscuits distributed from a bag.[32]

These caveats aside, it is possible to make a conservative estimate of the frequency of mutinous proceedings on convict vessels bound for Van Diemen's Land. A survey of 155 male ships arriving in the period 1825–1845 found evidence of a conspiracy on 16 separate voyages, a rate of just over 10 per cent. Since the surgeon's comments entered onto the conduct registers, the principal source of information upon which this survey was based, were missing for 43 voyages and were incomplete for many others, this is a conservative estimate. The rate on female transports was lower, although they too were not immune from mutiny.

The taking of a vessel was by definition a collective exercise. It could not be undertaken by a small number of individuals – something more than honour amongst thieves was required to set mutiny in motion. In this sense the very notion that convicts might seize a transport vessel was liberational in that it threatened the state's ability, not just to exile convicts physically, but also to strip them of identity. Thus, mutinous proceedings could have effects that were as contagious as any below-deck infection. As Atkinson eloquently put it: "when any single convict stood up for shared principle it was as if he declared (looking about him), 'I *rebel* – therefore we *exist*'".[33]

Rediker points out in relation to slavery that the ship was a factory in the sense that it produced a commodity for the market. At the start of the voyage it loaded a multi-ethnic collection of people. By the time it had reached its destination those that had survived had been converted into slaves.[34] A similar process occurred on the long voyage to Australia.

The first words that Surgeon Superintendent Colin Browning uttered to his charges on the *Elphinstone* were: "This day commences a new era in your existence."[35] Convicts were subjected to a system of regimentation from the moment they were delivered on board. They were divided into messes, grouped in turn into divisions, each under the eye a "captain" handpicked by the surgeon. Each division was bathed in seawater in rotation, ensuring that every convict got a cold dunking once every four days. At six bells all bedding was passed up on deck to be aired and stowed in the nettings. After breakfast two messes were selected to clean the prison. Depending on the weather, the decks were either washed and scrubbed or dry scraped with holy stones and sprinkled with lime.

---

32. *The Australian*, 5 August 1831; *The Courier*, 20 August 1831.
33. Atkinson, "Four Patterns of Convict Protest", p. 50.
34. M. Rediker, *The Slave Ship: A Human History* (London, 2007), pp. 9–10.
35. Colin Arrott Browning, *England's Exiles; or A View of a System of Instruction and Discipline as Carried into Effect During the Voyage to the Penal Colonies of Australia* (London, 1842), p. 5.

At seven bells the prisoners were fed and then mustered on the quarter-deck where the surgeon ensured that every charge drunk their draft of anti-scorbutic. At 10.30 on Sundays and Thursdays the prisoners were inspected to make sure that they were shaved clean. Clothes were washed every Tuesday and Friday. At other times the seamen and mechanics amongst the convicts were employed in tasks about the vessel and the rest in picking oakum – that is pulling apart strands of old rope, a task often reserved for prisoners.[36]

With the exception of the private cabins reserved for officers and full paying passengers, a ship was public space.[37] It was thus well suited to the introduction of industrial discipline. The surgeon appointed boatswains, or deck constables, on male vessels, and mess, or deck matrons, on female vessels to oversee the convicts at work. Such trustees supplemented the formal security provided by the military detachment and could expect a favourable recommendation on arrival in Australia. Many were former soldiers or were prisoners who were otherwise large and thus physically imposing.[38]

While the rituals of daily life on a convict vessel were crucial to maintaining hygiene, they had an important ancillary function in that they created "docile bodies". Just like a factory town, the convict vessel was organized so that every aspect of life, including domestic routines and leisure, could contribute to the wider goal of preparing the convict for a life of colonial servitude.[39] The ship, in this sense, was an institution – or, perhaps more accurately, a floating collection of institutions. Each vessel contained a prison, a hospital, and a schoolroom – spaces where convicts were regimented in preparation for their disembarkation in Australia.[40] Convict vessels adapted the technology and knowledge of both the slave ship and the man of war. They had strengthened bulwarks, supplies of leg irons and handcuffs, and hatches that could be guarded, but they were also spaces where industrial discipline could be imposed and effectively monitored. As floating institutions they ensured the continuity of power from the gaols and hulks of Britain and Ireland to the penitentiaries, female factories, and other sites of exploitation in the colonies.

That convict vessels were multi-functional increased their symbolic value. As well as resisting the process of being exiled, mutineers thus also conspired to carry an engine of the state off into the wide blue yonder. To

---

36. NA, ADM101/1/8.
37. G. Denning, *Mr Bligh's Bad Language: Passion, Power and Theatre on the Bounty* (Cambridge, 1992), pp. 18–34.
38. NA, ADM101/1/8.
39. W.M. Robbins, "Spatial Escape and the Hyde Park Barracks", *Journal of Australian Colonial History*, 7 (2005), pp. 81–96, 83.
40. J. Damousi, *Depraved and Disorderly: Female Convicts, Sexuality and Gender in Colonial Australia* (Cambridge, 1997), pp. 15–16.

put it another way, prisoners do not normally steal the gaols in which they are incarcerated.

Convict mutineers threatened to unpack themselves in other ways too. Navigational skills were crucial. While convicts might threaten to slit the throats of all on board, they were only truly dangerous when they transcended their status as prisoners. David Bracewell, described by the surgeon on the 1826 voyage of the *Layton* as "mutinous", and "a very bad fellow", was especially threatening because of his trade – he was a seaman.[41] Much the same could be said of the boatman Charles Ecclestone, charged with "using mutinous language to a sentinel". The words he uttered had more bite since they were issued by one familiar with his environment to a landlubber, who, though equipped with a Brown Bess, was otherwise literally all at sea.[42] It was, let us remind ourselves, the pre-transportation histories of the men aboard the *Argyle* that made them a threat. Their collective knowledge of the sea confirmed their guilt just as securely as it gave the lie to the notion that the transported were members of the idle poor who chose not to work, living instead by crime and crime alone.

In the case of the *Argyle* there is a sting in the tale that proves the point. As punishment for using his epitome to plot the progress of the vessel, William Philip was sent to the ultra-coercive penal station at Macquarie Harbour. There he gave clandestine lessons in navigation to the construction crew of the *Frederick*, the last vessel to be built at the site. Thus it was that Philip evened the score – the *Frederick* was successfully seized by ten convicts in January 1834 and sailed to Valdivia in Chile.[43] Four of the ten were subsequently recaptured in South America, clapped in irons, and placed on board the transport *Sarah* to be conveyed to Van Diemen's Land. The *Sarah* did not have an unproblematic voyage. Plans to put into Rio de Janeiro were shelved when a plot to seize the vessel was leaked. The *Frederick* pirates were named as the original conspirators, having enlisted the aid of several other prisoners, including two Spaniards with whom they could communicate thanks to their South American sojourn. The tale reveals the extent to which conspiracies circulated from one convict to another, passing, in this case, from sea to land and then back to sea again. It was a story, however, with a sequel. At least one of the convicts who cut out the *Frederick* eventually managed to effect his escape from Australia. James Porter absconded on the brig *Sir John Byng* in May 1847, twenty-three years after he had originally been transported. He was never heard of again.[44]

41. TAHO, Con 23/1, and Con 31/1, p. 244.

42. TAHO, Con 31/11, p. 171, and Con 18/13.

43. Maxwell-Stewart, *Closing Hell's Gates*, p. 265, and R. Davey (ed.), *The Travails of Jimmy Porter: A Memoir* (Strahan, 2003), pp. 40–44.

44. H. Maxwell-Stewart, "Seven Tales for a Man with Seven Sides", in L. Frost and H. Maxwell-Stewart (eds), *Chain Letters: Narrating Convict Lives* (Melbourne, 2001), pp. 64–76.

As the surgeon superintendent on the *Katherine Stewart Forbes* pointed out, securing those accused of mutiny during the passage to Australia was not necessarily the end of the matter. He reported how he had discovered that a "numerous gang" amongst the convicts had plotted in the hulks to seize the vessel and carry her to the United States of America. His subsequent investigations had uncovered a second plan to take a boat immediately after the vessel arrived in port in order to get ashore previous "to a description of their persons being taken".[45] This demonstrated both an alarming degree of familiarity with the procedure for processing convicts and the failure of the punishments inflicted on board the vessel to stamp out self-liberational desires.

Plans to seize vessels were often hatched prior to departure. The papers forwarded from the hulks regularly identified those amongst the convicts thought to be potential threats. In some cases prisoners had already disclosed their hand. At least twenty of the convicts embarked on board the *Coromandel* in 1838 had already been charged with mutiny. The disturbance was serious enough for the Secretary of State to order that they all be sent to road parties and penal stations upon disembarkation in Van Diemen's Land.[46]

Most plots could be traced to a small core, usually members of the same mess. Messes appear to have been self-organized. Thus on the *East London*, sailing in 1843, the women from Ulster messed together, as did those from Cavan, Cork, Dublin, and Westmeath.[47] On male vessels, prisoners boarded from the same hulk were usually permitted to keep together and as a result it was not unusual for messmates to share pre-voyage experiences. Such billeting arrangements fostered a system of fictive kinship – "messmate" was a term often employed by convicts.[48] Many of those accused of conspiring to take vessels shared native places, or similar prior experiences, which indicated that they are likely to have messed together. Four of the eleven conspirators on the *Isabella* in 1842 had been convicted in courts in Lancaster and another three had been court martialled in Halifax, Nova Scotia. Convicts convicted in Canada also featured in the plot to take the *Sarah* in 1837. Of the eleven ringleaders, three had been convicted in Montreal and a fourth in nearby Three Rivers. By the time they had embarked on the *Sarah*, all had already shared the experience of being shipped as prisoners across the Atlantic.

In order to put a plot into action the initial core of conspirators had to be expanded – it took more than one mess to take a convict vessel.

---

45. TAHO, CSO1/605/13784.
46. See TAHO Con 31/3, pp. 248, 250; Con 31/8, p. 49; Con 31/12, pp. 116, 139; Con 31/17, pp. 20–21, 23; Con 31/25, pp. 1, 278, 280–283; Con 31/32, pp. 48, 50; Con 31/36, p. 54.
47. TAHO, Con 19/2, pp. 274–343, and CSO 22/88/1859.
48. See, for example, Memoranda by Convict Davis, State Library New South Wales, Dixson Library Q168.

Beyond sheer numbers specialists needed to be recruited. These included navigators and those in positions of trust who might have access to such items as keys and arms. This was always dangerous. If those approached refused to participate they might give the game away. This is especially true if they were outsiders. The conspiracy to take the *Navarino* was hatched by six Ulstermen, but was betrayed by a forty-five-year-old Catholic labourer from Limerick.[49]

Some mutineers attempted to bind others to the plot through the use of oaths and other devices. William Chapman reported that while he was lying in his berth on the *Argyle* he was asked by Frampton, one his neighbours: "If you had a ship what would you do?" He was then asked to sign a piece of paper, an attempt to secure his allegiance. Chapman had cold feet from the start. According to his later testimony, he asked Frampton what would happen to the soldiers and sailors, only to be told they would be heaved over the side of the vessel. To this he replied "we must never see our country again if any thing of that happens". Frampton then said "Damn and bugger the country, can't we live as well in another?". This appears to have had little appeal to Chapman.[50] A former poacher who had been transported for stealing a faggot of wood and a pickaxe, he had left a wife and a child behind in Dorchester.[51] The information that he provided to the surgeon superintendent secured a favourable recommendation, useful for securing future indulgences including a possible assisted passage for his family. The wives and children of deserving convicts were sometimes permitted to travel to the Australian colonies to be reunited with their husbands.[52] A perpetual problem that convict mutineers faced was that their self-liberational desires provided opportunities for others.

Richard Jones, transported on the *Isabella Watson* in 1842, drew on his considerable experience of conspiratorial movements in an attempt to control loose tongues. A clerk by training, Jones had been the secretary of the Dublin Ribbon Society, an anti-Protestant republican organization that also operated as a quasi-benefit society. As well as corresponding with other Ribbonmen, he was believed by the Dublin police to have been party to an 1836 attempt to blow up a statue of William III. According to Garvin, Jones was instrumental in attempting to link the Dublin society to other Ribbon groups in northern Leinster and Ulster.[53] The majority of

---

49. State Library New South Wales, Tas Papers 30, pp. 429–460, and D5.
50. *Colonial Times*, 7 September 1831.
51. TAHO, Con 31/7, p. 98.
52. For the process of family reunion see P. McIntyre, *Free Passage: The Reunion of Irish Convicts and Their Families in Australia 1788–1852* (Dublin, 2011), pp. 51–68.
53. Tom Garvin, "Defenders, Ribbonmen and Others: Underground Political Networks in Pre-Famine Ireland", *Past and Present*, 96 (1982), pp. 133–155.

his co-mutineers on the *Isabella Watson* came from precisely this region. Four were from County Cavan, two from Longford, and one from Meath. All the conspirators gave their religion as Catholic. Ribbon societies used a system of passwords, oaths, and secret signs to organize members. According to the farm labourer James Byrne, Jones approached him on 15 May to ask him if he "would be one of the party". He then took a book out of his pocket, probably the catechism used at Ribbon meetings, in order to bind Byrne to the plan. The oath may have been effective at keeping some quiet. Francis Gafney confessed that he too had been asked to join the conspiracy, but on the advice of his brother and another prisoner had shunned the plotters. Yet although he refused to join the plot he did not turn informer.[54]

Radicalism on convict vessels was not limited to prisoners. Part of the crew on the *Prince Regent* mutinied on 17 December 1830. For the rest of the voyage they were put in irons – joining the convicts.[55] Whereas the surgeon and ship's officers could force the free to inhabit spaces normally reserved for the unfree, this served only to strengthen the similarities between crew and convict. Sailors too could be flogged and placed in the solitary confinement box that was secured to the deck of many transport vessels. The diet that convicts were fed was based on naval rations, and every surgeon charged with maintaining discipline during the voyage was naval trained. While the industrial landscape of the ship was used to regulate the lives of convict passengers, this was also true of the men who were employed to sail it. They too worked to ship time. While they did not come on board with their feet shackled in irons, the vessels that they served on were nevertheless coercive institutions.[56]

When James McTerman on the *Sarah* uncovered a plot to seize the vessel, he was alarmed to find that at least one member of the crew was implicated. As he informed the Colonial Secretary on arrival in Hobart Town: "I found Wilson, one of the sailors, so unequivocally involved, not only as an abettor, but as one whom by his promise, their chief reliance rested as well for information as for aid by conveying arms to the mutineers."[57]

This was McTerman's tenth voyage as a surgeon superintendent and he had already had at least one other run-in with would-be mutineers. On the *Ocean* sailing to New South Wales in 1823 he had placed five ring-leaders in irons, whom he thought were determined to possess the vessel. Rather than selecting a military guard to watch over the miscreants,

54. State Library New South Wales, Dixson Library, Add 537.
55. TAHO, CSO1/442/9841.
56. P. Linebaugh and M. Rediker, *The Many-Headed Hydra: Sailors, Slaves, Commoners and the Hidden History of the Revolutionary Atlantic* (Boston, MA, 2000), pp. 143–173.
57. TAHO, CSO 5/19/398.

he picked twelve "good" convicts to watch them at night.[58] This may have reflected a desire to keep security inhouse. John McDonald, the master on board the *Isabella Watson* sailing to Van Diemen's Land in 1842, became so concerned about reports that some amongst the military detachment had conspired with the convicts to seize the vessel that he armed the crew with cutlasses and boarding pikes, effectively turning them into an alternative guard.[59] Despite the explicit instructions provided to officers on transport vessels, relations between surgeons, masters, and military officers were often strained by voyage end.[60]

Indeed, it is noticeable that the only successful mutiny on a convict vessel – the seizure of the *Lady Shore* in 1797 – was put into effect by a confederation of disaffected crew and guard. The event illustrates the extent to which the line between convict, seaman, and soldier could become blurred.

The detachment of New South Wales Corps detailed to act as guard on this vessel contained a large number of "recruits" from the Savoy military prison. Deserters were routinely transported as convicts while Britain was at peace. When at war, however, both military and civilian convicts were pressed into service.[61] Amongst these unwilling recruits were several who had been enlisted from gaol as well as a number of prisoners of war including a helmsman and pilot from the captured French corvette, *La Bonne Citoyenne*. The convicts they were charged with guarding consisted of sixty-six women and two men, one of whom was the "notorious" adventurer and swindler Major Semple Lisle. Lisle later wrote an account of the affair in which he explicitly linked the troubles encountered during the voyage to the display of radicalism that those on board witnessed while anchored at Spithead. As he described it, the "British fleet laying close to us, was then in a state of open rebellion".[62] The Spithead mutiny broke out on 16 April when sixteen ships of the line refused to weigh anchor when ordered to join the blockade of Brest. The dispute lasted until 15 May, when the government conceded to the bulk of the mutineers' demands.[63] By then the *Lady Shore* had set sail. Lisle alleged that it was a somewhat hurried departure spurred on by a desire to

58. Brooke and Brandon, *Bound for Botany Bay*, p. 146.

59. State Library New South Wales, CY 4980 item 3.

60. British Parliamentary Papers, "Instructions to Surgeons Superintendent on Board Convict Ships Proceeding to New South Wales or Van Diemen's Land, 1832", *Correspondence and Papers Relating to Convict Transportation 1810–1841* (Shannon, 1972), VI, pp. 253–258.

61. H. Maxwell-Stewart, "Convict Transportation from Britain and Ireland, 1615-1870", *History Compass*, 8 (2010), pp. 1221–1242.

62. J. Semple Lisle, *The Life of Major J.G. Semple Lisle containing a Faithful Narrative of his Alternate Vicissitudes of Splendor and Misfortune* (London, 1799), p. 181.

63. N.A.M. Rodger, *The Command of the Ocean: A Naval History of Britain, 1649–1815* (London, 2004), pp. 446–453.

distance the convict vessel from the "mutiny then raging on board His Majesty's ships, by which we were surrounded".[64]

To the casual observer the *Lady Shore* may well have appeared to represent a distortion of the proper state of affairs on a transport vessel. After all, when she hastily set sail, Lisle, a member of the officer class, was numbered amongst the felons, while several former convicts could be counted amongst the ranks of the soldiers.

The mutiny broke out early on the morning of 1 August 1797 to cries of "Vive la République". In all, twenty-two soldiers and crew participated, nine of whom were former French prisoners of war. The insurrection had been carefully timed; in the words of one of the female convicts, the mutineers "managed their business extremely well". The plot was hatched by the soldiers and sailors of the morning watch, who loaded four of the ship's guns with broken glass and pointed two aft to cover the officers and passengers' quarters while tilting the other two so that they could be discharged down the hatches should there be an attempt to retake the vessel from below. The captain, first mate, and one of the mutineers were killed in the ensuing struggle, but the crew and soldiers belonging to the other watches did little to resist. The surviving officers were then compelled to sign certificates declaring that they would not take up arms against the French for a year and a day and absolving the surgeon, ship's petty officers, and crew from any blame for the loss of the vessel. The mutineers then donned the uniforms of their erstwhile superiors before setting all who did not want to join the venture adrift in one of the ship's boats. They then set course for Montevideo, where to their surprise they were detained by the Spanish, who sold the *Lady Shore* as a prize and distributed the female convicts to the houses of local notables.[65]

While the voyage was hardly typical, it did serve to illustrate the fine line that separated convict, soldier, and sailor. As far as the Naval Board was concerned, however, the female convicts below decks were far from innocent bystanders. It was widely thought that the affair was sexually charged and that social and physical intercourse between convicts and guard had led to the loss of the vessel. Attempts to prevent soldiers and crew from gaining access to the convict women had certainly soured relations. They had also proved largely ineffectual. At least one of the sailors confessed that he had been in bed with his convict lover when the mutiny broke.[66] Some of the female convicts openly consorted with the

64. Semple Lisle, *The Life of Major J.G. Semple Lisle*, p. 182.
65. John Black, *An Authentic Narrative of the Mutiny on Board the Ship Lady Shore* (London, 1798), pp. 15–17; *The True Britton*, 18 May 1798; *The Morning Chronicle*, 29 December 1804; W.D. Edmonds and T.G. Parsons, "Jacobinism Afloat – The Insurrection on the 'Lady Shore' in 1797", *History Today*, 34:11 (1984), pp. 11–15.
66. *General Evening Post*, 3 December 1799.

mutineers and, given the extent to which relationships developed between the crew and their convict charges prior to the mutiny, it is likely that some had been privy to the conspiracy. After the taking of the *Lady Shore* military detachments ceased to be placed on female transports because the risk that the guard would fraternize with their charges was considered too great.[67]

Damousi has argued that "mutiny and disorder came to carry different meanings for male and female convicts". As she puts it: "For women, notions of disorder were conceived in sexual terms and a particular form of surveillance was undertaken accordingly".[68] While this is true, there is a danger of overlooking the threat that female convicts posed to security. Attempted mutinies were certainly not restricted to male vessels. When James Hall attempted to crack down on what he referred to as "prostitution" amongst the female convicts on the *Brothers* in 1824 he claimed that "Six women conspired to murder me [...] and did actually form a mutiny of an alarming nature, in which I was knocked down in the prison, beaten and kicked". He alleged that the revolt had been instigated by James Thompson Meach, the chief mate, who had offered the women a bottle of rum in return for dispensing with Hall. While Meach was subsequently cleared of instigating mutiny, the incident confirmed that sexual relations on female transports were policed for more than ideological reasons.[69]

For all the attempts to separate convicts spatially and socially from crew and soldiers, conspiracies continued to be uncovered that involved those located both within and outside the ship's prison. One problem was that while those who sailed and guarded the ship might technically be free, the circumstances they faced were close enough to those experienced by convicts to highlight the coercive nature of both forecastle and the barrack room. If this applied to sailors, it was especially the case for soldiers. As the rank and file pressed from the Savoy prison into service with the New South Wales Corps understood, to be shipped as a soldier to Botany Bay was to receive a sentence of exile – it was de facto transportation. The military units that replaced the New South Wales Corps did a tour of duty that routinely encompassed first service in the Australian colonies and then British India. Rankers were often away for seven years, the length of the minimum sentence to transportation. Indeed, some soldiers deliberately offended in order to get court-martialled, reasoning that a sentence of transportation was preferable to the privations of barrack life.[70]

67. Bateson, *Convict Ships*, p. 26.
68. Damousi, *Depraved and Disorderly*, p. 19.
69. Bateson *Convict Ships*, pp. 225-226.
70. P. Hilton, "'Branded D on the Left Side': A Study of Former Soldiers and Marines Transported to Van Diemen's Land" (Ph.D. thesis, University of Tasmania, 2010).

As Colonel Breton, who commanded a regiment in New South Wales revealed in his evidence to a British Parliamentary Inquiry: "demoralization was [...] produced amongst the troops by their intercourse with the prison population, which could not be prevented, because many of the men found their fathers, brothers, and other relatives amongst the convicts".[71] Even where there were no kinship ties there were plenty of convicts who had served time in the forces. On board the *Somersetshire* bound for Hobart in 1841 a plot was uncovered that involved both convicts and guards. One of the convict ringleaders was William McCauley, a groom from County Fermanagh who had previously served nine years in the Enniskillen Dragoons. McCauley and his co-accused, Arthur Hewiett and John Winkfield, managed to persuade three privates and a bugler of the 99th Regiment to join the conspiracy. It was subsequently alleged that their plan was to kill the officers and set any remaining loyalists adrift in the ship's boats while the mutineers sailed to South America. So serious was the threat that the ship put into Cape Town so that a court martial could be assembled. The four soldiers were put on trial for "conspiracy to take forcible possession of the ship and do forcible injury to the officers on board", although one of them subsequently turned Queen's evidence. Of the remaining three, John Agnew was sentenced to be shot by firing squad and Walter Chisolm and John Kelly transported for life.[72]

After a plot to take the *Isabella Watson* was uncovered it emerged that the conspirators included at least one soldier. While relieving himself at the heads, Private Barney Macanally told two prisoners that there were some amongst the guard who would not participate in any attempt to put down a mutiny. Instead they would, as he put it, "make their water on the pistols and flintlocks so that they would not go off". Later in the voyage another Irish soldier ordered to stand guard over the conspirators was ironed after he was seen making Ribbonman signals to one of his prisoners.[73] Following three attempts to seize vessels between April and August 1842 Franklin, the Governor of Van Diemen's Land, requested that navy ships be selected as convict transports in the future. As the *Launceston Examiner* put it: "There are many two-deckers cruising, about

---

71. Sir William Molesworth, *Report from the Select Committee of the House of Commons on Transportation together with a Letter from the Archbishop of Dublin on the same Subject and Notes by Sir William Molesworth, Bart, Chairman of the Committee* (South Australia, 1967 [1838]), p. 16.
72. *Colonial Times*, 31 May 1842; *Launceston Examiner*, 4 June 1842. Although he spent ten days in the condemned cell, Agnew's sentence was commuted to life imprisonment. Incarcerated for nine months on Robben Island, Agnew was eventually forwarded to Van Diemen's Land on the *John Renwick* in 1843, Walter Chisolm and John Kelly having arrived the previous year on the *Surrey*; Dixson Library, Add 537, p. 239, and Mitchell Library, D 5.
73. State Library of New South Wales, MLMSS 1808/Box 1.

the British Channel which might be advantageously spared for this duty". Such measure would increase discipline and remove the added danger of "the too frequent insubordination of sailors in the merchant service".[74]

In conclusion, the voyage to Australia was designed to be an informative experience – part and parcel of the process of turning the convicted into penal labourers.[75] Despite the isolation of the voyage and the daily regime of deck scrubbing, washing, and oakum picking, that process was contested. If the four months spent at sea was designed to atomize convicts, then the surgeon superintendents failed in their duties.

Whereas it is difficult to count mutiny attempts, they were certainly not infrequent. Convicts were routinely punished for mutinous actions in the hulks and during the voyage itself. Plots hatched amongst small groups of conspirators had necessarily to be transmitted to a wider circle of confederates in order to put into action. While convicts outnumbered crew and military detachments, transport vessels doubled as prisons, the seaborne inmates of which were always under surveillance – especially when on deck. Attempts to recruit beyond the initial core usually led to betrayal despite the use of oaths, signed agreements, and other devices. The main reason for this was that informers stood to gain considerable advantages. Despite the high level of betrayal, ships' officers and colonial officials continued to be wary of the threat of mutiny.

The conspirators were drawn from a wide variety of backgrounds. Whereas it has been argued that those transported for political offences kept themselves aloof from the general body of prisoners, they could certainly be found amongst the ranks of mutineers.[76] Those who plotted to seize convict vessels were drawn from both rural and urban areas and from the length and breadth of the British Isles. Some had been sentenced in other parts of the Empire, and this was especially the case with soldiers.

Both former soldiers and sailors featured prominently amongst those identified as ringleaders. Not all of those who participated in plots to take transport vessels were convicts. Throughout the transportation era, ships' officers and colonial officials were surprised by the extent to which the "dreams of mutiny" hatched in prisons below deck spread into the quarters of the ship occupied by the guard and crew. This was in stark contrast to slave vessels, where race formed an effective partition blocking inter-deck fraternization.

74. *Launceston Examiner*, 23 September 1842.
75. R. Evans and W. Thorpe, "Power, Punishment and Penal Labour: Convict Workers and Moreton Bay", *Australian Historical Studies*, 25 (1992), pp. 90–111.
76. J.B. Hirst, *Convict Society and its Enemies* (Sydney, 1983), p. 138, and R.W. Connell and T.H. Irving, *Class Structure in Australian History: Documents, Narrative and Argument* (Melbourne, 1984), p. 50.

On convict transports there were many more ties that helped to foster common cause between bondsmen and women and those charged with sailing and securing the vessel. It was, after all, former sailors who had been pressed into service with the New South Wales Corps who played the lead in the capture of the *Lady Shore* in 1797. That mutineers had almost certainly acted in partnership with the female convicts was not lost on the government, which henceforth removed military detachments from female convict vessels. The fact was that "those lads" who "contrived a plan", to quote from the convict ballad the *Cyprus Brig*, were not necessarily lads nor necessarily lagged.

The experience of radicalism at sea had implications for convict management on land. Whereas the state attempted to use the process of transportation as a means of producing docile bodies, the convicted had other ideas. Although all bar one attempt to seize a transport vessel failed, the prisoners disgorged onto the shores of the Australian colonies were certainly not done with attempts at self-liberation. Those that failed at sea often became absconders, pirates, or mutineers of a different sort once they reached Australia.

IRSH 58 (2013), Special Issue, pp. 197–227 doi:10.1017/S0020859013000278
© 2013 Internationaal Instituut voor Sociale Geschiedenis

Cutting Out and Taking Liberties: Australia's Convict Pirates, 1790–1829

IAN DUFFIELD

Honorary Fellow, University of Edinburgh
19/3F2 Dundas Street, Edinburgh EH3 6QG, UK

E-mail: Ian.Duffield1@btinternet.com

ABSTRACT: The 104 identified piratical incidents in Australian waters between 1790 and 1829 indicate a neglected but substantial and historically significant resistance practice, not a scattering of unrelated spontaneous bolts by ships of fools. The pirates' ideologies, cultural baggage, techniques, and motivations are identified, interrogated, and interpreted. So are the connections between convict piracy and bushranging; how piracy affected colonial state power and private interests; and piracy's relationship to "age of revolution" ultra-radicalism elsewhere.

HIDDEN HISTORY

Transported convicts piratically seized at least eighty-two ships, vessels, and boats in Australian waters between 1790 and 1829. Unsuccessful piratical ventures involved at least twenty-two more. Somewhat more episodes occurred from 1830 to 1859,[1] but until the 2000s this extensive phenomenon remained unrecognized among academic Australianists[2] and

---

1. See Tables 1–7. Their data are drawn from my research, identifying 172 incidents, 1790–1859. Graeme Broxam has generously given me a draft of his forthcoming book on convict piracies. It identifies 39 incidents previously unknown to me – hence a current 1790–1859 total of 211. I do not discuss the incidents I know of only through Broxam.
2. For the exclusion of convict pirates, see Alan Atkinson, *The Europeans in Australia*, I and II (Oxford [etc.], 1997, 2004); Manning Clark, *A History of Australia*, I and II (Carlton, 1962, 1968); Grace Karskens, *The Rocks: Life in Early Sydney* (Carlton, 1997). On convict piracy's absence from academic Australian history, see *idem*, "'This Spirit of Emigration': The Nature and Meanings of Escape in Early New South Wales", in David Roberts (ed.), *Escape: Essays on Convict Australia*, special issue, *Journal of Australian Colonial History*, 7 (2005), pp. 1–34, 1–5. Other relevant post-2000 academic studies include James Boyce, *Van Diemen's Land* (Melbourne, 2008), pp. 15–19, and *idem*, *1835: The Founding of Melbourne and the Conquest of Australia* (Collingwood, 2011), ch. 2; Ian Duffield, "'Haul Away the Anchor Girls'; Charlotte Badger, Tall Stories and the Pirates of the 'Bad Ship *Venus*'", in Roberts, *Escape*, pp. 35–64; and Ian Duffield, "Identity Fraud: Interrogating the Impostures of 'Robert de Bruce Keith Stewart'"

maritime historians globally. Freelance Australianists' lively narratives lack convincing interpretation and fail to grasp the sheer extent of convict piracy.[3]

Thus, Robert Hughes's bestseller *The Fatal Shore* mentions fewer than twenty incidents, collectively represented as random frantic bolting from Britain's horrendous gulag but never as a fraction of something far larger.[4] To me, Hughes's pain-reflex piracies[5] resemble "running amok" on the supposed Malay model. Convict pirates, however, were not "running amok", and this point is not ethnological. Within colonialist culture, that phrase denied rational meaning to Malay peoples' sudden uprisings in colonial south-east Asia. Hughes imposes much the same on convict piracy. In the present volume, Matthias van Rossum historicizes and deconstructs notions of amok as a ferociously irrational Malay psychological trait. Rather, his 1782 mutiny of Balinese slave marines aboard the *Mercuur*, and similar contemporary events, were "collective and rational" acts.[6] I interpret Australia's convict piracies similarly.

It seems probable that convicts' old-world cultural baggage influenced their piracies. These did not simply mimic Kidd- and Blackbeard-era piracy, as represented in British popular culture. The convict pirates lacked Jolly Rogers, but aboard a newly pirated vessel they enacted liberty by literally and symbolically deciding their course and destination. That, plus collectively devising shipboard regulations and electing leaders, capsized their penal bondage. Similar acts also occurred during the "Golden Age of Piracy"[7] and aboard ships seized by mutineers elsewhere in the age of revolution.[8] Escape from transportation was a capital offence.

in Early Nineteenth-Century Penang and Calcutta", in Clare Anderson (ed.), *The Indian Ocean*, special issue, *Journal of Social History: Societies & Cultures*, 45 (2011), pp. 390–415; Erin Ihde, "Pirates of the Pacific: The Convict Seizure of the *Wellington*", *The Great Circle*, 30 (2008), pp. 3–17.

3. See, for instance, Thomas Dunbabin, *Sailing the World's Edge: Sea Stories from Old Sydney* (London, 1931), pp. 157–177; Robert Hughes, *The Fatal Shore* (London, 1987), ch. 7; Geoffrey C. Ingleton, *True Patriots All* (Sydney, 1952); Marjorie Tipping, *Convicts Unbound: The Story of the Calcutta Convicts and Their Settlement in Australia* (Ringwood, 1988), ch. 25; Warwick Hirst, *Great Convict Escapes in Colonial Australia* (East Roseville, rev. 2nd edn, 2003); *idem*, *The Man Who Stole the* Cyprus (Dural, 2008).

4. Hughes, *The Fatal Shore*, ch. 7, entitled "Bolters and Bushrangers".

5. My critique of Hughes here broadly coincides with Karskens, "'This Spirit of Emigration'", p. 2, on such aspects of *The Fatal Shore*.

6. Matthias van Rossum, "'Amok!': Mutinies and Slaves on Dutch East Indiamen in the 1780s", in the present volume.

7. See Marcus Rediker, *Villains of All Nations: Atlantic Pirates in the Golden Age* (Boston, MA, 2004), ch. 4; David Cordingly, *Under the Black Flag: The Romance and the Reality of Life Among the Pirates* (New York, 1995), pp. 12–14.

8. See in the present volume Anita Rupprecht, "'All We Have Done, We Have Done for Freedom': The *Creole* Slave-Ship Revolt (1841) and the Revolutionary Atlantic";

Escape by piracy – also a capital offence – inherently proclaimed "liberty or death", a widespread age of revolution slogan.

Here, a convict ballad (sometimes attributed to Francis MacNamara),[9] on the 1829 seizure of the *Cyprus*, is illustrative. The ballad's opening[10] rallies convict audiences to liberty's cause: "Come all you sons of Freedom, a chorus join with me,/I'll sing a song of heroes and glorious liberty." This suggests not mere flight but "liberty or death" confrontation with tyranny: "By tyranny we've been oppressed, by your Colonial laws,/But we'll bid adieu to slavery, or die in freedom's cause." The collective selects an appropriate commander: "We elected William Swallow, and obey'd our Captain's word [...]. For navigating smartly Bill Swallow was the man." The ballad is neither strictly factual nor sheer fiction but a manifesto created and circulated within convict society, expressing "a whole epistemological 'otherness' – ways of knowing set implacably against authority and empire".[11] It extols the piracy as anti-tyranny and pro an egalitarian and libertarian order, with its own "outlaw heroes" (here, Swallow),[12] and concludes with defiant celebration:

> Then sound your golden trumpets boys, play on your tuneful notes,
> The Cyprus Brig is sailing, how proudly now she floats.
> May fortune help th' Noble lads, and keep them ever free
> From Gags, and Cats, and Chains, and Traps, and Cruel Tyranny.

The eminent historian Alan Atkinson wrongly asserted that European pirates never troubled early colonial Australia, but he admits their presence in disembarking convicts' mental cultural baggage.[13] Pirates strongly featured in Britain's Georgian print culture. Ballads were transmitted orally and through print. Illiterates accessed print media through vocal readings by literate kinsfolk, neighbours, or workmates. Piracy also provided a popular theme for Georgian popular theatre. A notable example was John Gay's operetta *Polly* (1729). It was immediately banned

Marcus Rediker, "The African Origins of the *Amistad* Rebellion, 1839"; and Aaron Jaffer, "'Lord of the Forecastle': *Serangs, Tindals,* and Lascar Mutiny, c.1780–1860". See also Clare Anderson, "'The Ferringees are Flying – The Ship is Ours!' The Convict Middle Passage in Colonial South and Southeast Asia, 1790–1860", *Indian Economic and Social History Review*, 41:2 (2005), pp. 43–86.

9. See, for example, Ingleton, *True Patriots All*, p. 269, n. 93. Not so Bob Reece – see his "Frank the Poet", in *idem* (ed.), *Exiles from Erin: Convict Lives in Ireland and Australia* (Basingstoke, 1991), pp. 151–183.

10. Version quoted is in Ingleton, *True Patriots All*, p. 129.

11. Karskens, "'This Spirit of Emigration'", p. 3 and n. 13, citing Paul Carter, *The Road to Botany Bay* (London, 1987), pp. 295, 300ff, 301.

12. For an evidence-based account, see Hirst, *The Man Who Stole the* Cyprus, pp. 48–53, 60–67. My analysis follows Graham Seal, *The Outlaw Legend: A Cultural Tradition in Britain, America and Australia* (Cambridge, 1996).

13. Atkinson, *Europeans in Australia*, I, p. 36.

from performance, Gay's preceding smash hit *The Beggars' Opera* having satirically subverted Walpole's corrupt Whig government. However, *Polly* proved a lucrative multi-edition publication. Once unbanned in 1772, *Polly* flourished long-term in Britain's theatrical repertoire.[14] Such works delighted plebeian theatregoers, including thieves, fraudsters, prostitutes, and pickpockets.[15] Unfortunately, British popular representations of pirates cannot be linked directly with specific piracies in Australia.

James C. Scott's "hidden transcripts" concept helps here. Historically, Scott argues, clandestine subversive cultural forms were crucial to underlings' "arts of resistance", providing a template, under favourable circumstances, for overt challenges to existing power relations. Sudden militant confrontation by hitherto docile-seeming subalterns baffled dominant circles that were unaware of "hidden transcripts".[16] In Australia, officialdom regularly denounced piratical escapes as witless folly, inviting shipwreck, drowning, or murder by "savages".[17] This line absolved government from admitting – even perceiving – the pirates' rationality. Piracies sometimes precipitated tighter port security measures intended to prevent their recurrence.

Even before the "age of revolution", miniature "worlds turned upside down" existed aboard Atlantic pirate ships.[18] From the late seventeenth century Atlantic seamen faced increasingly severe shipboard discipline, intensification of the arbitrary authority of officers – especially captains – and deteriorating employment terms. In riposte, many seamen turned pirate.[19] Convicts transported to Australia experienced a similar jeopardy. There, arbitrary magistrates' courts could severely punish breaches of convict regulations as well as crimes by floggings, hard labour in irons, extensions of existing sentences of up to three years, and relocation to remote, harsh-regime penal stations.[20]

---

14. Duffield, "'Haul Away the Anchor Girls'", pp. 43–48; Hans Turley, *Rum, Sodomy and the Lash: Piracy, Sexuality, and Masculine Identity* (New York [etc.], 1999), ch. 5.

15. Robert Jordan, *Convict Theatres of Early Australia* (Hatfield, 2002), pp. 16–21; Suzanne Rickard, *George Barrington's Voyage to Botany Bay* (London [etc.], 2001), pp. 3–17.

16. This summarizes key points in James C. Scott, *Domination and the Arts of Resistance* (New Haven, CT, 1990).

17. See also Karskens, "'This Spirit of Emigration'", pp. 11–15.

18. See, for example, Rediker, *Villains of All Nations*, pp. 38–42; *ibid.*, ch. 4, *passim*; *idem*, "Hydrarchy and Libertalia: The Utopian Dimensions of Atlantic Piracy in the Early Eighteenth Century", in David. J. Starkey, Els van Eyck van Heslinga, and J.A. de Moor (eds), *Pirates and Privateers: New Perspectives on the War on Trade in the Eighteenth and Nineteenth Centuries* (Exeter, 1997), pp. 29–46, 31–36.

19. Marcus Rediker, *Between the Devil and the Deep Blue Sea: Merchant Seamen, Pirates and the Anglo-American Maritime World, 1700–1750* (Cambridge, 1987), ch. 5 *passim*.

20. See Raymond Evans and William Thorpe, "Power, Punishment and Penal Labour: *Convict Workers* and Moreton Bay", *Australian Historical Studies*, 25:98 (1992), pp. 90–111; Hamish Maxwell-Stewart, "Convict Workers, 'Penal Labour' and Sarah Island: Life at Macquarie

Can Australia's convict pirates be directly linked to age of revolution politics? Until their prosopography is better known, that remains problematic – excepting United Irishmen connections. Originally the United Irishmen were a Protestant middle-class constitutional movement seeking Ireland's autonomy, albeit under the British Crown, and an end to the Anglican-ascendancy monopoly of Ireland's electoral franchise, elected public posts, and remunerated Crown offices. Catholics especially, but also Presbyterians and Dissenters, were excluded from full civil and political rights. The French Revolution's republican turn inspired the United Irishmen, especially when persecuted following France's 1793 declaration of war on Britain, to become pro-French, secular republican revolutionaries. Prospective French military intervention, though never effectively realized, panicked Ireland's established order into extreme repression. Through the 1790s, the United Irishmen infiltrated their ideology and practices into hitherto localized Catholic agrarian "Defender" secret societies, thus gaining nearly 300,000 sworn members by 1797. They provided a rank and file for armed uprisings in 1798 and 1803–1804.[21]

Irish political radicals transported in the 1790s and early 1800s proved dangerous ship's cargo. In 1793 mutiny scares occurred on the *Sugar Cane* and *Boddington* convict transports from Ireland. At Sydney, some *Boddington* convicts declared they had intended killing every officer on taking the ship, except the first mate and agent. They were to die after navigating the mutineers close to their chosen destination. In 1796, Irish prisoners aboard the *Marquis Cornwallis* (allegedly plus the boatswain's mate and some soldiers) plotted to kill the officers, and then sail to the USA.[22] On 29 December 1801, thirteen prisoners on the *Hercules* were killed before a mutiny was suppressed.[23]

The United Irishmen's engagement with revolutionary republicanism internationalized their outlook and connections.[24] Considerable education and an enlightenment outlook gave some United Irishmen the confidence to seek escape from Australia by piracy. In February 1800, around forty United Irishmen, from a much larger group recently arrived in Sydney on

Harbour, 1822–1834", in Ian Duffield and James Bradley (eds), *Representing Convicts: New Perspectives on Convict Forced Labour Migration* (London, 1997), pp. 142–163.
21. Kevin Whelan, "The United Irishmen, the Enlightenment and Popular Culture", in David Dickson, Daire Keogh, and Kevin Whelan (eds), *The United Irishmen: Republicanism, and Rebellion* (Dublin, 1993), pp. 269–296, 281–283, 288–294.
22. Con Costello, *Botany Bay* (Dublin [etc.], 1987), pp. 20–21; Emma Christopher, "'Ten Thousand Times Worse than the Convicts'; Rebellious Sailors, Convict Transportation and the Struggle for Freedom, 1787–1800", *Journal of Australian Colonial History*, 5 (2004), pp. 30–46, 42.
23. Costello, *Botany Bay*, pp. 18–21, 56.
24. See Marianne Elliott, *Partners in Revolution: The United Irishmen and France* (New Haven, CT, 1982); Whelan, "The United Irishmen"; Paul Weber, *On the Road to Rebellion: The United Irishmen and Hamburg, 1796–1803* (Dublin, 1997).

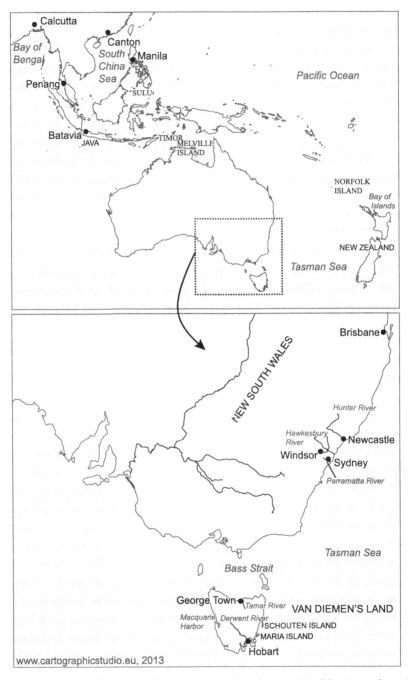

Figure 1. New South Wales and Van Diemen's Land, with the principal locations of convict piratical seizures, 1790–1829.
The author acknowledges Hamish Maxwell-Stewart for the draft of this map.

the *Minerva*, conspired to take the *Minerva* by night and compel officers and crew to take the ship out to sea. Informers, however, secured the conspirators' last-minute arrest. Nevertheless, officials were horrified: controlling shipping was crucial to convict transportation. Soon after, multiple Sydney Harbour shipping seizures were allegedly intrinsic to an Irish plot to overthrow the colonial government.[25]

As a coda to these troubles, on 1 April 1804 seven Irish convict fugitives from the recently crushed Castle Hill Rebellion were captured on the Hawkesbury River. Allegedly, they had planned "to seize upon the first boat to present itself, and […] commit themselves to the peril of the sea".[26] Many Castle Hill rebels had participated in Ireland's 1798 and 1803 risings.[27] After 1804, while Irish convicts participated in piracies alongside others,[28] their motivation was not perceived as revolutionary republicanism.

COLONIAL NEWSPAPERS AND CONVICT PIRACY

In June 1826 a Sydney *Monitor* correspondent recalled a recent sea passage from Sydney to Newcastle, New South Wales: "This is a pleasant packet, and the Captain a very pleasant gentlemanly fellow. The cabin is […] ornamented with muskets, pistols and cutlasses, in case of pirates – there are also two cannon […] on deck."[29] Insouciance notwithstanding, convict piracy evidently threatened shipping that connected the coastal settlements where most colonists, convict or free, dwelt.

Transportation to Australia did not automatically entail incarceration. On arrival, most convicts were assigned to free private employers, a minority being retained for government work. Especially in Sydney and Hobart, convicts could access newspapers in free time permitted, or when illicitly at large after hours – for example in taverns and sly-grog shops – and so read, or hear read, reports of local and world-wide piracies.[30] In the period addressed here, all Australian newspapers were published in port towns, where overseas newspapers too were landed. Shipping arrivals

---

25. *Historical Records of Australia* [hereafter *HRA*], Series 1, II, pp. 575–580.
26. *Sydney Gazette* [hereafter *SG*], 1 April 1804, p. 2c; Patrick O'Farrell, *The Irish in Australia* (Kensington, 1987), pp. 37–38; Atkinson, *Europeans in Australia*, I, pp. 251–256.
27. J.E. Gallagher, "The Revolutionary Irish", *Push from the Bush*, 19 (1985), pp. 2–33.
28. See, for example, the *Trial* piracy of 12 September 1816 – of the convicts listed in *SG*, 14 September 1816, p. 2a, as having seized the *Trial*, eleven were Irish, one English, one Spanish, one Portuguese, and yet no press reports called it an Irish event. See *SG*, 14 September 1816, p. 2c; 21 September 1816, p. 2d; 28 September 1816, Supplement, p. 2b; and *Hobart Town Gazette and Southern Reporter* [hereafter *HTG&SR*], 26 October 1816, p. 2a–b; 21 December 1816, p. 1b; 28 December 1816, p. 1b.
29. *Monitor*, Sydney, 9 June 1826, p. 2a.
30. On convict literacy, see Stephen Nicholas and Peter R. Shergold, "Convicts as Workers", and Deborah Oxley, "Females as Convicts", both in Stephen Nicholas (ed.), *Convict Workers: Reinterpreting Australia's Past* (Cambridge, 1988), pp. 75–78 and 91–94.

guaranteed repeated inflows of oral sea gossip. Sydney's Hyde Park Barracks, completed in 1819, provided accommodation for male convicts in government employ, hitherto privately lodged about the town. Mostly these men were set to public works outside the barracks. Sydney's assigned convicts continued to live at employers' premises or to find private lodgings.[31] In Hobart, where the Convict Barracks was incomplete until 1821, similar arrangements occurred. As in Sydney, convicts had access to printed and oral news stories, but anti-piracy sentiments and measures featured in the colonial press had little if any effect.

Information gleaned by port town convicts circulated further afield, becoming part of convict society's autonomous collective knowledge. My electronic scan of the *Sydney Gazette* from 1 January 1815 to 31 December 1817 reveals frequent local and global piracy reports.[32] The Principal Superintendent of Convicts' press notices of absentees included escapees by piracy. Fellow convicts could therefore track outcomes. Those who pirated the *Speedwell* from Newcastle on 7 April 1814 were gazetted in most subsequent *Sydney Gazettes* to December 1817.[33] As no report of their death or recapture appeared, fellow convicts could celebrate an apparently successful collective self-liberation. On 14, 21, and 28 September 1816, extensive identifying information was published about the men who had recently pirated the *Trial* from off Sydney Harbour's South Head.[34] From 5 October 1816 to beyond 1817, these men were gazetted alongside the *Speedwell* pirates in a section of the Principal Superintendent of Convicts' absentee lists, sub-headed "Pirates".[35] On 29 November 1817 those who had seized the *William Cossar* from Sydney Cove were featured beyond 1817. The last 1817 absentee list added five new pirates.[36]

From the 1803 debut of Australia's first newspaper, the *Sydney Gazette*, convict piracies were much reported. Thirteen ironed-gang convicts loading the *Eclipse* cutter at Newcastle on 11 May 1825 suddenly shed their irons – evidently tampered with in preparation – seized the *Eclipse*, and sailed seawards. Five Sydney press reports ensued, two in Hobart.[37]

31. J.B. Hirst, *Convict Society and its Enemies: A History of Early New South Wales* (Sydney, 1983), pp. 41–45; Karskens, *The Rocks*, pp. 30–31, 34–35, 167–168, 175.

32. I searched the *Sydney Gazette* using http://trove.nla.gov.au/newspaper, the National Library of Australia's facilities for searching digitized Australian newspapers. The following search terms were used: piracies, piracy, pirate, pirated, pirates, piratical, piratically, and pirating.

33. *SG*, 7 January 1815, p. 1d; and 27 December 1817, p. 2a. Similar notices appeared between those dates.

34. *SG*, 14 September 1816, p. 2; 21 September 1816, p. 2; 28 September 1816, p. 1.

35. *SG*, 5 October 1816, p. 1.

36. *SG*, 29 November 1817, p. 1, and 27 December 1817, p. 2.

37. *The Australian*, 19 May 1825, p. 4c; and 26 May 1825, p. 4c; *SG*, 26 May 1825, p. 2e; 2 June 1825, p. 2c; and 4 August 1825, p. 3d; *Hobart Town Gazette* [hereafter *HTG*], 1 July 1825, p. 4c; 2 July 1825, p. 2c.

On 25 November 1825, five convicts seized the *Maria*, carrying provisions for the Maria Island Penal Station, Van Diemen's Land. Two of these pirates, Henry Leonard and John Bogle, were convict crewmen. Three more lay concealed aboard till called to action. Two press reports ensued.[38] Reporting such events could only, if unintentionally, encourage convict piracy. Employing convict seamen cut shipowners' labour costs but was officially forbidden and inherently unsafe.

Until the 1820s, the only newspapers published in New South Wales and Van Diemen's Land were government organs – the *Sydney* and *Hobart Gazettes*. Naturally, they routinely condemned convict piracy as wicked folly – the official line. For instance, in 1807 the *Sydney Gazette* ridiculed six convicts who escaped in a stolen boat as "miserably provided for carrying such a determination into effect with any other prospect than [...] perishing".[39] Certain early recapture was regularly incanted, as when the *Hobart Town Gazette* reported the midnight seizure of the *Blue-Eyed Maid* by Matthew Brady and his bushranger gang on 3 December 1825.[40] As so often, Brady's gang made a mockery of cocksure recapture predictions. Indeed, the *Gazettes* often slid into sheer absurdity. The *Sydney Gazette* wrote of the *Speedwell* pirates: "they have no boat with them, and consequently can procure no supply of necessaries without the utmost risque [*sic*] to the vessel and their own lives". Lack of a ship's boat was disadvantageous, but it hardly presaged disaster. Such common exaggerations could only be counterproductive.

Even for the *Gazettes*, let alone competing private-enterprise newspapers emerging from the 1820s, piracies provided irresistible opportunities for colourful copy. That was fine when events delivered the "right" message, as when on 19 June 1818 a pirate boat was repelled in Sydney Cove by a brig's alert armed watch.[41] Altogether different impressions transpired when reports implied pirates had shown skill, resolution, and daring while, in contrast, port security regulations had been neglected and pursuit was tardy, bumbling, and fruitless. An instance is the *Sydney Gazette*'s original reporting of the seizure and ensuing pursuit of the *Harrington* brig in May 1808.[42] A clumsy subsequent attempt to remedy matters by drumming up these pirates' impending nasty fate probably aroused convict derision.[43]

Reporting of successful foreign piracies and mutinies may also have stimulated convict piracy. Though outside the formal chronological limits of this study, it is notable that the Atlantic slave mutinies aboard the

38. *HTG*, 3 December 1825, p. 2d; *The Australian*, 29 December 1825, p. 4b.
39. *SG*, 25 January 1807, p. 1c.
40. *HTG*, 3 December 1825, p. 2d.
41. *SG*, 20 June 1818, p. 2b–c.
42. *Ibid.*, 22 May 1808, p. 2a–b.
43. *Ibid.*, 29 May 1808, p. 2a.

Amistad (1839) and *Creole* (1841) were reported in Australia at a time when convict piracy was still endemic.[44] These reports (especially those concerning the *Creole*) sympathized with the slaves. Presumably convicts felt their own piratical escapes were equally justified and their superiors were humbugs to maintain otherwise. Convict culture held that convicts were treated as Hebrew slaves were by the pharaoh, while some prominent officials thought that, properly, convicts *were* virtually slaves.[45]

On occasion, the independent newspapers that appeared in the 1820s were more sympathetic to convict piracy than was possible in the *Gazettes*. Edward Smith Hall, a free immigrant and the Sydney *Monitor's* radical editor-proprietor, sometimes argued that escape from transportation exhibited an essentially English manly love of liberty.[46] His ideal manly Englishman was elastic. Thus, he praised the "frank, open, mild, but enterprising bold vivacious countenance" and "martial spirit" of the Isle-of-Wight born African diaspora convict, John Goff. This was during Goff's self-defence at his 1827 Sydney trial, for murder while leading an 1826 uprising on Norfolk Island. The *Sydney Gazette's* Goff was a savage monster.[47]

TWO MODES OF CONVICT PIRACY

Scant evidence suggests that plunder motivated convict pirates who voyaged afar to gain freedom. Others, however, navigated Australia's coasts, sometimes raiding isolated coastal settlements. Two broad modes of convict piracy thus emerge. Both prioritized taking "liberties" – afloat at sea, then at a distant friendly port, or by establishing master-less "rough crew" enclaves beyond government reach. Unauthorized masculine-libertarian settlements spread from the Bass Strait Islands to the Swan River in Western Australia.[48]

44. The only *Amistad* mutiny report is in the *Colonial Times*, Hobart, 2 March 1841, p. 2d. The *Creole* mutiny was repeatedly reported, for instance, in the New South Wales press, *Sydney Herald* [hereafter *SH*], 10 May 1841, p. 2b–c; 26 June 1841, p. 1d; and Supplement, 27 June 1841, p. 2d; *The Australian*, 26 August 1842, p. 2; 4 July 1842, p. 4; *SG*, 28 June 1842, p. 2. The *Creole* affair reports in Van Diemen's Land include: the *Launceston Examiner*, 28 May 1842, morning, p. 7b–c, evening, p. 7b–c; *The Courier*, Hobart, 4 November 1842, p. 4c; 9 December 1842, p. 4b; 13 January 1843, p. 3b; *Launceston Examiner*, 21 January 1843, p. 6d. For new interpretations of these mutinies see Rupprecht, "'All We Have Done, We Have Done for Freedom'", and Rediker, "African Origins of the *Amistad* Rebellion", in the present volume.
45. See "A Convict's Lament", verse 4, in Ingleton, *True Patriots All*, p. 121; Hamish Maxwell-Stewart, *Closing Hell's Gates: The Death of a Convict Station* (Crow's Nest, 2008), p. 155.
46. Erin Ihde, "'Bold, Manly-Minded Men' and 'Sly Cunning Base Convicts': The Double Standard of Escape", in Roberts, *Escape*, pp. 123–138, 127–131; and Erin Ihde, *Edward Smith Hall and the Sydney Monitor: 1826–1840* (Melbourne, 2004), ch. 5. For Hall on Goff, see *Monitor*, 24 September 1827, pp. 6b–c and 7a.
47. *Monitor*, 24 September 1827, p. 6c; *SG*, 24 September 1827, pp. 2f and 3a.
48. Boyce, *Van Diemen's Land*, ch. 1, and *idem*, *1835: The Founding of Melbourne and the Conquest of Australia*, ch. 2; Thomas Gunn, "Out from 'Under the Cloak of Nefarious

Unlike some eighteenth-century pirate settlements,[49] there is no case that these were utopian. Commonly, coerced Aboriginal women provided sexual, domestic, and general labour for a melange of pirates, other convict runaways, freelance sealers, ships' deserters, and castaways. Such autonomous, fluid, armed, and mobile combinations jangled official nerves.[50] However, coercive exploitation of Aborigines was not invariable. Five convicts escaped from Sydney on 26 September 1790 in a small stolen boat. The authorities deemed them foolish ignoramuses, throwing their lives away. In 1795 four survivors were found living, tranquilly assimilated, among Aboriginals at Port Stephens (180 kilometres from European settlements). They were "rescued", that is removed from Aboriginal wives and society and returned to Sydney.[51]

Atkinson's dismissal of convict piracy predated revisionist revelations.[52] Such mitigation is unavailable to Ian Hoskins's *Sydney Harbour* (2009). It mentions only the (discursively) hackneyed Mary Bryant episode of 1791 – worth briefly reprising here as the first convict piratical seizure motivated by dreams of faraway liberty. Bryant, her children, husband, and seven other male convicts departed Sydney Harbour in Governor Phillip's little cutter, eventually reaching Dutch Timor, where, briefly, they passed as shipwreck survivors.[53] Mary Bryant subsequently survived, became celebrated, and received a pardon. Colonial contemporaries, however, noticed better-founded long-distance piratical escapes from Sydney Harbour (see Tables 1–3). After dark, on 16 May 1808, 30 to 50 armed convicts stealthily boarded the 13-gun, 182-ton *Harrington* from stolen boats. This and the *Harrington*'s cutting out were undertaken with naval efficiency. The *Harrington*'s disappearance remained undetected till after sunrise. The pirates sailed 5,000 kilometres to Manila Bay, flying United States colours, and carrying forged ship's papers. When seized, the *Harrington* was moored in Farm Cove, not Sydney Cove, and lacked a

Practices' – Four Men in a Boat and Escape from Flinders Island 1836", in George Town Historical Society (ed.), *Crime on the High Seas* (George Town, 2007), pp. 30–37; Dunbabin, *Sailing the World's Edge*, pp. 157–177.
49. Rediker, "Hydrarchy and Libertalia", pp. 31–36.
50. See, for example, *HTG*, 10 June 1826, p. 4b–d.
51. David Collins, *An Account of the English Colony in New South Wales [...]*, Brian Fletcher (ed.) (Sydney, 1975; 1st edn, London, 1802), I, pp. 126, 128–130, 131, 222; Michael Flynn, *The Second Fleet: Britain's Grim Convict Armada of 1790* (North Sydney, 1993), pp. 400–401, 559, 582–583, 589–589; Hunter to Portland, 10 January 1798, *HRA*, Series 1, II, p. 116.
52. Hirst, *Great Convict Escapes*, is empirically revisionist. For analytical revision see Christopher, "'Ten Thousand Times Worse than the Convicts'"; Duffield, "'Haul Away the Anchor Girls'"; Karskens, "'This Spirit of Emigration'"; Ihde, "Pirates of the Pacific". Earlier freelancers discussed convict pirates piecemeal. See, for example, Dunbabin, *Sailing the World's Edge*; Ingleton, *True Patriots All*.
53. Ian Hoskins, *Sydney Harbour: A History* (Sydney, 2009), pp. 50–51, 53–55.

Table 1. *Vessels and ships seized by convict pirates, 1790–1829.*

No.	Name	Type	Tonnage	Owner(s)	Where seized	When seized
1	Cumberland	Schooner	28	NSW Government	NSW Broken Bay	5.9.1797
2	Norfolk	Sloop	25	NSW Government	NSW between Broken Bay & Sydney Harbour	October 1800
3	—	Small vessel	?	Private owner	NSW Hunter Estuary	Late 1800
4	Flinders	Pilot cutter	?	VDL Government	VDL Sullivan Cove	February 1806
5	Venus	Brig	45	Robert Campbell, Sydney	VDL Port Dalrymple	17.6.1806
6	Marcia	Schooner	26	Kable & Underwood, Sydney	Bass Strait	post 21.1.1806, prior to 1808
7	Harrington	Brig	182	William Campbell, Sydney	NSW Farm Cove	16.5.1808
8	Unity	Schooner	35	W.H. Mansel, Hobart	VDL Hobart	23.4.1813
9	Speedwell	Schooner or sloop	21	M'Kellop & Brown, Sydney	NSW Newcastle	7.4.1814
10	Argo	Ship	150	Payne & Tyrce, Calcutta	VDL Derwent Estuary	12.6.1814
11	Trial	Brig	20	Simeon Lord, Sydney	NSW inside Heads, Sydney Harbour	12.9.1816
12	William Cossar	Vessel	20	NSW Government after seizure	NSW Sydney Cove	7.7.1817
13	—	Bushranger-built vessel	?	Appropriated by VDL Government	VDL Hobart	11.4.1818
14	Young Lachlan	Schooner	44	J. Thomson, Hobart?	VDL Derwent Estuary	27.1.1819
15	—	Schooner	?	A.F. Kemp, Hobart	VDL Derwent Estuary	Post 23.10.1821, prior to 24.6.822
16	Seaflower	Schooner	Small	? – hired by George Meredith	VDL Pirates Bay	Shortly prior to 2.2.1822
17	Angelina	Sloop	16	?	NSW Broken Bay	30.10.1824
18	Isabella	Small craft	37	Richard Kelly, Hawkesbury	NSW Port Macquarie	Prior to 12.10.1824
19	Eclipse	Cutter	45	Reibey & Atkinson, Sydney	NSW Newcastle	11.5.1825
20	Maria	Cutter	?	VDL Government	VDL near Hobart	25.11.1825

Table 1.   *(continued)*

No.	Name	Type	Tonnage	Owner(s)	Where seized	When seized
21	*Glutton*	Sloop	?	Mr Campbell, VDL	VDL Schouten Island	2.12.1825
22	*Garnet/Gurnet*	Brig or schooner	20	?	NSW Newcastle	8.4.1826
23	*Wellington*	Brig	182	Chartered to NSW Government	250 miles from Norfolk Island	21.12.1826
24	*Ellen*	Sloop or cutter	22	M. Purdon	VDL Cape Roule	15.1.1827
25	*Phoebe*	Brig	24	Berry & Wollstonecraft, Sydney	NSW Shoalhaven River	14.12.1827
26	*Mary*	Vessel	Small	Williams (a baker), Sydney	NSW Darling Harbour	18.3.1828
27	*Cyprus*	Brig	108	VDL Government	VDL Recherche Bay	16.8.1829

NSW = New South Wales; VDL = Van Diemen's Land (now Tasmania).
Sources: Too numerous to list here, but especially *HRA* and contemporaneous colonial newspapers.

Table 2. *Vessels and ships unsuccessfully targeted by convict pirates, 1790–1829.*

No.	Name	Type	Tonnage	Owner(s)	Where, how, and by whom targeted	When attempted/planned
1	*Minerva*	Convict ship	578	Robert Larnock, London	NSW Sydney Cove: c.40 Irishmen recently arrived on the *Minerva*	Early February 1800
2	*Buffalo*	Naval store ship	462	Royal Navy	NSW Sydney Harbour: Irishmen	Between February & September 1800
3	*Governor Hunter*	Schooner	35	J. Nichols, Sydney	VDL at sea between Hobart & Oyster Bay: Robert Stewart & party	26.6.1805
4	*Flinders*	Pilot cutter	?	H. Hacking, Sullivan Cove	VDL: Stewart & party, to board the *Estramina*	February 1806
5	*Estramina*	Schooner	102	NSW Government	VDL south coast: Stewart & party	February 1806
6	*Governor Hunter*	Schooner	35	J. Nichols, Sydney	VDL Port Dalrymple: 4 convicts aboard	Late June–early July 1806
7	*Topaz*	Whaler	?	Mayhew, Boston	VDL Storm Bay Passage (a): convicts from boat	October 1807
8	*Aurora*	Brig	180	Thomas Wolden etc., New York	NSW at/near Sydney: convict conspiracy	Between 19.7.1810 & 18.9.1810
9	—	Vessel	?	—	NSW Sydney: convict conspiracy	Early May 1815
10	*Harriet*	Ship	450	Sold to Sydney merchants for 6,000 guineas 1817 (b)	On Hobart–Cape Town passage: 16 male, 5 female convict stowaways, some crew	Late 1817–early 1818
11	*Sophia*	Brig	60	T.W. Birch, Hobart	NSW Sydney: boatload of convicts	19.6.1818

Table 2.   *(continued)*

No.	Name	Type	Tonnage	Owner(s)	Where, how, and by whom targeted	When attempted/planned
12	*Castle Forbes*	Convict ship	459	Unknown	VDL Huon Estuary: 28 convicts	Mid-March 1820
13	*Hope*	Brig	226	Birnie & Co., Sydney	NSW Sydney: 16 convicts, leader M. Coogan	18.11.1820
14	*Sinbad*	Schooner	?	Robert Campbell, Sydney	NSW Government wharf, Windsor: 25 convicts arrested	Prior to 30.11.1820
15	*Prince Leopold*	Brig	92	VDL Government	VDL George Town: several convicts already aboard	2.3.1826
16	*Liberty*	Schooner	45	Unknown	NSW Sydney Harbour: 13 convicts with boat, leader Coogan	Early hours of 31.3.1827
17	*Emma Kemp*	Cutter	36	Richard Kemp, Hobart	VDL Derwent Estuary: 9–10 convicts from boat	14.12.1827

NSW = New South Wales; VDL = Van Diemen's Land (now Tasmania)
(a) Now D'Entrecasteaux Channel.
(b) *SG*, 7 June 1817, p. 3b.
Sources: Too numerous to list here, but especially *HRA* and contemporaneous colonial newspapers.

Table 3. *Seizures and attempted seizures of boats by convicts, 1790–1829.*

No.	Type	Owner(s)	Where seizure attempted	When attempted	Success or failure?
1–2	Punt, small rigged boat	?	NSW Rose Hill: Sydney Harbour Heads	26.9.1790	Success
3	6-oar cutter	Governor's boat	NSW Sydney Cove	28.3.1791	Success
4	Boat	?	NSW	Early September 1797	Success
5	Boat	?	NSW Parramatta	2.10.1797	Success
6	Boat	?	NSW Parramatta	November 1797	Failure
7	Boat	Owen Cavanagh	NSW Broken Bay	10.1.1798	Success
8	Boat	Richard Hawke	NSW Kissing Point	15 or 16.6.1803	Success
9	Boat	J. Mountgarret	VDL Risdon Cove	c.8.10.1803	Success
10	Boat	Sergeant Day	NSW Parramatta	Prior to 3.3.1804	Success
11	Boat	Revd Knopwood	VDL Sullivan Cove	24.7.1805	Success
12	Boat	?	VDL Derwent Estuary	February1806	Success
13	Boat	NSW Government?	NSW Newcastle PS	1.4.1806	Success
14	Boat	E. Willis, Sydney	NSW Sydney Harbour	19.1.1807	Success
15	Small boat	?	VDL Derwent Estuary	October 1807	Success
16–17	Boats: at least 2	?	NSW Sydney Harbour	16.5.1808	Success
18	Boat	?	NSW Hawkesbury River	Late 1813/early 1814	Failure
19	Pilot boat	VDL Government	VDL George Town	1.4.1814	Success
20	Pilot boat	VDL Government	VDL George Town	5.10.1814	Success
21	Boat	?	VDL	By July 1814	Success
22	Boat	?	NSW Sydney Harbour Heads	12.9.1816	Success
23	Whaleboat	NSW Government	NSW Newcastle PS	Shortly prior to 30.11.1816	Success
24–25	2 boats	VDL Government	VDL George Town	10.6.1817	Success
26	Longboat	VDL Government	VDL Port Dalrymple	Mid-June 1817	Success
27	Boat	William Thomas	NSW Rushcutters Bay	9.10.1817	Success
28–29	2 boats	VDL Government	VDL Sullivan Cove	8.4.1818	Success
30	Boat	?	NSW Sydney Harbour	On or prior to 19.6.1818	Failure
31	Boat	?	NSW Sydney Harbour	By 19.6.1818	Success
32	Boat	?	NSW Sydney Harbour	By 19.6.1818	Success

Table 3. *(continued)*

No.	Type	Owner(s)	Where seizure attempted	When attempted	Success or failure?
33–35	Boats: at least 3	?	NSW Sydney Harbour	Late July/early August 1818	Success
36	Boat	?	VDL Derwent Estuary	27.1.1819	Success
37	Boat	?	NSW Sydney Harbour	Mid-March 1819	Success
38	Whaleboat	Owners, whaler *Regalia*	VDL Hobart	Prior to May 1820	Success
39	Pilot boat	NSW Government	NSW Newcastle PS	June 1820	Success
40	Boat	?	VDL New Norfolk	c.28.11.1820	Success
41	Whaleboat	?	NSW Cockle Bay	25–26/12/1820	Success
42	Pilot boat	VDL Government	VDL Derwent Estuary	Between 23.10.1821 & 24.6.1822	Success
43–44	Boat: whaleboat	VDL Government	VDL Macquarie Harbour PS	7.6.1824	Success
45	Gig-boat	Commandant's boat	NSW Newcastle PS	Shortly prior to 11.5.1825	Success
46	Whaleboat	?	VDL Derwent Estuary	May 1825	Success
47	Boat	Major Honner	VDL Derwent Estuary	9.9.1825	Success
48	Boat	Mr Pechey	VDL Huon River Estuary	c.September 1825	Success
49	Whaleboat	George Meredith Esq.	VDL near Great Swan Port	8.10.1825	Success
50	Whaleboat	VDL Government	VDL Spring Bay	2.12.1825	Success
51–53	3 boats	NSW Government	NSW Norfolk Island PS	25.9.1826	Success
54	Boat	?	VDL Hobart	13.1.1827	Success
55	Boat	?	NSW Sydney Harbour	By 31.3.1827	Success
56	Boat	Mr Young	VDL Hobart	13.12.1827	Success
57–58	2 boats	T. Hyde, Sydney: one unknown	NSW Sydney Harbour	30.4.1828	Failure
59	Whaleboat, rigged	VDL Government	VDL Macquarie Harbour PS	December 1828	Success
60	Boat 3.5 tons	Dr Halloran, Parramatta	NSW Parramatta	16.8.1829	Success

VDL = Van Diemen's Land (now Tasmania); NSW = New South Wales; PS = Penal Station
Sources: Too numerous to list here, but especially *HRA* and contemporaneous colonial newspapers.

night watch – both against port regulations. Everything needful for a long trading voyage to Fiji was aboard.[54] Selecting such inviting prey implies these pirates operated effective prior surveillance and planning.

Van Diemen's Land experienced many boat seizures, and often its bushrangers were also boat and small vessel pirates. On 10 June 1817, bushrangers looted George Town's commissary store, escaping in two stolen boats with five convict recruits.[55] Around midnight on 3 December 1825, Matthew Brady and thirteen of his gang seized Maria Island's ferryboat, *Blue-Eyed Maid*.[56] Later that day, Brady and his men used this boat to take a sloop off nearby Schouten Island. Rising winds persuaded them to return, sink the sloop, and head for the Van Diemen's Land's interior.[57] The Brady Gang had commenced bushranging with a boat escape from the Macquarie Harbour Penal Station.[58] They and others became as much sea rangers as bushrangers. Bushrangers stole boats to access remote coastal and insular hideaways and to raid isolated coastal settlements, destabilizing existing power relations. Lieutenant-Governor Arthur – who rarely admitted failures – conceded "the skill and conduct of this extraordinary Man [Brady] [...] baffled the united efforts of the Civil and Military power".[59]

Three spectacular Tasman Sea incidents occurred between 1826 and 1827. On 25 September 1826, fifty-seven convicts fled in seized government boats from the Norfolk Island Penal Station, a general uprising having failed. John Goff led the evacuation under fire from troops. Often flogged, condemned at differing times to every other contemporaneous penal station, he escaped from them all. At Pieman's River, Van Diemen's Land, and on the Hastings River, New South Wales, he had stood alongside fellow runaways in firefights with troops.[60] After landing at nearby Philip Island, the 1826 Norfolk Island escapers contested the landing of a military pursuit party that took some captives and the runaways' boats. Subsequent seaborne infantry sorties recaptured piecemeal the marooned remnant, including Goff. He and two comrades were hanged in 1827 after a Sydney Supreme Court show trial.[61]

54. Duffield, "Identity Fraud", pp. 390–415; *SG*, 22 May 1808, p. 2a–b.
55. *HTG*, 5 July 1817, p. 1a; *SG*, 4 October 1817, p. 3a–b.
56. *HTG*, 3 December 1825, p. 2d.
57. *Ibid*; I.H. Nicholson, *Shipping Arrivals and Departures Tasmania*, I, *1803–1833* (Canberra, 1983), Pt I, p. 110.
58. Maxwell-Stewart, *Closing Hell's Gates*, pp. 183–186.
59. Arthur to Bathurst, 11 April 1826, in E. FitzSymonds (ed.), *Brady [...] and Associates* (Adelaide, 1979), pp. 151–152.
60. Maxwell-Stewart, *Closing Hell's Gates*, p. 176; Jack Bushman, "Passages from the Life of a 'Lifer'", ch. 2, *Moreton Bay Courier*, 9 April 1859, p. 4c.
61. Ian Duffield, "The Life and Death of 'Black' John Goff: Aspects of the Black Convict Contribution to Resistance Patterns During the Transportation Era in Eastern Australia",

Figure 2. Item 3 from *Panorama of Hobart*, 1825, watercolour, by Augustus Earle. The Van Diemen's Land government brig *Cyprus*, piratically seized by convicts in 1829, is the two-masted vessel second from the left.
Dixson Gallery, State Library of New South Wales. Used with permission.

On 21 December 1826, over forty out of sixty-six convicts bound from Sydney to Norfolk Island seized the government brig *Wellington*. The pirates chose an ex-army officer, John Walton, to command and (like "Golden Age" pirates) elected a council. A log was kept, offenders against collectively agreed articles were disciplined, and imprisoned opponents treated decently. Advised by the *Wellington*'s lawful commander, they called at New Zealand's Bay of Islands for water, preparatory to sailing for South America. Two British whaler captains, encouraged by the Revd Henry Williams, a resident Bay of Islands missionary and former naval officer, became suspicious. After a cannonade from the whalers, Walton surrendered, never having returned fire.[62] Nevertheless, similar ventures recurred. On 4 August 1827, eighteen out of twenty-one convicts bound from Hobart to Macquarie Harbour seized the *Cyprus* when it was storm-bound in Recherche Bay. Their elected commander, William Swallow,

Australian Journal of Politics and History, 33 (1987), pp. 30–44; Hamish Maxwell-Stewart, "The Search for the Invisible Man", in Lucy Frost and Hamish Maxwell-Stewart (eds), *Chain Letters: Narrating Convict Lives* (Carlton South, 2001), pp. 53–54; Maxwell-Stewart, *Closing Hell's Gates*, p. 176.
62. Ihde, "Pirates of the Pacific"; Hirst, *Great Convict Escapes*, ch. 5.

navigated the *Cyprus* via Japan to near Canton. Then, they scuttled the
Cyprus and tried – but failed – to pass as castaways, recalling the Bryant
episode. Two of them became the last pirates hanged at Wapping's
Execution Dock.[63]

VICTIMS, LOSSES, LASCARS, AND THE COLONIAL STATE'S INCAPACITY

Given the many convict piracies and the analytical deficit in popular
studies of them, it is necessary to identify and interrogate salient themes
from my reading of the sources that constitute my convict pirate archive.
The generic "who whom" problematics of archives preclude regarding
this archive as a neutral objective record. Therefore, I interrogate it to
unpackage state incapacity to curb convict piracy, reveal the range and
identify the victims of material losses inflicted, and air an unresolved
puzzle concerning alleged lascar connections.

Official reactions calibrate the piracies' effects, as do losses inflicted.
Both piratical incidents and fears about consequent convict responses
intensified endemic official and free settler anxieties about imagined
insurrectionary conspiracies.[64] Free colonists sometimes requested
countermeasures. At Windsor, New South Wales, a November 1824
Grand Jury fruitlessly requested a police boat based at the Hawkesbury
River's mouth "to prevent piratical seizures".[65] Even Sydney Harbour had
only a regular Row Guard from 5 February 1820. Two masters, two
boatswains, and six sailors were to provide two crews, one for day and
one for night service.[66] Convicts served in this Lilliputian outfit, as in the
police ashore. Foreseeable problems ensued. For example, on 2 September
1820 convict Row Guard sailor William Jones absconded. Coxswain
Bernard Williams reputedly flourished by smuggling spirits.[67] The
original Row Guard supposedly policed Sydney Harbour's labyrinthine
waterways, with their 317 kilometres of shoreline. Unsurprisingly, the
authorities had to expand the force rapidly, despite cost implications, to
36 boats and 140 men by 1822.[68]

---

63. On the London trial and execution of *Cyprus* pirates, see Hirst, *The Man Who Stole the Cyprus*, pp. 148–176.
64. Paula Jane Byrne, *Criminal Law and Colonial Subject: New South Wales, 1810–1830* (Cambridge, 1993), ch. 5; Michael Sturma, *Vice in a Vicious Society: Crime and Convicts in Mid Nineteenth-Century New South Wales* (St Lucia, 1983); Boyce, *Van Diemen's Land*, ch. 8.
65. *SG*, 2 December 1824, p. 3b.
66. *SG*, 5 February 1818, p. 1a–b; State Records of New South Wales [hereafter SRNSW], Colonial Secretary's Records [hereafter CSR], 5 February 1820, reel 6049, 4/1744, pp. 168–175; reel 6039, SZ756, pp. 53–55; 8 February 1820, reel 6007, 4/3501, pp. 237–238.
67. *SG*, 2 September 1818, p. 2a; Karskens, *The Rocks*, p. 185.
68. *Ibid.*, p. 184.

That had limited effects. There were only four Sydney Harbour/ Parramatta River incidents from 1821 to 1829. The small vessel *Mary* (1828) and two boats (1827 and 1829) were taken. The 1827 attempt on the schooner *Liberty* failed, but without Row Guard intervention.[69] However, this paucity of Sydney Harbour incidents during that period may indicate Row Guard deterrence. This is offset by the fact that most New South Wales convict piracies between 1821 and 1829 were at smaller ports or (once) on the high seas. There were seven such incidents, only one unsuccessful, involving vessels or ships and three, all successful, involving boats (see the data in Tables 1–3).

In June 1826, the *Hobart Town Gazette* bewailed Hobart's lack of "a well regulated excise or guard" for twenty-four-hour harbour and Derwent Estuary surveillance.[70] Eight months on, this official medium requested "a small Colonial armed vessel" to prevent piracy and smuggling in the Derwent and "round the coast". It added: "The Guard Boat, a most necessary establishment which rows round the vessels in the Harbour at night", should be of "the lightest and swiftest construction" and employ only "upright characters".[71] Implicitly, one lumbering guard boat and nefarious crew now existed, but only undertaking night duty in Sullivan Cove, Hobart's harbour. However, when a boat approached the cutter *Emma Kemp*, moored in the Derwent, at night on 28 June 1827, escaped prisoners replied "guard-boat" when challenged by the cutter's watch but sheered off when further questioned.[72] Port regulations threatened stiff fines on shipping without armed night watches, but, this incident notwithstanding, compliance remained patchy.

British naval units only intermittently visited New South Wales and Van Diemen's Land, while each operated just a few small, lightly armed government vessels. In May 1827, three small brigs comprised Sydney-based New South Wales sea power. A schooner was "permanently attached" to Melville Island and another designated for Port Essington,[73] outposts vastly nearer Timor than Sydney. In 1825, Governor Brisbane implored London to provide two modest-sized armed schooners for Sydney and a smaller one for Hobart, with costs falling on Britain's Treasury. A caustic refusal ensued.[74] In similar stingy vein, the New South Wales Police Fund – a multi-purpose government cash tank – swallowed

69. *Monitor*, 6 April 1827, p. 2b–c.
70. *HTG*, 10 June 1826, p. 4b.
71. *HTG*, 10 February 1827, p. 4a.
72. *Colonial Times and Tasmanian Advertiser* [hereafter *CT&TA*], 29 June 1827, p. 2a; *The Australian*, 18 July 1826, p. 4a.
73. Darling to Hay, 14 May 1827, *HRA*, Series 1, XIII, p. 304.
74. Brisbane to Bathurst, 8 July 1824, *HRA*, Series 1, XI, p. 303; Bathurst to Brisbane, 7 January 1825, *ibid.*, p. 469.

two-thirds of the revenue raised by selling Sydney Row Guard prizes. The remainder was distributed among Guard personnel: predominantly to masters, secondarily to boatswains, the residuum to sailors.[75] As seen, armed shipboard night watches could deter pirates. When a pirate boat attempted night seizure of the *Sophia* in Sydney Cove on 19 June 1818, James Kelly, the brig's master, led the vessel's armed watch in driving the pirates away with musketry.[76] Despite Kelly's resultant acclaim, port security regulation observance remained lax and pirates confident. Soon after, convicts seized several boats around Sydney Harbour – in order, officials worried, to seize a seagoing vessel.

A fourteen-strong escaped convict gang triggered the request for a Hawkesbury police boat. Led by William Skivener, on 30 October 1824 the gang seized the sloop *Angelina* in the Hawkesbury, after taking a boat carrying "wine, porter, sugar, tea, etc.", thus enhancing stolen basic provisions already cached at their Mullet Island rendezvous. The gang also possessed stolen charts, a sextant, quadrants, a compass, and a gold–cased chronometer – all useful for navigating a blue-water getaway. Among the gang were men with navigation skills. Skivener – no navigator but elected commander for his leadership talents – and five others embarked on the *Angelina*. Their comrades confidently expected "to take another vessel".[77] Small farmers (often time-served convicts) dominated Hawkesbury settler demography. The pirates' loot, if modest compared to that of contemporaneous Sulu and South China Sea pirates,[78] would have hurt many Hawkesbury households. Humbler members of colonial society, not just substantial merchants and ship-owners, suffered losses from convict piracy.

On the Hawkesbury Estuary and its Broken Bay extension, piracy began early. On 5 September 1797 fifteen convicts (some crewmen, some boarding from a boat) seized the government schooner *Cumberland*, laden with stores for the new Hawkesbury settlements. The pirates included the 1790 piratical escapers, George Lee and John Turwood.[79] The *Cumberland*, according to Governor Hunter, was the best vessel in the colony and sorely missed.[80] A replacement *Cumberland*, for pursuing absconded convicts "who were [...] in the practice of carrying off boats"

---

75. *SG*, 5 February 1818, p. 1a–b.
76. *SG*, 20 June 1818, p. 2b–c.
77. *The Australian*, 11 November 1824, p. 3b.
78. Robert J. Anthony, *Like Froth Floating on the Sea: The World of Pirates and Seafarers in Late Imperial South China* (Berkeley, CA, 2003); Dian H. Murray, *Pirates of the South China Coast, 1790–1810* (Stanford, CA, 1987); James Francis Warren, *Iranun and Balangingi: Globalization, Maritime Raiding, and the Birth of Ethnicity* (Quezon City, 2001).
79. Flynn, *The Second Fleet*, pp. 400–401, 572–573.
80. Collins, *Account of the English Colony in New South Wales*, II, p. 38; Hirst, *Great Convict Escapes*, p. 32; Hughes, *The Fatal Shore*, p. 213.

was nearing launch in July 1800.[81] That month, the government sloop *Norfolk*, laden with wheat for Sydney, was taken in the Hawkesbury and then shipwrecked.[82] Such events taxed the infant colony's fiscal resources.

As an indication of the value of small colonial craft, in March 1824 the new 33-ton schooner *Governor Sorell* was auctioned at Hobart for £380. Its small boat fetched £10.[83] A loss of around £10 would hurt petty proprietors; £380 might bankrupt modestly prosperous ones. In 1828 a man in a boat raided Johnson's Bay, on the Parramatta River, stealing a mast and sails belonging to Dr Laurence Hynes Halloran, a prominent but hard-up emancipist. After vigorous pursuit, Halloran and two of his sons recovered their property, the thief's boat, and a boat in tow. Both boats proved stolen.[84] Halloran was targeted again on the night of 16 August 1829: his 3.25-ton boat, used for commercial wood carrying, was taken. A handsome $20 reward (probably 20 Spanish dollars, then worth £4) was offered for its return.[85] Halloran declared the boat "the principal support of a large Family".[86] Though proliferating boat thefts were hard on victims, they could not unite the colonial poor, a fluctuating, heterogeneous element, in self-defence. Boat ownership offered small proprietors a chance to better themselves materially as self-employed watermen, but other poorer Sydneysiders were constantly making off with boats, to grab a free harbour crossing, escape justice, or undertake criminal enterprises.[87]

Concerning larger losses, information collected by J.T. Bigge, ahead of his Parliamentary Reports on New South Wales and Van Diemen's Land, is revealing. Robert Campbell, formerly Sydney's leading merchant, wrote to Bigge on 30 June 1820 fretting that the pirating of his brig the *Venus* in 1806, when under government hire, remained uncompensated. He estimated his loss at a painful £3,200.[88] What further galled him was that London had ordered large grants of New South Wales land and government livestock to William Campbell. In effect, if not formally, that settled his £4,000 1812

81. *HRA*, Series 1, II, p. 619.

82. SRNSW, CSR, 4/1719, microfilm reel 6041, pp. 109–112; Hirst, *Great Convict Escapes*, p. 33.

83. *SG*, 8 April 1824, p. 2c; Nicholson, *Shipping Arrivals and Departures Tasmania*, Pt 1, p. 95. This study's 2010 sterling values were calculated in comparative retail price index terms using www.measuringworth.com/calculators/ppoweruk/; £380 and £10 (1824) = £27,100 and £686 (2010).

84. *Monitor*, 3 May 1828, p. 8b.

85. *The Australian*, 19 August 1829, p. 4e. For converting Spanish dollars into sterling, see R.B. Allen, *Slaves, Freedmen and Independent Laborers in Colonial Mauritius* (Cambridge, 1999), p. xvii.

86. *The Australian*, 19 August 1829, p. 4e; £4 (1829) = £275 (2010).

87. Karskens, *The Rocks*, pp. 183–184, 186.

88. Campbell to J.T. Bigge, 30 June 1820, Mitchell Library, Sydney, Bonwick Transcripts, Box 25, microfilm reel CY 1506 – Bigge, J.T. – Report, Appendix, p. 4568; Margaret Steven, *Merchant Campbell 1769–1846: A Study of Colonial Trade* (Melbourne, 1965), chs 7–10, p. 137; £3,200 (1806) = £202,000 (2010).

claim for compensation for the *Harrington* piracy.[89] Yet, when seized, the *Harrington* was not chartered to the government and was breaching port regulations. When, occasionally, compensation was awarded, patronage rather than merit seemingly triumphed.

Bigge's antidote to disorder in Sydney, Hobart, and other coastal settlements – move all convicts well inland – was unworkable. Large piracy losses continued after his reports. The 1825 *Eclipse* piracy lost the owners £1,000.[90] Bigge commented tartly on "the frequency of piratical seizures [...] by the convicts of Sydney Cove" during Macquarie's governorship.[91] At least sixteen Sydney Harbour craft were targeted in that period, the pirates succeeding on eleven occasions (see Tables 1–3). However, only two successful incidents involved ships or vessels, against four failures (see Tables 1–2).

In Van Diemen's Land, Bigge's key informant was James Kelly,[92] a Derwent pilot and from 1819 Hobart's Harbour Master.[93] Following his *Sophia* triumph, Kelly had twice pursued Derwent pirates – unsuccessfully.[94] Oddly, Kelly informed Bigge, "Vessels that are most in danger are the Brigs from India manned by Lascars".[95] Frustratingly, this alleged "lascar connection" to convict piracy remains enigmatic, for lascars in early colonial Australia await serious scholarly attention and no "lascar connection" emerges from this study's many other sources. Kelly's own narrow escape from Otago Harbour in 1818, when Maori killed some of his crew, perhaps prejudiced his mind. He believed a Maori- and English-speaking lascar resident there, who managed the relevant Otago ruler's dealings with foreigners, had ensnared the *Sophia*'s shore party.[96] Bigge learned from Kelly about several Derwent piracies: *Unity* (23 April 1814); *Argo* (12 June 1814); an odd bushranger-built craft (11 April 1818); and *Young Lachlan* (27 February 1819).[97] The Calcutta-owned *Argo* presumably had lascar crew, but no known evidence suggests they abetted piracy.

89. Mitchell Library, Sydney, Bonwick Transcripts, Box 25, microfilm reel CY 1506 – Bigge, J.T. – Report, Appendix, p. 4584; *HRA*, Series 1, VII, pp. 518–520, 756–759. William Campbell's 1812 £4,000 compensation claim = £208,000 (2010).

90. *SG*, 26 May 1825, p. 2e; £1,000 (1825) = £64,000 (2010).

91. *Report of the Commissioner of Inquiry on the Judicial Establishments of New South Wales and Van Diemen's Land*, Parliamentary Papers 1823 (33) X 515, p. 81.

92. *HRA*, Series 3, III, pp. 458–466.

93. *Ibid.*, p. 458; Sorell to Macquarie, 6 April 1819, *HRA*, Series 3, II, p. 389.

94. *HTG&SA*, 25 April 1818, pp. 1a–b and 2a; K.M. Bowden, *Captain James Kelly of Hobart Town* (Parkville, 1964), pp. 51–52.

95. *HRA*, Series 3, III, p. 458.

96. Bowden, *Captain James Kelly*, pp. 47–48. For New Zealand's lascar presence, see Anne Salmond, *Between Worlds: Early Exchanges Between Maori and Europeans, 1773–1815* (Auckland, 1997), pp. 235, 290, 312.

97. *HTG*, 6 March 1819, p. 1a–b; 13 March 1819, pp. 1a–c and 2c; 27 March 1819, p. 2a–b; *SG*, 27 March 1819, p. 3a–b; 24 April 1819, p. 3a; Sorell to Macquarie, 26 March 1819, *HRA*, Series 3, II, pp. 386–387; Macquarie to Sorell, 15 June 1819, *ibid.*, p. 393; Hirst, *Great Convict Escapes*, p. 41.

The *Young Lachlan* seizure further illustrates the perils of neglecting port security regulations. Moored at owner Captain Howard's desire off his Macquarie Point store, when regulations stipulated Sullivan Cove, *Young Lachlan*'s sails, rudder, and the rudder's securing bolt remained on deck too. Regulations required their lock-up ashore. Some of the sails were already bent. These infractions facilitated a quick departure. There was neither night watch kept nor ammunition on board. The master having departed up-country, the four seamen on the *Young Lachlan* neglected all duty.[98] These unconcealed follies invited piracy. To cap it all, Lieutenant-Governor Sorell had condoned the *Young Lachlan*'s irregular mooring – though not the other security breaches.[99]

Because taken on a dark night, the *Young Lachlan* sailed invisible to Hobart's gunners at The Battery.[100] Sorell was informed of the seizure just after 5 a.m. on 28 February 1819. Beyond oared boats, only Thomas Birch's *Sophia* brig and twenty-ton sailing boat were in harbour.[101] The pirates' course at sea was sheer guesswork to their pursuers. Kelly accepted command of Birch's sailing boat. It was unready to sail till noon. Soldiers plus sea captains Howard and Bunster accompanied Kelly – two captains too many for one command? The pursuit merely rescued *Young Lachlan*'s crew, dumped by the pirates on Bruny Island. Nevertheless, Birch would have been recompensed. For a previous similar service, he was exempt customs duty on a substantial quantity of imported spirits.[102] Whenever a private craft was hired to pursue convict pirates, the owners were paid regardless of the outcome, making dead loss for some good business for others.

When taken, the *Young Lachlan* carried no water and few water casks, allowing assertions that it could not sail far. New standing orders obliged Hobart's gunners to keep their artillery loaded and "fire upon any Vessel [...] moving out of the Port past the Point, or down the River, during the night". It was reiterated that colonial and small vessels must moor close in at Sullivan Cove. Delinquents whose rudders and sails were not "landed and lodged in a Place of Security" faced embargo from trading till they complied.[103] Such papery severity lacked deterrent force, while the *Young Lachlan*'s pirates certainly obtained water somewhere, for they reached Java.[104] Self-interest ensured neglect of port regulations when conducting

98. *HTG*, 6 March 1819, p. 1a–b, and 13 March 1819, pp. 1a–c and 2c.
99. Sorell to Macquarie, 26 March 1819, *HRA*, Series 3, II, pp. 386–387.
100. *Ibid.*, p. 386.
101. *Ibid.*, p. 387.
102. Sorell to Macquarie, 23 May 1818, and Macquarie to Sorell, 3 June 1818, in *HRA*, Series 3, II, pp. 321, 327.
103. *HTG*, 13 March 1819, pp. 1a–b and 2c; *SG*, 27 March 1819, p. 3a–b, and 24 April 1819, p. 3a.
104. Hirst, *Great Convict Escapes*, p. 41.

legitimate trade, let alone smuggling (then rife). In 1817, Sorell fruitlessly requested Macquarie's permission to construct a government cutter, to prevent "improper proceedings" in the Derwent.[105] However, on 1 December 1818 Macquarie undertook to send Sorell the 92-ton brig *Prince Leopold* – purchased in Sydney for £1,200. That plus £167 18s towards refitting was charged to the Van Diemen's Land's Police Fund. The New South Wales government itself spent £562 2s 8d on refitting.[106] In Van Diemen's Land service, the *Prince Leopold* flopped – its draught was too deep for some Van Diemen's Land ports.[107] Meagre colonial fiscal resources had been wasted. The period 1820 to 1825 brought at least fourteen more Van Diemen's Land piratical incidents, and 1826 saw an attempt on the *Prince Leopold* itself.

THE GROUNDS OF PIRATE SUCCESS OR FAILURE

What constituted "successful" seizure? Here, success is not understood in absolute terms but as taking a prize and escaping – at least for a while. Successful seizures predominated. That required trustworthy, motivated confederates who would not blab indiscreetly or inform for reward. Also needed were: relevant skills among the gang; good intelligence gathering; acquisition of necessary implements (weapons, for example); and well-planned and executed tactics. Often, convict pirates stole a boat or boats for approaching, boarding, and cutting out a moored target – operations requiring skill and resolution.

An instance is the *Speedwell* piracy, committed by four runaways from the Newcastle Penal Station. John Pearce, Edward Scarr, and Herbert Stiles were capital respites on life sentences; Joseph Burridge was serving a fourteen-year sentence.[108] Such sentences served at a harsh penal station provided obvious motives for escape. Stiles had been convicted of piracy and sentenced at Calcutta, 4 December 1809.[109] After arrival at Sydney in 1811, he was forwarded to Newcastle and soon rumoured to be planning a piratical escape.[110] In April 1813 he escaped into the bush, but returned, injured by Aboriginals.[111] His subsequent gang boarded the *Speedwell* in rain at night on 7 April 1814, from a boat stolen from a government

---

105. Sorell to Macquarie, 26 June 1817, *HRA*, Series 3, II, p. 234.
106. The two 1818 charges to the Van Diemen's Land government for this vessel amounted to £80,640 (2010 prices). Refitting costs met by the New South Wales government were £33,300 (2010 prices).
107. Macquarie to Sorell, 1 December 1819, *HRA*, Series 3, II, pp. 369–370; Macquarie to Bigge, 22 January 1821, *HRA*, Series 1, X, p. 401.
108. Macquarie to Bathurst, 7 May 1814, *HRA*, Series 1, VIII, p. 251.
109. *Ibid.*
110. SRNSW, CSR, 10 October 1811, reel 6003, 4/3492, p. 74.
111. *Ibid.*, 2 October 1813, reel 6003, 4/3492, p. 215.

schooner aground nearby. Aboard the *Speedwell*, in the name of Newcastle's Commandant, they successfully requested the loan of a grapnel. With it, they promptly felled the *Speedwell*'s master, secured his wife and a seaman (the only others present), and sailed off.[112]

The *Sydney Gazette* stated that with scant water and provisions and no boat to put ashore for water, the seizure was doomed. Gazetting these pirates ceased after eleven months – tacit acknowledgement of a sustained escape. In fact, when seized the *Speedwell* carried one month's provisions and 60 gallons of water:[113] sufficient to reach New Zealand. A makeshift raft would assist conveying fresh water and food from landfalls. If necessary, drag anchors could be devised from rocks and cables. Island-hopping enabled a small vessel to cross the South Pacific. In 1806–1807, the pirated 45-ton brig *Venus* island hopped from New Zealand to Chile.[114] From 1790 to 1829, out of 60 identified boat incidents only 5 failed (see Tables 6 and 7). Seizing a vessel or ship was trickier: of 44 known incidents 17 failed.

Tables 4 and 5 show an inverse ratio between the size of ships and vessels and success. As much as 63 per cent of successes involved vessels of 50 tons or less. No attempt on craft of 200 tons or more succeeded (see Tables 4 and 5). Larger craft, like the 578-ton *Minerva* and the 459-ton *Castle Forbes*, were targeted by larger escape parties – potentially less cohesive than smaller parties. Colonial police shone at recruiting informers – this secured the *Castle Forbes*[115] and the *Minerva* from seizure. The known seizures and attempts from 1790 to 1829 directly involved around 900 men[116] and 8 women. Of all known ship or vessel incidents, 61.4% were successful, as were 91.7% of boat incidents (see Tables 6 and 7). Hughesian bolting or sheer luck could hardly achieve those success rates; rather, a predominance of well-planned and executed incidents is implied.

In late Georgian Britain, many people, though not oceanic seafarers, were "accustomed to the sea". Naval manning during the 1793–1815 wars against France required massive resort to the press gang, leading to high desertion rates. After 1815, there were probably more transported convicts "accustomed to the sea", or who concealed wartime naval service because of desertion, than the authorities reckoned. For self-advantage, in Australia the convict pirates Robert Stewart and John William Lancashire

---

112. Macquarie to Bathurst, 7 May 1814, *HRA*, Series 1, VIII, p. 250; *SG*, 23 April 1814, p. 2c.
113. *SG*, 23 April 1814, p. 2c.
114. Eugenio Pereira Salas, "Las primeras relaciones entre Chile y Australia", *Boletin de la Academia Chilena de la Historia*, 53 (1955), pp. 22–24; C.W. Vennell, *The Brown Frontier: New Zealand 1806–1877* (Wellington, 1967), ch. 1. Unaware of these works when writing "'Haul Away the Anchor Girls'", I recycled a chain of errors about the *Venus* piracy's end.
115. *HRA*, Series 3, III, p. 460.
116. Some engaged in multiple incidents – including George Lee, John Turwood, and Robert Stewart.

Table 4. *Tonnage, 27 ships and vessels seized by transported convicts,*
1790–1829.

16–50 tons	51–100 tons	101–200 tons	Tonnage unknown
17	—	4	6

Sources: Too numerous to list here, but especially *HRA* and contemporaneous
colonial newspapers.

Table 5. *Tonnage, 17 failed ships and vessel seizures by transported*
convicts, 1790–1829.

35–50 tons	51–100 tons	101–200 tons	201–300 tons	301–400 tons	401–500 tons	501–600 tons	Tonnage unknown
4	2	2	1	—	3	1	4

Sources: Too numerous to list here, but especially *HRA* and contemporaneous
colonial newspapers.

concealed wartime naval desertions.[117] Among convict pirates a minority
had significant seafaring skills. William Wales, a fine mathematician and
notable scientific and practical navigator, taught Stewart astral navigation
at the Royal Institute of Mathematics, London. In the navy, Stewart rose
to sailing master's mate. Sailing masters were warrant officers in charge
of the practical sailing of a warship. Necessarily, they and their mates
understood astral navigation. Stewart certainly could have navigated the
Harrington.

The twelve absconders from Hobart Prisoners' Barracks who seized the
cutter *Ellen* off Cape Pilar on 16 January 1827 further reveal how and
why convicts came together to seize a vessel. Among them, Alexander
Stirling was a former collier's mate, John Clarke a mariner, and James
Nelson a seaman. James Thompson (tried at Aberdeen, on the same
date as Stirling)[118] was a rope maker, Henry Alderson a cooper, and
William Ironmonger a carpenter – useful skills at sea. Five *Ellen* pirates
arrived in Australia on the *Medway* 2, two on the *Medina*. Convict
transport shipmates often sustained ongoing mutual loyalties. Alderson,
Thompson, and Stirling were *Medway* 2 men. Stirling's sea officer experience
probably swayed his fellow pirates to elect him their commander.[119]

117. Duffield, "Identity Fraud", p. 390; Jordan, *Convict Theatres*, pp. 227–231.
118. National Archives of Scotland, Edinburgh: AD 14/25/102, JC 26/1825/29, AD 14/25/73,
JC 26/1825/34.
119. Other sources for this paragraph: *HTG*, 19 January 1827, p. 4a; 20 January 1827, p. 2b;
27 January 1827, pp. 2b and 3a–b; and 3 February 1827, pp. 2a and 4a; *CT&T*, 2 February 1827,
p. 3d; *Monitor*, 3 February 1827, p. 5b.

Table 6. *Successful transported convict piratical seizures, 1790–1829.*

1790–1799		1800–1809		1810–1819		1820–1829	
Boats	Ships or vessels	Boats	Ships or vessels	Boats	Ships or vessels	Boats	Ships or vessels
6	1	10	6	18	7	21	13

82 craft seized: 55 boats; 27 ships or vessels
Sources: Too numerous to list here, but especially *HRA* and contemporaneous colonial newspapers.

Table 7. *Failed transported convict piratical seizures, 1790–1829.*

1790–1799		1800–1809		1810–1819		1820–1829	
Boats	Ships or vessels	Boats	Ships or vessels	Boats	Ships or vessels	Boats	Ships or vessels
1	—	—	7	2	4	2	6

22 craft, seizure failed: 5 boats; 17 ships or vessels
Sources: Too numerous to list here, but especially *HRA* and contemporaneous colonial newspapers.

Remember here that Herbert Stiles, leader of the *Speedwell* pirates, had prior sea experience *as a pirate*, a circumstance paralleled in Clare Anderson's study in the present volume.[120]

Few convict pirates underwent Supreme Court trials. Some were charged with other offences promising easier convictions. Magistrates summarily convicted and sentenced many pirates. Almost all penal stations had maritime locations necessitating boat and shipping services – and inviting inmate piracy. In the period 1806–1829 at least seven boats and four vessels were seized from penal stations, and two vessels were seized when bound for penal stations (see Tables 1 and 3).

Many more convict men and women escaped by stowing away on departing shipping or striking deals with short-handed ships' masters than by piracy, despite official countermeasures. The colonial authorities particularly hated United States ships' captains cutting deals with convict escapers, perhaps because their defiance of British authority revived painful memories of the American Revolution. However, some British captains behaved similarly, including a naval commander.[121] Other convicts

120. Clare Anderson, "The Age of Revolution in the Indian Ocean, Bay of Bengal, and South China Sea: A Maritime Perspective", in the present volume.
121. He was William Chase, HMS *Samarang*. See Macquarie to Croker, 3 August 1813, *HRA*, Series 1, VIII, p. 32.

achieved sea escape through shady deals with free settlers. In 1814 the
Calcutta-owned *Argo* left the Derwent without clearance – a serious
breach of port regulations. The *Argo*'s master Captain Dixon, apparently
in league with two Hobart merchants, Loane and Carr, received piratical
assistance from twelve convict escapers.[122] This looks like a deal between
big smugglers and their convict agents. Governor Macquarie wanted
Dixon tried for piracy if caught, and regretted that inadequate evidence
precluded Loane's or Carr's prosecution.[123] Dixon had been heavily fined
on 15 May 1814 for assaulting and slandering Hobart's Naval Officer,
James Gordon.[124] Collecting customs revenues and preventing smuggling
were prominent among Gordon's duties. Convicts, it seems, might
sometimes consort with their "betters" in smuggling and piracy.

An 1818 episode connected stowing away and piratical escape. Voyaging
from Sydney via Cape Town to London in 1818, the 450-ton merchantman
Harriet called unscheduled at Hobart for repairs and to land several convict
stowaways.[125] Nevertheless, twenty-one convicts – fifteen men, five
women, and one boy – left Hobart secreted on board the *Harriet*. An
informer betrayed them before the *Harriet* reached Cape Town, alleging
these stowaways, crewmen, and unspecified others planned "to take the
vessel, after the cargo had been received on board at the Cape, and carry her
into South America". Officers, passengers, and a military contingent (mostly
invalids) kept constant guard till the vessel had anchored in Table Bay.[126]
The male stowaways were returned to Sydney,[127] but not the women.
Possibly the Cape Town authorities found their disposal too problematic for
decisive action. Historically, many "successful" pirates eventually suffered
sticky ends. Once taken by the Dutch, the *Young Lachlan*'s pirates mostly
died in Batavia's noisome gaol. Five were repatriated to Hobart. Malcolm
Campbell, the youngest, saved himself and ensured his comrades' execution
by turning approver.[128]

CONCLUSION: CONVICT PIRACIES AND GEOGRAPHIES OF DISCONTENT

That convict pirates confidently put to sea hints at significant geographical knowledge among them. However, landfall experiences varied.

122. *SG*, 16 July 1814, p. 2a.
123. Macquarie to Davey, 27 May 1814, *HRA*, Series 3, II, p. 63.
124. *SG*, 4 June 1814, p. 2a.
125. *HTG*, 3 January 1818, p. 2b.
126. *SG*, 27 December 1817, p. 3a; 16 May 1818, p. 3b–c; Macquarie to Bathurst, 16 May 1818, *HRA*, Series 1, IX, pp. 792–793.
127. *SG*, 9 May 1818, p. 3b.
128. *Hobart Town Gazette & Van Diemen's Land Advertiser*, 27 January 1821, Supplement, p. 1b–c.

In a Dutch colony, incarceration in a pestilential gaol, with survivors eventually deported to British territory and the gallows, could ensue. Maori rulers sometimes conferred protection and other benefits. King Kamehameha I of Hawaii conscripted escaped convicts, castaways, and ship's deserters to crew his new navy and valued them.[129] Does the Indian and Pacific Ocean diaspora of convict sea-escapers slot these people into the ranks of those elite elements in the British Empire who wielded to their profit what Alan Lester has called the "new geographies of connection"?[130]

Australia's convict pirates fit awkwardly among Lester's colonial officials, officers, merchants, entrepreneurial missionaries, and commercial land-owners, etc. The convicts utilized geographies of *dis*connection from such superiors. Kerry Ward has shown that forced migrants in the Dutch East India Company's empire – exiles, convicts, and slaves – remained autonomous historical actors.[131] Likewise, historians have recently explored subaltern networks in the Indian Ocean region, through life stories of "soldiers, slaves, convicts, pirates, rebels, traders and travelers".[132] For Ward, imperial "geographies of connection" faced challenges from subversive counterparts. Convict pirates too were not mere historical flotsam and jetsam but were articulated in surprising if (often) indirect ways to the complex maritime struggles of the age of revolution. Colonial Australia began as a project of the new geographies of connection. How fitting, then, that it should generate a convict piracy antithesis.

129. Salmond, *Between Worlds*, pp. 254, 263–264, 356–359, 466–467; Mary Louise Ormsby, "Charlotte Badger", in W.H. Oliver (ed.), *A People's History* (Wellington, 1992), pp. 1–2. Isaac Land kindly communicated information on Kamehameha I's naval personnel.
130. Alan Lester, *Imperial Networks: Creating Identities in Nineteenth-Century South Africa and Britain* (London, 2001).
131. Kerry Ward, *Networks of Empire: Forced Migration in the Dutch East India Company* (Cambridge, 2009).
132. For example, throughout Anderson, *The Indian Ocean*. The quote is from Anderson's introduction, p. 335.

IRSH 58 (2013), Special Issue, pp. 229–251 doi:10.1017/S0020859013000229
© 2013 Internationaal Instituut voor Sociale Geschiedenis

The Age of Revolution in the Indian Ocean, Bay of Bengal, and South China Sea: A Maritime Perspective

C L A R E   A N D E R S O N

School of Historical Studies, University of Leicester
3–5 Salisbury Road, Leicester LE1 7QR, UK

E-mail: ca26@le.ac.uk

ABSTRACT: This essay explores the history of empire and rebellion from a seaborne perspective, through a focus on convict-ship mutiny in the Indian Ocean. It will show that the age of revolution did not necessarily spread outward from Europe and North America into colonies and empires, but rather complex sets of interconnected phenomena circulated regionally and globally in all directions. Convict transportation and mutiny formed a circuit that connected together imperial expansion and native resistance. As unfree labour, convicts might be positioned in global histories of the Industrial Revolution. And, as mutinous or insurgent colonial subjects, they bring together the history of peasant unrest and rebellion in south Asia with piracy in south-east Asia and the Pearl River delta. A subaltern history of convict transportation in the Indian Ocean thus has much to offer for an understanding of the maritime dimensions of the age of revolution.

INTRODUCTION

Two oceans away from revolutionary ferment in North America and Europe, maritime unrest in the Indian Ocean, Bay of Bengal, and South China Sea forms a critical part of the larger story of the great age of revolution. If we know, *pace* Eric Hobsbawm, that in the first half of the nineteenth century the French Revolution and the Industrial Revolution were the great motors (or, as he prefers it, midwives) of history, we also understand, *pace* Peter Linebaugh and Marcus Rediker, the importance of the American Revolution and proletarian radicalism in both connecting together and challenging the spread of industrial spaces of production across the Atlantic world. As they put it, the great irony of this important global process was that European expansion overseas itself created the conditions for the circulation of experience and resistance among the huge masses of labour that it set in motion.[1] Further, as recent work by David Armitage and Sanjay Subrahmanyam has shown, the age of revolution did not necessarily spread outward from Europe and North America into colonies and empires, but rather complex sets of interconnected phenomena – ideas about sovereignty, rights, and independence, as well as industrialization, revolt, and revolution – circulated in all directions.[2] Their perspective enables historians to produce connections, comparisons, and patterns of causation that do not simply place the age of revolution in a more expansive, world history framework but, more radically, still allows us to rearticulate the relationship between the local and the global across multiple centres of change.[3]

To take the example of industrialization, economic productivity, and labour mobility, the Industrial Revolution was previously understood by historians as a specifically European revolution, but it is now clear that the English Lancashire mills made famous by Friedrich Engels were part of a complex economic chain of resource extraction and piece production that stretched from the plantations of the Americas to the factories and mills of Bombay and Calcutta, and to the port cities of Singapore and Canton. Historians have paid much attention to industrialization and "the great divergence" between Europe and China, to the great migrations associated with global shifts in the movement of capital and resources, and also to the importance of resistance and rebellion in challenging them. They have centred in their narrative land, labour, and statecraft; the enslavement and indenture of millions of Africans, Europeans, and Asians in European factories and plantations worldwide; and the global circulations of soldiers, sailors, merchants, and traders. Resources and commodities such as cotton, sugar, spices, tea, and tobacco are at the heart of this story, with the tiniest of threads, grains, nuts, seeds, powders, and leaves underpinning the largest of regional, imperial, and global histories.

This essay seeks to bring together Armitage and Subrahmanyam's ideas about the "multiple logics of transformation"[4] with Linebaugh and Rediker's attention to maritime radicalism within the age of revolution. It will explore the history of empire, mobility, and rebellion from a seaborne

---

1. Peter Linebaugh and Marcus Rediker, *The Many-Headed Hydra: Sailors, Slaves, Commoners, and the Hidden History of the Revolutionary Atlantic* (Boston, MA, 2008), pp. 150, 152.

2. David Armitage and Sanjay Subrahmanyam (eds), *The Age of Revolutions in Global Context, c.1760–1840* (Basingstoke, 2009).

3. Miles Taylor demonstrates connections of other kinds, showing that Britain used its empire to ease political and fiscal pressures at home: through the transportation of rioters and rebels to penal colonies in Australia, and through drastic domestic retrenchment which was underpinned by the downscaling of imperial military forces. See Miles Taylor, "The 1848 Revolutions and the British Empire", *Past and Present*, 166 (2000), pp. 146–180.

4. Armitage and Subrahmanyam, "Introduction", in *idem* (eds), *The Age of Revolutions*, p. xxix.

perspective and, shifting our gaze beyond the revolutionary textures of Europe and North America, it will pay attention to the subaltern world of the Indian Ocean. I will take one strand of the complex web of imperialism, migration, labour, and resistance that underpinned the great political, ideological, and geographical shifts of the late eighteenth to mid-nineteenth centuries, and situate it within an expansive global framework. That thread is convict transportation, for it is one of the great paradoxes of the age that just as radical thinkers were working in the context of the radicalism of enslaved peoples to abolish the slave trade in the Atlantic world, the British East India Company busied itself simultaneously with the establishment of multi-directional flows of forced labour that cut across the seas of south, south-east, and east Asia.

Convict transportation brought together imperial understandings and desires regarding punishment and labour. The East India Company found it an attractive deterrent against crime because it believed that for cultural and religious reasons Asians especially feared it. But most importantly, the Company viewed it as a cheap and easy means of satisfying the labour demands associated with ongoing regional expansion into forts, port cities, littorals, and interiors. During the period 1787 to 1857 it shipped overseas some 30,000 convict workers, for which incipient Company settlements frequently competed. Subsequently, under the purview of the British Crown (which assumed control of India in 1858) three times as many convicts were sent to the Andamans penal colony. And yet these transportations have rarely featured in subaltern, maritime, or global history. This is curious, for convicts can be made to form a sort of circuit that connects together imperial expansion and native resistance. As unfree labour, convicts might be positioned in global histories of the Industrial Revolution. And, as mutinous or insurgent colonial subjects, they bring together peasant unrest and rebellion in south Asia with piracy in south-east Asia and the Pearl River delta and convict mutiny at sea. In both respects, convict transportation in the Indian Ocean has much to offer for an understanding of the maritime dimensions of the age of revolution – most particularly as a global process characterized by what Armitage and Subrahmanyam call "empire-making and empire-breaking".[5]

SUBALTERN CIRCUITS: CONVICTS AND COLONIALISM

In south Asia, near-constant murmurings against East India Company land settlement and taxation regimes as well as outright peasant rebellion and resistance characterized the first half of the nineteenth century. The incursions of the East India Company were not so much characterized by

5. *Ibid.*, p. xix.

a smooth implementation of *Pax Britannica* as constant warfare against a discontented countryside.[6] In fact, if we bring together and place the European revolutions in a global context, the age of revolution itself can be argued to have lasted well beyond 1848, and to have had a wide geographical reach. In the Bengal Presidency of India, for instance, tribal rebellions from the 1830s were succeeded in 1857 by unrest across large swathes of northern India in what Europeans called the mutiny, or great uprising, and Indian nationalists later came to call the first war of independence against the British. These were land-based rebellions provoked by the East India Company's many economic, social, and cultural interventions into everyday life.

Across the Bay of Bengal, predating the establishment of European trading ports in the Pearl River delta and their invigoration and exploitation of the lucrative opium trade, vast networks of pirates preyed on the opium-carrying boats and junks of what historian Dian Murray has called the indistinct boundaries of *water world*.[7] If European, North American, and Parsi (Indian) boats made it out of China, they faced further risks of piracy in the waters of the Straits of Malacca, the danger zone that stretched from Singapore to Penang and the tip of southern Burma, bordering the Andaman Sea. If the historical geography of peasant resistance in sub-continental south Asia was largely land-based, the coastlines, littorals, and inlets of south-east and east Asia lent it a distinctly maritime dimension. Of course both types predated the arrival of profit-seeking foreign traders, but even if unrest, rebellion, and piracy did not themselves intensify, the official response to their multi-pronged challenge to imperial interests certainly did.[8]

Though we usually think of imperialism as a process of territorial conquest effected across oceans, one way of connecting together nodes of colonization, rebellion, and resource extraction – and thus land, bay, and sea – is to consider the importance of the transportation of Asian convict *challans*[9] – their *trans-port*-ation – to fledgling British imperial settlements. These stretched from the south-east Asian littorals to military outposts and labour-hungry plantations. The port cities that knitted together this extensive penal network were part of a much larger global story of convict transportation. Law was used to criminalize individuals and communities, and to create new kinds of labour power. Ultimately this twin process created entirely new markets for free and unfree labour, for convicts were used to open up new areas for colonial expansion.

6. C.A. Bayly, *Indian Society and the Making of the British Empire* (Cambridge, 1988).
7. Dian Murray, *Pirates of the South China Coast, 1790–1810* (Stanford, CA, 1987).
8. *Ibid.*; John Carroll, *Edge of Empires: Chinese Elites and British Colonials in Hong Kong* (Cambridge, MA, 2005), ch. 1.
9. *Challans* = chain gangs, or batches of convicts.

For our purposes, the British story began with the shipment of convicted felons from Britain and Ireland to the plantations of Virginia, Chesapeake, and the Caribbean in the seventeenth and eighteenth centuries. It continued with their closure as convict destinations in the aftermath of the American War of Independence and their replacement with transportation to Australia in 1787. And – in an important detail of history that is always missed in world history accounts that centre on Europe and North America – its scope was at the same time widened substantially through the setting up of intra-regional or south–south Asian convict flows. This began with the foundation of a penal settlement in Bencoolen in 1787, two years before the French Revolution gave birth to the great shifts in economy and ideology that concern us here. It continued in the eighteenth century with transportation to Penang (1789–1857) and the Andaman Islands (1793–1796), and accelerated in the nineteenth century to encompass sites in Mauritius (1815–1837), Malacca and Singapore (1825–1857), Arakan and Tenasserim in Burma (1828–1857), Aden (1841–1849), and once again the Andamans (1858–1939). Collectively, these settlements received convicts from mainland south and south-east Asia, and the islands of Ceylon and Hong Kong – the latter of which also transported convicts to Van Diemen's Land and Sindh in western India. The East India Company shipped convicts outward to India too, with Chinese and Malay prisoners transported to the southern hill station of Ootacamund and the summer capital of the Bombay Presidency, Mahabaleshwar, during the mid-nineteenth century. Though the British Empire was reconstituted in the aftermath of the American Revolution, there were remarkable continuities over time with respect to the articulation and rearticulation of penal transportation – and its relationship to enslavement and indenture (European and Asian).[10]

The rationale for convict transportation in the south Asian context was deeply rooted in colonial concerns. The British believed that Hindus who journeyed across the black water, or *kala pani*, were outcaste, and so the authorities thought that transportation was a punishment worse than death. Certainly, caste was compromised when convicts of all classes and religions were chained and messed together. Many Indians had never before seen, let alone been to sea, rendering the ship an important tool of convicts' cultural and geographical displacement. In particular, normal practices regarding the preparation and eating of food, drinking, washing, and the performance of ablutions could not be respected. For high-caste or high-status convicts, this made the journey itself an important element of the punishment.[11]

10. Clare Anderson, *Subaltern Lives: Biographies of Colonialism in the Indian Ocean World, 1790–1920* (Cambridge, 2012).
11. *Idem*, "The Politics of Convict Space: Indian Penal Settlements and the Andaman Islands", in Alison Bashford and Carolyn Strange (eds), *Isolation: Places and Practices of Exclusion* (London, 2003), pp. 41–45.

2234 *Clare Anderson*

Likewise, the British in south-east Asia and Hong Kong believed that Malay and Chinese convicts especially feared transportation to unknown lands, because, having cut their family ties, after death they would not enjoy the burial rites necessary for their support in the afterlife.[12] For this reason, what the Colonial Secretary described as "distant and strange" destinations such as Sindh were chosen for Chinese convicts over the more geographically proximate and culturally familiar Straits Settlements or Tenasserim Provinces.[13]

Though the social impact of transportation made it an important element of the colonial penal repertoire across these Asian contexts, the East India Company also engaged convicts as a huge and seemingly unlimited work-force. In the ports, littorals, and interiors of islands and continents in the Indian Ocean, gangs laboured in occupations including jungle clearance; bund, bridge, and road building; infrastructural work; plantation agriculture; salt extraction; silk cultivation; prison manufacture; and tin mining. Thus, punishment and labour were brought together to remarkable effect. Convict work was said to be rehabilitative and reformative, but it also laid the infrastructural foundations for colonial settlement across the Indian Ocean and Bay of Bengal. Convicts enabled the expansion of trade, worked the land, and engaged in industrial production.

If convicts built and networked empire, convict transportation also created subaltern circuits of mobility, rebellion, and resistance. Some of the first Indian convicts transported to south-east Asia were Polygars from Malabar in South India, convicted in the wake of war against the East India Company at the turn of the nineteenth century.[14] Convicts were also transported out of the Kol, Bhil, and Santal *adivasi* (tribal) communities, after they resisted colonial incursions into land and increasing revenue demands in the Bengal and Bombay presidencies during the period 1830–1855.[15]

Pirates were sentenced to transportation in Hong Kong after it was ceded to the British Crown under the Treaty of Nanking (1841). The British were

12. Christopher Munn, "The Transportation of Chinese Convicts from Hong Kong, 1844–1858", *Journal of the Canadian Historical Association*, 8 (1997), pp. 113–145, 122; India Office Records, British Library, London [hereafter IOR], P/142/38 Bengal Judicial Consultations [hereafter BJC], 1 October 1845: J. Davis, Secretary to Government of Hong Kong, to Lord Stanley, 29 January 1845.
13. IOR P/404/3 Bombay Judicial Consultations [hereafter BomJC], 11 August 1846: W.A. Bruce, Colonial Secretary Hong Kong, to G.A. Bushby, Secretary to Government of India, 30 April 1846; Bushby to Bruce, 11 July 1846.
14. Tamil Nadu State Archives, Chennai [hereafter TNSA], Madras Judicial Consultations vol. 98 (1814): F.H. Baber, Magistrate North Malabar, to the Officer Commanding the Mysore Division, 11 July 1814.
15. Clare Anderson, *Convicts in the Indian Ocean: Transportation from South Asia to Mauritius, 1815–53* (Basingstoke, 2000), pp. 28–32. These early transportations anticipated the shipment to the Andamans from south Asia of 1857 rebels and mutineers, Wahabis, Manipuris, Kukas, Mapilahs, and nationalist agitators into the 1920s. See N. Iqbal Singh, *The Andaman Story* (New Delhi, 1978), pp. 176–204.

concerned about the island's apparent lawlessness as well the negative impact that the constant threat of piracy had on merchant vessels (and the opium trade) in what had become an important commercial port. There, and elsewhere in the South China Sea, they were especially fearful of maritime subcultures apparently beyond their control. They sought by turns both to criminalize piracy and to incorporate boat-dwellers into the colonial state.[16] Unlike the radical analysis of piracy-as-Atlantic-social-protest offered by Linebaugh and Rediker, it seems that piracy in the South China Sea was not so much revolutionary as entrepreneurial in character.[17] But, though it is difficult to trace relationships between piracy and the anti-dynastic or proto-nationalism that characterized the age of revolution in Europe, North America, and the colonies, with traders and sailors from all over the world passing through east Asia's trading ports and with pirates transported as convicts into south and south-east Asian penal regimes, the region nevertheless became networked into new colonial spheres of productivity and resistance in unprecedented ways.

The layers of subaltern connection evident in links between colonial economic imperatives and transportation can be seen also in convict resistance on board ships and in penal settlements and colonies, most especially when convicts transported for "political" crimes later joined together in open mutiny. For instance, convicts who had been transported for "insurrection and bearing arms" when the princely state of Kolhapur was in a state of rebellion against the East India Company led a violent escape attempt in Aden 1845.[18] And, when mutineers and rebels were shipped to the Andamans after the Great Indian Revolt of 1857, numerous escape attempts were underpinned by subaltern beliefs that there was a sympathetic rajah living in the jungles of Great Andaman or that there was a high road connecting the islands to south-east Asia. Many convicts believed that they could find service with the "King of Burma" and return to the Andamans to destroy the penal colony.[19] One mutinous *sipahi* [sepoy; soldier] later told British officials that he and other convicts thought that this man could be found after ten days' march into the jungles.[20]

16. Munn, "Transportation of Chinese Convicts", p. 115; Carroll, *Edge of Empires*, pp. 20–23.

17. As argued in Murray, *Pirates of the South China Coast*.

18. IOR P/403/47 BomJC, 13 August 1845: Political Agent, Aden to W. Escombe, Secretary to Government of Bombay, 27 June 1845; Governor's minute, n.d. On the history of Kolhapur in the nineteenth century, see *Imperial Gazetteer of India* (Oxford, 1908), XV, p. 383.

19. IOR P/206/61 India Judicial Proceedings [hereafter IJP], 29 July 1859: Dr Browne's report on the sanitary state of the Andamans.

20. IOR P/206/61 IJP, 29 July 1859: statement of convict no. 276 Doodnath Tewarry, 26 May 1859; M.V. Portman, *A History of our Relations with the Andamanese* (Calcutta, 1899), I, pp. 279–286; IOR P/188/53 India Judicial Consultations, 7 May 1858: Superintendent J.P. Walker to C. Beadon, Secretary to Government of India, 23 April 1858; Beadon to Walker, 7 May 1858; National Archives of India, New Delhi, Home Judicial Consultations, 28 May 1858: Walker to Beadon, 1 May 1858.

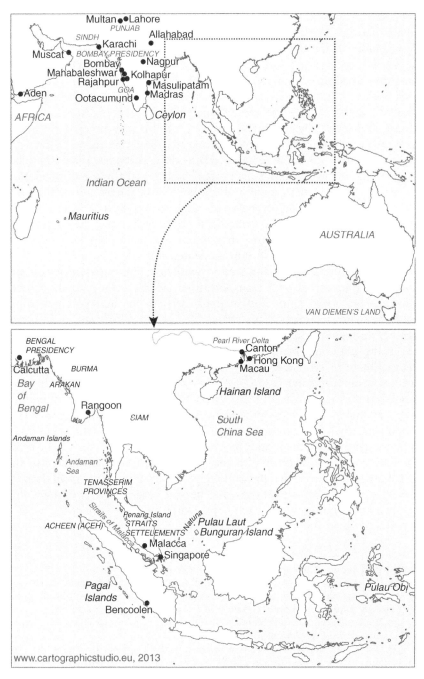

Figure 1. Mutiny and Piracy in the Bay of Bengal and South China Sea.

That penal transportation created networks and imagined geographies of anti-colonial resistance is evident in places like Aden and the mid-nineteenth-century Andamans. But the act of transportation itself – along rivers and across oceans – also supported the extension of terrestrial rebellion on to ships. Just like the merchant vessels of the Atlantic world described by Linebaugh and Rediker, convict ships were both engines of capitalism *and* spaces of resistance. They were especial conduits for the realization of colonial imperatives concerning punishment and labour as well as potential sites of violent anti-colonial struggle. Convict ship mutinies thus add a crucial maritime dimension to our understanding of subaltern resistance and unrest during this period, and offer a more expansive conceptual framework within which to trace both its character and its diffusion across land and sea around the Indian Ocean during the first half of the nineteenth century.

CONVICTS AND PIRATES: MUTINY AT SEA

Up to twenty convict ships left south and south-east Asian ports each year, carrying anything from a dozen to over 200 men – and occasionally one or two women. Until 1858 there were no ships specially fitted out for convicts. Rather, in the years before it lost its trading monopoly in 1834, the East India Company transported convicts on its China fleet, keeping them below decks under armed guard side by side with other cargo. Later, the Company put transportation out for tender, and henceforth convicts were carried overseas on private trading vessels. Arrangements became irregular and piecemeal, and though ships could not get insurance against uprisings they often kept costs down by skimping on armed guards. Convicts were accommodated between decks; if there was room they were kept in temporary prisons, otherwise these cargos of human capital slept next to bales of cotton, reels of silk, sacks of sugar, chests of opium, packs of dates, and sacks of betel nut.[21] Convicts were allowed to come up for air for just two hours per day, and even then only if the weather was good. In squally conditions the state of the convicts' quarters deteriorated fast. As on boats carrying African slaves and Indian indentured labourers later on, "dancing masters" cracked whips to encourage exercise.[22]

It was during the period after 1834 that there was most convict unrest at sea – in total, during the period to 1858 there were two attempted mutinies, one upriver outbreak, and more than a dozen seaborne uprisings. This represented a very small proportion of transportation ships – far fewer

21. IOR P/142/16 BJC, 27 May 1844: S. Garling, Resident Councillor Penang, to W.J. Butterworth, Governor of Straits Settlements, 28 February 1844.
22. IOR P/403/6 BomJC, 2 March 1842: Court of Judicature, Penang, 7 June 1841, testimony of Salamon.

than the estimated 10 per cent of Atlantic slave ships that mutinied.[23] However, unlike the ships of the slave trade, convict transportation was regulated publicly, and so mutinies were subject to government enquiries. An extensive archive survives, and it opens up extraordinary insights into convict mutineers' motives and desires.

Convict mutinies were always opportunistic, and without exception they arose out of failures to properly inspect, accommodate, or guard convicts.[24] Convicts were able to smuggle on to ships knives, small files, iron nails, and emery boards, sewn into the folds and ends of their bedding.[25] Their irons were frequently lightweight or rusted. Crews allowed them above decks in large numbers, or left muskets loaded or unsecured.[26] Furthermore, men were commonly locked on a single chain padlocked at one end only. If one man was released, the remaining convicts could slip out.[27] Convicts were ingenious in the use of waxed silk thread to cut through their fetters, stuffing the breaches with cement made from wax and dye so that they could not be detected.[28] Men also took advantage of any unsecured convict women on board, to obtain information in planning outbreaks about the ship's routine, the location of arms, and other matters.[29]

Further, mutiny rarely broke out on vessels unless they were carrying convicts who had been soldiers, sailors, or pirates – for the simple reason that those convicts knew how to use weapons or had previously been to sea, and so possessed the skills necessary to take a ship. That is why mutinies overwhelmingly occurred on vessels sailing out of Bombay, the Straits Settlements, and Hong Kong, rather than Bengal or Madras. The *Ararat* (Singapore to Bombay, 1859), for instance, embarked fifty-two pirates;[30] they secreted a knife on board, and used it to cut themselves free.

---

23. Stephen D. Behrendt, David Eltis, and David Richardson, "The Costs of Coercion: African Agency in the Pre-modern Atlantic World", *Economic History Review*, 54 (2001), pp. 454–476.
24. David Richardson, "Shipboard Revolts, African Authority, and the Atlantic Slave Trade", *William and Mary Quarterly*, 58 (2001), pp. 69–92, 75.
25. *Bengal Hurkaru*, 15 September 1859; IOR P/145/32 BJC, 14 February 1856: H. Fergusson, Superintendent Alipur Jail, to A.W. Russell, Under Secretary to Government of Bengal, 24 January 1856.
26. IOR P/402/39 BomJC, 31 December 1839: P.W. Le Geyt, Acting Senior Magistrate Police Bombay, to J.P. Willoughby, Secretary to Government of Bombay, 24 December 1839; P/402/2 BomJC, 24 June 1846: Willoughby's minute, 9 June 1846; P/404/3 BomJC, 6 August 1846: W.F. Curtis, Superintendent Convicts Bombay, to Escombe, 18 July 1846; IOR P/143/51 BJC, 31 July 1850: E.H. Lushington, Magistrate Patna, to J.P. Grant, Secretary to Government of Bengal, 23 June 1850.
27. IOR P/143/51 BJC, 31 July 1850: Capt. H.M. Nation, Commanding Behar Station Guards, to J.W. Dalrymple, Under Secretary to Government of Bengal, 25 June 1850.
28. IOR P/145/32 BJC, 14 February 1856: Fergusson to Russell, 24 January 1856.
29. IOR P/402/30 BJC, 30 January 1839: information of Captain F.N. Pendygrass (*Catherine*), 19 January 1839.
30. *Bengal Hurkaru*, 14 September 1859.

There followed an extraordinarily bloody uprising. The crew largely escaped injury, but before it resumed control of the ship thirty-five of the seventy-four convicts had either been shot dead or had jumped overboard and drowned.[31]

Eight of the sixteen convict mutineers on board the *Harriet Scott* (Penang to Bombay, 1843) were convicted pirates. Each had been doubly ironed, and chained together, but a rusty shackle proved the ship's downfall. The convicts freed themselves, armed themselves with pikes, and locked the crew below deck. They killed Captain Philip Benyon and cut his body into pieces. They got into the quarter boat, lowered it down, and escaped from the ship. The chief mate, who had himself sustained a serious head injury, took revenge on a convict who had not been involved in the uprising, shooting him dead and killing others who had been badly injured.[32] The escaped men were found exhausted and hungry by another vessel. They were given food, and confessed that they were escaped convicts. They were promised a free passage if they remained quiet, but instead were taken to Penang and handed over to the authorities.[33] They were tried and sentenced to hang, and were said to have mounted the scaffold "with great firmness". Their bodies were cut down and taken to the pauper hospital for dissection. Subsequently, the government urged ships to check that convicts had nothing in their possession with which they could cut their fetters, and to examine their irons twice a day.[34]

Hong Kong convicts gained an especial reputation for violent disorder. The *General Wood* (Hong Kong to Penang, via Singapore, 1848) carried ninety-two convicted pirates on board – most from Hong Kong, but also including one "notorious Macau Portuguese". The day after the ship sailed out of Singapore harbour on the final leg of its journey to the island of Penang, there was what was later described as an uproar. The convicts seized the ship's firearms, threw fifty lascars (sailors) overboard, killed Captain William Stokoe and the three mates, and left just three Europeans alive: the newly wed Lieutenant and Mrs L.W. Seymour, and a passenger called Andrew Farquhar. They made plain that had Mrs Seymour been the wife of Deputy Police Superintendent Caldwell at Hong Kong, they would have "chopped her into pieces". For thirteen days the convicts

31. *Ibid.*, 15 September 1859.
32. IOR P/142/8 BJC, 13 November 1843: Butterworth to A. Turnbull, Under Secretary to Government of Bengal, 7 October 1843; IOR P/142/9 BJC, 27 November 1843: Garling to Butterworth, 25 September 1843, enc. deposition of Thomas Jones, second mate of the *Harriet Scott*, n.d.
33. IOR P/142/8 BJC, 27 November 1843: deposition of Sheck Hyder Aly, a passenger on the *Brig Harsingar*, n.d.
34. IOR P/142/15 BJC, 29 April 1844: memorandum for the information of commanders of vessels engaged for the conveyance of convicts, 29 February 1844; *Penang Gazette*, 16 December 1843.

steered for Pulau Laut, a small island in the Natuna archipelago of the
South China Sea. When they arrived, they lowered the boats to shore,
leaving ten men behind to kill the remaining lascars and blow up the ship.
Hearing of their arrival, some local Malays came to meet the party, and
while the convicts were distracted they managed to spirit away Lieutenant
and Mrs Seymour and Mr Farquhar, saving their lives. They dispatched a
note to the "rajah" Orang Kaya (described as "principal chieftain" of the
Natunas) who lived on the island of Bunguran.

I take up the story in the words of his deputy, Datoo Buntara:

> On that night at 2 o'clock, two men in a small Boat arrived with a letter to me.
> I read it, it mentioned that ship wrecked men had landed at Pulo Si Lout;
> Europeans three, 2 males and 1 female; Lascars, and a very great number of
> Chinese who wanted to have killed the Europeans, but we have rescued and run
> away with them up the Hill. We are now much afraid that if Dattoo does not
> come to our assistance we will be in trouble to night. I immediately wrote to the
> Orang Kaya at Pulo Lemadang requesting him to bring Prows armed to Pulo Si
> Lout as our men there were in danger. After which I assembled all the men and
> desired them to prepare and arm themselves [...]. In a short time say in ¼ of
> an hour they were ready 14 Prows with 400 men and we proceeded to Pulo
> Si Lout – at 6 o'clock I arrived the men told me the Chinese had left during the
> night leaving ½ their number behind, also 1 Portuguese, in all 19 men – I then
> ordered the Prows to go in search of the runaways amongst the neighbouring
> Islands [...]. The Chinese on shore were watched. I then went on the Hill to see
> the Europeans and found 2 Gentlemen and a Lady – I enquired how this
> had occurred, they replied that the Chinese convicts had seized the ship and
> murdered the Captain, Mate and others. I told them to remain where they were
> as I intended to go after the escaped Chinese – on going I found a broken boat
> drifting. Some of the men in the other Prows found 4 Lascars in a small boat
> who informed me that the ship had gone down. The boats returned after a
> fruitless search [...]. After being on the Island one week a convict hung himself
> consequently I ordered the others to be handcuffed and watched. I afterwards
> spoke to the Orang Kaya about sending them all to Singapore [...]. After a stay
> of 2 weeks we departed touching at Pulo Dadap for wood and water and were
> there detained from stress of weather for one week during which time all our
> provisions were consumed and we were compelled to return for a fresh stock.
> We then sailed again and in 5 days reached Pulo Punoo sooh where we were
> overtaken by a storm when a convict in the bustle and confusion jumped
> overboard – the next morning we reached the Harbour. Mr Andrew Farquhar
> landed, then Mr George came on board to land Mr and Mrs Seymour after which
> the Constables and Peons came and took the convicts and Lascars on shore.

The British subsequently gifted the Orang a substantial Spanish $300 cash
reward, half a dozen flint muskets, a six-pounder gun bearing what was
described as a "suitable inscription", and – at his request – a "document to
show his neighbours and commanders of vessels". To the "gallant Malays"
who protected the Europeans were given money, rifles, and muskets.

Twenty-eight other convicts were later recaptured further south on Pulau Obi, and they told British officers that the remainder had left for Siam, Singapore, or Hainan Island off the coast of southern China.[35] The Pulau Obi convicts had in their possession various articles that they had plundered from the *General Wood*, some clearly useful equipment, and some of potential sale value. They were: a two-day chronometer manufactured by Koskell of Liverpool; a ship's timepiece; a Chinese lacquer box containing opium; an ivory card case that contained a paper written by Mrs Seymour; a pocket compass; a London-made telescope; a silver watch case; and a silver table fork and a silver salt spoon, presumably the property of the Seymours for they were marked with the initials "W&MS" and "WS" respectively.

Found on the person of one of the men was a piece of "Chinese writing", which was translated as follows:

If any of us should die, the death of such person is to be made known to the survivors.

If any of us should succeed in procuring a boat the same is to be made known to all of us.

None of us are to leave the Island [Pulau Obi] until we have fed and lived well so as not to be recognized as convicts when we get to China.

When I go to China, no one save God will know who I am.

We are to share alike in every thing, if we procure food we are to share alike.

If one of us procure[s] a boat the same is to be made known to all of us, that we may go together.

We all swear to assist and stand by one another to the last.

God only besides ourselves shall know our actions and what is in our possession.[36]

The paper was not signed. In the Atlantic world, such "round robins" were a common feature of piratical seizures. They captured what Rediker has elsewhere described as the "collective logic" behind mutiny, for they were used to organize uprisings without revealing individual identities to the authorities.[37] That the same tactic was used in the inlets and islands of

---

35. IOR P/143/21 BJC, 12 July 1848: Butterworth to A.R. Young, Under Secretary to Government of Bengal, 6 March 1848; statement of Lieutenant L.W. Seymour, n.d., Butterworth to Dalrymple, 6 May 1848; "memorandum of mine Datoo Buntara Yayah regarding the ship wrecked men within the limits of Pulo Bungoran", n.d.; *Straits Times Extra*, 20 February 1848; *Bengal Hurkaru*, 25 March 1848. The case of the *General Wood* fed into a growing ambivalence in Singapore about the continued transportation of Chinese convicts to a by now flourishing colonial settlement. See C.M. Turnbull, "Convicts in the Straits Settlements 1826–1867", *Journal of the Malaysian Branch of the Royal Asiatic Society*, 43 (1970), pp. 97–103, 88–89.

36. IOR P/143/21 BJC, 12 July 1848: list of articles found on different parts of Pulo Oly [Ubin] in possession of the Chinese now prisoners; translation of a Chinese writing found on the person of a Chinese convict at Pulo Oly [Ubin], n.d.

37. Marcus Rediker, *Between the Devil and the Deep Blue Sea: Merchant Seamen, Pirates and the Anglo-American Maritime World, 1700–1750* (Cambridge, 1987), pp. 234–235.

east and south-east Asia reveals something remarkable about an apparently borderless maritime world of mutual codes of honour. That said, once the pirates had been captured, one of the men turned on the others, pointing out two individuals who he claimed had killed Captain Stokoe. They jumped overboard as they sailed from Pulau Obi to Singapore; one man was picked up, but the other drowned.[38]

As for Indian transportation ships, two of the thirty-four *Virginia* convicts (Bombay to Singapore, 1839)[39] had been professional sailors – one a *caffree* and the other a *sydee* (both words implying African in maritime parlance).[40] They escaped the ship and made for the shore just south of Goa; some headed for their home villages, and others travelled towards the eastern Indian port of Masulipatam, with the intention of taking a ship to Muscat. But the men were recaptured, at the time complaining that they had mutinied because they had been short rationed, and otherwise "starved and ill-treated".[41] The *Virginia* convicts were re-embarked on the *Freak* (Bombay to Singapore, 1841), and, incredibly, they again broke out in mutiny. This time they succeeded in murdering the captain and chief mate. They took control of the vessel, stopping on the Pagai Islands close to Bencoolen, in the mistaken belief that they were the Nicobars; they then steered up the coast of Sumatra, and eventually landed at Acheen. They said they were traders with opium, cotton, dates, and piece goods to sell. The Rajah heard rumours of the arrival of a batch of convict mutineers, came to shore, and inspected the ship. The convicts presented him with a chronometer, the captain's watch, sword, and gun, and upon learning of events he personally enlisted fourteen of the mutineers as sepoys in his service, including the man who had been implicated in the murder of Captain Whiffen of the *Virginia*.[42]

At least one of the convicts shipped on the *Catherine* (Bombay to Singapore, 1838) had previously worked as a lascar. That ship was carrying sixty men, almost double the number it was certified to take. The captain became aware that the convicts were planning to take the ship, and so returned to Bombay. Re-embarked with a strengthened guard, when it finally landed in Singapore the senior police magistrate of the port

38. IOR P/143/21 BJC, 12 July 1848: Captain George Nibbett, Commander *Phlegathon*, to Captain P. McQuhae, Senior Officer Straits Settlements, n.d., enc. "Names of the convicts captured on Pulo Oly [Ubin] by the HCSV Phlegathon as given by themselves".
39. IOR P/402/39 BomJC, 31 December 1839: Le Geyt to Willoughby, 24 December 1839.
40. IOR P/402/39 BomJC, 31 December 1839: deposition of *seacunnie* [steersman] Charles de Cruz, n.d., minute of Governor J.R. Carnac, 28 December 1839; IOR P/402/43 BomJC, 11 March 1840: Willoughby's summary, 27 February 1840.
41. *Bombay Gazette*, 20 July 1840. See also IOR P/402/39 BomJC, 31 December 1839: deposition of *seacunnie* Charles de Cruz.
42. IOR P/403/6 BomJC, 2 March 1842: Court of Judicature, Penang, 7 June 1841; *Penang Gazette*, 10 April 1841; *Bombay Gazette*, 22 May 1841, 9 June 1841; *The Times*, 6 September 1841.

wrote that the smell below deck was so disgusting that he could not find words to describe it. He discovered several of the convicts sick with venereal and other diseases, and opined there had been no medical attendant on board.[43] A further dimension to the conviction of sailors and pirates was that shorthanded captains on occasion employed them as crew. Sheikh Ramran, a *sipahi* guard on the mutinous *Clarissa* (Bengal to Penang, 1854), claimed that the captain had even placed a convict in charge of his swords and muskets, which as we will see was a fatal miscalculation on his part.[44]

But there was a more radical dimension to convict mutiny than some of these cases might suggest, for it was sometimes expressive of subaltern desires for freedom, not solely from transportation or carceral restraint, but from colonial domination more generally. As such, maritime radicalism in the Indian Ocean drew on wider-ranging socio-political, and anti-colonial grievances that characterized the age of revolution within the more expansive global framework that I am proposing here. In this respect, it is important to note that there were significant connections between the land-based rebellions for which Indian convicts were transported and subsequent outbreaks at sea. Convicted rebels sometimes carefully planned mutinies, often while they were still in jail awaiting their embarkation overseas.[45]

Two of the convict leaders on board the *Catherine*, for example, were *bhils* who were transported in the context of *bhil* campaigns against British territorial expansion into the forests of western India during the 1830s. They planned the uprising before the ship had even left port, deciding upon the morning after Christmas when "the Captain and Officers would make themselves merry [and] they could have a better opportunity". A "conjuring book" pointed to 3 am as the best time. It further advised them to divide themselves up, avoid Portuguese Goa, and head for "Chitripoore Ram Rajah's country [...] Rajahpoor" – presumably the established Hindu Saraswat Brahmin community in Kannada – for protection. They would "eat and drink and live there as nobody would be there to molest them".[46] Likewise, a dozen of the seventy-nine convicts shipped on the *Recovery* (Bombay to Singapore, 1846) were *marattas*,

43. IOR P/402/30 BomJC, 23 January 1839: depositions of Captain F.N. Pendygrass, 12, 19 January 1839.
44. IOR P/145/18 BJC, 13 September 1855: deposition of Sheikh Ramran, son of Russub Alla, sepoy Alipur Militia, 17 June 1854. For corroboration see also the deposition of Hwikh Joomur, son of Sheikh Talib, sepoy Alipur Militia, 17 June 1854.
45. IOR P/402/30 BomJC, 30 January 1839: deposition of Pendygrass, 19 January 1839; J.A. Forbes, Acting Senior Magistrate Police, to Willoughby, 22 January 1839.
46. IOR P/402/30 BomJC, 23 January 1839: depositions of Sahola Fuzul, Rama Balloo, and Juttoo Bin Mahomed Adky, 25 December 1838. On *bhil* resistance, see Ajay Skaria, *Hybrid Histories: Forests, Frontiers and Wildness in Western India* (New Delhi, 1999), p. 42.

convicted and transported for insurrection, rebellion, or treason in the districts of the Bombay Presidency. It was these men who wrote a mutiny plan in jail, and then after they left port broke out of the holds, over-powered the sentries and guards, and got up on deck – though the crew managed to force them into retreat, killing one man and wounding five.[47]

More dramatically, in the aftermath of the Anglo-Sikh Wars of the 1840s, Punjabi convicts became notorious for their violent resistance to British control. In 1850, a *challan* of Punjabis travelling up river from Allahabad to Calcutta for transportation to Burma seized a steamer called the *Kaleegunga*. They had been locked on a single chain, padlocked at one end. When two men were let off to answer calls of nature, the remaining convicts escaped.[48] Eighteen loaded guns had been stored within arm's reach of their sleeping quarters; they grabbed them, killed three guards, and jumped off the boat to shore. Their leader was described as a "notorious Sikh general", Narain Singh, who had been convicted of treason in the aftermath of Britain's annexation of the Punjab in 1849.[49]

Another mutiny, on the *Clarissa* in 1854, was an uprising of unprece-dented scale, and underlines especially well the connections that can be drawn between radicalism on land, mutiny at sea, and anti-British military campaigns. The bulk of the 133 convicts on board were Punjabis; they mutinied, murdered Captain Johnson, the chief and second mates, and half the crew and guard (31 men), and escaped.[50] One convict claimed that during the uprising leader Soor Singh had called out: "The Ferringees [foreigners] are flying – the ship is ours!"[51] Earlier the convicts had complained about the overcrowding and heat below decks,[52] but the mutiny had been sparked when one man complained about his water ration, and struck the *sipahi* guard on the head with his brass *lotah* [drinking vessel].[53] One convict put it like this: "In the ship we all got cheated out of our provisions. Short measure and not enough water.

47. IOR P/403/55 BomJC, 4 February 1846: list of convicts under sentence of transportation to Singapore, n.d.; IOR P/404/2 BomJC, 24 June 1846: Captain J. Johnson to J. Church, Resident Councillor Singapore, 15 April 1846, enc. "Names of those killed and wounded on board the *Recovery* on the 5th February in a revolt of the convicts".

48. IOR P/143/51 BJC, 31 July 1850: Nation to Dalrymple, 25 June 1850.

49. IOR P/143/51 BJC, 23 June 1850: Lushington to Grant, 23 June 1850. For a detailed biography of Narain Singh, see Anderson, *Subaltern Lives*, ch. 4.

50. IOR P/145/18 BJC, 13 September 1855: S.R. Tickell, Principal Assistant Commissioner and District Magistrate Amherst, to W. Grey, Secretary to Government of Bengal, enc. matter of the Queen v. the life convicts on board the *Clarissa* for affray attended with homicide and for murder on the high seas, 14 July 1854.

51. IOR P/145/18 BJC, 13 September 1855: deposition of Shaik Sooiah, son of Chambale, convict no. 72, 30 June 1854.

52. IOR P/145/18 BJC, 13 September 1855: deposition of Goolab, 14 June 1854.

53. IOR P/144/61 BJC, 15 June 1854: deposition of Sheikh Suvraj, son of Sheikh Kitaboodeen aged 30 – *burra tindal* [boatswain's chief mate] of the *Clarissa*, 19 May 1854.

All men discontented and began to be alarmed at our fate."[54] Having taken the vessel, the convicts destroyed the convict register and logbook, ran the ship aground, armed themselves, and waded to the southern Burmese shore.[55]

But this was no simple protest about shipboard conditions. Leader Soor Singh took charge, putting on the captain's coat and boots, and the gold necklace, sword, and sash belonging to the *subadar* (head) of the guard. He armed six other convicts, gave them "caps and accoutrements", and called them "his sepoys".[56] Another central figure in the mutiny was Kurrim Singh (who later turned informer), who had previously been an artilleryman in the fifth company at Rangoon, and understood a little Burmese.[57] He described how the convicts were assembled on the beach, Soor Singh sitting before them in a chair.[58] He told them: "you shall be taken to the Burma Raja's and there be all free men".[59] Thinking that they were in lands as yet uncolonized by the British, the seven leaders made their way to his district, planning to offer him their services in anti-British campaigns. But they were mistaken, for the East India Company had annexed Lower Burma following the Second Anglo-Burmese War (1852). They found the Rajah, but a gunfight broke out, and Soor Singh and his six men were killed.[60]

The surviving convicts (129 in number) were captured and brought before the Burmese magistrate for an initial hearing. Ill-equipped to cope with even this stage of such a complex case,[61] he sent them back to Bengal, where they were put to trial in Calcutta's supreme court.[62] The chief judge, Sir J. Colville, stated that it was the most serious trial that he had ever come across.[63] Eighteen men were charged with the murder of the captain, three more with the murder of the *subadar* and *havildar* (deputy) guard, and one with shooting a lascar after he jumped overboard. All faced trial for piratical seizure of the vessel, their offence in law.

54. IOR P/145/18 BJC, 13 September 1855: deposition of Boor Singh, son of Humeer Singh, convict no. 115, 6 July 1854.
55. IOR P/144/61 BJC, 15 June 1854: Tickell to A. Bogle, Commissioner Tenasserim Provinces, 18 May 1854; *Bengal Hurkaru*, 6 July 1854.
56. Many of the witnesses testified to this military display. For example: IOR P/145/18 BJC, 13 September 1855: deposition of *edoo serang* [boatswain], 13 June 1854.
57. *Bengal Hurkaru*, 16 August 1854.
58. IOR P/145/18 BJC, 13 September 1855: deposition of Sheikh Suvraj.
59. IOR P/145/18 BJC, 13 September 1855: deposition of Beejah Sing, son of Punchum Sing, convict no. 5, 21 June 1854.
60. IOR P/145/18 BJC, 13 September 1855: deposition of Kurrim Singh, son of Hennath Singh, convict no. 1, 8 June 1854.
61. IOR P/145/18 BJC, 13 September 1855: Tickell to Grey, 14 July 1854.
62. IOR P/144/61 BJC, 15 June 1854: Advocate General C.R. Prinsep's opinion, 9 June 1854.
63. *Bengal Hurkaru*, 12 August 1854. For further reports of the Supreme Court trial, see *Bengal Hurkaru*, 14, 16–19 August 1854.

Assah Singh deposed: "I came all the way from Lahore to Calcutta a thousand coss if I had wishes to rebel outbreak from confinement could I not have done so more easily during that long journey on land than at sea?"[64] He was one of four convicts sentenced to death, and when the sentence was read out it was said that he gave a "sneering contemptuous laugh which made one shudder".[65] The remainder of the convicts were transported as per their original sentence. They were not allowed to progress through the penal classes, like other convicts in the Straits Settlements. Instead it was directed that they were to be kept at hard labour during their entire term.[66]

There were at least two outbreaks on convict ships in the aftermath of the Indian Revolt of 1857, through which previously land-based military and peasant resistance was carried overseas. In February 1858 forty-four convicts, including sepoys convicted of mutiny, were embarked on the *Julia* for Singapore, in the weeks before the announcement of the new penal colony in the Andamans. When the ship's carpenter entered the below-decks prison they took the chance to grab his tools, and kill and disarm the chief guard and his sentry. The ship's officers accessed the hatches, opened fire, and shot two convicts dead. They ordered the remainder up on deck, and chained them to the bower cable and anchor, where they left them in the shadow of the loaded forecastle gun. Three convicts died overnight.[67] When the ship arrived in Singapore the authorities promptly ordered it on to the Andamans, without putting the convicts on trial for mutiny, perhaps fearing the spread of unrest.[68] At the end of 1858 another thirty-seven rebels were sent from Multan to Karachi on the *Frere*, ready for shipment to the Andamans. Despite the fact they had previously tried to escape from jail, no special instructions were given to the ship's commander. They were able to slip their fetters off and rush the deck. Before the ship's command took control seven convicts had gone missing and two were dead. "Unless a prisoner is secured in a manner which humanity must forbid", the subsequent enquiry opined, "he cannot be kept in safe custody unless he is constantly watched".[69]

64. IOR P/145/18 BJC, 13 September 1855: deposition of Assah Singh, son of Chur Sing, convict no. 91, 3 July 1854. A *coss* is approximately one and a half miles.
65. *Bengal Hurkaru*, 19 August 1854.
66. *Ibid.*
67. *The Maitland Mercury and Hunter River General Advertiser*, 17 August 1858.
68. IOR P/407/10 BomJC, 6 July 1858: Beadon to C.J. Buckland, Junior Secretary to Government of Bengal, 24 April 1858; IOR P/407/13 BomJC, 21 September 1858: G.W. Blundell, Resident Councillor Penang, to G.W. Anderson, Governor of Bombay, 15 June 1858; *Singapore Free Press*, 22 July 1858.
69. IOR P/407/30 Bombay Judicial Proceedings [hereafter BomJP] 4 July 1859: H.B.E. Frere, Commissioner Sindh, to Anderson, 4 June 1859; G.W. Hamilton, Commissioner Multan, to Judicial Commissioner Panjab, 8 November 1858.

There was an associated politico-religious dimension to some shipboard rebellions too. The convicts on the *Recovery* were said to have sworn on the Qur'an to mutiny before the ship had even set sail. Rumours reached the authorities that some "Arabic" vessels would be waiting in the harbour to help the convicts escape. When the ships did not appear, Captain Thomas Johnson dropped his guard, and it was then that the convicts rose. The signal for mutiny was *"din"*, the cry of Koranic devotion and duty.[70] A convict informer from the *Freak* claimed that after killing the captain and chief mate, one of the convicts had declared: "now all the poison all the liquor is coming out". He then threw the crews' shoes overboard, declaring them "infidels' things".[71] The second mate added that the convicts had decided to go to Mecca, but, believing that they would get caught, decided to make for Aceh instead.[72] The leader, Hadjee Hussain, had asked the second mate whose country it was:

> [H]e said a Mohamedan country, the inhabitants are Malay. Hadjee Hussain asked if there are any English? [T]he 2nd mate said "No" if the English go there they are killed and if an English vessel go there, all the men are killed and the ship plundered, Hadjee Hussain asked how large is the country 2nd mate said 14 miles broad and 200 long. The Rajah and Troops reside there, and 12 Governors in different parts, so Hadjee Hussain said "take the vessel there" and the 2nd mate steered for Aceh.[73]

The second mate of the *Freak*, Francis Ward, stated later that the crew had been "very familiar with the convicts" and thought that they must have known of the convicts' intentions. His suspicions remained, however, entirely speculative.[74]

JUSTICE AND RETRIBUTION AT SEA

It is well known that maritime authority was violent and arbitrary, with British officers boasting that they were lords of the oceans.[75] With respect to transportation, there were very real risks associated with carrying convicts, and land-based authorities often congratulated captains for floggings, beatings, or shootings during episodic unrest. In 1841, for example, convicts on the *Singapore Packet* complained about their rations and stormed the deck. The Governor of the Straits Settlements, S.G. Bonham, joined the local press in congratulating Captain Tingate for

---

70. IOR P/403/56 BomJC, 11 March 1846: J. Geddes, Marshall Bombay County Jail, to W.F. Curtis, Superintendent of Convicts Bombay, 1 February 1846.
71. IOR P/403/6 BomJC, 2 March 1842: deposition of convict Michael Anthony, 7 June 1841.
72. IOR P/403/6 BomJC, 2 March 1842: deposition of second mate Francis Ward, 7 June 1841.
73. IOR P/403/6 BomJC, 2 March 1842: deposition of convict Michael Anthony.
74. IOR P/403/6 BomJC, 2 March 1842: deposition of second mate Francis Ward.
75. Rediker, *Between the Devil and the Deep Blue Sea*, ch. 5.

his "bold and manly conduct" in quelling the outbreak, as a result of which four convicts had died.[76] Attempted mutiny on board another Bombay ship, the *Recovery*, was suppressed with even more brutality. Captain Johnson gave every convict who had been on deck at the time three dozen lashes, and twenty others "as much as they could take".[77] After a convict outbreak on the *Ararat*, Captain Correya stripped the survivors naked, and gave all of them, including twenty-eight men who had played no part in the mutiny, three or four dozen lashes.[78]

Here, we see tensions between governance at sea and on land, for while the *Bengal Hurkaru* congratulated Correya for his "courage and pluck" in staving off disaster,[79] both the Secretary of State for India and the Madras authorities banned him from captaining convict ships in the future.[80] The captain himself claimed that he had removed the convicts' clothing to make sure that none had hidden weapons,[81] but there is no doubt that the public removal of garments was also an emasculating punishment which was part of the armoury of colonial penal practice during the first half of the nineteenth century.[82] The tensions between land and sea are illustrated also in the case of the *Harriet Scott*. At the time of the convict mutiny, chief mate John MacDuff was drunk, and in this state of intoxication he shot dead two convicts who had taken no part in the mutiny. Fearing what might happen next, the passengers and crew placed him in irons.[83] The authorities arrested him when the ship arrived back in Penang and indicted him for manslaughter, but he was acquitted. Though the judge congratulated MacDuff on the verdict, the secretary to the government of Bombay later wrote that he was disappointed that he had not been convicted.[84]

The archives are peppered with the noise of the slaps, kicks, and threats that were dished out to convicts, routinely and with little contemporary comment[85] – unless of course they provoked mutiny. The attempt to seize

76. *Bombay Gazette*, 6 July 1841.
77. *Bengal Hurkaru*, 23 May 1846.
78. IOR P/407/36 BomJP, 11 October 1859: Advocate General's opinion, 27 September 1859.
79. *Bengal Hurkaru*, 14 September 1859.
80. IOR P/407/36 BomJP, 11 October 1859: Resolution of the Board, 3 October 1859; TNSA Madras Judicial Proceedings, 14 December 1860, nos 101–102: extract dispatch from HM's Secretary of State for India, 20 September 1860.
81. IOR P/407/36 BomJP, 11 October 1859: Advocate General's opinion, 27 September 1859.
82. Clare Anderson, *Legible Bodies: Race, Criminality and Colonialism in South Asia* (Oxford, 2004), p. 39.
83. IOR P/142/9 BJC, 27 November 1843: deposition of Robert Cort, n.d.; IOR P/142/12 BJC, 22 January 1844: deposition of Thomas Jones, 25 September 1843.
84. IOR P/142/15 BJC, 29 April 1844: C. Norris, Secretary to Government of Bombay, to Butterworth, 7 February 1844.
85. IOR P/402/30 BomJC, 23 January 1839: deposition of Rama Balloo, another convict, 25 December 1838; IOR P/402/30 BomJC, 30 January 1839: information of Pendygrass, 19 January 1839; *Bombay Gazette*, 30 July 1840.

the *Catherine*, for example, took place after a convict called Kondajee Bapoo complained to the captain about his treatment. The captain slapped Kondajee around the face, and threatened him with a flogging. Another convict stated that later that evening Kondajee had resolved to murder him.[86] One of the *Virginia* convicts, Hameer Rhadoo, claimed that before mutiny erupted Captain Whiffen had threatened to throw any man who was seasick overboard. Other convicts spoke of being kicked and thrown down by him.[87]

It is far from surprising then that convict mutineers mirrored this everyday brutality, and in this they were also intensely justice-seeking and mutinies were deeply performative. The *Virginia* convicts for example beat Captain Whiffen to a pulp.[88] Those on the *Clarissa* gave a great collective shout when they fatally injured the captain.[89] The symbolism of this physical anti-authoritarian violence ran deep. One convict informer (*Freak*) testified that the mutinous convicts tied up Captain Suffield, and when he asked for water told him he should have only two tin pots (the convicts' usual ration). They slit his throat, and threw him overboard, according to the informer saying "now this chain has been so many days on your legs is now on their's".[90] Convicts also targeted ships' papers for destruction. They ripped up or burnt logbooks, indents, and convict rolls, in the hope that it would prevent their later identification. The *Freak* convicts were unwilling to take any chances, and because they were illiterate they threw overboard all the books and papers found in the captain's cabin.[91] The *Clarissa* convicts too ransacked the ship, and destroyed all its papers.[92]

After taking ships, convicts commonly removed their simple prison issue *dhotis* (waist cloths) and put on the clothes of the captain and his officers. This careful dressing up was supposed to present a façade of normality to passing ships.[93] Yet it was also a visual expression of their newly acquired status and power. Convict leaders wore the captain's coat, sash, and sword; others took silk handkerchiefs and knotted them around their necks. Mutinies became carnivalesque, as convicts slaughtered livestock, made pilaf and curry, dissolved sugar into sherbet, drank and feasted. One of the first things the *Clarissa* convicts did after seizing the

---

86. IOR P/402/30 BomJC, 23 January 1839: deposition of Rama Balloo; IOR P/402/30 BomJC, 30 January 1839: information of Pendygrass.
87. *Bombay Gazette*, 30 July 1840.
88. *Ibid.*, 20 July 1840.
89. *Bengal Hurkaru*, 18 August 1854.
90. IOR P/403/6 BomJC, 2 March 1842: deposition of Michael Anthony.
91. IOR P/403/5 BomJC, 16 February 1842: J.W. Salmond, Resident Councillor Penang, to Willoughby, 15 July 1841.
92. IOR P/145/18 BJC, 13 September 1855: Tickell to Bogle, 8 June 1854.
93. As claimed in the *Bengal Hurkaru*, 27 March 1848.

ship was to make a drink by mixing some sugar that they found in the hold with seawater.⁹⁴ Convicts drew their own lines of cultural distinction as they ate separately from those of other religions and castes, but all joined in dancing, singing, and making merry.⁹⁵ Dressed in the garb of colonial authority to feast at the captain's table, these extraordinary scenes call out for our interpretation as the metaphorical capsizing of transportation ships, of the topsy-turvy world of the age of revolution.

And yet mutinous ships were not always radical or egalitarian spaces. First officer James Squire said the mutinous *Clarissa* convicts fought continually over rations. The Bengali convicts on board later testified that they had nothing to do with the mutiny; the Sikhs were responsible, they said, they had locked them below deck and appropriated most of the rations. When the ship ran aground, the Bengalis had been forced to work as porters. One of the recaptured *Clarissa* convicts Verream Singh stated in his defence: "I am a cultivator [...]. I never knew how to hold a musket how could I have fired one on board[?]."⁹⁶

CONCLUSION

A maritime focus on the age of revolution in the Indian Ocean necessarily incorporates subaltern perspectives, and suggests the importance of adding new layers of connection to the study of Europe, North America, and European colonies during the eighteenth and nineteenth centuries. My purpose here has been to unpack networks of empire, productivity, labour, and resistance in the Bay of Bengal and Indian Ocean, and in so doing to link together aspects of the age of rebellion across the region's rivers, seas, islands, littorals, and lands. Clearly, in the colonial context convict ships were both conduits for and sites of rebellion. They provided floating locales for mutiny and subversion; they were spaces in which peasants, pirates, and mutineers staged efforts to win freedom from a colonial nexus that linked punishment with voyaging and unfree labour; and they provided a means for the circulation of more generalized and ambitious forms of anti-colonial resistance and solidarity – as well as for the replication of established land-based forms of hierarchy.

There are important points of comparison here with a range of other contexts: with slave-ship mutinies and Australian convict piracy, with the downing of tools and petitioning of sailors and lascars, and with the libertarian, democratic, and "amok" desires and moments that frequently

94. IOR P/145/18 BJC, 13 September 1855: deposition of *edoo serang*.
95. IOR P/403/6 BJC, 2 March 1842: depositions of Michael Anthony, 7, 8 June 1841; *Bombay Gazette*, 20 July 1840.
96. IOR P/145/18 BJC, 13 September 1855: deposition of convict Verream Sing, son of Joe Sing no. 105, 5 July 1854.

underpinned them all. Furthermore, proletarian and subaltern subversion moved around, and local struggles became generalized, within and across the very spaces that constituted "the age" of the age of revolution – that is, as a time of unfreedom, forced labour circulation, and exploitation. Mutiny, piracy, anti-colonialism, and proto-nationalism in the European, Atlantic, and Indian Ocean worlds: each reveals that we must necessarily bring into view the multiple connections between land and sea, and take a more expansive geographical approach to questions of resistance and revolution in the eighteenth and nineteenth centuries.

IRSH 58 (2013), Special Issue, pp. 253–277 doi:10.1017/S0020859013000254
© 2013 Internationaal Instituut voor Sociale Geschiedenis

"All We Have Done, We Have Done for Freedom": The *Creole* Slave-Ship Revolt (1841) and the Revolutionary Atlantic

ANITA RUPPRECHT

School of Humanities, University of Brighton
10–11 Pavilion Parade, Brighton, East Sussex BN1 1RA, UK

E-mail: A.Rupprecht@brighton.ac.uk

ABSTRACT: The revolt aboard the American slaving ship the *Creole* (1841) was an unprecedented success. A minority of the 135 captive African Americans aboard seized the vessel as it sailed from Norfolk, Virginia, to the New Orleans slave markets. They forced the crew to sail to the Bahamas, where they claimed their freedom. Building on previous studies of the *Creole*, this article argues that the revolt succeeded due to the circulation of radical struggle. Condensed in collective memory, political solidarity, and active protest and resistance, this circulation breached the boundaries between land and ocean, and gave shape to the revolutionary Atlantic. These mutineers achieved their ultimate aim of freedom due to their own prior experiences of resistance, their preparedness to risk death in violent insurrection, and because they sailed into a Bahamian context in which black Atlantic cooperation from below forced the British to serve the letter of their own law.

When news of the extraordinary success of the slave revolt aboard the *Creole* broke in 1841, it was hailed as another *Amistad*. On 7 November the American slaving brig, having left Norfolk, Virginia, sailed into Nassau with 135 self-emancipated African Americans aboard. A minority of the captives had risen, killed a slaving agent, severely wounded the captain, and forced the crew to sail them into free waters, the British having abolished slavery three years earlier.[1] Occurring less than three

---

1. Howard Jones, "The Peculiar Institution and National Honor: The Case of the *Creole* Slave Revolt", *Civil War History*, 21 (1975), pp. 28–33; Edward D. Jervey and C. Harold Huber, "The *Creole* Affair", *Journal of Negro History*, 65 (1980), pp. 196–211; George Hendrick and Willene Hendrick, *The Creole Mutiny: A Tale of a Revolt Aboard a Slave Ship* (Chicago, IL, 2003); Walter Johnson, "White Lies: Human Property and Domestic Slavery Aboard the Slave Ship *Creole*", *Atlantic Studies*, 5 (2008), pp. 237–263. Depositions of the *Creole*'s crew are published

years after the *Amistad* rebellion, and two days before those Africans sailed for Sierra Leone, American slaveholders were thrown into a "great fever" at the event.[2] Unlike the *Amistad* rebellion, which had been a strike against Caribbean slavery under Spanish rule, the *Creole* struck at the very heart of American slavery under American rule. More broadly, the mutiny reaffirmed for the plantocracy that the great Atlantic wave of militant black anti-slavery rebellion and resistance shaped by the American, French, and Haitian revolutions rolled on.

Virginia had already been the site of two highly planned but ultimately unsuccessful slave plots that had deeply threatened the planter class. Gabriel Prosser's Richmond plot in 1800 was betrayed before it could be enacted, but Nat Turner's, which erupted in Southampton County in 1831, was the bloodiest of all slave rebellions prior to the Civil War. In 1822, Denmark Vesey, who had laboured in Haiti, plotted to take Charleston, South Carolina, on Bastille Day. In 1835, the enslaved rose in Bahia, Brazil. They were wearing images of Dessalines. The huge upsurge of resistance spurred the Atlantic-wide abolitionist movement to radicalize and gather pace. In the Caribbean, the Demerara Rebellion in 1823 rejuvenated the British campaigns. In Jamaica, Sam Sharpe's "Baptist War" of 1831–1832 mobilized tens of thousands of the enslaved, accelerating the British decision to pass their Abolition Acts in 1833 and 1838. On the other side of the ocean, David Walker's incendiary *Appeal [...] to the Coloured Citizens of the World*, published in 1829, circulated widely. William Lloyd Garrison founded *The Liberator* two years later.

The *Creole* looms large within African-American history and cultural memory, where Madison Washington, leader of the insurrection, has become immortalized as one of the great slave rebel leaders. This article offers a narrative of the mutiny that reflects on how Washington and his fellow insurgents were able to overthrow shipboard authority when so many maritime slave revolts ended in failure. It argues that the insurrection was an extraordinary achievement, but that the context in which it took place – the revolutionary Atlantic – was also pivotal to its ultimate success. The rebels rose as they were sailing along a porous eastern American seaboard, already enmeshed within wider networks of communication

in Sen. Docs. No. 51, 27th Cong., 2nd sess., 1842, II, pp. 1–46. The depositions are available too in *Parliamentary Papers*, 1843, [485], "Class D. Correspondence with foreign powers, not parties to conventions. Giving right of search of vessels suspected of the slave trade" [hereafter *PP*, 1843, [485]], and it is this source that has been used in the present article. For an account of the public rhetoric surrounding the event see Maggie Sale, *The Slumbering Volcano: American Slave Ship Revolts and the Production of Rebellious Masculinity* (Durham, NC, 1997), pp. 120–145.

2. *Oberlin Evangelist*, 12 October 1842, p. 167.

and resistance, and thus situated at the very edges of freedom. Stories of courageous slave-ship risings were circulating in American harbours when the *Creole* captives were forcibly embarked. Moreover, many were aware that hundreds of African Americans had claimed their freedom in the Bahamas in a variety of unexpected ways. Once the rebels had taken the ship, their liberation was secured because they sailed into an Atlantic vortex shaped by official British abolitionism from above, and by black Atlantic solidarity from below.

THE VOYAGE OF THE *CREOLE*

The Americans outlawed their transatlantic slave trade in 1808. While an illegal trade continued, as the slave markets of the southern states boomed in the face of increasing demand for labour, a rapidly commercializing and legal domestic slave trade quickly developed. By 1841, hundreds of slaving ships had voyaged down the south-eastern coast of North America, and along the Gulf Coast to New Orleans. There was nothing unusual about the route or the routine of the *Creole*.[3]

The brig departed from Richmond, Virginia, at midnight on Monday 25 October 1841, under the command of Captain Robert Ensor. By the time she reached open water a week later, the vessel had accumulated a "cargo" of 135 human beings, and several hogsheads of processed tobacco. She was bound for New Orleans. The majority of the enslaved belonged to the owners of the brig, Johnson & Eperson, but 26 were the property of Thomas McCargo, a well-known Virginian slave trader who was also aboard. The first mate was Zephaniah Gifford, an experienced mariner; his second mate was Lucius Stevens. In addition, there were ten crew, eight black servants, and four passengers aboard. Jacob Leitner, a Prussian, assisted the steward as mate. Three of the passengers were responsible for overseeing the captives. John Hewell had particular charge of the slaves of McCargo. William Merritt, as overseer, had general charge and superintendence of all the slaves aboard ship.

Even though this was a slaving voyage, it was also something of a family affair. Ensor's wife, baby daughter, and his fifteen-year-old niece were travelling with him. McCargo's young nephew, Theophilus, was also aboard to be tutored in the business of human trafficking. The presence of the children suggests that the traders were not contemplating, or did not allow themselves to contemplate, the risk of resistance. Perhaps their nerves were soothed by the fact that five insurance policies had been put

3. Robert H. Gudmestad, *A Troublesome Commerce: The Transformation of the Interstate Slave Trade* (Baton Rouge, LA, 2003); Adam Rothman, *Slave Country: American Expansion and the Origins of the Deep South* (Cambridge, MA, 2005); Steven Deyle, *Carry Me Back: The Domestic Slave Trade in American Life* (New York, 2005).

in place to cover any unlikely losses, but only three of these included any mention of slave revolt.

As was usual on these domestic voyages, the enslaved were able to occupy the deck during the day. At night, however, the women and men were confined below, separated by stacks of boxed tobacco as a way of preventing intimacies that might compromise their value. These conditions meant that four men, Madison Washington, Elijah Morris, Doc Ruffin, and Ben Blacksmith, were able to consolidate their bonds of "fictive kinship",[4] and collectively to map, with at least fifteen others, the spaces of the vessel and to watch and wait as shipboard routines settled down into a daily rhythm. Washington, as "head cook of the slaves" was in a unique position to assess the possibilities for mutiny. Serving meals to the captives twice a day provided a regular opportunity to identify potential allies, locate possible weapons, and watch the crew's movements.

No record exists of the process whereby the four captives planned their course of action. Nevertheless, Solomon Northup, kidnapped and transported from Richmond for sale in New Orleans only a few months before the *Creole* departed, described his part in plotting a shipboard revolt in his autobiography. As for the rebels aboard the *Creole,* Northup and his fellow conspirators were faced with the problems of knowing whom of their compatriots they could trust, and how to trigger the surprise and exact the violence necessary for a successful mutiny. They knew the uprising should begin at night, and therefore needed to find a way to avoid being locked in the hold. Northup describes how they debated these problems, and how he trial ran a potential plan by secreting himself under an upturned ship's boat at nightfall. The success of the trial determined that Northup and his fellow rebel, Arthur, would hide themselves until they were able to emerge and attack and kill the captain and mate as they slept in their bunks.[5]

Although the plot was not carried through, Northup's description offers an important counter to assumptions that maritime slave revolts were always spontaneous and undirected outbursts doomed by lack of leadership and planning. It is clear that rebel leaders aboard the *Creole* had also choreographed significant aspects of their attack carefully, including enlisting the support of at least some of the captive women to help trigger the assault, and identifying in advance a set of weapons.

4. This phrase is most often used in relation to specific bonds forged aboard transatlantic slaving vessels and carried into the Americas, though they are relevant with respect to wider maritime communities during the period. Given what transpired, they are applicable here. See Sidney W. Minz and Richard Price, *The Birth of African-American Culture: An Anthropological Perspective* (Boston, MA, 1992).
5. Solomon Northup, *Twelve Years a Slave* (New York, 1855), pp. 68–72.

UNITED STATES SLAVE TRADE.
1830.

Figure 1. The domestic slave trade figured prominently in American anti-slavery propaganda. The copper plate from which this image was engraved was discovered in the ruins of the Anti-Slavery Hall in Philadelphia which was burned down by anti-abolitionists in 1838 in reaction to the radicalization of the movement. The image references key elements of abolitionist iconography including the coffle, the forcible separation of families, the use of the whip, and maritime trafficking. Capitol Hill in the background signals the fact that, as the slave trade was supported legally by the Constitution, Congress had the power to outlaw the practice. *Library of Congress Prints and Photographs Division. Used with permission.*

THE MUTINY

The mutiny occurred a week into the voyage, and about 130 miles northeast of the Hole in the Wall. The captain, believing that he was closer to Abaco than he thought, ordered the brig to heave to for the night. All was calm, quiet, and dark; the rest of the crew and passengers were asleep. Gifford and three other mariners were on first watch. Washington had illicitly positioned himself in the women's hold. The women were silent. At about 9 o'clock, Morris approached the mate. Seeming to betray his co-conspirator, he reported that "one of the men had gone aft among the women". Gifford went back to wake the overseer, Merritt. The two of them returned, Merritt bringing a match and a lamp. Gifford stopped at the hatchway while Merritt descended into the darkness of the hold, and struck his match to light the lamp. When lit, it revealed Washington, who was standing behind him. Startled, Merritt said, "You are the last man on the brig I expected to find here". Washington replied, "Yes sir, it is me", and immediately leapt towards the ladder saying, "I'm going up, I cannot stay here."

Washington overpowered both men but Gifford stumbled to the deck as Washington emerged from the hold. Morris, who was still standing nearby, drew a pistol. He fired at Gifford, the ball grazing the back of his head. Washington ran towards the men's quarters in the forward part of the hold shouting directions, in order to signal that the uprising had begun. "We have begun, and must go through; rush boys aft, and we have them." It was vital that he stirred the slaves above and below into action either by fear or fury, and he yelled into the hold, "Come up, every damned one of you; if you don't and lend a hand, I will kill you and throw you overboard."[6]

A group of waiting rebels came at Merritt with handspikes as he clambered up to the deck after Washington. He dodged a blow so that the weapon hit another rebel instead, allowing Merritt to break free and run down the ship towards the cabin. The rebels pursued both him and Gifford along the deck, and down the ladder into the corridor, Gifford shouting the alarm, "There's been a mutiny on deck, I've been shot." Other rebels quickly surrounded the entrance and the skylights on the quarterdeck above. As the rebels crowded down into the corridor, Hewell, one of the other passengers, grabbed a musket, and came out to confront the slaves. Faced with the firearm, the rebels retreated. Hewell followed them back up the ladder, and tried to defend the cabin. He fired the gun but it contained no shot. One of the rebels pulled it from him, so he grabbed a handspike, brandishing it in the dark. Not being able to see clearly, the rebels retreated further, momentarily thinking it to be another musket.[7]

During the moments that Hewell held back the rebels, Captain Ensor, armed with a bowie knife, rushed out through the forecastle further to rouse the crew members. A vicious fight began between the rebels and sailors, both groups armed with clubs, knives, and sticks. Ensor was felled in the starboard scuppers where the rebels repeatedly clubbed and stabbed him, yelling, "Kill the son-of-a-bitch, kill him."[8] Ben Blacksmith grabbed Ensor's bowie knife lying on the deck, and went for Hewell who, despite multiple wounds, was still fighting. Blacksmith stabbed him in the chest. Mortally wounded, Hewell got himself back down the ladder, and into Theophilus McCargo's berth, where he bled to death. His mutilated body was later thrown overboard on the orders of Washington, Blacksmith, and Morris. Severely wounded, Ensor crawled away from the melee and, with nowhere else to hide, struggled up the main shroud and secreted himself in the maintop.

With vicious fighting going on above, and all exits guarded, Merritt realized that he was trapped below decks. He tried to hide under the bedclothes while two of the women cabin servants sat on him but, terrified, they soon moved away. Two of the rebels burst into the room, one shouting,

6. "Protest", *New Orleans Advertiser*, 8 December 1841.
7. "Deposition of William H. Merritt", 9 November 1841, *PP*, 1843, [485], p. 148.
8. "Deposition of Zephaniah C. Gifford", 9 November 1841, *PP*, 1843, [485], p. 149.

"Kill the son-of-a-bitch, don't spare him; and kill every white person on board, don't spare one."[9] Merritt had no idea who was dead by this time, and who was alive. Neither could the rebels be sure. Thinking quickly, with a knife to his neck, he told the insurgents that he had once been a ship's mate, and could navigate.[10]

Gifford did not stay to fight long. The rebels attacked him with clubs and sticks, and one slashed through his clothes at his breast, with what he later identified as a large meat knife taken from the galley.[11] Battered and terrified, he climbed the rigging into the darkness of the maintop. Once there, he found the severely wounded captain virtually unconscious, and, as the ship was pitching about violently, he tied the captain so that he would not fall, and then lay there listening as the rebels shouted to each other in the dark as they searched about for the ship's captain and mate.

The success of the revolt had depended on unleashing the full fury of the insurgents, but Gifford heard shouted orders revealing efforts to direct and limit the violence. While Merritt was hiding under his bed sheets, he heard shouts amid the chaos of, "Don't hurt the steward, don't hurt Jacob, or Mrs. Ensor."[12] Jacob Leitner hid in his berth until he could not bear it any longer, and came up on deck to meet what he thought was his certain death. Morris, fully committed to maintaining the momentum of the revolt, ran out of the cabin at him shouting, "Kill every God damn white person on board the vessel, and if none else will, I will!" Leitner brought him up short by confronting him, "Will you kill me, Morris?" Morris stopped in his tracks, and assured him that he would not but demanded that he go down into the after hatch out of harm's way.[13]

The incident signals the ways in which the necessity of exacting the violence necessary to take the ship might easily have tipped into an indiscriminate and revengeful blood lust with potentially catastrophic consequences. Morris's sparing of Leitner also demonstrates that events were shaped by complicated relations between black and white, crew and enslaved. When rebels set to kill Jacques Lacombe, Washington warned them off, shouting that he was French, and could not speak English. This might not have been the only reason. Lacombe had remained steadfastly at the wheel throughout the battle. He may have done so through fear, or because he was unwilling to take sides.

Searching for ship's officers, the rebels entered the staterooms, and found the captain's wife, the children, and the steward, all of whom they

9. "Protest".
10. "Deposition of William H. Merritt", 9 November 1841, pp. 141–142.
11. Merritt M. Robinson, *Reports of the Cases Argued and Determined in the Supreme Court of Louisiana* (New Orleans, LA, 1845), X, p. 207.
12. *Ibid.*, p. 142.
13. "Deposition of Jacob Leitner", *PP*, 1843, [485], p. 143.

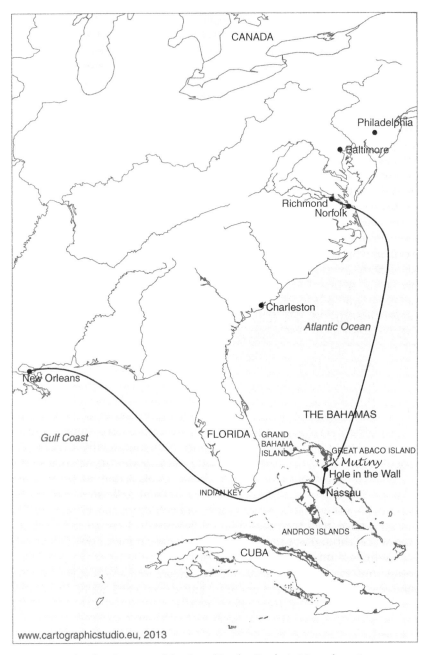

Figure 2. Map showing the route of the slave ship, the *Creole*, in November, 1841.

secured in the hold. They discovered Stevens, the second mate, hiding in his cabin. The rebels burst in on him, one firing a musket. They chased him up onto the deck and attacked him with a piece of flagstaff, and knives. Wounded, Stevens scrambled up the fore shrouds on to the fore-royal yard, and stayed there. The three senior ship's officers were now aloft, and out of sight.

By about 1 am, the rebels felt confident enough to acknowledge that the ship was theirs. In a symbolic celebratory performance of upturned hierarchies, they called Leitner, the steward's mate, to the cabin, where he served them apples and bread and the officers' brandy. Leitner was clearly not regarded as an enemy. When one of the rebels took his watch, it was returned when it was realized that it did not belong to the captain. The rebels rifled the personal trunks, donned new clothes, and pulled the officers' stockings over their own. The search was not one of merely joyous subversion however. They were also looking for further weapons to secure their position. Apart from the officers who were aloft, and of whom they were still unaware, the upper deck was, for that moment, theirs. Determined to occupy previously forbidden space, as many who could fit in it slept in the cabin.[14]

The discovery of the ship's officers in the rigging at dawn revealed that tensions remained high, and the chain of command not entirely settled. The rebels were not in agreement about whether the officers should be killed. Amongst the crew, there was confusion about whose orders had precedence. Gifford, once returned to the deck, complained, "Some say make sail, and others say not, who shall I obey?". Stevens descended reluctantly, which infuriated some rebels who threatened to pitch him overboard. Gifford told them that Ensor was aloft and seriously wounded. At this point, Washington asserted his leadership, making it clear that he did not want any more killing. He ordered that Ensor be lowered to the deck, and then secured in the hold with his family after his wounds had been dressed. Nevertheless, Morris and Blacksmith kept threatening Stevens the next day, and that evening someone took a potshot at him as he walked along the quarterdeck in the dark, the bullet whistling past his head.[15] It was the last shot of the mutiny.

BACKGROUND TO THE *CREOLE* REVOLT

The *Creole* rebels achieved their extraordinary success because, as Eugene Genovese noted with more general reference to shipboard revolts, "the appearance of favorable conditions and a genuine chance of success could

---

14. *Ibid.*, pp. 143–144.
15. "Deposition of Lucius Stevens", Nassau, 10 November 1841, *PP*, 1843, [485], p. 140.

trigger bold action".[16] The rising was possible, in part, because of the lax conditions aboard the *Creole*. As Marcus Rediker has argued, transatlantic slave ships were vicious machines dedicated to the violent production of slaves, ruthlessly recalibrating African lives and bodies into human commodities as they plied the Middle Passage.[17] The coastwise slaving vessels were not engaged in the production of slaves so much as transporting human beings understood by American traffickers to have already been "made" into slaves. It seems clear that slavers had grown complacent about the possible resistance of their human cargoes. They mixed them with other sundry merchandise, from bricks to tobacco, and from millstones to seeds. Why else did the *Creole* carry a slave trader's young family members? Why else was there only one musket between them all? Why else were none of the 135 African Americans either chained or restrained?

Allowing the captives a certain amount of mobility aboard may have been designed to prevent the build-up of tension, but the policy thereby enabled the captives to learn the layout of the ship, identify and collect together weapons – the meat knife from the galley, handspikes, "left forward by the windlass, where they could be picked up by anybody" – whisper, plan, and organize themselves.[18] It does not appear that the hatches were secure by 9 o'clock on the night of the rising. Washington had managed to leave one hold and enter the other without drawing any attention to himself, while no issue was made about Morris and several other slaves remaining on deck in the dark. As the captives had not even been searched when they were boarded, they may also have smuggled weapons on board.[19]

This last fact is significant for it highlights the fact that the *idea* of mutiny preceded embarkation. While practical details might have been worked out covertly during the first week at sea, a core commitment had already been formed on shore with the goal of taking the ship. The leaders of the rising, Washington, Ruffin, Morris, and Blacksmith, had been sold into the slave trade from different parts of the north, and would not have known each other until they met in the stinking slave pens. Washington is the only one of the *Creole* mutineers about whom there exists biographical detail, although it is probable that the other three men had prior contact with, or knowledge of, runaways and abolitionists. It would have been while awaiting their transportation that the *Creole* rebels first formed their alliances, told their stories, shared information, and forged a bond of trust that they then carried on to the slaver.

16. Eugene D. Genovese, *From Rebellion to Revolution: Afro-American Slave Revolts in the Making of the Modern World* (Baton Rouge, LA, 1992), p. 6.
17. Marcus Rediker, *The Slave Ship: A Human History* (London, 2007), pp. 41–45.
18. Robinson, *Reports of the Cases*, p. 336.
19. *Ibid.*, pp. 217–218.

Washington's fragmented story not only confirms an intense desire for freedom but also that, as a fugitive slave, he had moved covertly through radical abolitionist networks of communication and asylum prior to his recapture. Here, he had listened to the arguments for violent resistance, and, even more specifically, he had been presented with a heroic figure and a model for successful action. Washington was born a slave in Virginia. In late 1839 he had fled to Canada using the Underground Railroad. In early 1841, against the advice of well-known abolitionist activists, Hiram Wilson, Henry Garnet, and Robert Purvis, he travelled back down the railroad to Virginia in search of his wife. He returned via Philadelphia where he stayed with Purvis, who had previously helped him reach Canada.

Fifty years later Purvis recalled Washington's surprising visit. He had arrived on the same day that Purvis took possession of a striking portrait entitled, "Sinque, the Hero of the Amistad", painted by the abolitionist artist Nathaniel Joceylyn. Washington was "intensely interested" in the picture and in the story of the famous rebellion. Purvis recalled that "[h]e drank in every word, and greatly admired the hero's courage and intelligence".[20] Washington was recaptured in Virginia in early 1841, and sold to Thomas McCargo. Burning with rage, and holed up in the Norfolk slave pen, the recent memory of Cinqué's portrait must have galvanized Washington, while relaying the story of the *Amistad* to his fellow captives surely provided inspiration and vital coordinates for calculating the possibility of another shipboard rebellion.

Slave pens existed all around the harbours of the eastern seaboard for holding captives while traders acquired enough human property to fill a hold. Captives were also trans-shipped between vessels while they were at anchor. This enabled conspiracies to travel from shore to ship, and from ship to ship. At least fifteen other captives took part in the *Creole* revolt. It is not clear whether the four met them on shore, or recruited them to the cause once aboard. Nevertheless, what is clear is that planned mutiny had already dramatically breached the division between shipboard and the Norfolk shoreside on previous occasions. If stories of the *Amistad* rebellion were circulating in 1841, they would have mixed with those of earlier slave-ship revolts inspired by the revolution in, and proximity of, Saint-Domingue.

In 1826, rebels took the slave ship *Decatur* after it had departed from Baltimore and ordered that it be sailed to Saint-Domingue. The mutiny was quelled before it reached the island.[21] Perhaps inspired by the attempt, another revolt occurred on the *Lafayette*, which departed from Norfolk harbour in 1829. As with the *Creole*, reports suggest the

20. *Philadelphia Inquirer*, 26 December 1889.
21. For reports of the mutiny aboard the *Decatur* see the *Essex Register*, Salem, MA, 22 May 1826, p. 3; *City Gazette and Commercial*, Charleston, South Carolina, 26 May 1826, p. 2; *Alexandria Gazette*, Alexandria, Virginia, 22 May 1826, p. 2.

complacency of the captain and crew in the face of the potential for an uprising. The large slaver also carried extra cargo, and other white passengers. The 197 male and female slaves had been separated by using a ship's boat stowed bottom up and athwart the ship as a bulkhead. It could, as Solomon Northup later affirmed, be used to spark an insurrection. The ship's crew managed to overpower the rebels during a vicious fight. Later, under interrogation, twenty-five men, deemed to be the leaders of the affray, revealed the magnitude of the plot.

The rising had been organized amongst the group of slaves previously held aboard another slaver, the *Ajax*, while it lay in Norfolk harbour. Those who were transferred to the *Lafayette* had taken the plan with them. The *Ajax* had sailed a few days after the *Lafayette*, and it was later confirmed that a planned revolt on the *Ajax* had reputedly been betrayed before it could be staged. The *Lafayette* rebels undercut whatever reassurance might have been supplied to the enemy by the revelation of fragile solidarities. They told their interrogators that the slaver, the *Transport*, following on behind the *Ajax*, was also carrying captives who were committed to the same plan.[22]

Even though these insurrections were unsuccessful, the prospect of rolling waves of shipboard mutinies, each one copying the next, exacerbated the already well-established alarm amongst southern slave owners.[23] The fact that the militants, like those aboard the *Decatur*, had "confessed that their object was to slay the whites and run the vessel to St Domingo" simply confirmed for them that slave revolt haunted them at every turn. The *New Orleans Courier*, reflecting on the *Lafayette* conspiracy, glossed its incendiary nature by claiming that the revolts were the result of moral degeneracy rather than political impetus. The editors argued that they were "among many of the evil consequences attendant upon the system followed by our northern neighbors of sending the most worthless and abandoned portion of their slave population to this place".[24]

The geographical and historical proximity of Saint-Domingue exerted an extraordinarily powerful motivating force on both enslaved African Americans, immobilized on the plantations, and on those funnelled into overland and maritime slaving routes.[25] In 1841, however, the *Creole* rebels chose not to steer for the new republic. By this time, another possible maritime route to freedom had more immediate valency, of which the rebels also had prior knowledge and which determined the next stage of the mutiny.

22. *New Orleans Courier*, 14 December 1829.
23. Rothman, *Slave Country*, pp. 165–216.
24. *New Orleans Courier*, 14 December 1829.
25. Alfred N. Hunt, *Haiti's Influence on Antebellum America: Slumbering Volcano in the Caribbean* (Baton Rouge, LA, 1988), pp. 107–188.

VOYAGE TO THE BAHAMAS

After gaining final control of the *Creole*, Washington took Merritt into one of the staterooms and – perhaps remembering Cinqué – told him that they wanted to sail for Liberia. Merritt replied that the ship was equipped with neither provisions nor water to make a transatlantic crossing. Then Blacksmith and several others said, "they wanted to go to the British islands; they did not want to go anywhere else but where Mr Lumpkin's Negroes went last year". They were referring to the slave ship *Hermosa*, which had been wrecked off Abaco the year before. They knew that having been rescued by Bahamian wreckers and taken into Nassau, "Mr. Lumpkin's Negroes" had been freed by the British colonials.[26]

The *Hermosa* was not an isolated case, even if it was the most recent. As the prospect of British emancipation loomed across the West Indies, a set of shipwrecks off the Bahamian islands had resulted in the loss of hundreds of thousands of dollars for American traffickers, and freedom for several hundred African-American slaves. American slaveholders and their government had been serially scandalized by what they saw as tyrannical British interference in property rights, and sought compensation. The rebels' demand to sail to the Bahamas shows that enslaved African Americans knew the details of these earlier shipwrecks, or near shipwrecks, and came to view the Bahamas, less than 200 miles from the coast of Florida, as a vital coordinate in their contemporary geopolitical map of freedom.[27] Moreover, unlike the rebels aboard the *Amistad*, the new masters of the *Creole* also had a smattering of vital maritime knowledge that would help them to get there.

Whether he had been employed at sea previously is not clear, but Pompey Garrison, one of the rebels, had apparently sailed to New Orleans before, and knew the route. George Cortlock and Doc Ruffin "knew the letters of the compass". Once Merritt had ordered his crew to set sail for Nassau, the rebel leaders took turns to watch the compass, forbidding Merritt and Gifford, on pain of death, from speaking to each other, or from taking their reckonings in writing in case they were secretly communicating. It could not be taken for granted that the crew, or the rest of the enslaved, or even the rebel leaders, would submit peacefully to the plan. The rebel leaders took stations around the ship in order to maintain their control. Morris intimated that all was not fully agreed amongst them when he was asked whether the intention was to kill all the sailors. He replied, "No: I expect we shall rise again among ourselves, but the white

26. Philip Troutman, "Grapevine in the Slave Market: African American Geopolitical Literacy and the 1841 *Creole* Revolt", in Walter Johnson (ed.), *The Chattel Principle: Internal Slave Trades in the Americas* (New Haven, CT, 2004), pp. 203–233.
27. *Ibid.*, p. 209.

Figure 3. Madison Washington saw this portrait of Cinqué, leader of the *Amistad* mutiny, at the home of Robert Purvis with whom he stayed in 1841 prior to his recapture and the mutiny aboard the *Creole*.
Yale University Art Gallery

people shall not be hurt."[28] No such divisions occurred, however, the rebels ensuring that their authority over both captives and crew remained secure until they reached Nassau.

As the *Creole* approached the harbour on the morning of 9 November, a pilot boat came out to meet the brig. The rebels jettisoned their weapons into the sea, and, leaving their watch positions, began to mix amongst the captives. Despite the fact that British post-emancipation law recognized African Americans as free persons, at this moment there could be no certainty about how that law would be translated once the colonial authorities knew about the conditions under which this ship had arrived. Merritt recalled that "the other Negroes were laughing and looking on and appeared much animated as they would had there been no mutiny", although the rebels seemed anxious.[29]

If they were not quite ready to let their guard down, however, their first contact with local Bahamians set terms for an extraordinary set of solidarities and identifications that would develop and spread over the coming days. As he boarded, one of the pilot boat's black crew told the African Americans that "he came out from Charleston, and that he got free by coming out there in that way". He may well have been captive aboard the *Enconium*, another American slaver that had been shipwrecked off Abaco eight years earlier. The meeting produced jubilation on the *Creole*. One white witness noted that the African Americans "kissed the negroes that came on board and said, you are my brothers, &c. The negroes of the *Creole* laughed, and appeared much rejoiced, particularly those who heard the negro say, that he had got free in that way".[30]

For obvious reasons, Gifford did not board the pilot boat. He went on shore in the quarantine boat to inform the American Consul, Bacon, of the mutiny. Bacon immediately requested that the Governor send a guard on board until it was clear what should happen next. The Governor acceded by sending twenty-four Second West India Regiment troops armed with muskets, bayonets fixed. The soldiers were Africans to a man, with the exception of their captain. Like many of the inhabitants of Nassau, the soldiers had been kidnapped from the coasts of West Africa, and had endured the Middle Passage aboard illegally operating slaving vessels. Intercepted by the British, these Africans were rescued under the terms of the Abolition Acts that funnelled them, involuntarily, into the British Army, or, prior to emancipation, ensured they were "apprenticed" for a maximum of fourteen years.

28. "Protest".
29. Johnson, "White Lies", p. 244.
30. *McCargo v. New Orleans Insurance Company*, printed testimony of Jacob Leidner, pp. 1–2, Dockett 4409, New Orleans Public Library.

In the years between the passing of the Acts and 1841, at least two dozen ships landed over 6,000 rescued Africans in the Bahamas.[31] Those who were not recruited into the military were initially bonded in a variety of situations across the mixed economy, including in plantation agriculture, maritime occupations such as fishing, sponging, wrecking, and salt-raking, and in a variety of skilled and semi-skilled trades and shopkeeping in Nassau. The African troops boarded the *Creole*, and with the aid of the crew identified the leaders of the mutiny, Washington, Ruffin, Morris, and Blacksmith, and tied them down in a long boat. Over the next few days, the Consul and the British Attorney General travelled out to the vessel to begin deposing the *Creole*'s officers and crew.

The troops secured the rebel leaders but ignored the order not to communicate with their charges and were, apparently, in continual and familiar and even intimate contact with them throughout the week. The Americans were alarmed at the resulting subversion of racial and social hierarchies on board, while Merritt felt that the soldiers purposefully undermined his position as a senior ship's officer. When he raised the issue with the commanding officer, "who he found conversing with a coloured female with his cloak around her", he was, Merritt reported, simply brushed off.[32] Even more shockingly, the commanding officer apparently

> [...] told Mary, one of the slaves owned by Thomas McCargo, in presence of many of the other slaves, how foolish they were, that they had not when they rose killed all the whites on board, and run the vessel ashore, and then they would all have been free, and there would have been no more trouble about it.[33]

Meanwhile, Consul Bacon knew what had happened in the cases of the shipwrecked *Comet* and the *Enconium*, and had been Consul when "Mr. Lumpkin's Negroes" had been freed from the *Hermosa* the year before. He was determined that the British would not embarrass him again. He approached Captain Woodside, Master of the *Congress*, another American vessel docked in the harbour and, together with the *Creole*'s officers, they devised a plot to retake the ship with the aid of Woodside's crew. They planned to sail it to Indian Key, where there was an American man-of-war permanently based – as a result, amongst other things, of the Seminole Wars that were raging in Florida – which could facilitate their onward journey to New Orleans. If the ship was to be reclaimed by force, however, the crew of the *Creole* required rearming as the mutineers had

---

31. Rosanne Adderley, *"New Negroes from Africa": Slave Trade Abolition and Free African Settlement in the Nineteenth-Century Caribbean* (Indianapolis, IN, 2006), p. 10.
32. "Deposition of William H. Merritt", Nassau, Bahamas, 13 November 1841, *PP*, 1843, [485], p. 132.
33. "Protest".

jettisoned the few weapons that were originally aboard. Bacon and Gifford undertook to go into town and purchase new guns.

Their mission revealed that news about the mutiny had already spread like wildfire around Nassau. It seemed that everyone knew that there were American slaves being held aboard the *Creole*. Crowds began to gather around the harbour front. If the Bahamian mariners and the African troops were in solidarity with the rebels' cause, it transpired that so too were Nassau's weapons dealers. They all refused to sell to the Americans. It also seemed that everyone already knew exactly who Gifford was, and as he walked down the street he was subjected to jeers and insults from both black and white residents. He reported that he heard them say, "There goes one of the damned pirates and slavers".[34] Defeated, Gifford and Bacon decided to scrape together what spare guns they could procure from two other American vessels. Their preferred plan was to wait until the nineteen rebels had been taken from the *Creole*. Clearly, it was worth the loss of the most dangerous slaves in order to secure the rest for the New Orleans markets. Thus, they waited as the endless depositions were accumulated, and the tension mounted in Nassau, Woodside, with the Consul checking with the *Creole*'s crew day by day as to the appropriate moment to strike. While British officials appeared to be in no hurry to act, however, it began to look as if local Bahamians might.

LOCAL SOLIDARITY AND THE THREAT OF REVOLT

The pattern of social protest that followed drew directly on the experience of previous struggles. Many Afro-Bahamians who acted would have remembered the day the slaves were liberated from the *Hermosa* only the previous year. Some might have remembered the shipwrecked *Comet* or the *Enconium* in 1831 and 1833. Others, like the black mariner, may even "have got free in that way". In each prior case, Bahamians had been key in minimizing British vacillation about freeing enslaved Americans, and blocking interference by American traders, resident slaveholders, or illegal traffickers. In each prior case, British colonials had acted on a clause in their anti-slave trade legislation that had determined that captives who survived shipwrecks in the West Indies were freed, but it was the local community who created the conditions in which it would have been extremely difficult for the British to have acted otherwise. To this extent the *Creole* mutineers sailed into, and were embraced by, another sphere of the wider tradition of black Atlantic resistance and cooperation.

When the *Comet* and the *Enconium* foundered off Abaco in the early 1830s, it was the same group of Bahamian wreckers who rescued each

---

34. Robinson, *Reports of the Cases*, p. 213.

vessel's captain, crew, and slaves, insisting that they travel to Nassau. Bahamian "rackers" had long scouted the out islands for the valuable salvage thrown up as European and American vessels foundered on the reefs as they entered and exited the Caribbean. Made up of poor whites, escaped slaves, and their descendants, and later liberated Africans, the wreckers had a reputation for being little other than smugglers and pirates.[35] Yet, it was wreckers that helped ferry black Seminoles and runaway slaves, escaping extermination in Florida, to the Andros Islands during the 1820s.[36]

The intervention by the wreckers meant that the captives did not arrive at Nassau under an American flag. Once arrived, the captain of the *Comet* was served with a writ which stated that the slaves were to be seized and freed.[37] All but three (who refused to disembark) of the sixty-one captives who had been aboard the *Enconium* were also landed and legally freed. They were then fed and accommodated in the army barracks by liberated African soldiers.[38]

Both cases infuriated the southern press, the American government, and the Bahamian assembly. The day before the authorities seized the captives from the *Comet*, the assembly sent a hysterical and unanimously signed letter of protest to the colony's governor. Resurrecting earlier fears about the arrival of the liberated Africans and echoing southern planter fear and prejudice, they wrote:

> The sudden irruption [...] of this large body of strange Creole slaves, also combining as the American negroes generally do the Intelligence and cunning of the lower order of Freemen, with the characteristic want of thought and fore-sight almost inseparable from a state of Slavery, the profligate habits, the vices, the crimes, which have notoriously been the frequent occasion of the deportation of Slaves, from the Atlantic States to the Western settlements of North America would be but too justly calculated to inspire fears in this quarter of the most alarming character.[39]

Despite their remonstrations, six months after the passing of the British Abolition Act, another seventy-eight enslaved Americans found freedom in nearby Bermuda. They had been aboard the slaver, *Enterprize*, en route

35. Virgil Henry Storr, *Enterprising Slaves & Master Pirates: Understanding Economic Life in the Bahamas* (New York, 2004), pp. 47–48.
36. Rosalyn Howard, "The 'Wild Indians' of Andros Island: Black Seminole Legacy in the Bahamas", *Journal of Black Studies*, 37 (2006), pp. 275–298; Irvin D.S. Winsboro and Joe Knetsch, "Florida Slaves, the 'Saltwater Railroad' to the Bahamas, and Anglo–American Diplomacy", *Journal of Southern History*, 79 (2013), pp. 51–78.
37. National Archives, London [hereafter NA], CO 23/92.
38. The *Enconium* was sailing from Charleston to New Orleans carrying sixty-four captives, rice, naval stores, millstones, and sundry merchandise. See "Protest" by Captain Staples of the *Enconium*, n.d., NA, CO 23/92.
39. "Bahamas House of Assembly", 14 January 1831, NA CO 23/92.

from Alexandria to Charleston.[40] Damaged in a storm, the brig was forced into Hamilton Harbour, but once repairs were completed local customs officials refused to give clearance for the vessel until a legal ruling had been made regarding the status of the captives on board.

Over several days, word spread across the island that American slaves, most of them children, had been discovered in the vessel's hold (they were not listed on the ship's manifest). Again, the planter class expressed their concern about the consequences of releasing enslaved Americans in the colony.[41] The newly apprenticed and free black Bermudan population, on the other hand, rapidly mobilized amongst themselves. They took immediate action when the captain, Elliott, made ready to sail. Crowds gathered as an Afro-Bermudan named Tucker, leader of a newly instituted Young Men's Friendly Lodge – one of the many post-emancipation collectives founded by the free blacks to provide mutual welfare, support, and to campaign for political and labour rights – obtained a writ of habeus corpus against Elliott.[42] Elliott watched helplessly as the captives disembarked to the cheers of an immense crowd that surged along with them, and then packed the courthouse late into the night determined to see justice done.[43]

All but one woman and her five children elected to claim their liberty. The crowd immediately began a collection amongst themselves to provide for the ex-slaves' needs. The members of the Friendly Institution also arranged for their temporary accommodation by securing an empty house in the town, "and the next day by the interposition of their Society nearly all [...] obtained places in different parts of the Colony".[44] As these examples demonstrate, maritime and land-based traditions from below – of mutual aid and local anti-slavery activism – played a crucial part in successive liberations of American slaves in the Bahamas and Bermuda well before the *Creole*'s triumphant arrival in Nassau. The story of the *Hermosa*, which proved to be so pivotal for the *Creole* rebels, further bolstered these traditions.

The *Hermosa* foundered off Abaco on 19 October 1840. Also sailing from Richmond for New Orleans, the slaver was carrying a cargo of cotton goods, tobacco, and forty-eight slaves. Again, Bahamian wreckers

---

40. Governor of Bermuda to Earl of Aberdeen, 28 February 1835, NA, CO 37/96. The *Enterprise* carried no mounted guns, and, together with 3 paying passengers, was loaded with a cargo of 40,000 bricks, 6 hogsheads of tobacco, a large supply of seeds, and 78 captives.
41. *Ibid.*
42. Howard Johnson, "Friendly Societies in the Bahamas 1834–1910", *Slavery & Abolition*, 12:3 (1991), pp. 183–199. Although Johnson focuses his study on the Bahamas, he notes at the outset that, "Until the development of viable trade unions in the late 1930s, the Friendly Society remained the characteristic working-class organisation in many areas of the British Caribbean", p. 183.
43. Nellie Musson, *Mind the Onion Seed* (Nashville, TN, 1979), pp. 65–67.
44. NA, CO 37/96.

rescued all who were aboard, salvaged the cargo, and sailed for Green Turtle Key. While the captain, Chattin, was ashore arguing with the customs officers, stipendiary magistrates and a priest boarded the wreckers to advise the forty-eight that they were free.

Chattin sought support from Consul Bacon once they arrived in Nassau, but the captives were disembarked before they could complete their protest. At the magistrate's office, Chattin reported that he could not hear what was being said because "the mob was so great", and that he and Bacon were "forced out of doors". The British West India Corps, heavily armed, later prevented him from communicating with the African Americans as they spent their first night of freedom housed in Crown buildings. He made another attempt to claim them the next morning, but the entire group had already disappeared into the Nassau market crowds.[45]

Even if it was inevitable that, in each case, colonial officials (without the support of the planter class) would have legally pronounced the enslaved Americans free, the local community's identification with the captives forced the issue in a moment of danger. In the case of the *Enterprize* and the *Hermosa*, it was the direct action of the crowd that prevented the ships' masters from absconding. By insisting on bearing witness, and in huge numbers, they ensured that the captives were recognized as full rights-bearing subjects before the law, and offered their support thereafter. They were determined that the same should happen for those on the *Creole*.

The *Creole* had been lying in the harbour for four days when the tension intensified dramatically. Crowds again lined the waterfront, and surrounding balconies were packed with men and women with spyglasses trained on the *Creole*. Rumours that the "blacks of the island" were planning forcibly to rescue the captives that day were rippling through the town. It quickly became clear to Bacon that the local community was once again mobilizing. He was accosted repeatedly by "respectable" whites, one of whom told him that their servants had been meeting at night, and planned to assist in the liberation of the slaves that day. Another gestured towards the harbour, informing the Consul that the launch heading out towards the *Creole* belonged to him, and had been commandeered, and "that the slaves were to be liberated by the blacks by means of boats".[46] By the time Bacon arrived at the brig, it looked to him that the rescue attempt had begun. The crowd had taken to the water. The *Creole* was completely surrounded by at least fifty small boats, and a large sloop, packed with Bahamians armed with clubs, had been towed out and anchored near the brig. The men aboard the sloop were distributing the

45. "Further Protest and Deposition of the Master of the *Hermosa*", New Orleans, *PP*, 1843, [485], p. 201.
46. Robinson, *Reports of the Cases*, p. 227.

clubs amongst the smaller boats. Bacon was told that one attempt had already been made to board the *Creole*.

Pinder, the Police Magistrate, concerned about public order, decided he could do nothing about the bristling "mosquito fleet", and so went instead to where the crowds were assembled.[47] Bacon also decided it would be unwise to board the vessel, given its now highly seditious context. He returned to his office to warn the Governor of the volatile situation in the harbour, and to request support. Gifford, frightened for the safety of his crew and of losing his property, was waiting for him when he arrived.

Having sent his letter, Bacon must have realized that there was limited time before the Governor's forces would act. In any case, it looked as if the Bahamians were about to overwhelm the ship. If it was going to stay in American hands, if indeed it still was, then the plan that he had concocted with Woodside and the officers of the *Creole* to take the ship by force had to be enacted immediately. Bacon ordered Creasy, the mate of the *Congress*, to take four sailors, and the few muskets and cutlasses that they had gleaned, and row out to the *Creole*. This could no longer be a covert operation; it was broad daylight, and there were at least 2,000 people watching. According to the later "Protest" (interestingly, no individual deponent mentioned this incident at the time, except Woodside), "a negro in a boat" spotted them loading the boat, the arms concealed in an American flag, and following them across the harbour "gave the alarm to the British officer in command on board". The crowd watched, "the excitement increasing", as Creasy's tiny army approached the brig, only to be told by the British officer on board that they would be fired on if they came too near.[48] With a line of twenty-four West India muskets, with fixed bayonets, trained down on them, and surrounded by masses of armed fishermen, stevedores, and droughers, they had no option but to withdraw.

Aboard the *Creole*, the Americans became increasingly anxious as the fleet accumulated around them. As the confusion intensified, the boundaries of the vessel, and between the parties aboard, were further breached as first Woodside boarded, and then two clergymen who, ignoring the Americans, engaged in "familiar conversation with the slaves", seemingly readying them for their departure. The women began "patting their bonnets", and packing up their belongings.[49] Stevens recalled that the black pilot urgently called up from the sloop, "Come get through with your business on board, we want to commence ours". Woodside disembarked to tell the Consul what he already knew, that the brig was "literally surrounded with boats full of black people armed with clubs".[50]

47. *Ibid.*
48. *Ibid.*, p. 228.
49. "Deposition of William Woodside", 13 November 1841, *PP*, 1843, [485], p. 131.
50. "Deposition of Zephaniah C. Gifford", 9 November 1841, p. 133.

Back on shore, Bacon was summoned to a rapidly convened council session where he had a testy discussion with the Governor. The Governor knew about the American plot, and that the situation in the harbour was now on a knife-edge. He informed Bacon that he was finally sending the Attorney General out to the *Creole* to identify those implicated in the murder, remove the troops, and to oversee the landing of the rest of the party of slaves. There was nothing Bacon could do except rush back, and advise Gifford and Woodside to return to the *Creole* as fast as possible, and to do all they could to protest at the liberation of the slaves. It was all over an hour later.

The Attorney General's initial report offers a measured and procedural narrative of the subsequent events in which he reported that he successfully reasserted British authority over the amassed Bahamians by ordering them to throw their clubs overboard. (Later, in the insurance trials, he was to deny that "the boats were subject to his orders").[51] Boarding the *Creole*, he informed Washington and his eighteen compatriot rebels that they were charged with "mutiny and murder", and would be taken into custody by the troops to await word from London. He placated the *Creole*'s officers and crew regarding their fear that the Bahamians would exact violent revenge, and then informed the rest of the assembled captives that, as far as the authorities were concerned, they were no longer subject to any restrictions on their movements. The news, he reported, gave them "great pleasure". Later, he added that he "called upon them to say what they would do", whereupon a "shout almost immediately rose from among the coloured persons [...] with one voice to express their determination to quit the vessel".[52] He said that he then made a signal, and observed from a small boat as the captives crowded over the side of the ship into their waiting, and welcoming, ferries.[53]

Merritt, Gifford, and Stevens gave a more chaotic and contingent representation of events as they apparently struggled to maintain a hold over the slaves in the face of terrible intimidation by the Bahamians, and the interference of the British. Merritt reported that he strenuously tried to persuade the captives to stay aboard, while "white persons were telling the captives that they would probably be punished if they went to New Orleans". The depositions suggest that either the British officials were happy to exploit the Americans' anxiety, or that their own authority was less secure than it appeared to be. Merritt asked a magistrate what "all this meant, the boats and the launches being full of men armed with clubs". The magistrate told him that as "soon as the troops were removed, they

51. Robinson, *Reports of the Cases*, p. 251.
52. *Ibid.*, p. 249.
53. "Report of G.C. Anderson, Attorney General of the Bahamas", 13 November 1841, *PP*, 1843, [485], pp. 129–130.

would probably come on board, when there would probably be blood-shed". The Americans also reported that only "some" Bahamians threw their arms overboard at the behest of the Attorney General, and that throughout the proceedings the troops were having difficulty keeping the Bahamians from repeatedly attempting to board the vessel. Merritt reported that he had asked for protection "as he feared that those in the launches and boats, when they came alongside, would commit some violence".[54] Gifford reported his "serious fears", and the "agitation of the moment", in which he may, or may not, have said of the slaves, "Let them go". He could not recall. Others certainly did recall that he had done so.[55]

Stevens was also fixated by the "threatening state of things". He stated that the men aboard the small vessels "showed fight" with their clubs, "swinging them about in a threatening manner, at the same time using insulting language".[56] Later in the insurance trials, he noted that the Attorney General, after informing the slaves that they were "at liberty", turned around and "waived his handkerchief to the boats which surrounded the brig; as did the other magistrates", signalling them to approach.[57] The fluttering of handkerchiefs, presumably white, by the highest representatives of colonial law, was an ambiguously laden sign. It was a signal that the slaves could be disembarked. But, if read as the universal referent for surrender, it might also point to the critical issue: that quite who was surrendering what, and to whom, had never been completely certain.

Stevens' testimony is redolent of the Americans' confusion as their world turned upside down for a second time. He recalled the enormous cheer that erupted around the harbour as the captives disembarked, and simultaneously the alien sight of black slaves being treated with decorous, and very British, propriety. He reported that he heard two magistrates say, as they assisted the departing women over the side of the brig, "Here ladies, this is a nice boat on purpose for ladies get in here".[58]

It suited the slavers to construct a narrative that helped to secure their status as victimized patriots harassed by British imperial tyranny. Simultaneously, British authority required the veneer of colonial control throughout this last phase of the revolt. Both sets of narratives are compromised, however, by the collective action taken by the Bahamian crowd both on land and afloat during the last phase of the *Creole*'s story. The justice-seeking "mosquito fleet" had been, at least in part, organized in advance, and drew on previous patterns of political action. It showed

54. "Deposition of William H. Merritt", 13 November 1841, pp. 132–133.
55. Robinson, *Reports of the Cases*, p. 254.
56. "Deposition of Lucius Stevens", 10 November 1841, p. 131.
57. Robinson, *Reports of the Cases*, p. 223.
58. "Deposition of Lucius Stevens", 10 November 1841, p. 131.

impatient restraint as the boats waited to ferry the captives to shore while the spectacle of their numbers, their noise, and the threat of violence that accompanied their presence helped to prevent the Americans from recapturing the ship, and forced the issue of the captives' release. To adapt E.P. Thompson's famous terms, the water-borne crowd had, as its "legitimising notion", the revolutionary right to freedom, while British colonial abolitionism signalled the "measure of licence afforded by the authorities" necessary for the assertion of those rights.[59] The multiple and fractured recollections of the events recorded in the official archive gesture at what was unspeakable for both the Americans and the British: that things might have taken, and nearly had taken, a very different route.

The black pilot who had pressed so hard for the slaves' emancipation ensured that all the captives were safely ferried to shore, although he could not persuade Rachel Glover, a young girl named Mary, two other women, and one of their sons, to claim their freedom. They, like the unnamed woman and her five children on the *Enterprize*, chose rather to sail for New Orleans. Their decisions mark the complications that gender brought to the unforeseen prospect of Caribbean freedom. It is impossible to know exactly why the women did not disembark, but they may have been in search of husbands or children previously sold away to New Orleans. They may have had relationships with the *Creole*'s crew members, or they may have been fearful of further exploitation if left legally free but vulnerable, and with children to care for, in a strange country. Of the rest, many took up a British offer of passage to Jamaica almost immediately. The British held the nineteen identified as "mutineers" for nearly six months but, in the end, the charge of piracy collapsed. Like the groups of African Americans previously freed from the wrecked vessels, Washington and his compatriots disappear into the Atlantic vortex at this point, leaving the imperial nations to squabble for years over the irreducibly liquid boundaries of the sea, so-called property rights in persons, and the fictions of "race" in the determination of universal freedom.

CONCLUSION

The revolt aboard the *Creole* has taken its place in the epic tradition of black anti-slavery revolts against white American colonial authorities. Madison Washington's leadership is repeatedly cited alongside that of Nat Turner, Denmark Vesey, and Gabriel Prosser. The story of the *Creole* reaches far beyond the boundaries of national history or memory, however,

59. E.P. Thompson, "The Moral Economy of the English Crowd in the Eighteenth Century", *Past & Present*, 50 (1971), pp. 76–136, 78.

and beyond the singular brilliance of its leader. The enslaved Americans liberated themselves by staging a mutiny within a geopolitical context that breached land and sea in a myriad of imagined and material ways. Their extraordinary success is testimony to the circulation of radical struggle, the wider currents of political action, and the power of fugitive connections that together defined the collective nature of the revolutionary Atlantic.

GUIDELINES FOR CONTRIBUTORS

Manuscripts are considered for publication on the understanding that they are not currently under consideration elsewhere and that the material – in substance as well as form – has not been previously published. Two copies of the manuscript should be submitted. Each article should be accompanied by a summary, not exceeding 100 words, outlining the principal conclusions and methods in the context of currently accepted views on the subject. All material – including quotations and notes – must be double-spaced with generous margins. Use of dot-matrix printers is discouraged. Notes should be numbered consecutively and placed at the end of the text. Spelling should be consistent throughout (e.g. Labour and Labor are both acceptable, but only one of these forms should be used in an article). Turns of phrase using masculine forms as universals are not acceptable.

Sample citation forms

Book: E.P. Thompson, *The Making of the English Working Class* (London, 1963), pp. 320–322. Journal: Walter Galenson, "The Unionization of the American Steel Industry", *International Review of Social History*, 1 (1956), pp. 8–40. Detailed instructions for contributors are available from http://www.iisg.nl/irsh/irshstyl.php. Twenty-five free offprints of each article are provided, and authors may purchase additional copies provided these are ordered at proof stage.

DISCLAIMER

The Internationaal Instituut voor Sociale Geschiedenis (IISG) has used its best endeavours to ensure that the URLs for external websites referred to in this journal are correct and active at the time of going to press. However, the IISG has no responsibility for the websites and can make no guarantee that a site will remain live or that the content is or will remain appropriate.

Every effort has been made to trace all copyright holders, but if any have been inadvertently overlooked the Internationaal Instituut voor Sociale Geschiedenis (IISG) will be pleased to include any necessary credits in any subsequent issue.

This journal issue has been printed on FSC-certified paper and cover board. FSC is an independent, non-governmental, not-for-profit organization established to promote the responsible management of the world's forests. Please see www.fsc.org for information.